# THE UNITED METHODIST MUSIC AND WORSHIP PLANNER

## 2015–2016

David L. Bone
and
Mary J. Scifres

Abingdon Press
*Nashville*

---



ISBN 978-1-4267-9810-8



15 16 17 18 19 20 21 22 23 24—10 9 8 7 6 5 4 3 2 1

MANUFACTURED IN THE UNITED STATES OF AMERICA

# Do you have the book you need?

We want you to have the best planner, designed to meet your specific needs. How do you know if you have the right resource? Simply complete this one-question quiz:

## Do you lead worship in a United Methodist congregation?

### Yes.

Use *The United Methodist Music and Worship Planner, 2015–2016* (ISBN: 9781426798108)

### No.

Use *Prepare! An Ecumenical Music and Worship Planner, 2015–2016* (ISBN: 9781426798092)

To order these resources, call Cokesbury toll-free at 1-877-877-8674, or shop online at www.cokesbury.com. Do you find yourself rushing at the last minute to order your new planner? Subscribe today and receive your new *The United Methodist Music and Worship Planner* or *Prepare!* automatically next year and every year. Call toll-free 1-800-672-1789 to request a subscription.

# USING THIS PLANNER

## How We Organize the Resource Lists

This *United Methodist Music and Worship Planner (UM Planner)* is designed to give you as many ideas as possible about a given worship service. Use it alongside a worship plan notebook that you create and copies of *The United Methodist Hymnal, The United Methodist Book of Worship, The Faith We Sing,* and *Worship & Song*. Features of the *UM Planner* include:

- The lectionary verses found on left-hand pages of the *UM Planner* come from the Common English Bible (CEB), published through Abingdon Press in 2011. While the full lectionary text is provided for most readings, we might use only the first two verses of some psalms. NOTE: The CEB italicizes Old Testament quotations in the New Testament. Where available, we have added psalter numbers from the *UM Hymnal*.
- Each week **Primary Hymns and Songs for the Day** are suggested first. These suggestions include various helps for singing the hymns. These hymns and songs have the closest relationship to the scriptures and are widely known. The lengthier lists of **Additional Hymn Suggestions** and **Additional Contemporary Suggestions** will add variety to your musical selections.
- The musical suggestions are chosen to suggest a wide variety of styles, using *The United Methodist Hymnal, The Faith We Sing,* and *Worship & Song* to their fullest.
- Each item is referenced to scripture or occasion.
- **Opening (O)** and **Closing (C) hymns** are suggested for each worship service.
- At least one **Communion hymn** is recommended for the first Sunday of each month and liturgical season. When appropriate, communion hymns related to the scriptures are noted on other days as well.
- **Additional Contemporary Suggestions** include not only praise choruses but also global and ethnic music, folk music, and meditative music from traditions such as Taizé. Information about resources referenced in this section can be found on page 7.
- **Vocal Solos** and **Anthems** provide ideas for vocal music "performance" offerings, but may also inspire ideas for additional congregational selections.
- The recommended **Vocal Solos** are taken from a group of eleven collections that range from contemporary settings of hymn texts and praise choruses to spirituals to well-known classics (see p. 7). Augment these suggestions from your own library.
- The **Anthems** suggestions include new works as well as generally known works that are already in many church choral libraries. Your study of the scripture and hymn texts will lead you to anthems in your church library that are appropriate.
- **One word of advice:** Be sure to consult all the music suggestions regardless of the type of service you are planning. In the changing world of worship, no one style defines a song or a worship service. Many items appropriate for contemporary and emergent styles are listed under the **Additional Hymn Suggestions** and many resources for traditional and blended services can be found in the **Additional Contemporary Suggestions** list. **Vocal Solos**, **Anthems**, and **Other Suggestions** may be appropriate for congregational use as well. Don't let the "category" here deter you from using any item that will enhance your worship service. Planners should consult all lists when choosing congregational music.
- Suggestions for "**Visuals**" are offered for each service. See the article "Visuals in Worship" (p. 4) for discussion of these suggestions. Visual ideas are found in the **Other Suggestions** lists. They have been compiled by Ashley M. Calhoun and supplemented by our authors. Ashley is known for his inventive use of "found" items in creating visual worship settings. Worship committees, visual artists, dancers, and altar guilds can use these ideas to create their own unique worship centers, altar pieces, banners, and dance images. Screen visual artists can use these themes to select appropriate background and theme screens for worship.
- **Other Suggestions** also include words for worship, primarily from *The United Methodist Book of Worship* and *Worship & Song* (Worship Resources edition); suggestions for choral introits ("Call to Worship") and sung benedictions; and ideas for musical responses related to the spoken liturgy.
- A two-year, at-a-glance **2015–2016 Calendar** follows the **Worship Planning Sheets** (see pages 137-39). It includes a note on the lectionary years covered in this edition of *The UM Music and Worship Planner.*

## Planning Worship with These Resources

When planning any worship service, it is always best to start with the scripture and let it guide your thoughts and plans. If your church is not using the Revised Common Lectionary, but you do know what the scripture text will be for a service, look up that text in the **Index of Scriptures Referenced** on page 133.

As you read and study the Scripture passages, read all of the suggested hymn texts. The hymns may remind you of anthems, solos, or keyboard selections. It is wise to mark your hymnal with the dates individual hymns are sung to avoid singing some too frequently. The **Hymn Resources** (see p. 7) can enhance congregational singing, but should be used sparingly.

Use a three-ring binder to organize your plans. For each service of worship, include a copy of one of the **Worship Planning Sheets** found on pages 137–139 (or design your own!) along with blank paper for listing further ideas. Do not simply "fill in the blanks" for each service, but use the Planning Sheet to guide your work.

Use the suggestions in the *UM Planner* along with your own page of ideas to begin making decisions about worship. Will the choir sing a "Call to Worship"? Can a hymn verse serve as a prayer response? Can a particular anthem or vocal solo give direction to the sermon? What prayers will be used?

Once your decisions are made, complete the **Worship Planning Sheet**. Make a separate list of tasks related to that service. Planning worship is an awesome responsibility, but one that can be accomplished with an organized effort along with spiritual guidance.

# VISUALS IN WORSHIP

## Ashley M. Calhoun

The suggestions for visuals in this planner are meant to help worship leaders use objects and images to increase the impact of the gospel on a people who are increasingly visually oriented. These suggestions can be incorporated into many visual elements: hanging and processional banners, worship settings (whether on the altar or in the chancel or narthex), worship folder covers, and bulletin boards. The ideas can also be used to suggest ways to use classical and contemporary works of art, sculpture, needlework, and photography in worship services

With more churches incorporating screens and video walls into their worship spaces, there is tremendous potential for the use of still or moving imagery. Also, interpretive movement and drama can be very strong in visual impact.

The visual suggestions in this *Planner* have several characteristics:

- The suggestions are not meant to give detailed plans, but to spark your imagination and creativity.
- Some are drawn literally from the lessons; others are thematic.
- The suggestions are organized by reference to the lectionary passages:

**O** Old Testament or Easter season, Acts reading
**P** Psalm reading or Canticle
**E** Epistle or New Testament reading
**G** Gospel reading

- Chapter and verse numbers are sometimes given to indicate actual phrases in the scripture passage that can serve as visual elements.
- Themes such as "forgiveness," "love," or "rejoicing," are offered to encourage creative use of video and photographic images of people engaged in demonstrating those themes.

So much about worship is visual and intended to strengthen the proclamation of the gospel. The worship space is filled with visual elements that send a message. The church year is a treasure trove of color, texture, symbolism, and visual imagery. Special Sundays and special days in the cultural and denominational calendars also offer opportunities for visual expression. Evaluate the visual aspects of your worship services and find ways to enhance the worship experience with thoughtful, intentional use of visual elements and images.

# PLANNING WORSHIP IN ALTERNATIVE STYLES

Mary J. Scifres

Various forms of nontraditional worship have become increasingly popular in the last thirty years, mass labeled as "contemporary." These alternative styles of worship may be foreign to the experience of traditional worship planners. Nevertheless, the popularity of modern music and public events, the increasing diversity of today's culture, the growing comfort with informal approaches to worship, and the high energy of young people may encourage you to use contemporary resources and alternative styles in one or more of your worship services.

Planning alternative worship provides an exciting opportunity for church staff members and volunteers to work together as a team. Such planning can also provide a vehicle in which worship committees find new opportunity for ministry.

If alternative or contemporary worship is new to you, spend time in prayer and planning long before your first service. Know your own gifts and those of your congregation, and observe what other churches and worship leaders are doing around your community and around the country. If you're beginning an added worship service, build the necessary groundwork to support this new mission of the church by recruiting leadership from within your congregation, advertising the event before it happens, and setting a goal for this mission. If you are integrating new elements into an existing worship service, include your current leadership alongside young adults and new leadership in planning for the changes. As you embark on this new venture, be careful not to abandon your current worshiping congregation or set up a competition between existing worship services and new ones. As you explore the possibility of new worship styles, be open not only to contemporary praise music and alternative Christian music, but also to global praise music or quieter forms of contemporary worship using folk music or Taizé music. Secular resources and music may also be of help in developing new styles of worship. With these things in mind, you are ready to begin the planning process.

As you design your alternative worship service, several decisions need to be made:

- Whom do you want to reach? (traditions, faith backgrounds, ages, theology?)
- What type of worship experience shall you start or improve? (You may want to consider blending styles.)
- How much are you willing to spend?

With those decisions in mind, you are ready to build your planning team. "Team?" you may ask. "Our pastor does all the worship planning!" If that is the case, this is the perfect opportunity to explore a new model of planning worship. Contemporary expressions of worship are foreign to many pastors and musicians. Increasing the number of planners will expand the diversity and creativity of ideas—important elements of alternative worship! With this resource, we hope that many pastors, musicians, and worship leaders find encouragement and assistance planning worship in advance and in cooperation with one another.

Planning team members may include musicians, artists, organizers, writers, and pastors. All members of the worship planning team meet regularly, at least biannually. Some worship teams find weekly, monthly, or seasonal planning meetings helpful, but even two meetings a year can improve communication and coordination efforts immensely. Planning meetings are necessary, common, and often frequent in alternative worship planning.

However often one plans, pastors need to know the time requirements for planning music and other artistic elements of worship. Each pianist or song leader can communicate to the pastor the average length of time needed to pick new songs, order the music or songbooks, obtain copyright permissions, and rehearse the songs prior to Sunday morning. Each drama coordinator can decide the length of time needed to write or find a vignette to illustrate the scripture or sermon topic. Visual coordinators can let worship planners know the time needed to locate photographs, develop altar displays, or prepare electronic slide shows for worship. Finally, musicians and artists can communicate with the pastor their visions for music and art ministry in the context of worship.

Pastors, likewise, need to inform musicians of special needs for musical and visual support. Some pastors establish cues to alert the musician that light background music is needed during an unexpected situation in worship. A pastor can tell artists of expectations regarding worship leadership roles (e.g., listen attentively to the sermon, smile during the opening songs, stand or kneel during the prayer). Additionally, pastors can communicate their visions for the music and worship arts ministry of the church. These initial communications are essential when worship planners begin to work together and when there are personnel changes in the worship planning team.

Many models for the actual planning might be used, but we offer one model to help a team in starting integrated planning. In order to use this model, the team needs several copies of this *Planner* (particularly for scripture readings and song lists), a Bible (if lectionary is not being used or for team members who do not have access to a copy of this *Planner*), hymnals and/or songbooks. You may also wish to have a copy of *The Abingdon Worship Annual* and *The United Methodist Book of Worship.* Musicians may find it helpful to have copies of each of the music collections suggested in this guide as well as a single copy file of the song collection of your church. Copies of the planning sheet from pages 137–139 can be distributed to each team member for each Sunday being discussed.

- Before the meeting, the pastor(s) prepares scripture and sermon outlines; musicians prepare repertoire lists as well as repertoire wish lists.
- Team meets for a designated time. (A retreat setting is appropriate, especially if this is to be only a biannual event.)
- Open meeting with prayer and discussion of worship.
- Read scriptures (perhaps in advance of meeting), and select specific scriptures for each Sunday being planned.
- The pastor(s) introduces and outlines sermon topics or emphases.
- Discuss and outline seasonal needs.
- Choose songs and/or hymns, keeping in mind: thematic and scriptural emphases, musical abilities, sermon topics, congregational music preferences, and desire for introduction of new songs in a helpful way.
- Visual artists begin outlining plans for visual emphases or focal points.
- Introduce and discuss special ideas or plans for specific worship services (e.g., Easter, new member celebration, children's Sunday, stewardship Sunday).
- Write or choose spoken prayers, responses, and other worship words (full team or subgroup, depending on number of people participating). *The Abingdon Worship Annual, Worship & Song Worship Resources Edition,* and *The United Methodist Book of Worship* are particularly helpful resources here.
- Choose vocal and instrumental music (full team or subgroup, depending on number of people participating).
- Review services for integration and unity as well as diversity.
- Discuss concerns regarding specific services and plans for improvement.
- Close meeting with song and prayer.

In planning alternative worship, you want to offer a quality experience; planning with a team can help. At any step, members of the planning team may have valuable input. A pastor may have an idea for a dramatic sketch to enhance a sermon idea; a musician may have insight into a sermon topic as it relates to the congregation. Members of the team will find helpful suggestions in this *Planner* at any of these steps. The text of each scripture reading is provided, season and color are noted, music and visual suggestions are offered, liturgical suggestions are provided, and other ideas are mentioned that may spark interest in innovations for your worship service.

When planning alternative worship, try to:

- Offer a high-quality experience of worship
- Employ your heritage creatively
- Offer as many opportunities for participation as possible
- Use language and theology that affirms
- Use creative, diverse, understandable language and music
- Be honest, open, and genuine in word and action
- Offer a welcoming experience for visitors
- Use a variety of media (video, drama, live music, visual arts)
- Avoid dependence on handouts (such as bulletins)
- Obtain a copyright license if you plan to duplicate for overhead projection or bulletins (Christian Copyright License at ccli.com or One License at Onelicense.net).
- Have fun!

Alternative worship planning need not be a point of departure for a worship staff. Rather, it can be an opportunity for unity and team building. The team that works together models corporate worship for the congregation. If we want people who enter the church on Sunday mornings from their many walks of life to have a community experience, we need to offer worship that incorporates many ideas from different voices to connect with our congregation's diverse journeys of faith. In so doing, we will find that the Holy Spirit has found a new freedom in which to work.

# RESOURCE KEY

UM — Young, Carlton R., ed. *The United Methodist Hymnal.* Nashville. The United Methodist Publishing House, 1989. ISBN #9780687431328.

2000 or S2000 — Hickman, Hoyt L., ed. *The Faith We Sing.* Nashville: Abingdon Press, 2000. Cokesbury Order #090547 (Pew Edition). NOTE: All hymn numbers 2000 and higher are from this hymnal.

3000 or WS3000 — Smith, Gary Alan, ed. *Worship & Song.* Nashville: Abingdon Press, 2011. Accompaniment, singer, guitar, and planning editions available. Cokesbury Order #090547 (Pew edition). NOTE: All hymn numbers 3000 and higher are from this hymnal.

WSL — Smith, Gary Alan, ed. *Worship & Song Leader's Edition.* Nashville: Abingdon Press, 2011. Cokesbury Order # (Leader's edition). These resources *WSL1–WSL222* refer to the written words for worship (prayers, litanies, benedictions) available in worship resource editions of Worship & Song.

BOW — Langford, Andy, ed. *The United Methodist Book of Worship.* Nashville: Abingdon Press, 1992. Leader and accompaniment editions available. ISBN #9780687035724.

## HYMN RESOURCES

S-1 — Smith, Gary Alan, ed. *The United Methodist Hymnal: Music Supplement.* Nashville: Abingdon Press, 1991. Cokesbury Order #431476.

S-2 — Bennett, Robert C., ed. *The United Methodist Hymnal: Music Supplement II.* Nashville: Abingdon Press, 1993. Cokesbury Order #430135.

H-3 — Hopson, Hal H. *The Creative Church Musician Series.* Carol Stream, IL: Hope Publishing Co.
**Hbl** Vol. 1. *The Creative Use of Handbells in Worship. 1997.* Cokesbury Order #921992.
**Chr** Vol. 2. *The Creative Use of Choirs in Worship. 1999.* Cokesbury Order #732807.
**Desc** *The Creative Use of Descants in Worship. 1999.* Cokesbury Item #732864.
**Org** *The Creative Use of the Organ in Worship. 1997.* Cokesbury Order #323904.

## VOCAL SUGGESTION RESOURCES

V-1 — Kimbrough, Steven, ed. *Sweet Singer: Hymns of Charles Wesley.* Chapel Hill, NC: Hinshaw Music, 1987. Catalogue #CV-1 Cokesbury Order #811712

V-2 — Handel, George Frederick. *Messiah.* Various editions available.

V-3 — Hayes, Mark. *The Mark Hayes Vocal Solo Collection*
**V-3 (1)** *Ten Spirituals for Solo Voice.* Alfred Music Publishing, 2007. ISBN#9780882848808.
**V-3 (2)** *Seven Praise and Worship Songs for Solo Voice.* Alfred Music Publishing, 2010. ISBN#9780739037249.
**V-3 (3)** *Ten Hymns and Gospel Songs for Solo Voice.* ISBN#9780739006979.

V-4 — Scott, K. Lee. *Sing a Song of Joy.* Minneapolis, MN: Augsburg Fortress, 1989. ISBN #9780800647889 (Medium High Voice) ISBN #9780800647889 (Medium Low Voice) ISBN #9780800652821.

V-5 — Various Editors. *With All My Heart: Contemporary Vocal Solos.* Minneapolis, MN: Augsburg Fortress, 2004.
**Volume 1**: Autumn and Winter
**Volume 2**: Spring and Summer
**Volume 3**: Baptisms, Weddings, and Funerals

V-6 — Walters, Richard, arr. *Hymn Classics: Concert Arrangements of Traditional Hymns for Voice and Piano.* Milwaukee, WI: Hal Leonard Publishing, 1993. ISBN #9780793560080. High Voice: Cokesbury Order #811290. Low Voice: Cokesbury Item #811233.

V-7 — Johnson, Hall, arr. *Thirty (30) Spirituals.* New York: G. Schirmer, Inc., 1949. ISBN10#0793548039.

V-8 — Wilson, John F., Don Doig, and Jack Schrader, eds. *Everything for the Church Soloist.* Carol Stream, IL: Hope Publishing Company, 1980. Cokesbury Order #810103.

V-9 — Scott, K. Lee. *Rejoice Now My Spirit: Vocal Solos for the Church Year.* Minneapolis, MN: Augsburg Fortress, 1992. ISBN #9780800651084.

V-10 — Hayes, Mark, et al. *From the Manger to the Cross—Seasonal Solos for Medium Voice.* Dayton, OH: The Lorenz Corporation, 2006. Cokesbury Order #526369.

V-11 — Pote, Allen. *A Song of Joy.* Carol Stream, IL: Hope Publishing, 2003. Cokesbury Order #505068.

## CONTEMPORARY RESOURCES

SP — Various. *Songs for Praise and Worship Singalong Edition.* Waco, TX: Word Music, 1992. ISBN #9783010203494.

M1-M55 — Barker, Ken, ed. *More Songs for Praise and Worship Choir/Worship Team Edition.* Waco, TX: Word Music, 2000. Cokesbury Order #509802 (*Keyboard Edition*: Cokesbury Order #509776. *Piano/Guitar/Vocal Edition*: Cokesbury Order #509764).

M56-M115 — Barker, Ken, ed. *More Songs for Praise and Worship 2 Choir/Worship Team Edition.* Waco, TX: Word Music, 2002. Cokesbury Order #512053 (*Keyboard Edition*: Cokesbury Order #512075. *Piano/Guitar/Vocal Edition*: Cokesbury Order #080689314186).

M116-M168 — Barker, Ken, ed. *More Songs for Praise and Worship 3 Choir/Worship Team Edition.* Waco, TX: Word Music, 2005. Cokesbury Order #523357 (*Keyboard Edition*: Cokesbury Order # 523418. *Piano/Guitar/Vocal Edition*: Cokesbury Order #523369).

M169-M219 — Barker, Ken, ed. *More Songs for Praise and Worship 4 Choir/Worship Team Edition.* Waco, TX: Word Music, 2006. Cokesbury Order # 529198 (*Keyboard Edition*: Cokesbury Order # 529244. *Piano/Guitar/Vocal Edition*: ISBN #9785557996822).

M220-M279 — McClure, Mark and Sarah G. Huffman, eds. *More Songs for Praise and Worship 5.* Waco, TX: Word Music, 2011. (*Piano/Guitar/Vocal Edition:* ISBN#9781458418807. *Choir/Worship Team Edition:* ISBN#9781458418814. *Keyboard/SATB Edition:* Catalogue #0-80689-50087-9.)

See also Vocal Solo suggestions from V-3.

**Proverbs 22:1-2, 8-9, 22-23**

A good reputation is better than much wealth;
high esteem is better than silver and gold.
2 The rich and the poor have this in common:
the LORD made them both.

. . . . . . . . . . . . . . . . . . . . . . . . .

8 Those who sow injustice will harvest evil;
the rod of their fury will come to an end.
9 Happy are generous people,
because they give some of their food to the poor.

. . . . . . . . . . . . . . . . . . . . . . . . .

22 Don't steal from the poor, because they are poor.
Don't oppress the needy in the gate.
23 The LORD will take up their case
and press the life out of those who oppress them.

---

**Psalm 125**

The people who trust in the LORD
are like Mount Zion:
never shaken, lasting forever.
2 Mountains surround Jerusalem.
That's how the LORD surrounds his people
from now until forever from now!
3 The wicked rod won't remain
in the land given to the righteous
so that they don't use their hands to do anything wrong.
4 LORD, do good to people who are good,
to people whose hearts are right.
5 But as for those people who turn to their own twisted ways—
may the LORD march them off with other evildoers!
Peace be on Israel!

---

**James 2:1-10 (11-13), 14-17**

My brothers and sisters, when you show favoritism you
deny the faithfulness of our Lord Jesus Christ, who has been
resurrected in glory. 2 Imagine two people coming into your
meeting. One has a gold ring and fine clothes, while the
other is poor, dressed in filthy rags. 3 Then suppose that you
were to take special notice of the one wearing fine clothes,
saying, "Here's an excellent place. Sit here." But to the poor
person you say, "Stand over there"; or, "Here, sit at my feet."
4 Wouldn't you have shown favoritism among yourselves and
become evil-minded judges?

5 My dear brothers and sisters, listen! Hasn't God chosen
those who are poor by worldly standards to be rich in terms
of faith? Hasn't God chosen the poor as heirs of the kingdom he has promised to those who love him? 6 But you have
dishonored the poor. Don't the wealthy make life difficult for
you? Aren't they the ones who drag you into court? 7 Aren't
they the ones who insult the good name spoken over you at
your baptism?

8 You do well when you really fulfill the royal law found in
scripture, *Love your neighbor as yourself.* 9 But when you show
favoritism, you are committing a sin, and by that same law
you are exposed as a lawbreaker. 10 Anyone who tries to keep
all of the Law but fails at one point is guilty of failing to keep
all of it. 11 The one who said, *Don't commit adultery,* also said,
*Don't commit murder.* So if you don't commit adultery but do
commit murder, you are a lawbreaker. 12 In every way, then,
speak and act as people who will be judged by the law of
freedom. 13 There will be no mercy in judgment for anyone
who hasn't shown mercy. Mercy overrules judgment.

14 My brothers and sisters, what good is it if people say they
have faith but do nothing to show it? Claiming to have faith
can't save anyone, can it? 15 Imagine a brother or sister who
is naked and never has enough food to eat. 16 What if one of
you said, "Go in peace! Stay warm! Have a nice meal!"? What
good is it if you don't actually give them what their body
needs? 17 In the same way, faith is dead when it doesn't result
in faithful activity.

---

**Mark 7:24-37**

24 Jesus left that place and went into the region of Tyre. He
didn't want anyone to know that he had entered a house, but
he couldn't hide. 25 In fact, a woman whose young daughter
was possessed by an unclean spirit heard about him right
away. She came and fell at his feet. 26 The woman was Greek,
Syrophoenician by birth. She begged Jesus to throw the
demon out of her daughter. 27 He responded, "The children
have to be fed first. It isn't right to take the children's bread
and toss it to the dogs."

28 But she answered, "Lord, even the dogs under the table
eat the children's crumbs."

29 "Good answer!" he said. "Go on home. The demon has
already left your daughter." 30 When she returned to her
house, she found the child lying on the bed and the demon
gone.

31 After leaving the region of Tyre, Jesus went through
Sidon toward the Galilee Sea through the region of the Ten
Cities. 32 Some people brought to him a man who was deaf
and could hardly speak, and they begged him to place his
hand on the man for healing. 33 Jesus took him away from
the crowd by himself and put his fingers in the man's ears.
Then he spit and touched the man's tongue. 34 Looking into
heaven, Jesus sighed deeply and said, *"Ephphatha,"* which
means, "Open up." 35 At once, his ears opened, his twisted
tongue was released, and he began to speak clearly.

36 Jesus gave the people strict orders not to tell anyone.
But the more he tried to silence them, the more eagerly
they shared the news. 37 People were overcome with wonder,
saying, "He does everything well! He even makes the deaf to
hear and gives speech to those who can't speak."

**Primary Hymns and Songs for the Day**

592 "When the Church of Jesus" (Prov, Jas) (O)
H-3 Chr-35; Org-65
S-2 #99. Desc.
434 "*Cuando el Pobre*" ("When the Poor Ones") (Prov, Jas, Mark)
427 "Where Cross the Crowded Ways of Life" (Jas)
H-3 Chr-178, 180; Org-44
S-1 #141-43 Various treatments
454 "Open My Eyes, That I May See" (Jas, Mark)
H-3 Chr-157; Org-108
2086 "Open Our Eyes, Lord" (Mark)
SP199
664 "Sent Forth by God's Blessing" (Jas) (C)
H-3 Chr-125; Org-9
S-1 #327. Desc.

**Additional Hymn Suggestions**

147 "All Things Bright and Beautiful" (Prov)
581 "Lord, Whose Love Through Humble Service" (Prov, Jas, Mark)
425 "O Crucified Redeemer" (Jas)
438 "Forth in Thy Name, O Lord" (Jas)
548 "In Christ There Is No East or West" (Jas)
634 "Now Let Us from This Table Rise" (Jas, Comm.)
2138 "Sunday's Palms Are Wednesday's Ashes" (Jas)
2245 "Within the Day-to-Day" ("A Hymn for Deacons") (Jas)
2254 "In Remembrance of Me" (Jas, Comm.)
2267 "Taste and See" (Jas, Comm.)
2149 "Living for Jesus" (Jas)
2175 "Together We Serve" (Jas, Mark)
2213 "Healer of Our Every Ill" (Jas, Mark)
3149 "A Place at the Table" (Jas, Mark, Comm.)
57 "O For a Thousand Tongues to Sing" (Mark)
262 "Heal Me, Hands of Jesus" (Mark)
263 "When Jesus the Healer Passed Through Galilee" (Mark)
265 "O Christ, the Healer" (Mark)
273 "Jesus' Hands Were Kind Hands" (Mark)
367 "He Touched Me" (Mark)
3001 "O For a Thousand Tongues to Sing" (Mark)

**Additional Contemporary Suggestions**

S2186 "Song of Hope" (Prov, Jas, Mark)
S2152 "Change My Heart, O God" (Prov, Pss, Jas)
SP195
S2179 "Live in Charity" ("*Ubi Caritas*") (Jas)
M101 "These Hands" (Jas, Stewardship)
UM432 "*Jesu, Jesu*" (Jas, Mark)
S-1 #63. Vocal part
S2040 "Awesome God" (Mark)
SP11
S2086 "Open Our Eyes, Lord" (Mark)
SP199
WS3008 "Open the Eyes of My Heart" (Mark)
M57
S2064 "O Lord, You're Beautiful" (Mark)
S2139 "I Know the Lord's Laid His Hands on Me" (Mark)
M26 "The Power of Your Love" (Mark)
M267 "Hear Us from Heaven" (Mark)

**Vocal Solos**

"Bright and Beautiful" (Prov)
V-3 (3) p. 10
"Jesus Revealed in Me" (Jas)
V-8 p. 347
"O For a Thousand Tongues to Sing" (Mark)
V-1 p. 32
V-6 p. 28

**Anthems**

"The Lord Made Them All" (Prov)
Ruth Elaine Schram; Jubilate/Alfred 42520
SATB with piano, opt. flute, children's choir/congregation

"The Very Thought of Thee" (Mark)
Arr. Brian L. Hanson; Choristers Guild CGA-1375
SATB with piano

**Other Suggestions**

Visuals:
**O** bread, generosity, ministering hands, mountain(s), scepter, ministry, (river, bird, snare)
**E** rich/poor, hands, ministry w/poor, clothes, food, blanket
**G** sick child/well child, healing hands, hearing impaired

*This would be an appropriate day to schedule a healing service in relation to the Mark reading. Use BOW, pp. 615–21, A Service of Healing I, with the Holy Communion liturgy printed there. Other resources related to healing can be found on pp. 622–29.*

Prayer of Confession: WSL90 (Prov, Jas)
Prayer: UM639. Bread and Justice (Prov, Jas, Comm.)
Prayer: UM456. For Courage to Do Justice (Prov, Jas, Mark)
Offertory Prayer: WSL114 (Jas)
Litany of Thanksgiving and Sending Forth: WSL175 (Mark)
Dismissal: BOW559 (Prov, Jas)
Great Thanksgiving for Season after Pentecost: BOW, pp. 70–71.
Sung Benediction: UM670. "Go Forth for God" (Pss)

**Proverbs 1:20-33**
20 Wisdom shouts in the street;
in the public square she raises her voice.
21 Above the noisy crowd, she calls out.
At the entrances of the city gates, she has her say:
22 "How long will you clueless people love your naïveté,
mockers hold their mocking dear,
and fools hate knowledge?
23 You should respond when I correct you.
Look, I'll pour out my spirit on you.
I'll reveal my words to you.
24 I invited you, but you rejected me;
I stretched out my hand to you,
but you paid no attention.
25 You ignored all my advice,
and you didn't want me to correct you.
26 So I'll laugh at your disaster;
I'll make fun of you when dread comes over you,
27 when terror hits you like a hurricane,
and your disaster comes in like a tornado,
when distress and oppression overcome you.
28 Then they will call me, but I won't answer;
they will seek me, but won't find me
29 because they hated knowledge
and didn't choose the fear of the Lord.
30 They didn't want my advice;
they rejected all my corrections.
31 They will eat from the fruit of their way,
and they'll be full of their own schemes.
32 The immature will die because they turn away;
smugness will destroy fools.
33 Those who obey me will dwell securely,
untroubled by the dread of harm."

**Psalm 19 (UM750)**
Heaven is declaring God's glory;
the sky is proclaiming his handiwork.
2 One day gushes the news to the next,
and one night informs another
what needs to be known. . . .

**James 3:1-12**
My brothers and sisters, not many of you should become
teachers, because we know that we teachers will be judged
more strictly. 2 We all make mistakes often, but those who don't
make mistakes with their words have reached full maturity.
Like a bridled horse, they can control themselves entirely. 3
When we bridle horses and put bits in their mouths to lead
them wherever we want, we can control their whole bodies.
4 Consider ships: They are so large that strong winds are
needed to drive them. But pilots direct their ships wherever
they want with a little rudder. 5 In the same way, even though
the tongue is a small part of the body, it boasts wildly.
Think about this: A small flame can set a whole forest on
fire. 6 The tongue is a small flame of fire, a world of evil at
work in us. It contaminates our entire lives. Because of it, the
circle of life is set on fire. The tongue itself is set on fire by
the flames of hell.
7 People can tame and already have tamed every kind of
animal, bird, reptile, and fish. 8 No one can tame the tongue,
though. It is a restless evil, full of deadly poison. 9 With it
we both bless the Lord and Father and curse human beings
made in God's likeness. 10 Blessing and cursing come from
the same mouth. My brothers and sisters, it just shouldn't be
this way!
11 Both fresh water and salt water don't come from the
same spring, do they? 12 My brothers and sisters, can a fig tree
produce olives? Can a grapevine produce figs? Of course not,
and fresh water doesn't flow from a saltwater spring either.

**Mark 8:27-38**
27 Jesus and his disciples went into the villages near Caesarea Philippi. On the way he asked his disciples, "Who do
people say that I am?"
28 They told him, "Some say John the Baptist, others Elijah,
and still others one of the prophets."
29 He asked them, "And what about you? Who do you say
that I am?"
Peter answered, "You are the Christ." 30 Jesus ordered them
not to tell anyone about him.
31 Then Jesus began to teach his disciples: "The Human
One must suffer many things and be rejected by the elders,
chief priests, and the legal experts, and be killed, and then,
after three days, rise from the dead." 32 He said this plainly.
But Peter took hold of Jesus and, scolding him, began to
correct him. 33 Jesus turned and looked at his disciples, then
sternly corrected Peter: "Get behind me, Satan. You are not
thinking God's thoughts but human thoughts."
34 After calling the crowd together with his disciples, Jesus
said to them, "All who want to come after me must say no
to themselves, take up their cross, and follow me. 35 All who
want to save their lives will lose them. But all who lose their
lives because of me and because of the good news will save
them. 36 Why would people gain the whole world but lose
their lives? 37 What will people give in exchange for their
lives? 38 Whoever is ashamed of me and my words in this
unfaithful and sinful generation, the Human One will be
ashamed of that person when he comes in the Father's glory
with the holy angels."

**Primary Hymns and Songs for the Day**

553 "And Are We Yet Alive" (Mark) (O)
H-3 Hbl-49; Chr-14; Desc-27; Org-25
451 "Be Thou My Vision" (Prov, Pss)
H-3 Hbl-15, 48; Chr-36; Org-153
S-1 #319. Arr. for organ and voices in canon
77 "How Great Thou Art" (Pss)
H-3 Chr-103; Org-105
S-1 #163. Harm.
3034 "God of Wonders" (Pss)
M80
2129 "I Have Decided to Follow Jesus" (Mark)
415 "Take Up Thy Cross" (Mark) (C)
H-3 Chr-178, 180; Org-44
S-1 #141-43 Various treatments

**Additional Hymn Suggestions**

598 "O Word of God Incarnate" (Prov)
145 "Morning Has Broken" (Prov, Pss)
152 "I Sing the Almighty Power of God" (Prov, Pss)
149 "*Cantemos al Señor*" ("Let's Sing unto the Lord") (Pss)
150 "God, Who Stretched the Spangled Heavens" (Pss)
685 "Now, On Land and Sea Descending" (Pss)
2004 "Praise the Source of Faith and Learning" (Pss)
2012 "Let Us with a Joyful Mind" (Pss)
157 "Jesus Shall Reign" (Jas)
463 "Lord, Speak to Me" (Jas)
549 "Where Charity and Love Prevail" (Jas)
2082 "Woke Up This Morning" (Jas)
159 "Lift High the Cross" (Mark) (O)
261 "Lord of the Dance" (Mark)
338 "Where He Leads Me" (Mark)
421 "Make Me a Captive, Lord" (Mark)
424 "Must Jesus Bear the Cross Alone" (Mark)
430 "O Master, Let Me Walk with Thee" (Mark)
439 "We Utter Our Cry" (Mark)
528 "Nearer, My God, to Thee" (Mark)
2101 "Two Fishermen" (Mark)
2102 "Swiftly Pass the Clouds of Glory" (Mark)
2137 "Would I Have Answered When You Called" (Mark)
2149 "Living for Jesus" (Mark)
2245 "Within the Day-to-Day" ("A Hymn for Deacons") (Mark)
568 "Christ for the World We Sing" (Mark) (C)

**Additional Contemporary Suggestions**

S2002 "I Will Call upon the Lord" (Pss, Jas)
SP224
S2065 "More Precious than Silver" (Pss)
SP99
S2066 "Praise the Name of Jesus" (Pss)
SP87
UM186 "Alleluia" (Pss)
SP108, S-2 #3-4. Desc. and Harm.
M58 "All Heaven Declares" (Pss)
M93 "Rock of Ages"
M111 "The Heavens Shall Declare" (Pss)
M126 "Famous One" (Pss)
M127 "Indescribable" (Pss)
M235 "Sing, Sing, Sing" (Pss)
S2165 "Cry of My Heart" (Mark)
M39
M53 "Let It Be Said of Us" (Mark)
M122 "Every Move I Make" (Mark)
M150 "Everyday" (Mark)
M157 "Surrender" (Mark)
M248 "One Way" (Mark)
M255 "Just to Be with You (Mark)

**Vocal Solos**

"The Heavens Declare His Glory" (Pss)
V-8 p. 248
"Lord of the Dance" (Mark)
V-3 (3) p. 34
"Christ Living Within You" (Mark)
V-8 p. 177
"Courage, My Heart" (Mark)
V-9 p. 20

**Anthems**

"The Heavens Are Telling" (Pss)
Richard McKinney; Concordia 98-3517
SAB with keyboard

"My Jesus Makes My Heart Rejoice" (Mark)
Buxtehude/Burkhardt; Choristers Guild CGA-1356
Unison with piano

**Other Suggestions**

Visuals:
**O** Crowded street corner, gates, storm, tornado, listening
**P** Light/darkness, rising/setting sun, gold, honeycomb, honey
**E** Teaching, bridle, ship rudder, fire
**G** Christ, teaching, rugged cross, descending Christ/angels

*This would be an appropriate day to dedicate new church school teachers and/or celebrate Christian Education Sunday in relation to the Proverbs and James readings.*

Opening Prayer: BOW461 (Pss)
Canticle: UM112. "Canticle of Wisdom" (Prov)
Song of Prayer: BOW193. "Prayer for Wisdom" (Prov)
Prayer: BOW525. For Wisdom (Prov)
Prayer: WSL47 (Prov)
Prayer for Illumination: WSL71 (Pss)
Responsive Prayer: BOW514. May This Mind Be in Us (Prov, Jas, Mark)
Dismissal: BOW189. "May This Mind Be in Us" (Prov, Jas)
Blessing: BOW564 (Prov, Jas)

**Proverbs 31:10-31**

10 A competent wife, how does one find her?
Her value is far above pearls.
11 Her husband entrusts his heart to her,
and with her he will have all he needs.
12 She brings him good and not trouble
all the days of her life.
13 She seeks out wool and flax;
she works joyfully with her hands.
14 She is like a fleet of merchant ships,
bringing food from a distance.
15 She gets up while it is still night,
providing food for her household,
even some for her female servants.
16 She surveys a field and acquires it;
from her own resources, she plants a vineyard.
17 She works energetically;
her arms are powerful.
18 She realizes that her trading is successful;
she doesn't put out her lamp at night.
19 She puts her hands to the spindle;
her palms grasp the whorl.
20 She reaches out to the needy;
she stretches out her hands to the poor.
21 She doesn't fear for her household when it snows,
because they are all dressed in warm clothes.
22 She makes bedspreads for herself;
fine linen and purple are her clothing.
23 Her husband is known in the city gates
when he sits with the elders of the land.
24 She makes garments and sells them;
she supplies sashes to traders.
25 Strength and honor are her clothing;
she is confident about the future.
26 Her mouth is full of wisdom;
kindly teaching is on her tongue.
27 She is vigilant over the activities of her household;
she doesn't eat the food of laziness.
28 Her children bless her;
her husband praises her:
29 "Many women act competently,
but you surpass them all!"
30 Charm is deceptive and beauty fleeting,
but a woman who fears the LORD is to be praised.
31 Let her share in the results of her work;
let her deeds praise her in the city gates.

**Psalm 1 (UM738)**

The truly happy person
doesn't follow wicked advice,
doesn't stand on the road of sinners,
and doesn't sit with the disrespectful.
2 Instead of doing those things,
these persons love the LORD's Instruction,
and they recite God's Instruction day and night!
3 They are like a tree replanted by streams of water,
which bears fruit at just the right time
and whose leaves don't fade.
Whatever they do succeeds.
4 That's not true for the wicked!
They are like dust that the wind blows away.
5 And that's why the wicked will have no standing in the court
of justice—
neither will sinners
in the assembly of the righteous.
6 The LORD is intimately acquainted
with the way of the righteous,
but the way of the wicked is destroyed.

**James 3:13–4:3, 7-8a**

13 Are any of you wise and understanding? Show that your
actions are good with a humble lifestyle that comes from
wisdom. 14 However, if you have bitter jealousy and selfish
ambition in your heart, then stop bragging and living in
ways that deny the truth. 15 This is not the wisdom that comes
down from above. Instead, it is from the earth, natural and
demonic. 16 Wherever there is jealousy and selfish ambition,
there is disorder and everything that is evil. 17 What of the wisdom from above? First, it is pure, and then peaceful, gentle,
obedient, filled with mercy and good actions, fair, and genuine. 18 Those who make peace sow the seeds of justice by their
peaceful acts.

4 1 What is the source of conflict among you? What is the
source of your disputes? Don't they come from your cravings
that are at war in your own lives? 2 You long for something
you don't have, so you commit murder. You are jealous for
something you can't get, so you struggle and fight. You don't
have because you don't ask. 3 You ask and don't have because
you ask with evil intentions, to waste it on your own cravings.
. . .

7 Therefore, submit to God. Resist the devil, and he will run
away from you. 8a Come near to God, and he will come near
to you.

**Mark 9:30-37**

30 From there Jesus and his followers went through Galilee,
but he didn't want anyone to know it. 31 This was because he
was teaching his disciples, "The Human One will be delivered into human hands. They will kill him. Three days after
he is killed he will rise up." 32 But they didn't understand this
kind of talk, and they were afraid to ask him.

33 They entered Capernaum. When they had come into a
house, he asked them, "What were you arguing about during the journey?" 34 They didn't respond, since on the way
they had been debating with each other about who was the
greatest. 35 He sat down, called the Twelve, and said to them,
"Whoever wants to be first must be least of all and the servant
of all." 36 Jesus reached for a little child, placed him among
the Twelve, and embraced him. Then he said,
37 "Whoever welcomes one of these children in my name welcomes me; and whoever welcomes me isn't actually welcoming me but rather the one who sent me."

**Primary Hymns and Songs for the Day**
2004 "Praise the Source of Faith and Learning" (Prov, Pss, Jas) (O)
H-3 Hbl-46; Chr-26, 134; Desc-53; Org-56
S-1 #168-171. Various treatments
598 "O Word of God Incarnate" (Prov, Pss)
H-3 Hbl-86; Chr-153; Org-95
S-1 #243. Harm.
402 "Lord, I Want to Be a Christian" (Jas, Mark)
H-3 Chr-130
432 "Jesu, Jesu" (Mark)
H-3 Chr-114; Org-19
S-1 #63. Vocal part
2176 "Make Me a Servant" (Mark)
SP193
421 "Make Me a Captive, Lord" (Mark) (C)
H-3 Hbl-55; Chr-60; Desc-30; Org-27
S-1 #86-88. Various treatments

**Additional Hymn Suggestions**
194 "Morning Glory, Starlit Sky" (Prov)
433 "All Who Love and Serve Your City" (Prov, Mark)
468 "Dear Jesus, in Whose Life I See" (Prov, Mark)
712 "I Sing a Song of the Saints of God" (Prov, Mark)
354 "I Surrender All" (Jas)
369 "Blessed Assurance" (Jas)
407 "Close to Thee" (Jas)
425 "O Crucified Redeemer" (Jas)
439 "We Utter Our Cry" (Jas)
2158 "Just a Closer Walk with Thee" (Jas)
2166 "Christ Beside Me" (Jas)
2181 "We Need a Faith" (Jas)
2185 "For One Great Peace" (Jas)
2196 "We Walk by Faith" (Jas)
2175 "Together We Serve" (Jas, Mark)
417 "O For a Heart to Praise My God" (Jas, Mark)
561 "Jesus, United by Thy Grace" (Jas, Mark)
562 "Jesus, Lord, We Look to Thee" (Jas, Mark)
191 "Jesus Loves Me" (Mark)
430 "O Master, Let Me Walk with Thee" (Mark)
530 "Are Ye Able" (Mark)
581 "Lord, Whose Love Through Humble Service" (Mark)
589 "The Church of Christ, in Every Age" (Mark)
712 "I Sing a Song of the Saints of God" (Mark)
2092 "Like a Child" (Mark)
2245 "Within the Day-to-Day" ("A Hymn for Deacons") (Mark)
2268 "As We Gather at Your Table" (Mark, Comm.)

**Additional Contemporary Suggestions**
S2270 "I Will Enter His Gates" (Pss)
SP168
UM601 "Thy Word Is a Lamp" (Pss)
SP183
S2131 "Humble Thyself in the Sight of the Lord" (Jas)
SP223
S2159 "Jesus, Draw Me Close" (Jas)
M48
S2186 "Song of Hope" (Jas)
S2223 "They'll Know We Are Christians" (Jas)
S2171 "Make Me a Channel of Your Peace" (Jas)
M26 "The Power of Your Love" (Jas)
M60 "Better Is One Day" (Jas)
S2222 "The Servant Song" (Mark)

**Vocal Solos**
"A Worthy Woman" (Prov)
V-8 p. 364
"Make Me a Channel of Your Peace" (Jas)
V-3 (2) p. 25
V-3 (3) p. 28
"Just a Closer Walk with Thee" (Jas)
V-5(2) p. 31
V-8 p. 323
"Ye Servants of God" (Mark)
V-1 p. 41
"Bright and Beautiful" (Mark)
V-3 (3) p. 10

**Anthems**
"A Prayer for Peace" (Jas)
Michael John Trotta; MorningStar MSM-50-8511
SATB *a cappella*

"Like a Child" (Mark)
arr. David Cherwien; Hope C5013
Two-part mixed with piano and opt. flute

**Other Suggestions**
Visuals:
**O** Jewels, women at work, speaking, laughing, praise
**P** Open Bible, chaff/wind, scales of justice
**E** Gentle touch, fruit/harvest, conflict/treaty, James 3:8
**G** Crucifixion/Resurrection, arguing, child, Mark 9:37
Introit: S2268. "As We Gather at Your Table" (Mark, Comm.)
Opening Prayer: BOW469 (Prov)
Opening Prayer: WSL54 (Jas, Mark)
Prayer of Confession: WSL95 (Jas) or BOW476 (Prov, Mark)
Response: S2275 or S2277. "*Kyrie*" ("Lord, Have Mercy") (Jas)
Prayer for Illumination: WSL72 (Prov, Pss, James)
Prayer: BOW528. A Prayer of Susanna Wesley (Prov)
Prayer: UM401. For Holiness of Heart (Jas)
Prayer: UM570. Prayer of Ignatius of Loyola (Mark)
Sung Benediction: S2186. "Song of Hope" (Jas)
*Resources related to the Proverbs theme of Wisdom can be found in last week's list of Other Suggestions.*

**Esther 7:1-6, 9-10; 9:20-22**

When the king and Haman came in for the banquet with
Queen Esther, 2 the king said to her, "This is the second day
we've met for wine. What is your wish, Queen Esther? I'll give
it to you. And what do you want? I'll do anything—even give
you half the kingdom."

3 Queen Esther answered, "If I please the king, and if the
king wishes, give me my life—that's my wish—and the lives
of my people too. That's my desire. 4 We have been sold—I
and my people—to be wiped out, killed, and destroyed. If we
simply had been sold as male and female slaves, I would have
said nothing. But no enemy can compensate the king for this
kind of damage."

5 King Ahasuerus said to Queen Esther, "Who is this person,
and where is he? Who would dare do such a thing?"

6 Esther replied, "A man who hates, an enemy—this wicked
Haman!" Haman was overcome with terror in the presence
of the king and queen. . . .

9 Harbona, one of the eunuchs serving the king, said, "Sir,
look! There's the stake that Haman made for Mordecai, the
man who spoke up and did something good for the king. It's
standing at Haman's house—seventy-five feet high."

"Impale him on it!" the king ordered. 10 So they impaled
Haman on the very pole that he had set up for Mordecai,
and the king's anger went away. . . .

9:20 Mordecai wrote these things down and sent letters to all
the Jews in all the provinces, both near and far, of King Ahasuerus. 21 He made it a rule that Jews keep the fourteenth and
fifteenth days of the month of Adar as special days each and
every year. 22 They are the days on which the Jews finally put
to rest the troubles with their enemies. The month is the one
when everything turned around for them from sadness to
joy, and from sad, loud crying to a holiday. They are to make
them days of feasts and joyous events, days to send food gifts
to each other and money gifts to the poor.

---

**Psalm 124 (UM846)**

If the LORD hadn't been for us—
  let Israel now repeat!—
2 if the LORD hadn't been for us,
    when those people attacked us
3 then they would have swallowed us up whole
    with their rage burning against us!
4 Then the waters would have drowned us;
  the torrent would have come over our necks;
5 then the raging waters would have come over our necks!
6 Bless the LORD
  because he didn't hand us over
  like food for our enemies' teeth!
7 We escaped like a bird from the hunters' trap;
  the trap was broken so we escaped!
8 Our help is in the name of the LORD,
  the maker of heaven and earth.

---

**James 5:13-20**

13 If any of you are suffering, they should pray. If any of
you are happy, they should sing. 14 If any of you are sick,
they should call for the elders of the church, and the elders
should pray over them, anointing them with oil in the name
of the Lord. 15 Prayer that comes from faith will heal the sick,
for the Lord will restore them to health. And if they have
sinned, they will be forgiven. 16 For this reason, confess your
sins to each other and pray for each other so that you may
be healed. The prayer of the righteous person is powerful in
what it can achieve. 17 Elijah was a person just like us. When
he earnestly prayed that it wouldn't rain, no rain fell for
three and a half years. 18 He prayed again, God sent rain, and
the earth produced its fruit.

19 My brothers and sisters, if any of you wander from the
truth and someone turns back the wanderer, 20 recognize
that whoever brings a sinner back from the wrong path will
save them from death and will bring about the forgiveness of
many sins.

---

**Mark 9:38-50**

38 John said to Jesus, "Teacher, we saw someone throwing
demons out in your name, and we tried to stop him because
he wasn't following us."

39 Jesus replied, "Don't stop him. No one who does powerful acts in my name can quickly turn around and curse me.
40 Whoever isn't against us is for us. 41 I assure you that whoever gives you a cup of water to drink because you belong to
Christ will certainly be rewarded.

42 "As for whoever causes these little ones who believe in me
to trip and fall into sin, it would be better for them to have a
huge stone hung around their necks and to be thrown into
the lake. 43 If your hand causes you to fall into sin, chop it off.
It's better for you to enter into life crippled than to go away
with two hands into the fire of hell, which can't be put out.
45 If your foot causes you to fall into sin, chop it off. It's better
for you to enter life lame than to be thrown into hell with
two feet. 47 If your eye causes you to fall into sin, tear it out.
It's better for you to enter God's kingdom with one eye than
to be thrown into hell with two. 48 That's a place *where worms*
*don't die and the fire never goes out.* 49 Everyone will be salted
with fire. 50 Salt is good; but if salt loses its saltiness, how will
it become salty again? Maintain salt among yourselves and
keep peace with each other."

**Primary Hymns and Songs for the Day**

126 "Sing Praise to God Who Reigns Above" (Esth, Jas) (O)
H-3 Hbl-92; Chr-173; Desc-76; Org-91
S-1 #237. Desc.
2053 "If It Had Not Been for the Lord" (Esth, Pss)
2223 "They'll Know We Are Christians" (Jas)
591 "Rescue the Perishing" (Jas, Mark)
583 "*Sois la Semilla*" ("You Are the Seed") (Mark)
670 "Go Forth for God" (Pss) (C)
S-1 #138-39. Harm. with desc.
#140. Harm.
H-3 Hbl-77; Chr-63; Org-106

**Additional Hymn Suggestions**

105 "God of Many Names" (Esth)
107 "*La Palabra Del Señor Es Recta*" ("Righteous and Just") (Esth)
506 "Wellspring of Wisdom" (Esth)
127 "Guide Me, O Thou Great Jehovah" (Esth, Pss)
128 "He Leadeth Me: O Blessed Thought" (Esth, Pss)
129 "Give to the Winds Thy Fears" (Esth, Pss)
131 "We Gather Together" (Esth, Pss)
139 "Praise to the Lord, the Almighty" (Esth, Pss)
142 "If Thou But Suffer God to Guide Thee" (Esth, Pss)
519 "Lift Every Voice and Sing" (Esth, Pss)
2146 "His Eye Is on the Sparrow" (Esth, Pss)
2210 "Joy Comes with the Dawn" (Esth, Pss)
2001 "We Sing to You, O God" (Esth, Jas)
2169 "God, How Can We Forgive" (Esth, Jas)
2202 "Come Away with Me" (Jas)
2205 "The Fragrance of Christ" (Jas)
2262 "Let Us Offer to the Father" (Jas)
93 "Let All the World in Every Corner Sing" (Jas)
343 "Come Back Quickly to the Lord" (Jas)
479 "Jesus, Lover of My Soul" (Jas)
492 "Prayer Is the Soul's Sincere Desire" (Jas)
526 "What a Friend We Have in Jesus" (Jas)
463 "Lord, Speak to Me" (Jas, Mark)
192 "There's a Spirit in the Air" (Mark)
396 "O Jesus, I Have Promised" (Mark)
410 "I Want a Principle Within" (Mark)
434 "*Cuando el Pobre*" ("When the Poor Ones") (Mark)
444 "O Young and Fearless Prophet" (Mark)
577 "God of Grace and God of Glory" (Mark)
596 "Blessed Jesus, at Thy Word" (Mark)
649 "How Shall They Hear the Word of God" (Mark)
2149 "Living for Jesus" (Mark)
2185 "For One Great Peace" (Mark)
2246 "Deep in the Shadows of the Past" (Mark)

**Additional Contemporary Suggestions**

WS3108 "Trading My Sorrows" (Esth)
M75
UM523 "*Saranam, Saranam*" ("Refuge") (Esth, Pss)
S2193 "Lord, Listen to Your Children Praying" (Jas)
S2200 "O Lord, Hear My Prayer" (Jas)
S2207 "Lord, Listen to Your Children" (Jas)
S2144 "Someone Asked the Question" (Jas)
S2273 "Jesus, We Are Here" ("*Yesu Tawa Pano*") (Jas)
S2176 "Make Me a Servant" (Jas, Mark)
SP193
S2278 "The Lord's Prayer" (Jas, Mark)
UM271, WS3068-WS3071
S2171 "Make Me a Channel of Your Peace" (Mark)
S2186 "Song of Hope" (Mark)

**Vocal Solos**

"God Will Make a Way" (with "He Leadeth Me") (Esth)
V-3 (2) p. 9
"Jesus, Thou Art Watching Ever" (Pss)
V-4 p. 6
"This Is My Commandment" (Jas)
V-8 p. 284
"In Jesus' Name" (Mark)
V-8 p. 188

**Anthems**

"If My People" (Jas)
Jonathan Adams; Choristers Guild CGA-1345
SATB with piano

"Let Us Talents and Tongues Employ" (Mark)
Arr. Austin Lovelace; Choristers Guild CGA-619
Two-part with piano and opt. guitar, bongo drums

**Other Suggestions**

Visuals:
**O** Hand, crown, festival, joy, food, gifts
**P** Flood, bird, snare
**E** Praying hands, oil, James 5:15a, parched earth/rain/harvest, return
**G** Cup of water, stumbling block, millstone/sea, hand/foot, eye, fire salt
Introit: S2271. "Come! Come! Everybody Worship" (Jas)
Greeting: BOW453 (Esth)
Greeting: BOW454 or BOW615 (Jas)
Prayer of Confession: BOW489 (Mark)
Prayer Response and Litany: S2201. "Prayers of the People" (Jas)
Prayer: WSL59 (Mark)
Prayers: BOW545 and BOW546. For Those Who Suffer (Jas)
Prayer: BOW547. For a Victim or Survivor of Crime or Oppression (Esth)
Litany of Faith: UM106. God Is Able (Esth)
Response: UM448, stanza 11, without refrain. "Go Down, Moses" (Esth)
Blessing: WSL176 (Esth, Jas, Mark)
Sung Benediction: S2171. "Make Me a Channel of Your Peace" (Mark)

**Job 1:1; 2:1-10**
A man in the land of Uz was named Job. That man was
honest, a person of absolute integrity; he feared God and
avoided evil. . . .
2 One day the divine beings came to present themselves
before the LORD. The Adversary also came among them to
present himself before the LORD. 2 The LORD said to the
Adversary, "Where have you come from?"
The Adversary answered the LORD, "From wandering
throughout the earth."
3 The LORD said to the Adversary, "Have you thought about
my servant Job, for there is no one like him on earth, a man
who is honest, who is of absolute integrity, who reveres God
and avoids evil? He still holds on to his integrity, even though
you incited me to ruin him for no reason."
4 The Adversary responded to the LORD, "Skin for skin—
people will give up everything they have in exchange for
their lives. 5 But stretch out your hand and strike his bones
and flesh. Then he will definitely curse you to your face."
6 The LORD answered the Adversary, "There he is—within
your power; only preserve his life."
7 The Adversary departed from the LORD's presence and
struck Job with severe sores from the sole of his foot to
the top of his head. 8 Job took a piece of broken pottery to
scratch himself and sat down on a mound of ashes. 9 Job's
wife said to him, "Are you still clinging to your integrity?
Curse God, and die."
10 Job said to her, "You're talking like a foolish woman. Will
we receive good from God but not also receive bad?" In all
this, Job didn't sin with his lips.

---

**Psalm 26**
Establish justice for me, LORD,
because I have walked with integrity.
I've trusted the LORD without wavering.
2 Examine me, LORD; put me to the test!
Purify my mind and my heart.
3 Because your faithful love is right in front of me—
I walk in your truth!
4 I don't spend time with people up to no good;
I don't keep company with liars.
5 I detest the company of evildoers,
and I don't sit with wicked people.
6 I wash my hands—they are innocent!
I walk all around your altar, LORD,
7 proclaiming out loud my thanks,
declaring all your wonderful deeds!
8 I love the beauty of your house, LORD;
I love the place where your glory resides.
9 Don't gather me up with the sinners,
taking my life along with violent people
10 in whose hands are evil schemes,
whose strong hands are full of bribes.
11 But me? I walk with integrity.
Save me! Have mercy on me!
12 My feet now stand on level ground.
I will bless the LORD in the great congregation.

---

**Hebrews 1:1-4; 2:5-12**
In the past, God spoke through the prophets to our ancestors in many times and many ways. 2 In these final days,
though, he spoke to us through a Son. God made his Son the
heir of everything and created the world through him.
3 The Son is the light of God's glory and the imprint of God's
being. He maintains everything with his powerful message.
After he carried out the cleansing of people from their sins,
he sat down at the right side of the highest majesty. 4 And
the Son became so much greater than the other messengers,
such as angels, that he received a more important title than
theirs. . . .
2 5 God didn't put the world that is coming (the world we
are talking about) under the angels' control. 6 Instead, someone declared somewhere,
*What is humanity that you think about them?*
*Or what are the human beings that you care about them?*
7 *For a while you made them lower than angels.*
*You crowned the human beings with glory and honor.*
8 *You put everything under their control.*
When he puts everything under their control, he doesn't
leave anything out of control. But right now, we don't see
everything under their control yet. 9 However, we do see the
one who was made lower in order than the angels for a little
while—it's Jesus! He's the one who is now crowned with glory
and honor because of the suffering of his death. He suffered
death so that he could taste death for everyone through
God's grace.
10 It was appropriate for God, for whom and through whom
everything exists, to use experiences of suffering to make
perfect the pioneer of salvation. This salvation belongs to
many sons and daughters whom he's leading to glory. 11 This
is because the one who makes people holy and the people
who are being made holy all come from one source. That
is why Jesus isn't ashamed to call them brothers and sisters
when he says,
12 *I will publicly announce your name to my brothers and sisters.*
*I will praise you in the middle of the assembly.*

---

**Mark 10:2-16**
2 Some Pharisees came and, trying to test him, they asked,
"Does the Law allow a man to divorce his wife?"
3 Jesus answered, "What did Moses command you?"
4 They said, "Moses allowed a man to write a divorce certificate and to divorce his wife."
5 Jesus said to them, "He wrote this commandment for
you because of your unyielding hearts. 6 At the beginning of
creation, *God made them male and female.* 7 *Because of this, a man
should leave his father and mother and be joined together with his
wife,* 8 *and the two will be one flesh.* So they are no longer two
but one flesh. 9 Therefore, humans must not pull apart what
God has put together."
10 Inside the house, the disciples asked him again about
this. 11 He said to them, "Whoever divorces his wife and marries another commits adultery against her; 12 and if a wife
divorces her husband and marries another, she commits
adultery."
13 People were bringing children to Jesus so that he would
bless them. But the disciples scolded them. 14 When Jesus saw
this, he grew angry and said to them, "Allow the children
to come to me. Don't forbid them, because God's kingdom
belongs to people like these children. 15 I assure you that
whoever doesn't welcome God's kingdom like a child will
never enter it." 16 Then he hugged the children and blessed
them.

**Primary Hymns and Songs for the Day**
277 "Tell Me the Stories of Jesus" (Mark) (O)
507 "Through It All" (Job)
708 "Rejoice in God's Saints" (Job)
H-3 Hbl-90, 105; Chr-221; Desc-49; Org-51
S-2 #71-74. Intro. and harm.
620 "One Bread, One Body" (World Comm.)
H-3 Chr-156
529 "How Firm a Foundation" (Job, Pss) (C)
H-3 Hbl-27, 69; Chr-102; Desc-41; Org-41
S-1 #133. Harm.
#134. Performance note

**Additional Hymn Suggestions**
505 "When Our Confidence Is Shaken" (Job)
506 "Wellspring of Wisdom" (Job)
517 "By Gracious Powers" (Job)
519 "Lift Every Voice and Sing" (Job)
2105 "Jesus, Tempted in the Desert" (Job)
2212 "My Life Flows On" ("How Can I Keep from Singing") (Job)
2216 "When We Are Called to Sing Your Praise" (Job)
2221 "In Unity We Lift Our Song" (Job, World Comm.)
368 "My Hope Is Built" (Job, Pss)
464 "I Will Trust in the Lord" (Job, Pss)
521 "I Want Jesus to Walk with Me" (Job, Pss)
141 "Children of the Heavenly Father" (Pss, Heb, Mark)
79 "Holy God, We Praise Thy Name" (Heb)
166 "All Praise to Thee, for Thou, O King Divine" (Heb)
326 "The Head That Once Was Crowned" (Heb)
363 "And Can It Be that I Should Gain" (Heb)
540 "I Love Thy Kingdom, Lord" (Heb)
679 "O Splendor of God's Glory Bright" (Heb)
189 "Fairest Lord Jesus" (Heb, Mark)
191 "Jesus Loves Me" (Mark)
273 "Jesus' Hands Were Kind Hands" (Mark)
447 "Our Parent, by Whose Name" (Mark)
479 "Jesus, Lover of My Soul" (Mark)
632 "Draw Us in the Spirit's Tether" (Mark, Comm.)
643 "When Love Is Found" (Mark, Comm.)
2092 "Like a Child" (Mark)
2197 "Lord of All Hopefulness" (Mark)
2245 "Within the Day-to-Day" ("A Hymn for Deacons") (Mark)
3149 "A Place at the Table" (Mark, World Comm.)
3173 "Table of Plenty" (Mark, World Comm.)
2238 "In the Midst of New Dimensions" (World Comm.)
617 "I Come with Joy" (World Comm.)
624 "Bread of the World" (World Comm.)
630 "Become to Us the Living Bread" (World Comm.)
637 "*Una Espiga*" ("Sheaves of Summer") (World Comm.)

**Additional Contemporary Suggestions**
UM63 "Blessed Be the Name" (Job)
M12, S2034, SF2034
WS3002 "Blessed Be Your Name" (Job)
M163
M73 "My Redeemer Lives" (Job)
M177 "How Can I Keep from Singing" (Job)
M262 "Desert Song" (Job)
WS3104 "Amazing Grace" ("My Chains Are Gone") (Job, Pss)
M205
WS3105 "In Christ Alone" ("My Hope Is Found") (Job, Pss)
M138
UM99 "My Tribute" ("To God Be the Glory") (Job, Heb)
V-8 p. 5 Vocal Solo
S2272 "Holy Ground" (Pss)
SP86
M60 "Better Is One Day" (Pss)
M26 "The Power of Your Love" (Pss, Mark)
S2188 "The Family Prayer Song" ("As for Me and My House") (Pss, Mark)
M54
S2023 "How Majestic Is Your Name" (Heb)
SP14
M15 "Agnus Dei" (Heb)
M21 "Blessing, Honour and Glory" (Heb)
M44 "Most Holy Lord" (Heb)
M94 "That's Why We Praise Him" (Heb)
M104 "There Is None Like You" (Mark)
S2233 "Where Children Belong" (Mark)
S2224 "Make Us One" (World Comm.)
SP137
S2226 "Bind Us Together" (World Comm.)
SP140
S2227 "We Are the Body of Christ" (World Comm.)

**Vocal Solos**
"A Contrite Heart" (Pss)
V-4 p. 10
"One Bread, One Body" (World Comm.)
V-3 (2) p. 40

**Anthems**
"Love Has Broken Down the Wall" (Heb, Mark)
Mark Miller; Choristers Guild CGA-1384
SATB with piano

"Bread of the World" (World Comm.)
C. Griffith Bratt; Paraclete Press PPM01305
SATB with organ

**Other Suggestions**
Visuals:
**O** Hand, sores, suffering, potsherd, ashes, man/woman
**P** Walking, heart, washing hands, singing, foot, broom
**E** Jesus, angels, crown, cross, pioneer
**G** Divorce decree, marriage (wedding rings, certificate), children, Mark 10:14, blessing
Greeting: BOW449 (Pss)
Call to Worship: WSL68 (World Comm.)
Opening Prayer: WSL67 (World Comm.)
Call to Prayer: BOW196. Call to Prayer (Job)
Prayer of Confession: WSL89 (Job, Pss)
Prayer of Confession: WSL43 (World Comm.)
Prayer: UM531. For Overcoming Adversity (Job)
Prayer: BOW545. For Those Who Suffer (Job)
Offertory Prayer: WSL116 (World Comm.)
Prayer of Thanksgiving: BOW554
Prayer: UM639. Bread and Justice (Mark, World Comm.)
World Communion Resources: BOW431, 488, 495, 501–506, p. 72
Sung Response: S2257 or WS3172. "Communion Setting"
Closing Prayer: WSL171 (World Comm.)

**Job 23:1-9, 16-17**

Job answered:
[2] Today my complaint is again bitter;
my strength is weighed down because of my groaning.
[3] Oh, that I could know how to find him—
come to his dwelling place;
[4] I would lay out my case before him,
fill my mouth with arguments,
[5] know the words with which he would answer,
understand what he would say to me.
[6] Would he contend with me through brute force?
No, he would surely listen to me.
[7] There those who do the right thing can argue with him;
I could escape from my judge forever.
[8] Look, I go east; he's not there,
west, and don't discover him;
[9] north in his activity, and I don't grasp him;
he turns south, and I don't see.

. . . . . . . . . . . . . . . . . . . . . . . . . .

[16] God has weakened my mind;
the Almighty has frightened me.
[17] Still I'm not annihilated by darkness;
he has hidden deep darkness from me.

**Psalm 22:1-15 (UM752)**

My God! My God,
why have you left me all alone?
Why are you so far from saving me—
so far from my anguished groans?
[2] My God, I cry out during the day,
but you don't answer;
even at nighttime I don't stop.
[3] You are the holy one, enthroned.
You are Israel's praise.
[4] Our ancestors trusted you—
they trusted you and you rescued them;
[5] they cried out to you and they were saved;
they trusted you and they weren't ashamed.
[6] But I'm just a worm, less than human;
insulted by one person, despised by another.
[7] All who see me make fun of me—
they gape, shaking their heads:
[8] "He committed himself to the LORD,
so let God rescue him;
let God deliver him
because God likes him so much."
[9] But you are the one who pulled me from the womb,
placing me safely at my mother's breasts.
[10] I was thrown on you from birth;
you've been my God
since I was in my mother's womb.
[11] Please don't be far from me,
because trouble is near
and there's no one to help.
[12] Many bulls surround me;
mighty bulls from Bashan encircle me.
[13] They open their mouths at me
like a lion ripping and roaring!
[14] I'm poured out like water.
All my bones have fallen apart.
My heart is like wax;
it melts inside me.
[15] My strength is dried up
like a piece of broken pottery.
My tongue sticks to the roof of my mouth;
you've set me down in the dirt of death.

**Hebrews 4:12-16**

[12] God's word is living, active, and sharper than any two-
edged sword. It penetrates to the point that it separates the
soul from the spirit and the joints from the marrow. It's able
to judge the heart's thoughts and intentions. [13] No creature is
hidden from it, but rather everything is naked and exposed
to the eyes of the one to whom we have to give an answer.
[14] Also, let's hold on to the confession since we have a great
high priest who passed through the heavens, who is Jesus,
God's Son; [15] because we don't have a high priest who can't
sympathize with our weaknesses but instead one who was
tempted in every way that we are, except without sin.
[16] Finally, let's draw near to the throne of favor with confidence so that we can receive mercy and find grace when we
need help.

**Mark 10:17-31**

[17] As Jesus continued down the road, a man ran up, knelt
before him, and asked, "Good Teacher, what must I do to
obtain eternal life?"
[18] Jesus replied, "Why do you call me good? No one is good
except the one God. [19] You know the commandments: *Don't
commit murder. Don't commit adultery. Don't steal. Don't give false
testimony.* Don't cheat. *Honor your father and mother.*"
[20] "Teacher," he responded, "I've kept all of these things
since I was a boy."
[21] Jesus looked at him carefully and loved him. He said,
"You are lacking one thing. Go, sell what you own, and
give the money to the poor. Then you will have treasure in
heaven. And come, follow me." [22] But the man was dismayed
at this statement and went away saddened, because he had
many possessions.
[23] Looking around, Jesus said to his disciples, "It will be very
hard for the wealthy to enter God's kingdom!" [24] His words
startled the disciples, so Jesus told them again, "Children, it's
difficult to enter God's kingdom! [25] It's easier for a camel to
squeeze through the eye of a needle than for a rich person to
enter God's kingdom."
[26] They were shocked even more and said to each other,
"Then who can be saved?"
[27] Jesus looked at them carefully and said, "It's impossible
with human beings, but not with God. All things are possible
for God."
[28] Peter said to him, "Look, we've left everything and followed you."
[29] Jesus said, "I assure you that anyone who has left house,
brothers, sisters, mother, father, children, or farms because
of me and because of the good news [30] will receive one hundred times as much now in this life—houses, brothers, sisters,
mothers, children, and farms (with harassment)—and in the
coming age, eternal life. [31] But many who are first will be last.
And many who are last will be first."

### Primary Hymns and Songs for the Day

463 "Lord, Speak to Me" (Job, Mark) (O)
H-3 Hbl-75; Chr-131; Desc-22; Org-18
S-1 #52. Desc.
474 "Precious Lord, Take My Hand" (Job, Pss)
H-3 Chr-164; Org-116
515 "Out of the Depths I Cry to You" (Job, Pss)
396 "O Jesus, I Have Promised" (Mark)
S-2 #9. Desc.
402 "Lord, I Want to Be a Christian" (Mark)
399 "Take My Life, and Let It Be" (Mark) (C)

### Additional Hymn Suggestions

103 "Immortal, Invisible, God Only Wise" (Job)
708 "Rejoice in God's Saints" (Job)
452 "My Faith Looks Up to Thee" (Job, Pss)
474 "Precious Lord, Take My Hand" (Job, Pss)
520 "Nobody Knows the Trouble I See" (Job, Pss)
2105 "Jesus, Tempted in the Desert" (Job, Pss)
2180 "Why Stand So Far Away, My God?" (Job, Pss)
2216 "When We Are Called to Sing Your Praise" (Job, Pss)
2217 "By the Babylonian Rivers" (Job, Pss)
521 "I Want Jesus to Walk with Me" (Pss)
473 "Lead Me, Lord" (Pss, Heb)
178 "Hope of the World" (Heb)
400 "Come, Thou Fount of Every Blessing" (Heb)
517 "By Gracious Powers" (Heb)
577 "God of Grace and God of Glory" (Heb)
598 "O Word of God Incarnate" (Heb)
2046 "Womb of Life" (Heb)
2050 "Mothering God, You Gave Me Birth" (Heb)
2084 "Come, Let Us with Our Lord Arise" (Heb)
2169 "God, How Can We Forgive" (Heb)
2264 "Come to the Table" (Heb)
468 "Dear Jesus, in Whose Life I See" (Heb, Mark)
415 "Take Up Thy Cross" (Mark)
2127 "Come and See" ("*Kyrie*") (Mark)
2130 "The Summons" (Mark)
2137 "Would I Have Answered When You Called" (Mark)
2268 "As We Gather at Your Table" (Mark, Comm.)

### Additional Contemporary Suggestions

S2219 "Goodness Is Stronger than Evil" (Job)
WS3112 "Breathe" (Job, Pss)
M61
M262 "Desert Song" (Job, Pss)
WS3184 "Word of God, Speak" (Job, Pss, Heb)
M148
M115 "When It's All Been Said and Done" (Job, Pss, Mark)
M37 "He Is Able" (Job, Mark)
UM601 "Thy Word Is a Lamp" (Heb)
SP183
M44 "Most Holy Lord" (Heb)
M74 "There Is Joy in the Lord" (Heb)
S2085 "He Came Down" (Heb)
S2244 "People Need the Lord" (Heb, Mark)
WS3040 "You Are My All in All" (Heb, Mark)
SP220
S2036 "Give Thanks" (Mark)
SP170
S2218 "You Are Mine" (Mark)
S2131 "Humble Thyself in the Sight of the Lord" (Mark)
SP223
S2176 "Make Me a Servant" (Mark)
SP193
S2165 "Cry of My Heart" (Mark)
M39
M34 "I Will Never Be" (the Same Again) (Mark)
WS3004 "Step by Step" (Mark)
M51
M41 "You're Worthy of My Praise" (Mark)
M92 "All Things Are Possible" (Mark)
M98 "Take This Life" (Mark)
M104 "There Is None Like You" (Mark)
M122 "Every Move I Make" (Mark)
M156 "Be the Centre" (Mark)
M157 "Surrender" (Mark)
M227 "I Will Boast" (Mark)

### Vocal Solos

"He Trusted in God" (Job, Pss)
V-2
"Steal Away to Heaven" (Job, Pss)
V-3 (1) p. 17
"Give Me a Clean Heart" (Mark)
V-5(2) p. 52
"Here I Am" (Mark)
V-11 p. 19

### Anthems

"I Lift Up My Eyes to the Mountains" (Pss, Heb)
Paul French; Paraclete Press PPM01315
SATB *divisi a cappella*

"Take My Life, and Let It Be" (Mark)
Arr. Margaret R. Tucker; Choristers Guild CGA-1111
Unison/Two-part with organ and opt. handbells

### Other Suggestions

Visuals:
**O** Briefcase, Job 23:3, courtroom, judge, scales, darkness
**P** Crying, worm, birth, nursing, bulls, lion, water, melted wax, dust
**E** Heb 4:12, open Bible, sword, scales, heart, Christ
**G** Kneeling, Jesus, Ten Commandments, rich/poor, camel/needle

Introit: S2265. "Time Now to Gather" (Heb, Comm.)
Greeting: BOW451 (Heb)
Prayer of Confession: BOW477 (Heb) or BOW485 (Mark)
Response: S2277. "Lord, Have Mercy" (Heb)
Prayer: UM597 (Heb) or UM403 (Mark)
Offertory Prayer: WSL156 (Mark)
Prayer of Thanksgiving: BOW550 (Pss, Heb, Mark)
Prayer of Thanksgiving: BOW557 (Job)

**Job 38:1-7, (34-41)**

Then the LORD answered Job from the whirlwind:
2 Who is this darkening counsel
with words lacking knowledge?
3 Prepare yourself like a man;
I will interrogate you, and you will respond to me.
4 Where were you when I laid the earth's foundations?
Tell me if you know.
5 Who set its measurements? Surely you know.
Who stretched a measuring tape on it?
6 On what were its footings sunk;
who laid its cornerstone,
7 while the morning stars sang in unison
and all the divine beings shouted?

. . . . . . . . . . . . . . . . . . . . . . . . . .

34 Can you issue an order to the clouds
so their abundant waters cover you?
35 Can you send lightning so that it goes
and then says to you, "I'm here"?
36 Who put wisdom in remote places,
or who gave understanding to a rooster?
37 Who is wise enough to count the clouds,
and who can tilt heaven's water containers
38 so that dust becomes mud
and clods of dirt adhere?
39 Can you hunt prey for the lion
or fill the cravings of lion cubs?
40 They lie in their den,
lie in ambush in their lair.
41 Who provides food for the raven
when its young cry to God,
move about without food?

---

**Psalm 104:1-9, 24, 35c (UM826)**

Let my whole being bless the LORD!
LORD my God, how fantastic you are!
You are clothed in glory and grandeur!
2 You wear light like a robe;
you open the skies like a curtain.
3 You build your lofty house on the waters;
you make the clouds your chariot,
going around on the wings of the wind.
4 You make the winds your messengers;
you make fire and flame your ministers.
5 You established the earth on its foundations
so that it will never ever fall.
6 You covered it with the watery deep like a piece of clothing;
the waters were higher than the mountains!
7 But at your rebuke they ran away;
they fled in fear at the sound of your thunder.
8 They flowed over the mountains,
streaming down the valleys
to the place you established for them.
9 You set a boundary they cannot cross
so they'll never again cover the earth.

. . . . . . . . . . . . . . . . . . . . . . . . . .

24 LORD, you have done so many things!
You made them all so wisely!
The earth is full of your creations!

. . . . . . . . . . . . . . . . . . . . . . . . . .

35c Praise the LORD!

**Hebrews 5:1-10**

Every high priest is taken from the people and put in
charge of things that relate to God for their sake, in order to
offer gifts and sacrifices for sins. 2 The high priest is able to
deal gently with the ignorant and those who are misled since
he himself is prone to weakness. 3 Because of his weakness, he
must offer sacrifices for his own sins as well as for the people.
4 No one takes this honor for themselves but takes it only
when they are called by God, just like Aaron.
5 In the same way Christ also didn't promote himself to
become high priest. Instead, it was the one who said to him,
*You are my Son.*
*Today I have become your Father,*
6 *as he also says in another place,*
*You are a priest forever,*
*according to the order of Melchizedek.*
7 During his days on earth, Christ offered prayers and
requests with loud cries and tears as his sacrifices to the one
who was able to save him from death. He was heard because
of his godly devotion. 8 Although he was a Son, he learned
obedience from what he suffered. 9 After he had been made
perfect, he became the source of eternal salvation for everyone who obeys him. 10 He was appointed by God to be a high
priest according to the order of Melchizedek.

---

**Mark 10:35-45**

35 James and John, Zebedee's sons, came to Jesus and said,
"Teacher, we want you to do for us whatever we ask."
36 "What do you want me to do for you?" he asked.
37 They said, "Allow one of us to sit on your right and the
other on your left when you enter your glory."
38 Jesus replied, "You don't know what you're asking! Can
you drink the cup I drink or receive the baptism I receive?"
39 "We can," they answered.
Jesus said, "You will drink the cup I drink and receive
the baptism I receive, 40 but to sit at my right or left hand
isn't mine to give. It belongs to those for whom it has been
prepared."
41 Now when the other ten disciples heard about this, they
became angry with James and John. 42 Jesus called them over
and said, "You know that the ones who are considered the
rulers by the Gentiles show off their authority over them and
their high-ranking officials order them around. 43 But that's
not the way it will be with you. Whoever wants to be great
among you will be your servant. 44 Whoever wants to be first
among you will be the slave of all, 45 for the Human One
didn't come to be served but rather to serve and to give his
life to liberate many people."

**Primary Hymns and Songs for the Day**

152 "I Sing the Almighty Power of God" (Job) (O)
H-3 Hbl-44; Chr-21; Desc-40; Org-40
S-1 #131-132. Intro. and desc.
165 "Hallelujah! What a Savior" (Heb)
H-3 Chr-134
432 "*Jesu, Jesu*" (Mark)
H-3 Chr-114; Org-19
S-1 #63. Vocal part
2222 "The Servant Song" (Mark)
530 "Are Ye Able" (Mark, Laity Sunday) (C)
S-2 #23. Intro.

**Additional Hymn Suggestions**

77 "How Great Thou Art" (Job)
110 "A Mighty Fortress Is Our God" (Job)
144 "This Is My Father's World" (Job)
150 "God, Who Stretched the Spangled Heavens" (Job)
153 "Thou Hidden Source of Calm Repose" (Job)
443 "O God Who Shaped Creation" (Job)
2004 "Praise the Source of Faith and Learning" (Job)
2191 "Eternal Father, Strong to Save" (Job)
2210 "Joy Comes with the Dawn" (Job)
3035 "Bless Christ Through Whom All Things Are Made" (Job)
414 "Thou Hidden Love of God" (Job, Heb, Mark)
89 "Joyful, Joyful, We Adore Thee" (Job, Pss)
148 "Many and Great, O God" (Job, Pss)
73 "O Worship the King" (Pss)
103 "Immortal, Invisible, God Only Wise" (Heb)
154 "All Hail the Power of Jesus' Name" (Heb)
155 "All Hail the Power of Jesus' Name" (Heb)
731 "Glorious Things of Thee Are Spoken" (Heb)
2083 "My Song Is Love Unknown" (Heb)
2149 "Living for Jesus" (Heb)
2259 "Victim Divine" (Heb)
2027 "Now Praise the Hidden God of Love" (Heb, Mark)
2100 "Thou Didst Leave Thy Throne" (Heb, Mark)
166 "All Praise to Thee, for Thou, O King Divine" (Heb, Mark)
425 "O Crucified Redeemer" (Heb, Mark)
181 "Ye Servants of God" (Mark)
415 "Take Up Thy Cross" (Mark)
421 "Make Me a Captive, Lord" (Mark)
517 "By Gracious Powers" (Mark)
579 "Lord God, Your Love Has Called Us Here" (Mark)
581 "Lord, Whose Love Through Humble Service" (Mark)
589 "The Church of Christ, in Every Age" (Mark)
2175 "Together We Serve" (Mark, Laity Sunday)
2261 "Life-Giving Bread" (Mark, Comm.)

**Additional Contemporary Suggestions**

WS3034 "God of Wonders" (Job, Pss)
M80
M127 "Indescribable" (Job, Pss)
M262 "Desert Song" (Job, Pss)
M73 "My Redeemer Lives" (Job, Heb)
SP32 "Bless the Lord, O My Soul" (Pss)
M4 "Let It Rise" (Pss)
M243 "Beautiful Savior" (Pss, Heb)
M78 "Once Again" (Heb)
M81 "Amazing Love" (Heb)
WS3040 "You Are My All in All" (Heb)
SP220
WS3102 "You Are My King" ("Amazing Love") (Heb)
M82
M94 "That's Why We Praise Him" (Heb)
M106 "I Come to the Cross" (Heb)
S2031 "We Bring the Sacrifice of Praise" (Heb)
SP1
S2131 "Humble Thyself in the Sight of the Lord" (Mark)
SP223
S2176 "Make Me a Servant" (Mark)
SP193
S2223 "They'll Know We Are Christians" (Mark)
M40 "More Love, More Power" (Mark)
M49 "Refresh My Heart" (Mark)
M53 "Let It Be Said of Us" (Mark)
M98 "Take This Life" (Mark)

**Vocal Solos**

"Holy Is the Lamb" (Heb)
V-5(1) p. 5
"Ah, Holy Jesus" (Heb)
V-6 p. 24

**Anthems**

"Within Creation" (Job, Pss)
Arr. Carolyn Hamlin; Hinshaw HMC2340
SATB with piano

"Many and Great, O God" (Job, Pss)
arr. Mitzi Scott; Choristers Guild CGA-1122
Unison/Two- or three-part with piano

**Other Suggestions**

Visuals:
**O** Whirlwind, creation, cornerstone, stars, storm
**P** Light, tent, clouds, wind, fire, sea, mountains
**E** Priest/sacrifice, Christ, Heb 5:5a, Jesus praying, cross
**G** Hands, chalice, baptism, cross, servant
Greeting: BOW452 (Job, Pss)
Call to Prayer: BOW194. "Teach Me to Hear in Silence" (Job)
Opening Prayer: BOW464 (Job, Pss)
Prayer of Confession: BOW478 (Job, Mark)
Prayer: UM570 (Mark) or BOW530 (Job)
Intercessory Prayer: BOW418. For Others (Mark)
Responsive Creed: WSL76 (Heb)
Prayer of Thanksgiving: BOW556 (Job, Pss)
Litany: BOW432 (Laity Sunday)

**Job 42:1-6, 10-17**

Job answered the LORD:
2 I know you can do anything;
no plan of yours can be opposed successfully.
3 You said, "Who is this darkening counsel without
knowledge?"
I have indeed spoken about things I didn't understand,
wonders beyond my comprehension.
4 You said, "Listen and I will speak;
I will question you and you will inform me."
5 My ears had heard about you,
but now my eyes have seen you.
6 Therefore, I relent and find comfort
on dust and ashes.

. . . . . . . . . . . . . . . . . . . . . . . . . . . . . . . . . . . . . . . . . . . .

10 Then the LORD changed Job's fortune when he prayed
for his friends, and the LORD doubled all Job's earlier possessions. 11 All his brothers, sisters, and acquaintances came
to him and ate food with him in his house. They comforted
and consoled him concerning all the disaster the LORD had
brought on him, and each one gave him a qesitah and a
gold ring. 12 Then the LORD blessed Job's latter days more
than his former ones. He had fourteen thousand sheep,
six thousand camels, one thousand yoke of oxen, and one
thousand female donkeys. 13 He also had seven sons and
three daughters. 14 He named one Jemimah, a second Keziah,
and the third Keren-happuch. 15 No women in all the land
were as beautiful as Job's daughters; and their father gave an
inheritance to them along with their brothers. 16 After this,
Job lived 140 years and saw four generations of his children.
17 Then Job died, old and satisfied.

**Psalm 34:1-8, (19-22) (UM769)**

I will bless the LORD at all times;
his praise will always be in my mouth.
2 I praise the LORD—
let the suffering listen and rejoice.
3 Magnify the LORD with me!
Together let us lift his name up high!
4 I sought the LORD and he answered me.
He delivered me from all my fears.
5 Those who look to God will shine;
their faces are never ashamed.
6 This suffering person cried out:
the LORD listened and saved him from every trouble.
7 On every side, the LORD's messenger protects those
who honor God; and he delivers them.
8 Taste and see how good the LORD is!
The one who takes refuge in him is truly happy!

. . . . . . . . . . . . . . . . . . . . . . . . . . . . . . . . . . . . . . . . . . . .

19 The righteous have many problems,
but the LORD delivers them from every one.
20 He protects all their bones;
not even one will be broken.
21 But just one problem will kill the wicked,
and those who hate the righteous will be held
responsible.
22 The LORD saves his servants' lives;
all those who take refuge in him
won't be held responsible for anything.

**Hebrews 7:23-28**

23 The others who became priests are numerous because
death prevented them from continuing to serve. 24 In contrast, he holds the office of priest permanently because he
continues to serve forever. 25 This is why he can completely
save those who are approaching God through him, because
he always lives to speak with God for them.
26 It's appropriate for us to have this kind of high priest:
holy, innocent, incorrupt, separate from sinners, and raised
high above the heavens. 27 He doesn't need to offer sacrifices
every day like the other high priests, first for their own sins
and then for the sins of the people. He did this once for all
when he offered himself. 28 The Law appoints people who
are prone to weakness as high priests, but the content of the
solemn pledge, which came after the Law, appointed a Son
who has been made perfect forever.

**Mark 10:46-52**

46 Jesus and his followers came into Jericho. As Jesus was
leaving Jericho, together with his disciples and a sizable
crowd, a blind beggar named Bartimaeus, Timaeus' son, was
sitting beside the road. 47 When he heard that Jesus of Nazareth was there, he began to shout, "Jesus, Son of David, show
me mercy!" 48 Many scolded him, telling him to be quiet, but
he shouted even louder, "Son of David, show me mercy!"
49 Jesus stopped and said, "Call him forward."
They called the blind man, "Be encouraged! Get up! He's
calling you."
50 Throwing his coat to the side, he jumped up and came to
Jesus.
51 Jesus asked him, "What do you want me to do for you?"
The blind man said, "Teacher, I want to see."

**Primary Hymns and Songs for the Day**
600 "Wonderful Words of Life" (Job, Heb) (O)
H-3 Chr-221; Org-186
351 "Pass Me Not, O Gentle Savior" (Mark)
H-3 Chr-159
452 "My Faith Looks Up to Thee" (Mark)
H-3 Hbl-77; Chr-138; Org-108
S-2 #142. Flute/violin desc.
454 "Open My Eyes, That I May See" (Mark)
H-3 Chr-157; Org-108
2086 "Open Our Eyes, Lord" (Mark)
SP199
110 "A Mighty Fortress Is Our God" (Job, Reformation) (C)
H-3 Chr-19; Desc-35; Org-34
S-1 #111-13. Various treatments

**Additional Hymn Suggestions**
101 "From All That Dwell Below the Skies" (Job)
505 "When Our Confidence Is Shaken" (Job)
2004 "Praise the Source of Faith and Learning" (Job)
2210 "Joy Comes with the Dawn" (Job)
2212 "My Life Flows On" (Job)
89 "Joyful, Joyful, We Adore Thee" (Job, Pss) (O)
142 "If Thou But Suffer God to Guide Thee" (Job, Mark)
2177 "Wounded World that Cries for Healing" (Job, Mark)
2126 "All Who Hunger" (Pss, Comm.)
2261 "Life-Giving Bread" (Pss, Comm.)
2267 "Taste and See" (Pss, Comm.)
169 "In Thee Is Gladness" (Heb)
173 "Christ, Whose Glory Fills the Skies" (Heb)
267 "O Love, How Deep" (Heb)
368 "My Hope Is Built" (Heb)
379 "Blow Ye the Trumpet, Blow" (Heb)
606 "Come, Let Us Use the Grace Divine" (Heb)
2169 "God, How Can We Forgive" (Heb)
170 "O How I Love Jesus" (Heb, Mark)
57 "O For a Thousand Tongues to Sing" (Mark)
59 "*Mil Voces Para Celebrar*" (Mark)
262 "Heal Me, Hands of Jesus" (Mark)
263 "When Jesus the Healer Passed Through Galilee" (Mark)
265 "O Christ, the Healer" (Mark)
266 "Heal Us, Emmanuel, Hear Our Prayer" (Mark)
348 "Softly and Tenderly Jesus Is Calling" (Mark)
451 "Be Thou My Vision" (Mark)
385 "Let Us Plead for Faith Alone" (Mark)
650 "Give Me the Faith Which Can Remove" (Mark)
2104 "An Outcast among Outcasts" (Mark)
2130 "The Summons" (Mark)
2199 "Stay with Us" (Mark)
2277 "Lord, Have Mercy" (Mark)
3001 "O For a Thousand Tongues to Sing" (Mark)
3110 "By Grace We Have Been Saved" (Mark)

**Additional Contemporary Suggestions**
UM507 "Through It All" (Job)
WS3002 "Blessed Be Your Name" (Job)
M163
S2203 "In His Time" (Job)
S2219 "Goodness Is Stronger than Evil" (Job)
S2244 "People Need the Lord" (Job, Mark)
M73 "My Redeemer Lives" (Job)
M177 "How Can I Keep from Singing" (Job)
M262 "Desert Song" (Job)
M60 "Better Is One Day" (Pss)
M113 "In the Presence of Jehovah" (Pss)
M178 "Majestic" (Pss)
SP18 "I Exalt You" (Pss)
SP77 "O Magnify the Lord" (Pss)
S2023 "How Majestic Is Your Name" (Pss)
SP14
S2071 "Jesus, Name Above All Names" (Heb)
SP76
WS3104 "Amazing Grace" ("My Chains Are Gone") (Heb)
M205
WS3105 "In Christ Alone" ("My Hope Is Found") (Heb)
M138
M65 "Before the Throne of God Above" (Heb)
M94 "That's Why We Praise Him" (Heb)
UM349 "Turn Your Eyes upon Jesus" (Mark)
SP218
UM394 "Something Beautiful" (Mark)
M26 "The Power of Your Love" (Mark)
M164 "Good to Me"
WS3008 "Open the Eyes of My Heart" (Mark)
M57

**Vocal Solos**
"God Will Make a Way" (with "He Leadeth Me") (Job)
V-3 (2) p. 9
"This Is My Father's World" (Job, Pss)
V-6 p. 42
"Redeeming Grace" (Mark)
V-4 p. 47
"Softly and Tenderly" (Mark)
V-5(3) p. 52

**Anthems**
"Sing to the Lord" (Pss)
Medema/Althouse; Alfred 42515
SATB with piano

"Lord, I Was Blind" (Mark)
David Rasbach; Choristers Guild CGA-1343
SATB with piano, opt. cello

**Other Suggestions**
Visuals:
**O** Dust/ashes, gold coins, rings, boys/girls
**P** Praise, Pss 34:8, taste: fruits, vegetables, sweets
**E** Christ, vestments on the altar
**G** Tattered cloak, blind man: dramatize, dance, mime
If you wish to emphasize the healing aspect of the Mark reading, see BOW resources, pp. 615–29.
Introit: S2132. "You Who Are Thirsty" (Pss, Comm.)
Greeting: BOW449 (Pss)
Opening Prayer: BOW461 (Job, Pss)
Prayer of Confession: BOW478 (Job)
Response: S2275. "*Kyrie*" (Mark)
Prayer: BOW545-546. For Those Who Suffer (Job, Mark)
Prayer: WSL70 (Job, Pss)
Prayer of Thanksgiving: BOW552 (Job, Mark)
Prayer: WSL193 (Reformation)
Reformation Day Resources: BOW444, 456, 501–6

**Isaiah 25:6-9**

6 On this mountain,
the LORD of heavenly forces will prepare for all peoples
a rich feast, a feast of choice wines,
of select foods rich in flavor,
of choice wines well refined.
7 He will swallow up on this mountain the veil that is veiling
all peoples,
the shroud enshrouding all nations.
8 He will swallow up death forever.
The LORD God will wipe tears from every face;
he will remove his people's disgrace from off the whole
earth,
for the Lord has spoken.
9 They will say on that day,
"Look! This is our God,
for whom we have waited—
and he has saved us!
This is the LORD, for whom we have waited;
let's be glad and rejoice in his salvation!"

---

**Psalm 24 (UM755)**

The earth is the LORD's and everything in it,
the world and its inhabitants too.
2 Because God is the one who established it on the seas;
God set it firmly on the waters.
3 Who can ascend the LORD's mountain?
Who can stand in his holy sanctuary?
4 Only the one with clean hands and a pure heart;
the one who hasn't made false promises,
the one who hasn't sworn dishonestly.
5 That kind of person receives blessings from the LORD
and righteousness from the God who saves.
6 And that's how things are
with the generation that seeks him—
that seeks the face of Jacob's God. *[Selah]*
7 Mighty gates: lift up your heads!
Ancient doors: rise up high!
So the glorious king can enter!
8 Who is this glorious king?
The LORD—strong and powerful!
The LORD—powerful in battle!
9 Mighty gates: lift up your heads!
Ancient doors: rise up high!
So the glorious king can enter!
10 Who is this glorious king?
The LORD of heavenly forces—
he is the glorious king! *[Selah]*

---

**Revelation 21:1-6a**

Then I saw a new heaven and a new earth, for the former
heaven and the former earth had passed away, and the sea
was no more. 2 I saw the holy city, New Jerusalem, coming
down out of heaven from God, made ready as a bride beautifully dressed for her husband. 3 I heard a loud voice from the
throne say, "Look! God's dwelling is here with humankind.
He will dwell with them, and they will be his peoples. God
himself will be with them as their God. 4 He will wipe away
every tear from their eyes. Death will be no more. There will
be no mourning, crying, or pain anymore, for the former
things have passed away." 5 Then the one seated on the
throne said, "Look! I'm making all things new." He also said,
"Write this down, for these words are trustworthy and true."
6a Then he said to me, "All is done. I am the Alpha and the
Omega, the beginning and the end."

---

**John 11:32-44**

32 When Mary arrived where Jesus was and saw him, she fell
at his feet and said, "Lord, if you had been here, my brother
wouldn't have died."
33 When Jesus saw her crying and the Jews who had come
with her crying also, he was deeply disturbed and troubled.
34 He asked, "Where have you laid him?"
They replied, "Lord, come and see."
35 Jesus began to cry. 36 The Jews said, "See how much he
loved him!" 37 But some of them said, "He healed the eyes
of the man born blind. Couldn't he have kept Lazarus from
dying?"
38 Jesus was deeply disturbed again when he came to the
tomb. It was a cave, and a stone covered the entrance. 39 Jesus
said, "Remove the stone."
Martha, the sister of the dead man, said, "Lord, the smell
will be awful! He's been dead four days."
40 Jesus replied, "Didn't I tell you that if you believe, you will
see God's glory?" 41 So they removed the stone. Jesus looked
up and said, "Father, thank you for hearing me. 42 I know
you always hear me. I say this for the benefit of the crowd
standing here so that they will believe that you sent me." 43
Having said this, Jesus shouted with a loud voice, "Lazarus,
come out!" 44 The dead man came out, his feet bound and
his hands tied, and his face covered with a cloth. Jesus said to
them, "Untie him and let him go."

**Primary Hymns and Songs for the Day**

213 "Lift Up Your Heads, Ye Mighty Gates" (Pss) (O)
H-3 Hbl-50; Chr-47; Desc-101; Org-167
S-1 #334-35. Desc. and harm.
711 "For All the Saints" (Pss, All Sts)
H-3 Hbl-58; Chr-65; Org-152
S-1 #314-18. Various treatments
2210 "Joy Comes with the Dawn" (Isa, Rev, John)
2272 "Holy Ground" (Pss, All Sts)
SP86
733 "Marching to Zion" (Isa, Rev) (C)
H-3 Chr-298

**Additional Hymn Suggestions**

722 "I Want to Be Ready" (Isa, Rev)
725 "Arise, Shine Out, Your Light Has Come" (Isa, Rev)
727 "O What Their Joy and Glory Must Be" (Isa, Rev)
729 "O Day of Peace That Dimly Shines" (Isa, Rev)
383 "This Is a Day of New Beginnings" (Isa, Rev, John, Comm.)
2126 "All Who Hunger" (Isa, Comm.)
2264 "Come to the Table" (Isa, Comm.)
2044 "My Gratitude Now Accept, O God" (Pss)
152 "I Sing the Almighty Power of God" (Pss)
312 "Hail the Day That Sees Him Rise" (Pss, Rev, John)
384 "Love Divine, All Loves Excelling" (Rev)
428 "For the Healing of the Nations" (Rev)
510 "Come, Ye Disconsolate" (Rev)
524 "Beams of Heaven as I Go" (Rev)
533 "We Shall Overcome" (Rev)
623 "Here, O My Lord, I See Thee" (Rev, Comm.)
653 "Christ the Victorious" (Rev)
702 "Sing with All the Saints in Glory" (Rev, All Sts)
726 "O Holy City, Seen of John" (Rev)
731 "Glorious Things of Thee Are Spoken" (Rev)
2142 "Blessed Quietness" (Rev)
2284 "Joy in the Morning" (Rev)
3094 "Come to Me" (Rev, All Sts)
551 "Awake, O Sleeper" (John, All Sts)
654 "How Blest Are They" (John, All Sts)
680 "Father, We Praise Thee" (All Sts)
708 "Rejoice in God's Saints" (All Sts)
712 "I Sing a Song of the Saints of God" (John)
2106 "When Jesus Wept" (John)
2110 "Why Has God Forsaken Me?" (John)
2042 "How Lovely, Lord, How Lovely" (All Sts)
2155 "Blest Are They" (All Sts)
2221 "In Unity We Lift Our Song" (All Sts)
2246 "Deep in the Shadows of the Past" (All Sts)
2268 "As We Gather at Your Table" (All Sts, Comm.)
2283 "For All the Saints" (All Sts)
3157 "Come, Let Us Dream" (All Sts)

**Additional Contemporary Suggestions**

S2132 "You Who Are Thirsty" (Isa, Rev)
M36 "Awesome in This Place" (Isa, Pss)
S2091 "The King of Glory Comes" (Pss)
M141 "Sing to the King" (Pss)
UM347 "Spirit Song" (Rev)
SP134
UM706 "Soon and Very Soon" (Rev)
S-2 #187. Piano Arr.
S2087 "We Will Glorify" (Rev)
SP68
UM171 "There's Something About That Name" (Rev)
SP89
M21 "Blessing, Honour and Glory" (Rev)
M23 "Hallelujah to the Lamb" (Rev)
WS3003 "How Great Is Our God" (Rev)
M117
M159 "All Who Are Thirsty" (Rev)
M260 "I Will Rise" (Rev, John)
M20 "Jesus Is Alive" (Rev, John)
M220 "All Because of Jesus" (John)
S2066 "Praise the Name of Jesus" (John)
SP87
WS3187 "We Fall Down" (All Sts)
M66

**Vocal Solos**

"Marchin' On Up" (Isa, Rev)
V-3 (3) p. 57
"Maybe the Rain" (Isa, Rev)
V-5(2) p. 27
"Then Shall the Righteous Shine Forth" (Rev, All Sts)
V-8 p. 274
"In Bright Mansions Above" (All Sts)
V-4 p. 39

**Anthems**

"The Church's One Foundation" (Rev, All Sts)
Arr. Michael Burkhardt; MorningStar MSM-50-9032
SATB with organ, opt. brass, handbells, congregation

"Ye Holy Angels Bright" (All Sts)
Arr. June Nixon; Paraclete Press PPM01356
SATB with organ and two trumpets

**Other Suggestions**

Visuals:
**O** Banquet, sheet, handkerchief, rejoicing
**P** Sea, river, hill, washing hands, heart, Pss 24:7, gates/doors
**E** Wedding, Alpha/Omega, joy, tears/handkerchief
**G** Woman weeping, open tomb, white linen, strips of cloth

Greeting: BOW414 (All Sts) or BOW453 (Isa, Rev)
Prayer of Confession: BOW494 (Pss)
Prayer for Illumination: WSL75 (Rev)
Prayer: UM713 or BOW415. All Saints (All Sts)
Memorial Prayers: UM461, UM656, BOW548
Great Thanksgiving for All Saints: BOW, pp. 74–75
Benediction: WSL46 (All Sts)
Alternate Scriptures for 23rd Sunday after Pentecost: Ruth 1:1-18; Ps 146:1-10; Heb 9:11-14; Mark 12:28-34

**Ruth 3:1-5; 4:13-17**

Naomi her mother-in-law said to her, "My daughter, shouldn't I seek security for you, so that things might go well for you?[2] Now isn't Boaz, whose young women you were with, our relative? Tonight he will be winnowing barley at the threshing floor. [3] You should bathe, put on some perfume, wear nice clothes, and then go down to the threshing floor. Don't make yourself known to the man until he has finished eating and drinking. [4] When he lies down, notice the place where he is lying. Then go, uncover his feet, and lie down. And he will tell you what to do."

[5] Ruth replied to her, "I'll do everything you are telling me." . . .

4 [13] So Boaz took Ruth, and she became his wife.

He was intimate with her, the LORD let her become pregnant, and she gave birth to a son. [14] The women said to Naomi, "May the LORD be blessed, who today hasn't left you without a redeemer. May his name be proclaimed in Israel. [15] He will restore your life and sustain you in your old age. Your daughter-in-law who loves you has given birth to him. She's better for you than seven sons." [16] Naomi took the child and held him to her breast, and she became his guardian. [17] The neighborhood women gave him a name, saying, "A son has been born to Naomi." They called his name Obed. He became Jesse's father and David's grandfather.

---

**Psalm 127**

Unless it is the LORD who builds the house,
the builders' work is pointless.
Unless it is the LORD who protects the city,
the guard on duty is pointless.
[2] It is pointless that you get up early and stay up late,
eating the bread of hard labor
because God gives sleep to those he loves.
[3] No doubt about it: children are a gift from the LORD;
the fruit of the womb is a divine reward.
[4] The children born when one is young
are like arrows in the hand of a warrior.
[5] The person who fills a quiver full with them is truly happy!
They won't be ashamed when arguing with their enemies
in the gate.

---

**Hebrews 9:24-28**

[24] Christ didn't enter the holy place (which is a copy of the true holy place) made by human hands, but into heaven itself, so that he now appears in God's presence for us. [25] He didn't enter to offer himself over and over again, like the high priest enters the earthly holy place every year with blood that isn't his. [26] If that were so, then Jesus would have to suffer many times since the foundation of the world. Instead, he has now appeared once at the end of the ages to get rid of sin by sacrificing himself. [27] People are destined to die once and then face judgment. [28] In the same way, Christ was also offered once to take on himself the sins of many people. He will appear a second time, not to take away sin but to save those who are eagerly waiting for him.

---

**Mark 12:38-44**

[38] As he was teaching, he said, "Watch out for the legal experts. They like to walk around in long robes. They want to be greeted with honor in the markets. [39] They long for places of honor in the synagogues and at banquets. [40] They are the ones who cheat widows out of their homes, and to show off they say long prayers. They will be judged most harshly."

[41] Jesus sat across from the collection box for the temple treasury and observed how the crowd gave their money. Many rich people were throwing in lots of money. [42] One poor widow came forward and put in two small copper coins worth a penny. [43] Jesus called his disciples to him and said, "I assure you that this poor widow has put in more than everyone who's been putting money in the treasury. [44] All of them are giving out of their spare change. But she from her hopeless poverty has given everything she had, even what she needed to live on."

**Primary Hymns and Songs for the Day**

384 "Love Divine, All Loves Excelling" (Ruth, Heb) (O)
H-3 Chr-134; Desc-18; Org-13
S-1 #41-42. Desc. and harm.
87 "What Gift Can We Bring" (Mark)
H-3 Chr-211
S-2 #10-11. Descs.
399 "Take My Life, and Let It Be" (Mark, Stewardship)
430 "O Master, Let Me Walk with Thee" (Mark) (C)
H-3 Hbl-81; Chr-147; Desc-74; Org-87
S-2 #118. Desc.

**Additional Hymn Suggestions**

97 "For the Fruits of This Creation" (Ruth)
115 "How Like a Gentle Spirit" (Ruth)
127 "Guide Me, O Thou Great Jehovah" (Ruth)
517 "By Gracious Powers" (Ruth)
643 "When Love Is Found" (Ruth)
2182 "When God Restored Our Common Life" (Ruth)
2230 "Lord, We Come to Ask Your Blessing" (Ruth)
118 "The Care the Eagle Gives Her Young" (Ruth, Pss)
105 "God of Many Names" (Ruth, Heb)
557 "Blest Be the Tie That Binds" (Ruth, Mark)
642 "As Man and Woman We Were Made" (Ruth, Mark)
647 "Your Love, O God, Has Called Us Here" (Ruth, Mark)
165 "Hallelujah! What a Savior" (Heb)
214 "Savior of the Nations, Come" (Heb)
470 "My God, I Love Thee" (Heb)
715 "Rejoice, the Lord Is King" (Heb)
716 "Rejoice, the Lord Is King" (Heb)
2149 "Living for Jesus" (Heb)
2151 "I'm So Glad Jesus Lifted Me" (Heb)
2259 "Victim Divine" (Heb, Comm.)
422 "Jesus, Thine All-Victorious Love" (Heb, Mark)
132 "All My Hope Is Firmly Grounded" (Mark)
408 "The Gift of Love" (Mark)
410 "I Want a Principle Within" (Mark)
427 "Where Cross the Crowded Ways of Life" (Mark)
432 "*Jesu, Jesu*" (Mark)
S-1 #63. Vocal part
434 "*Cuando el Pobre*" ("When the Poor Ones") (Mark)
441 "What Does the Lord Require" (Mark)
444 "O Young and Fearless Prophet" (Mark)
549 "Where Charity and Love Prevail" (Mark)
587 "Bless Thou the Gifts" (Mark, Stewardship)
2044 "My Gratitude Now Accept, O God ("*Gracias, Señor*") (Stewardship)
2153 "I'm Gonna Live So God Can Use Me" (Stewardship)

**Additional Contemporary Suggestions**

UM63 "Blessed Be the Name" (Ruth)
M12, S2034, SF2034
S2188 "The Family Prayer Song" ("As for Me and My House") (Ruth, Pss)
M54
M26 "The Power of Your Love" (Ruth, Pss)
S2053 "If It Had Not Been for the Lord" (Pss)
WS3040 "You Are My All in All" (Heb)
SP220
WS3085 "The Power of the Cross" (Heb)
M222
WS3102 "You Are My King" ("Amazing Love") (Heb)
M82
M36 "Awesome in this Place" (Heb)
M65 "Before the Throne of God Above" (Heb)
M81 "Amazing Love" (Heb)
M137 "How Deep the Father's Love for Us" (Heb)
M228 "Stronger" (Heb)
S2108 "Oh, How He Loves You and Me" (Heb)
SP113
S2272 "Holy Ground" (Heb)
SP86
WS3102 "You Are My King" ("Amazing Love") (Heb)
M82
S2003 "Praise You" (Mark, Stewardship)
M84
S2036 "Give Thanks" (Mark, Stewardship)
SP170
S2065 "More Precious than Silver" (Mark, Stewardship)
SP99
S2150 "Lord, Be Glorified" (Mark, Stewardship)
SP196
S2168 "Love the Lord Your God" (Mark)
S2174 "What Does the Lord Require of You" (Mark)
WS3106 "Your Grace Is Enough" (Mark)
M191
M98 "Take This Life" (Mark, Stewardship)
M101 "These Hands" (Mark, Stewardship)

**Vocal Solos**

"Whither Thou Goest" (Ruth)
V-8 p. 117
"Rejoice, The Lord Is King" (Heb)
V-1 p. 66
"Take My Life" (Mark, Stewardship)
V-3 (3) p. 17
V-8 p. 262

**Anthems**

"Sing Together! Psallite!" (Ruth)
Bach/Liebergen; Choristers Guild CGA-1354
Unison/Two-part with piano and two opt. flutes

"Take My Life, and Let It Be" (Mark, Stewardship)
Bruce Saylor; Paraclete Press PPM01114
SATB with organ

**Other Suggestions**

Visuals:
**O** Threshing, marriage, nursing woman, Jesse tree
**P** Building church, rising/sleeping, newborns, arrow/quiver
**E** Ascension, Crucifixion, Second Coming
**G** Long robe, greeting, banquet, widow, 2 coins
Greeting: BOW450 (Mark)
Canticle: UM646. "Canticle of Love" (Ruth, Pss)
Offertory Prayer: WSL99 (Mark)
The Mark reading can lead to a Stewardship focus.
Resources:
Greeting: BOW465
Canticle: UM406. "Canticle of Prayer"
Prayer of Confession: BOW485
Prayers: UM403 and BOW506
Prayer of Thanksgiving: BOW552
Dismissal: BOW559

**1 Samuel 1:4-20**

4 Whenever he sacrificed, Elkanah would give parts of
the sacrifice to his wife Peninnah and to all her sons and
daughters. 5 But he would give only one part of it to Hannah,
though he loved her, because theLORD had kept her from
conceiving. 6 And because the LORD had kept Hannah from
conceiving, her rival would make fun of her mercilessly, just
to bother her. 7 So that is what took place year after year.
Whenever Hannah went to the LORD's house, Peninnah
would make fun of her. Then she would cry and wouldn't eat
anything.

8 "Hannah, why are you crying?" her husband Elkanah
would say to her. "Why won't you eat? Why are you so sad?
Aren't I worth more to you than ten sons?"

9 One time, after eating and drinking in Shiloh, Hannah
got up and presented herself before the LORD. (Now Eli the
priest was sitting in the chair by the doorpost of the LORD's
temple.) 10 Hannah was very upset and couldn't stop crying
as she prayed to the LORD. 11 Then she made this promise:
"LORD of heavenly forces, just look at your servant's pain and
remember me! Don't forget your servant! Give her a boy!
Then I'll give him to the LORD for his entire life. No razor
will ever touch his head."

12 As she kept praying before the LORD, Eli watched her
mouth. 13 Now Hannah was praying in her heart; her lips
were moving, but her voice was silent, so Eli thought she was
drunk.

14 "How long will you act like a drunk? Sober up!" Eli told
her.

15 "No sir!" Hannah replied. "I'm just a very sad woman. I
haven't had any wine or beer but have been pouring out my
heart to the LORD. 16 Don't think your servant is some good-
for-nothing woman. This whole time I've been praying out of
my great worry and trouble!"

17 Eli responded, "Then go in peace. And may the God of
Israel give you what you've asked from him."

18 "Please think well of me, your servant," Hannah said.
Then the woman went on her way, ate some food, and wasn't
sad any longer.

19 They got up early the next morning and worshipped the
LORD. Then they went back home to Ramah. Elkanah had
sex with his wife Hannah, and the LORD remembered her.
20 So in the course of time, Hannah conceived and gave birth
to a son. She named him Samuel, which means "I asked the
LORD for him."

---

**1 Samuel 2:1-10**

Then Hannah prayed:
My heart rejoices in the LORD.
My strength rises up in the LORD!
My mouth mocks my enemies
because I rejoice in your deliverance.
2 No one is holy like the LORD—
no, no one except you!
There is no rock like our God! . . .

---

**Hebrews 10:11-14 (15-18) 19-25**

11 Every priest stands every day serving and offering the
same sacrifices over and over, sacrifices that can never take
away sins. 12 But when this priest offered one sacrifice for
sins for all time, he sat down at the right side of God. 13 Since
then, he's waiting until his enemies are made into a footstool
for his feet, 14 because he perfected the people who are being
made holy with one offering for all time.

15 The Holy Spirit affirms this when saying,
16 *This is the covenant that I will make with them.*
*After these days, says the Lord,*
*I will place my laws in their hearts*
*and write them on their minds.*
17 *And I won't remember their sins*
*and their lawless behavior anymore.*

18 When there is forgiveness for these things, there is no
longer an offering for sin.

19 Brothers and sisters, we have confidence that we can
enter the holy of holies by means of Jesus' blood, 20 through
a new and living way that he opened up for us through the
curtain, which is his body, 21 and we have a great high priest
over God's house.

22 Therefore, let's draw near with a genuine heart with
the certainty that our faith gives us, since our hearts are
sprinkled clean from an evil conscience and our bodies are
washed with pure water.

23 Let's hold on to the confession of our hope without
wavering, because the one who made the promises is reliable.

24 And let us consider each other carefully for the purpose
of sparking love and good deeds. 25 Don't stop meeting
together with other believers, which some people have got-
ten into the habit of doing. Instead, encourage each other,
especially as you see the day drawing near.

---

**Mark 13:1-8**

As Jesus left the temple, one of his disciples said to him,
"Teacher, look! What awesome stones and buildings!"

2 Jesus responded, "Do you see these enormous buildings?
Not even one stone will be left upon another. All will be
demolished."

3 Jesus was sitting on the Mount of Olives across from the
temple. Peter, James, John, and Andrew asked him privately,
4 "Tell us, when will these things happen? What sign will show
that all these things are about to come to an end?"

5 Jesus said, "Watch out that no one deceives you. 6 Many
people will come in my name, saying, 'I'm the one!' They will
deceive many people. 7 When you hear of wars and reports of
wars, don't be alarmed. These things must happen, but this
isn't the end yet. 8 Nations and kingdoms will fight against
each other, and there will be earthquakes and famines in all
sorts of places. These things are just the beginning of the sufferings associated with the end."

**Primary Hymns and Songs for the Day**

117 "O God, Our Help in Ages Past" (1 Sam) (O)
H-3 Hbl-33, 80; Chr-143; Desc-93; Org-132
S-1 #293-296. Various treatments
198 "My Soul Gives Glory to My God" (1 Sam)
H-3 Chr-139, 145; Desc-77
S-1 #241-42. Orff arr. and desc.
719 "My Lord, What a Morning" (Heb, Mark)
H-3 Chr-139
529 "How Firm a Foundation" (Mark)
H-3 Hbl-27, 69; Chr-102; Desc-41; Org-41
S-1 #133. Harm.
#134. Performance note
730 "O Day of God, Draw Nigh" (Mark) (C)
H-3 Hbl-79; Chr-141; Desc-95; Org-143
S-1 #306-8. Various treatments

**Additional Hymn Suggestions**

60 "I'll Praise My Maker While I've Breath" (1 Sam) (O)
73 "O Worship the King" (1 Sam)
139 "Praise to the Lord, the Almighty" (1 Sam)
118 "The Care the Eagle Gives Her Young" (1 Sam)
129 "Give to the Winds Thy Fears" (1 Sam)
200 "Tell Out, My Soul" (1 Sam)
361 "Rock of Ages, Cleft for Me" (1 Sam)
496 "Sweet Hour of Prayer" (1 Sam)
522 "Leave It There" (1 Sam)
2155 "Blest Are They" (1 Sam)
2189 "A Mother Lined a Basket" (1 Sam)
2247 "Wonder of Wonders" (1 Sam, Heb, Baptism)
140 "Great Is Thy Faithfulness" (1 Sam 1, Heb)
505 "When Our Confidence Is Shaken" (1 Sam, Heb)
175 "Jesus, the Very Thought of Thee" (Heb)
362 "Nothing but the Blood" (Heb)
417 "O For a Heart to Praise My God" (Heb)
419 "I Am Thine, O Lord" (Heb)
472 "Near to the Heart of God" (Heb)
605 "Wash, O God, Our Sons and Daughters" (Heb, Baptism)
2140 "Since Jesus Came into My Heart" (Heb)
2147 "There Are Some Things I May Not Know" (Heb)
2149 "Living for Jesus" (Heb)
2259 "Victim Divine" (Heb)
2268 "As We Gather at Your Table" (Heb, Comm.)
3110 "By Grace We Have Been Saved" (Heb)
655 "Fix Me, Jesus" (Heb, Mark)
703 "Swing Low, Sweet Chariot" (Heb, Mark)
704 "Steal Away to Jesus" (Heb, Mark)
720 "Wake, Awake, for Night Is Flying" (Heb, Mark)
722 "I Want to Be Ready" (Heb, Mark)
512 "Stand by Me" (Mark)
3048 "View the Present Through the Promise" (Mark)

**Additional Contemporary Suggestions**

S2029 "Praise to the Lord" (1 Sam 2)
S2036 "Give Thanks" (1 Sam 2)
SP170
S2188 "The Family Prayer Song" ("As for Me and My House") (1 Sam)
M54
WS3042 "Shout to the North" (1 Sam 2)
M99
M93 "Rock of Ages" (1 Sam 2)
M142 "Let the River Flow" (1 Sam 2)
M164 "Good to Me" (1 Sam 2)
M227 "I Will Boast" (1 Sam 2)
WS3040 "You Are My All in All" (1 Sam 2, Heb)
SP220
WS3085 "The Power of the Cross" (Heb)
M222
WS3102 "You Are My King" ("Amazing Love") (Heb)
M82
M35 "White as Snow" (Heb)
M65 "Before the Throne of God Above" (Heb)
M78 "Once Again" (Heb)
M81 "Amazing Love" (Heb)
M224 "Because of Your Love" (Heb)
M251 "Grace Like Rain" (Heb)
UM640 "Take Our Bread" (Heb, Comm.)
S2192 "Freedom Is Coming" (Mark)
S2194 "O Freedom" (Mark)
S2214 "Lead Me, Guide Me" (Mark)
WS3186 "Days of Elijah" (Mark)
M139
M50 "Refiner's Fire" (Mark)
M69 "Did You Feel the Mountains Tremble?" (Mark)

**Vocal Solos**

"Come, Thou Fount of Every Blessing" (1 Sam)
V-3 (3) p. 22
V-6 p. 4
"Strength to My Soul" (1 Sam)
V-8 p. 352
"Steal Away to Heaven" (Heb, Mark)
V-3 (1) p. 17
"My Lord, What a Mornin'" (Mark)
V-7 p. 68

**Anthems**

"God Is Our Refuge and Strength" (1 Sam)
Anna Laura Page; Choristers Guild CGA-1381
SATB with piano (opt. flute, trumpet, handbells)

"Great Is Thy Faithfulness" (1 Sam 1, Heb)
Arr. Joel Raney; Hope C-5834
SATB with piano

**Other Suggestions**

Visuals:
**O** Woman weeping/praying, old man, couple worshiping, newborn
**P** Praying, rock, broken bow, 4 pillars, scales
**E** Cross, footstool, curtain, water, baptism, worship
**G** Scattered stones, war, earthquake, famine, dawn
Introit: UM494. "*Kum Ba Yah*" (1 Sam)
Greeting: BOW245 (1 Sam) or BOW456 (Mark)
Canticle: UM199. "Canticle of Mary" ("*Magnificat*") (1 Sam)
Opening Prayer: BOW252 (1 Sam)
Prayer of Confession: BOW486 (Mark)
Prayer: UM495. The Sufficiency of God (1 Sam)
Prayer of Thanksgiving: BOW554 (1 Sam, Mark)
Blessing: BOW561 (1 Sam)
Sung Benediction: UM665. "Go Now in Peace" (1 Sam 1)

**2 Samuel 23:1-7**

These are David's last words:
This is the declaration of Jesse's son David,
the declaration of a man raised high,
a man anointed by the God of Jacob,
a man favored by the strong one of Israel.
2 The LORD's spirit speaks through me;
his word is on my tongue.
3 Israel's God has spoken,
Israel's rock said to me:
"Whoever rules rightly over people,
whoever rules in the fear of God,
4 is like the light of sunrise
on a morning with no clouds,
like the bright gleam after the rain
that brings grass from the ground."
5 Yes, my house is this way with God!
He has made an eternal covenant with me,
laid out and secure in every detail.
Yes, he provides every one of my victories
and brings my every desire to pass.
6 But despicable people are like thorns,
all of them good for nothing,
because they can't be carried by hand.
7 No one can touch them,
except with iron bar or the shaft of a spear.
They must be burned up with fire right on the spot!

---

**Psalm 132:1-12 (UM849)**

LORD, remember David—
all the ways he suffered
2 and how he swore to the LORD,
how he promised the strong one of Jacob:
3 "I won't enter my house,
won't get into my bed.
4 I won't let my eyes close,
won't let my eyelids sleep,
5 until I find a place for the LORD,
a dwelling place for the strong one of Jacob."
6 Yes, we heard about it in Ephrathah;
we found it in the fields of Jaar.
7 Let's enter God's dwelling place;
let's worship at the place God rests his feet!
8 Get up, LORD, go to your residence—
you and your powerful covenant chest!
9 Let your priests be dressed in righteousness;
let your faithful shout out with joy!
10 And for the sake of your servant David,
do not reject your anointed one.
11 The LORD swore to David
a true promise that God won't take back:
"I will put one of your own children on your throne.
12 And if your children keep my covenant
and the laws that I will teach them,
then their children too will rule on your throne forever."

---

**Revelation 1:4b-8**

4b Grace and peace to you from the one who is and was
and is coming, and from the seven spirits that are before
God's throne, 5 and from Jesus Christ—the faithful witness, the firstborn from among the dead, and the ruler of
the kings of the earth.
To the one who loves us and freed us from our sins by his
blood, 6 who made us a kingdom, priests to his God and
Father—to him be glory and power forever and always.
Amen.
7 Look, he is coming with the clouds! Every eye will see him,
including those who pierced him, and all the tribes of the
earth will mourn because of him. This is so. Amen. 8 "I am
the Alpha and the Omega," says the Lord God, "the one who
is and was and is coming, the Almighty."

---

**John 18:33-37**

33 Pilate went back into the palace. He summoned Jesus and
asked, "Are you the king of the Jews?"
34 Jesus answered, "Do you say this on your own or have others spoken to you about me?"
35 Pilate responded, "I'm not a Jew, am I? Your nation
and its chief priests handed you over to me. What have you
done?"
36 Jesus replied, "My kingdom doesn't originate from this
world. If it did, my guards would fight so that I wouldn't have
been arrested by the Jewish leaders. My kingdom isn't from
here."
37 "So you are a king?" Pilate said.

**Primary Hymns and Songs for the Day**
715 "Rejoice the Lord Is King" (Rev, Christ the King) (O)
H-3 Hbl-8, 53, 90; Chr-37; Desc-27; Org-24
S-1 #78-80. Various treatments
718 "Lo, He Comes With Clouds Descending" (2 Sam, Rev)
H-3 Hbl-93; Chr-129; Desc-50; Org-53
S-1 #157. Desc.
2070 "He Is Exalted" (Rev, Christ the King)
SP66
157 "Jesus Shall Reign" (Rev) (C)
H-3 Hbl-29, 58; Chr-117; Desc-31; Org-31
S-1 #100-103. Various treatments

**Additional Hymn Suggestions**
153 "Thou Hidden Source of Calm Repose" (2 Sam)
247 "O Morning Star, How Fair and Bright" (2 Sam)
327 "Crown Him with Many Crowns" (2 Sam)
361 "Rock of Ages, Cleft for Me" (2 Sam)
203 "Hail to the Lord's Anointed" (2 Sam, Rev) (O)
2279 "The Trees of the Field" (Pss)
64 "Holy, Holy, Holy" (Rev)
90 "Ye Watchers and Ye Holy Ones" (Rev)
103 "Immortal, Invisible, God Only Wise" (Rev)
139 "Praise to the Lord, the Almighty" (Rev)
154 "All Hail the Power of Jesus' Name" (Rev)
155 "All Hail the Power of Jesus' Name" (Rev)
185 "When Morning Gilds the Skies" (Rev)
184 "Of the Father's Love Begotten" (Rev, Comm.)
384 "Love Divine, All Loves Excelling" (Rev)
638 "This Is the Feast of Victory" (Rev, Comm.)
694 "Come, Ye Thankful People, Come" (Rev, Thanks.)
716 "Rejoice, the Lord Is King" (Rev, Christ the King)
2190 "Bring Forth the Kingdom" (Rev, Christ the King)
168 "At the Name of Jesus" (Rev, John)
194 "Morning Glory, Starlit Sky" (Rev, John)
325 "Hail, Thou Once Despised Jesus" (John)
3043 "You, Lord, Are Both Lamb and Shepherd" (John)
577 "God of Grace and God of Glory" (John)
626 "Let All Mortal Flesh Keep Silence" (John, Comm.)
2009 "O God Beyond All Praising" (Christ King, Thanks.)
2276 "Glory to God in the Highest" (Christ the King)

**Additional Contemporary Suggestions**
M93 "Rock of Ages" (2 Sam)
S2002 "I Will Call upon the Lord" (2 Sam)
SP224
S2066 "Praise the Name of Jesus" (2 Sam, Christ the King)
SP87
S2195 "In the Lord I'll Be Ever Thankful" (2 Sam)
S2018 "Honor and Praise" (Pss)
UM328 "Surely the Presence of the Lord" (Pss)
SP243; S-2 #200. Stanzas for soloist
UM349 "Turn Your Eyes upon Jesus" (Rev)
SP218
UM706 "Soon and Very Soon" (Rev, Christ the King)
S-2 #187. Piano Arr.
S2040 "Awesome God" (Rev, John, Christ the King)
SP11
S2063 "You Are Worthy" ("*Eres Digno*") (Rev, Christ the King)
S2075 "King of Kings" (Rev, Christ the King)
SP94
S2087 "We Will Glorify the King of Kings" (Rev, Christ the King)
SP68
WS3003 "How Great Is Our God" (Rev, Christ the King)
M117
M21 "Blessing, Honour and Glory" (Rev, Christ the King)
M24 "Jesus, We Crown You with Praise" (Rev, Christ the King)
M31 "I See the Lord" (Rev, Christ the King)
M55 "Jehovah Reigns" (Rev, Christ the King)
M240 "You Are" (Rev)
S2069 "All Hail King Jesus" (John, Christ the King)
SP63
SP64 "Our God Reigns" (Christ the King)
M22 "Crown Him King of Kings" (Christ the King)
M67 "We Want to See Jesus Lifted High" (Christ King)
M168 "He Reigns" (Christ the King)
M230 "The Highest and the Greatest" (Christ the King)
M237 "My Savior Lives" (Christ the King)
M275 "Prepare Ye the Way" ("You Reign on High") (Christ the King)

**Vocal Solos**
"Great Day!" (Rev)
V-7 p. 14
"Jesus Is Lord of All" (Christ the King)
V-8 p. 254
"King of Glory, King of Peace" (Christ the King)
V-9 p. 24
"Crown Him, the Risen King" (Christ the King)
V-10 p. 55

**Anthems**
"Jesus Shall Reign" (Rev)
Arr. Robert J. Powell; Paraclete Press PPM01307
SATB with organ, opt. trumpets, congregation

"We Hear Singing" (Christ the King)
Mary Elen Kerrick; Choristers Guild CGA-1351
Unison/Two-part with piano

**Other Suggestions**
Visuals: Cross/crown, lamb/cross
**O** Speaking, rock, sunrise, rain/grass, thorns, spear, fire
**P** Empty bed, ark, crown, throne, scepter
**E** Crown, scepter, cross, royal robe, fabric(gold/purple)
**G** Jesus/Pilate, shackles, John 18:36a, crown, listening
Introit: S2274. "Come, All You People" ("*Uyai Mose*") (Pss)
Greeting: BOW420 or BOW451 (Christ the King)
Canticle: UM734. "Canticle of Hope" (Rev)
Prayer of Confession: WSL91 (John, Christ the King)
Prayer of Confession: BOW, 478 (2 Sam, John)
Prayer: UM721 or BOW421. Christ the King (Rev, John)
Prayer: BOW511. For God's Reign (2 Sam, Rev, John)
Litany: BOW433 (Student Day)
Prayer of Thanksgiving: BOW556 (Rev)
Blessing: BOW563.
See BOW419 for additional Christ the King suggestions.
For Thanksgiving Sunday, see Thanksgiving Day Suggestions.

**Joel 2:21-27**

21 Don't fear, fertile land;
rejoice and be glad,
for the Lord is about to do great things!
22 Don't be afraid, animals of the field,
for the meadows of the wilderness will turn green;
the tree will bear its fruit;
the fig tree and grapevine will give their full yield.
23 Children of Zion,
rejoice and be glad in the LORD your God,
because he will give you the early rain as a sign of
righteousness;
he will pour down abundant rain for you,
the early and the late rain, as before.
24 The threshing floors will be full of grain;
the vats will overflow with new wine and fresh oil.
25 I will repay you for the years
that the cutting locust,
the swarming locust, the hopping locust, and the
devouring locust have eaten—
my great army, which I sent against you.
26 You will eat abundantly and be satisfied,
and you will praise the name of the LORD your God,
who has done wonders for you;
and my people will never again be put to shame.
27 You will know that I am in the midst of Israel,
and that I am the LORD your God—no other exists;
never again will my people be put to shame.

**Psalm 126 (UM847)**

When the LORD changed Zion's circumstances for the better,
it was like we had been dreaming.
2 Our mouths were suddenly filled with laughter;
our tongues were filled with joyful shouts.
It was even said, at that time, among the nations,
"The LORD has done great things for them!"
3 Yes, the LORD has done great things for us,
and we are overjoyed.
4 LORD, change our circumstances for the better,
like dry streams in the desert waste!
5 Let those who plant with tears
reap the harvest with joyful shouts.
6 Let those who go out,
crying and carrying their seed,
come home with joyful shouts,
carrying bales of grain!

**1 Timothy 2:1-7**

First of all, then, I ask that requests, prayers, petitions,
and thanksgiving be made for all people. 2 Pray for kings
and everyone who is in authority so that we can live a quiet
and peaceful life in complete godliness and dignity. 3 This is
right and it pleases God our savior, 4 who wants all people to
be saved and to come to a knowledge of the truth. 5 There
is one God and one mediator between God and humanity,
the human Christ Jesus, 6 who gave himself as a payment to
set all people free. This was a testimony that was given at the
right time. 7 I was appointed to be a preacher and apostle of
this testimony—I'm telling the truth and I'm not lying! I'm a
teacher of the Gentiles in faith and truth.

**Matthew 6:25-33**

25 "Therefore, I say to you, don't worry about your life, what
you'll eat or what you'll drink, or about your body, what
you'll wear. Isn't life more than food and the body more than
clothes? 26 Look at the birds in the sky. They don't sow seed
or harvest grain or gather crops into barns. Yet your heavenly
Father feeds them. Aren't you worth much more than they
are? 27 Who among you by worrying can add a single moment
to your life? 28 And why do you worry about clothes? Notice
how the lilies in the field grow. They don't wear themselves
out with work, and they don't spin cloth. 29 But I say to you
that even Solomon in all of his splendor wasn't dressed like
one of these. 30 If God dresses grass in the field so beautifully,
even though it's alive today and tomorrow it's thrown into
the furnace, won't God do much more for you, you people
of weak faith? 31 Therefore, don't worry and say, 'What are we
going to eat?' or 'What are we going to drink?' or 'What are
we going to wear?' 32 Gentiles long for all these things. Your
heavenly Father knows that you need them. 33 Instead, desire
first and foremost God's kingdom and God's righteousness,
and all these things will be given to you as well."

**Primary Hymns and Songs for the Day**
694 "Come, Ye Thankful People, Come" (Joel, Thanks.) (O)
H-3 Hbl-54; Chr-58; Desc-94; Org-137
S-1 #302-3. Harm. with desc.
131 "We Gather Together" (Joel, Matt, Thanks.)
H-3 Chr-206; Desc-61; Org-68
S-1 #192-94. Various treatments
130 "God Will Take Care of You" (Matt)
2146 "His Eye Is on the Sparrow" (Matt)
140 "Great Is Thy Faithfulness" (Pss, Matt) (C)
H-3 Chr-87; Desc-39; Org-39
S-2 #59. Piano arr.

**Additional Hymn Suggestions**
62 "All Creatures of Our God and King" (Joel, Thanks.)
67 "We, Thy People, Praise Thee" (Joel)
102 "Now Thank We All Our God" (Joel, Thanks.)
637 "*Una Espiga*" ("Sheaves of Summer") (Joel, Comm.)
2182 "When God Restored Our Common Life" (Pss)
2210 "Joy Comes with the Dawn" (Pss)
2248 "Baptized in Water" (1 Tim, Baptism)
85 "We Believe in One True God" (1 Tim)
97 "For the Fruits of This Creation" (Matt)
129 "Give to the Winds Thy Fears" (Matt)
138 "The King of Love My Shepherd Is" (Matt)
141 "Children of the Heavenly Father" (Matt)
147 "All Things Bright and Beautiful" (Matt
522 "Leave It There" (Matt)
629 "You Satisfy the Hungry Heart" (Matt, Comm.)
672 "God Be with You till We Meet Again" (Matt)
673 "God Be with You till We Meet Again" (Matt)
678 "Rise to Greet the Sun" (Matt)
2042 "How Lovely, Lord, How Lovely" (Matt)
2044 "My Gratitude Now Accept, O God ("*Gracias, Señor*") (Thanks.)
2061 "Praise Our God Above" ("Harvest Song") (Matt, Thanks.)
2190 "Bring Forth the Kingdom" (Matt)
2197 "Lord of All Hopefulness" (Matt)
2206 "Without Seeing You" (Matt)
2262 "Let Us Offer to the Father" (Matt, Thanks.)
2265 "Time Now to Gather" (Thanks., Comm.)
89 "Joyful, Joyful, We Adore Thee" (Thanks.)

**Additional Contemporary Suggestions**
S2086 "Open Our Eyes, Lord" (Joel)
SP199
M26 "The Power of Your Love" (Joel)
WS3008 "Open the Eyes of My Heart" (Joel)
M57
WS3108 "Trading My Sorrows" (Pss)
M75
M263 "From the Inside Out" (Pss)
M253 "Jesus Messiah" (1 Tim, Comm.)
UM405 "Seek Ye First" (Matt)
SP182
S2056 "God Is So Good" (Matt)
S2144 "Someone Asked the Question" (Matt)
S2215 "Cares Chorus" (Matt)
SP221
WS3026 "God Is Good All the Time" (Matt)
M45
M223 "Today Is the Day" (Matt)
M226 "Counting on God" (Matt)
UM84 "Thank You, Lord" (Thanks.)
S2036 "Give Thanks" (Thanks.)
SP170
S2081 "Thank You, Jesus" ("*Tino Tenda, Jesu*") (Thanks.)
M166 "Thank You, Lord" (Thanks.)

**Vocal Solos**
"Now Thank We All Our God" (Joel, Thanks.)
V-6 p. 8
"Bright and Beautiful" (Matt)
V-3 (3) p. 10
"Great Is Thy Faithfulness" (Matt, Thanks.)
V-8 p. 48
"His Eye Is on the Sparrow" (Matt)
V-8 p. 166
"My Shepherd Will Supply My Need" (Matt)
V-10 p. 4

**Anthems**
"Now Thank We All Our God" (Joel, Thanks.)
Arr. Randall Thompson; E.C. Schirmer 4008
SATB and keyboard

"For the Fruits of This Creation" (Matt, Thanks.)
Arr. Eugene Butler; Hope C-5822
SATB with keyboard

**Other Suggestions**
Visuals: cornucopia, fruit, vegetables, etc.
**O** Farm animals, green pastures, fruit trees, grapes
**P** Laughter, bounty, river, weeping/joy, sheaves
**E** Praying hands, one, Christ, cross, ransom note
**G** Food, clothing, birds, lilies, grass, water
Introit: S2271. "Come! Come! Everybody Worship" (Thanks.)
Greeting: BOW417 (Thanks.)
Call to Worship: WSL58 (Matt)
Act of Congregational Centering: BOW471 (Joel)
Canticle: UM91. "Canticle of Praise to God" (Pss)
Prayer of Confession: BOW485 (Thanks.)
Prayer: UM495. The Sufficiency of God (Matt)
Prayer: BOW418 (Thanks.)
Prayer of Thanksgiving: BOW557 (Joel) or BOW558 (Thanks.)
Response: S2195 or S2081 (Thanks.)
Offertory Hymn: BOW179. "For the Gift of Creation" (Joel)
Doxology: BOW182 (Thanks.)
Blessing: BOW562 (Thanks.)
Sung Benediction: S2279. "The Trees of the Field" (Pss)

**Jeremiah 33:14-16**

14 The time is coming, declares the LORD, when I will fulfill my gracious promise with the people of Israel and Judah. 15 In those days and at that time, I will raise up a righteous branch from David's line, who will do what is just and right in the land. 16 In those days, Judah will be saved and Jerusalem will live in safety. And this is what he will be called: The LORD Is Our Righteousness.

---

**Psalm 25:1-10 (UM756)**

I offer my life to you, LORD.
2 My God, I trust you.
Please don't let me be put to shame!
Don't let my enemies rejoice over me!
3 For that matter,
don't let anyone who hopes in you
be put to shame;
instead, let those who are treacherous without excuse be put to shame.
4 Make your ways known to me, LORD;
teach me your paths.
5 Lead me in your truth—teach it to me—
because you are the God who saves me.
I put my hope in you all day long.
6 LORD, remember your compassion and faithful love—
they are forever!
7 But don't remember the sins of my youth or my wrongdoing.
Remember me only according to your faithful love
for the sake of your goodness, LORD.
8 The LORD is good and does the right thing;
he teaches sinners which way they should go.
9 God guides the weak to justice,
teaching them his way.
10 All the LORD's paths are loving and faithful
for those who keep his covenant and laws.

---

**1 Thessalonians 3:9-13**

9 How can we thank God enough for you, given all the joy we have because of you before our God? 10 Night and day, we pray more than ever to see all of you in person and to complete whatever you still need for your faith. 11 Now may our God and Father himself guide us on our way back to you. 12 May the Lord cause you to increase and enrich your love for each other and for everyone in the same way as we also love you. 13 May the love cause your hearts to be strengthened, to be blameless in holiness before our God and Father when our Lord Jesus comes with all his people. Amen.

---

**Luke 21:25-36**

25 "There will be signs in the sun, moon, and stars. On the earth, there will be dismay among nations in their confusion over the roaring of the sea and surging waves. 26 The planets and other heavenly bodies will be shaken, causing people to faint from fear and foreboding of what is coming upon the world. 27 Then they will see the Human One coming on a cloud with power and great splendor. 28 Now when these things begin to happen, stand up straight and raise your heads, because your redemption is near."

29 Jesus told them a parable: "Look at the fig tree and all the trees. 30 When they sprout leaves, you can see for yourselves and know that summer is near. 31 In the same way, when you see these things happening, you know that God's kingdom is near. 32 I assure you that this generation won't pass away until everything has happened. 33 Heaven and earth will pass away, but my words will certainly not pass away.

34 "Take care that your hearts aren't dulled by drinking parties, drunkenness, and the anxieties of day-to-day life. Don't let that day fall upon you unexpectedly, 35 like a trap. It will come upon everyone who lives on the face of the whole earth. 36 Stay alert at all times, praying that you are strong enough to escape everything that is about to happen and to stand before the Human One."

**Primary Hymns and Songs for the Day**

211 "O Come, O Come, Emmanuel" (Jer) (O)
H-3 Hbl-14, 79; Chr-141; Org-168
S-1 #342. Handbell accompaniment
171 "There's Something About That Name" (Luke)
SP89
719 "My Lord, What a Morning" (Luke)
H-3 Chr-139
730 "O Day of God, Draw Nigh" (Luke)
H-3 Hbl-79; Chr-141; Desc-95; Org-143
S-1 #306-8. Various treatments
213 "Lift Up Your Heads, Ye Mighty Gates" (Jer, 1 Thess) (C)
H-3 Hbl-50; Chr-47; Desc-101; Org-167
S-1 #334-35. Desc. and harm.

**Additional Hymn Suggestions**

196 "Come, Thou Long-Expected Jesus" (Jer, Luke) (O)
203 "Hail to the Lord's Anointed" (Jer)
209 "Blessed Be the God of Israel" (Jer)
216 "Lo, How a Rose E'er Blooming" (Jer)
473 "Lead Me, Lord" (Jer, Pss)
2100 "Thou Didst Leave Thy Throne" (Jer, Advent)
2177 "Wounded World that Cries for Healing" (Jer)
2183 "Unsettled World" (Jer)
2214 "Lead Me, Guide Me" (Pss)
2254 "In Remembrance of Me" (Pss, Comm.)
368 "My Hope Is Built" (Pss)
411 "Dear Lord, Lead Me Day By Day" (Pss)
519 "Lift Every Voice and Sing" (Pss, Luke)
402 "Lord, I Want to Be a Christian" (1 Thess)
417 "O For a Heart to Praise My God" (1 Thess)
549 "Where Charity and Love Prevail" (1 Thess)
562 "Jesus, Lord, We Look to Thee" (1 Thess)
692 "Creator of the Stars of Night" (1 Thess)
2232 "Come Now, O Prince of Peace" ("*O-So-So*") (1 Thess)
206 "I Want to Walk as a Child of the Light" (1 Thess, Luke)
718 "Lo, He Comes With Clouds Descending" (1 Thess, Luke)
202 "People, Look East" (Luke)
221 "In the Bleak Midwinter" (Luke)
512 "Stand By Me" (Luke)
714 "I Know Whom I Have Believed" (Luke)
715 "Rejoice, the Lord Is King" (Luke)
716 "Rejoice, the Lord Is King" (Luke)
720 "Wake, Awake, for Night Is Flying" (Luke)
623 "Here, O My Lord, I See Thee" (Luke, Comm.)
633 "The Bread of Life for All Is Broken" (Advent, Comm.)
2265 "Time Now to Gather" (Comm.)

**Additional Contemporary Suggestions**

S2018 "Honor and Praise" (Jer)
S2091 "The King of Glory Comes" (Jer)
S2232 "Come Now, O Prince of Peace" ("*O-So-So*") (Jer, Advent)
M129 "You Are Holy" ("Prince of Peace") (Jer, Advent)
M141 "Sing to the King" (Jer)
S2032 "My Life Is in You, Lord" (Pss)
SP204
S2161 "To Know You More" (Pss)
S2165 "Cry of My Heart" (Pss)
M39
S2167 "More Like You" (Pss)
WS3099 "Falling on My Knees" (Pss)
M155
M30 "Knowing You" ("All I Once Held Dear") (Pss)
M38 "In the Secret" ("I Want to Know You") (Pss)
M63 "I Could Sing of Your Love Forever" (Pss)
M107 "Show Me Your Ways" (Pss)
M108 "Lead Me, Lord" (Pss)
M113 "In the Presence of Jehovah" (Pss, Advent)
M159 "All Who Are Thirsty" (Pss, Advent)
S2085 "He Came Down" (1 Thess)
WS3188 "Hosanna" (1 Thess, Luke)
M268
S2192 "Freedom Is Coming" (Luke)
S2194 "O Freedom" (Luke)
SP158 "The Battle Belongs to the Lord" (Luke)
M1 "Ancient of Days" (Luke)
M237 "My Savior Lives" (Advent)

**Vocal Solos**

"Sing for Christ Is Born" (Jer, Advent)
V-10 p. 16
"Alleluia, Sing to Jesus" (Jer, Luke)
V-3 (3) p. 50
"Lo, He Comes with Clouds Descending" (Luke)
V-1 p. 54
"My Lord, What a Mornin'" (Luke, Advent)
V-3 (1) p. 39
V-7 p. 68

**Anthems**

"O Come, O Come, Emmanuel" (Jer)
Joel Raney; Hope C-5841
SATB with piano and opt. instruments

"Give Me a Song" (Luke)
Pepper Choplin; Alfred 42531
SATB with keyboard

**Other Suggestions**

Visuals:
**O** Branch, Jesse tree, new buds
**P** Teaching, leading, path, open Bible
**E** Joy, praying hands, Jesus, Second Coming
**G** Sun, moon, earth, clouds, Christ descending, fig tree, budding tree, guard, praying, weights, Luke 21:36a

Introit: WS3048. "View the Present Through the Promise" (Luke)
Greeting: BOW240 (Pss) or BOW244 (Luke)
Opening Prayer: WSL10 (Luke, Advent)
Blessing of the Advent Wreath: BOW261
Advent Wreath Responses: S2090. "Light the Advent Candle"
Canticle: UM208. "Canticle of Zechariah" (Jer)
Opening Prayer: BOW254 (Luke)
Prayer of Confession: BOW483 (Pss)
Response: S2275. "*Kyrie*" (Pss)
Offertory Prayer: WSL115 (Advent)
Sung Benediction: S2184. "Sent Out in Jesus' Name" (Jer)
See BOW258 for an order of service for Hanging of the Greens.

**Malachi 3:1-4**
Look, I am sending my messenger who will clear the path
before me;
suddenly the LORD whom you are seeking will come to
his temple.
The messenger of the covenant in whom you take delight
is coming,
says the Lord of heavenly forces.
2 Who can endure the day of his coming?
Who can withstand his appearance?
He is like the refiner's fire or the cleaner's soap.
3 He will sit as a refiner and a purifier of silver.
He will purify the Levites
and refine them like gold and silver.
They will belong to the LORD,
presenting a righteous offering.
4 The offering of Judah and Jerusalem will be pleasing to the
LORD
as in ancient days and in former years.

---

**Luke 1:68-79**
68 "Bless the Lord God of Israel
because he has come to help and has delivered his
people.
69 He has raised up a mighty savior for us in his servant
David's house,
70 just as he said through the mouths of his holy prophets
long ago.
71 He has brought salvation from our enemies
and from the power of all those who hate us.
72 He has shown the mercy promised to our ancestors,
and remembered his holy covenant,
73 the solemn pledge he made to our ancestor Abraham.
He has granted 74 that we would be rescued
from the power of our enemies
so that we could serve him without fear,
75 in holiness and righteousness in God's eyes,
for as long as we live.
76 You, child, will be called a prophet of the Most High,
for you will go before the Lord to prepare his way.
77 You will tell his people how to be saved
through the forgiveness of their sins.
78 Because of our God's deep compassion,
the dawn from heaven will break upon us,
79 to give light to those who are sitting in darkness
and in the shadow of death,
to guide us on the path of peace."

---

**Philippians 1:3-11**
3 I thank my God every time I mention you in my prayers.
4 I'm thankful for all of you every time I pray, and it's always a
prayer full of joy. 5 I'm glad because of the way you have been
my partners in the ministry of the gospel from the time you
first believed it until now. 6 I'm sure about this: the one who
started a good work in you will stay with you to complete the
job by the day of Christ Jesus. 7 I have good reason to think
this way about all of you because I keep you in my heart. You
are all my partners in God's grace, both during my time in
prison and in the defense and support of the gospel. 8 God is
my witness that I feel affection for all of you with the compassion of Christ Jesus.
9 This is my prayer: that your love might become even more
and more rich with knowledge and all kinds of insight. 10 I
pray this so that you will be able to decide what really matters
and so you will be sincere and blameless on the day of Christ.
11 I pray that you will then be filled with the fruit of righteousness, which comes from Jesus Christ, in order to give glory
and praise to God.

---

**Luke 3:1-6**
In the fifteenth year of the rule of the emperor Tiberius—
when Pontius Pilate was governor over Judea and Herod was
ruler over Galilee, his brother Philip was ruler over Ituraea
and Trachonitis, and Lysanias was ruler over Abilene, 2 during the high priesthood of Annas and Caiaphas—God's word
came to John son of Zechariah in the wilderness. 3 John went
throughout the region of the Jordan River, calling for people
to be baptized to show that they were changing their hearts
and lives and wanted God to forgive their sins. 4 This is just as
it was written in the scroll of the words of Isaiah the prophet,
*A voice crying out in the wilderness:*
*"Prepare the way for the Lord;*
*make his paths straight.*
5 *Every valley will be filled,*
*and every mountain and hill will be leveled.*
*The crooked will be made straight*
*and the rough places made smooth.*
6 *All humanity will see God's salvation."*

**Primary Hymns and Songs for the Day**

567 "Heralds of Christ" (Luke) (O)
H-3 Hbl-64; Chr-78; Desc-78; Org-96
S-2 #131-32. Harm. with desc.
207 "Prepare the Way of the Lord" (Luke 3, Advent)
209 "Blessed Be the God of Israel" (Mal, Luke 1)
M50 "Refiner's Fire" (Mal)
2163 "He Who Began a Good Work in You" (Phil)
SP180
220 "Angels from the Realms of Glory" (Mal) (C)
H-3 Chr-30, 48, 62; Desc-89; Org-121
S-1 #280. Desc. and harm.

**Additional Hymn Suggestions**

382 "Have Thine Own Way, Lord" (Mal)
706 "Soon and Very Soon" (Mal)
S-2 #187. Piano Arr.
384 "Love Divine, All Loves Excelling" (Mal, Phil)
475 "Come Down, O Love Divine" (Mal, Phil)
2172 "We Are Called" (Mal, Luke 1)
2208 "Guide My Feet" (Luke 1)
2214 "Lead Me, Guide Me" (Luke 1)
2236 "Gather Us In" (Luke 1)
3046 "Come, O Redeemer, Come" (Luke 1)
196 "Come, Thou Long-Expected Jesus" (Mal, Luke 1)
210 "*Toda la Tierra*" ("All Earth Is Waiting") (Mal, Luke 3)
211 "O Come, O Come, Emmanuel" (Mal, Luke 1)
108 "God Hath Spoken by the Prophets" (Luke 1)
195 "Send Your Word" (Luke 1)
206 "I Want to Walk as a Child of the Light" (Luke 1)
209 "Blessed Be the God of Israel" (Luke 1)
216 "Lo, How a Rose E'er Blooming" (Luke 1)
223 "Break Forth, O Beauteous Heavenly Light" (Luke 1)
272 "Sing of Mary, Pure and Lowly" (Luke 1)
213 "Lift Up Your Heads, Ye Mighty Gates" (Phil, Advent)
388 "O Come and Dwell in Me" (Phil)
395 "Take Time to Be Holy" (Phil)
419 "I Am Thine, O Lord" (Phil)
422 "Jesus, Thine All-Victorious Love" (Phil)
453 "More Love to Thee, O Christ" (Phil)
612 "Deck Thyself, My Soul, with Gladness" (Phil, Comm.)
699 "Come, and Let Us Sweetly Join" (Phil, Luke 1)
202 "People, Look East" (Luke 1)
625 "Come, Let Us Eat" (Luke, Comm.)
2089 "Wild and Lone the Prophet's Voice" (Luke 3)
2092 "Like a Child" (Luke 1)
2107 "Wade in the Water" (Luke 3, Baptism)
2255 "In the Singing" (Luke, Comm.)

**Additional Contemporary Suggestions**

WS3042 "Shout to the North" (Mal, Advent)
M99
WS3103 "Purify My Heart" (Mal)
M90
S2143 "O Lord, Your Tenderness" (Mal)
M33 "Jesus, You Are My Life" (Mal)
M89 "Purified" (Mal)
M144 "Light the Fire Again" (Mal)
M145 "Move Me Again" (Mal)
M275 "Prepare Ye the Way" ("You Reign") (Mal, Luke)
S2036 "Give Thanks" (Luke)
SP170
S2204 "Light of the World" (Luke 1)
S2266 "Here Is Bread, Here Is Wine" (Luke 1, Comm.)
S2235-b "We Are Marching" ("*Siyahamba*") (Luke 1)
WS3003 "How Great Is Our God" (Luke 1, Advent)
M117
WS3026 "God Is Good All the Time" (Luke 1)
M45
WS3177 "Here I Am To Worship" (Luke 1, Advent)
M116
M19 "Shine on Us" (Luke 1, Advent)
M64 "Hear Our Praises" (Luke 1, Advent)
M150 "Everyday" (Luke 1, Advent)
UM186 "Alleluia" (Luke 3, Comm.)
SP108, S-2 #3-4. Desc. and harm.
M62 "Rise Up and Praise Him" (Luke 3)
M125 "Praise Adonai" (Luke 3)

**Vocal Solos**

"And He Shall Purify," "But Who May Abide," and "Thus Saith the Lord" from *Messiah* (Mal)
"Every Valley" from *Messiah* (Mal, Luke)
V-2
"God Will Make a Way" (with "He Leadeth Me") (Mal, Luke)
V-3 (2) p. 9
"Alleluia, Sing to Jesus" (Mal, Luke)
V-3 (3) p. 50
"Come, Thou Long-Expected Jesus" (Luke, Advent)
V-10 p. 11

**Anthems**

"Purify My Heart" (Mal)
Arr. Patrick Tierney; Hope C-5850
SATB with piano

"Blessed Be the God of Israel" (Mal, Luke 1)
Arr. Michael Burkhardt; MorningStar MSM-50-0002
SATB with organ and optional congregation

**Other Suggestions**

Visuals:
**O** Fire, soap, silver, gold, refining, silver polish
**P** Christ, child, dawn breaking, light/darkness
**E** Prayer, open Bible, heart, shackles, letter, robe, harvest
**G** John, baptism, Luke 3:4b, straight path, level ground, all nations
Introit: S2005, BOW216. "Arise, Shine" (Luke, Advent)
Greeting: BOW245 (Luke 1) or BOW241 (Luke 3)
Call to Worship: WSL4 (Luke, Phil, Advent)
Advent Wreath Litany: BOW208. "Come, Lord Jesus"
Canticle: UM205. "Canticle of Light and Darkness" (Luke 1)
Canticle: UM208. "Canticle of Zechariah" (Luke 1)
Opening Prayer: BOW252 (Mal, Luke)
Prayer of Confession: BOW479 (Luke)
Prayer: UM201. Advent (Luke)
Prayer: BOW510. For Discernment (Luke 1)
Offertory Prayer: WSL125 or WSL152 (Luke, Advent)

**Zephaniah 3:14-20**

14 Rejoice, Daughter Zion! Shout, Israel!
Rejoice and exult with all your heart, Daughter
Jerusalem.
15 The LORD has removed your judgment;
he has turned away your enemy.
The LORD, the king of Israel, is in your midst;
you will no longer fear evil.
16 On that day, it will be said to Jerusalem:
Don't fear, Zion.
Don't let your hands fall.
17 The LORD your God is in your midst—a warrior bringing
victory.
He will create calm with his love;
he will rejoice over you with singing.
18 I will remove from you those worried about the appointed
feasts.
They have been a burden for her, a reproach.
19 Watch what I am about to do to all your oppressors at
that time.
I will deliver the lame;
I will gather the outcast.
I will change their shame into praise and fame
throughout the earth.
20 At that time, I will bring all of you back,
at the time when I gather you.
I will give you fame and praise among all the neighboring
peoples
when I restore your possessions and you can see
them—says the LORD.

---

**Isaiah 12:2-6**

2 "God is indeed my salvation;
I will trust and won't be afraid.
Yah, the LORD, is my strength and my shield;
he has become my salvation."
3 You will draw water with joy from the springs of salvation.
4 And you will say on that day:
"Thank the LORD; call on God's name;
proclaim God's deeds among the peoples;
declare that God's name is exalted.
5 Sing to the LORD, who has done glorious things;
proclaim this throughout all the earth."
6 Shout and sing for joy, city of Zion,
because the holy one of Israel is great among you.

---

**Philippians 4:4-7**

4 Be glad in the Lord always! Again I say, be glad! 5 Let your
gentleness show in your treatment of all people. The Lord is
near. 6 Don't be anxious about anything; rather, bring up all
of your requests to God in your prayers and petitions, along
with giving thanks. 7 Then the peace of God that exceeds all
understanding will keep your hearts and minds safe in Christ
Jesus.

---

**Luke 3:7-18**

7 Then John said to the crowds who came to be baptized
by him, "You children of snakes! Who warned you to escape
from the angry judgment that is coming soon? 8 Produce fruit
that shows you have changed your hearts and lives. And don't
even think about saying to yourselves, Abraham is our father.
I tell you that God is able to raise up Abraham's children
from these stones. 9 The ax is already at the root of the trees.
Therefore, every tree that doesn't produce good fruit will be
chopped down and tossed into the fire."
10 The crowds asked him, "What then should we do?"
11 He answered, "Whoever has two shirts must share with
the one who has none, and whoever has food must do the
same."
12 Even tax collectors came to be baptized. They said to
him, "Teacher, what should we do?"
13 He replied, "Collect no more than you are authorized to
collect."
14 Soldiers asked, "What about us? What should we do?"
He answered, "Don't cheat or harass anyone, and be satisfied with your pay."
15 The people were filled with expectation, and everyone
wondered whether John might be the Christ. 16 John replied
to them all, "I baptize you with water, but the one who is
more powerful than me is coming. I'm not worthy to loosen
the strap of his sandals. He will baptize you with the Holy
Spirit and fire. 17 The shovel he uses to sift the wheat from the
husks is in his hands. He will clean out his threshing area and
bring the wheat into his barn. But he will burn the husks with
a fire that can't be put out." 18 With many other words John
appealed to them, proclaiming good news to the people.

**Primary Hymns and Songs for the Day**
203 "Hail to the Lord's Anointed" (Zeph) (O)
2030 "The First Song of Isaiah" (Isa)
224 "Good Christian Friends, Rejoice" (Phil, Luke)
H-3 Hbl-19, 30, 65; Chr-83; Desc-55; Org-62
S-1 #180. Rhythm instrument accompaniment
2089 "Wild and Lone the Prophet's Voice" (Luke)
196 "Come, Thou Long-Expected Jesus" (Zeph) (C)
H-3 Hbl-46; Chr-26, 134; Desc-53; Org-56
S-1 #168-71. Various treatments

**Additional Hymn Suggestions**
107 "*La Palabra Del Señor Es Recta*" ("Righteous and Just Is the Word of Our Lord") (Zeph)
195 "Send Your Word" (Zeph, Luke)
200 "Tell Out, My Soul" (Zeph, Isa, Phil, Luke)
209 "Blessed Be the God of Israel" (Zeph, Luke)
210 "*Toda la Tierra*" ("All Earth Is Waiting") (Zeph, Luke 3)
2218 "You Are Mine" (Zeph)
2236 "Gather Us In" (Zeph)
132 "All My Hope Is Firmly Grounded" (Isa)
149 "*Cantemos al Señor*" ("Let's Sing Unto the Lord") (Isa)
160 "Rejoice, Ye Pure in Heart" (Phil)
161 "Rejoice, Ye Pure in Heart" (Phil)
715 "Rejoice, the Lord Is King" (Phil)
716 "Rejoice, the Lord Is King" (Phil)
729 "O Day of Peace That Dimly Shines" (Phil, Luke)
2197 "Lord of All Hopefulness" (Phil, Advent)
3048 "View the Present Through the Promise" (Phil, Luke)
221 "In the Bleak Midwinter" (Luke)
388 "O Come and Dwell in Me" (Luke)
399 "Take My Life, and Let It Be" (Luke)
421 "Make Me a Captive, Lord" (Luke)
425 "O Crucified Redeemer" (Luke)
434 "*Cuando el Pobre*" ("When the Poor Ones") (Luke)
436 "The Voice of God Is Calling" (Luke)
441 "What Does the Lord Require" (Luke)
2060 "God the Sculptor of the Mountains" (Luke)
3045 "Down by the Jordan (Luke)

**Additional Contemporary Suggestions**
S2074 "Shout to the Lord" (Zeph, Isa)
M16; V-3 (2) p. 32 Vocal solo
S2091 "The King of Glory Comes" (Zeph)
WS3038 "Mighty to Save" (Zeph)
M246
WS3023 "Forever" (Isa)
M68
M164 "Good to Me" (Isa)
S2070 "He Is Exalted" (Isa)
SP66
S2144 "Someone Asked the Question" (Isa, Phil)
S2195 "In the Lord I'll Be Ever Thankful" (Isa, Phil)
S2270 "I Will Enter His Gates" (Isa, Phil)
SP168
S2145 "I've Got Peace Like a River" (Phil)
S2156 "Give Peace" ("*Da Pacem Cordium*") (Phil)
S2157 "Come and Fill Our Hearts" ("*Confitemini Domino*") (Phil)
S2164 "Sanctuary" (Phil)
M52
WS3148 "There's a Spirit of Love in This Place" (Phil)
M87 "Let the Peace of God Reign" (Phil)
M166 "Thank You, Lord" (Phil)
S2071 "Jesus, Name Above All Names" (Luke)
SP76
M34 "I Will Never Be" ("The Same Again") (Luke)
M50 "Refiner's Fire" (Luke, Advent)

**Vocal Solos**
"Rejoice, the Lord Is King" (Zeph)
V-1 p. 66
"Rejoice Greatly, O Daughter of Zion" (Zeph)
V-2
"Prepare Thyself, Zion" (Zeph)
V-9 p. 2
"A Song of Joy" (Zeph, Phil)
V-11 p. 2
"A Song of Trust" (Phil)
V-4 p. 20

**Anthems**
"Come, Thou Long-Expected Jesus" (Zeph)
Mark Shepperd; MorningStar MSM-50- 0047
SSAATBB with organ or flute/oboe, cello, and percussion

"An Advent Alleluia" (Zeph)
Douglas E. Wagner; Hope A680
SATB with keyboard

**Other Suggestions**
Visuals:
**O** Rejoicing, singing, festival, clock, saving
**P** Races/nations, singing, shouting, water/well
**E** Rejoicing, praying hands, Phil 4:4, 5b, 6a, b, peace
**G** Snakes, axe/root, Holy Spirit, fir, water, 2 coats, tax form, fruit, winnowing fork, wheat, service, trees bearing fruit and barren
Introit: UM315, stanza 1. "Come, Ye Faithful, Raise the Strain" (Zeph)
Greeting: BOW242 (Zeph)
Call to Worship: WSL9 (Zeph)
Opening Prayer: BOW250 (Zeph, Luke)
Call to Prayer: S2157. "Come and Fill Our Hearts" (Phil)
Prayer: UM201. Advent (Luke)
Canticle: UM208. "Canticle of Zechariah" (Zeph)
Prayer of Confession: UM366. For Guidance (Luke)
Prayer of Confession: BOW482 (Zeph, Luke)
Prayer for Mercy: UM597. For the Spirit of Truth (Luke)
Prayer of Thanksgiving and Intercession: BOW255 (Zeph)
Response: S2201. "Prayers of the People" (Phil)
Blessing: BOW561 (1 Thess)
Sung Benediction: S2279. "The Trees of the Field" (Isa)

**Micah 5:2-5a**

2 As for you, Bethlehem of Ephrathah,
though you are the least significant of Judah's forces,
one who is to be a ruler in Israel on my behalf will come out from you.
His origin is from remote times, from ancient days.
3 Therefore, he will give them up
until the time when she who is in labor gives birth.
The rest of his kin will return to the people of Israel.
4 He will stand and shepherd his flock in the strength of the LORD,
in the majesty of the name of the LORD his God.
They will dwell secure,
because he will surely become great throughout the earth;
5a he will become one of peace.

---

**Luke 1:47-55**

47 "In the depths of who I am I rejoice in God my savior.
48 He has looked with favor on the low status of his servant.
Look! From now on, everyone will consider me highly favored
49 because the mighty one has done great things for me.
Holy is his name.
50 He shows mercy to everyone,
from one generation to the next,
who honors him as God.
51 He has shown strength with his arm.
He has scattered those with arrogant thoughts and proud inclinations.
52 He has pulled the powerful down from their thrones
and lifted up the lowly.
53 He has filled the hungry with good things
and sent the rich away empty-handed.
54 He has come to the aid of his servant Israel,
remembering his mercy,
55 just as he promised to our ancestors,
to Abraham and to Abraham's descendants forever."

---

**Hebrews 10:5-10**

5 Therefore, when he comes into the world he says,
*You didn't want a sacrifice or an offering,*
*but you prepared a body for me;*
6 *you weren't pleased with entirely burned offerings or a sin offering.*
7 *So then I said,*
*"Look, I've come to do your will, God.*
*This has been written about me in the scroll."*
8 He says above, *You didn't want* and *you weren't pleased with*
*a sacrifice or an offering* or *with entirely burned offerings or a puri-*
*fication offering,* which are offered because the Law requires
them. 9 Then he said, *Look, I've come to do your will.* He puts an
end to the first to establish the second. 10 We have been made
holy by God's will through the offering of Jesus Christ's body
once for all.

---

**Luke 1:39-45**

39 Mary got up and hurried to a city in the Judean high-
lands. 40 She entered Zechariah's home and greeted Elizabeth. 41 When Elizabeth heard Mary's greeting, the child
leaped in her womb, and Elizabeth was filled with the Holy
Spirit. 42 With a loud voice she blurted out, "God has blessed
you above all women, and he has blessed the child you
carry. 43 Why do I have this honor, that the mother of my
Lord should come to me? 44 As soon as I heard your greeting,
the baby in my womb jumped for joy. 45 Happy is she who
believed that the Lord would fulfill the promises he made to
her."

**Primary Hymns and Songs for the Day**

234 "O Come, All Ye Faithful" (Luke) (O)
H-3 Hbl-78; Desc-12; Org-2
S-1 #7-13. Various treatments
230 "O Little Town of Bethlehem" (Mic)
H-3 Hbl-81; Chr-145; Desc-95; Org-141
S-1 #304. Harm.
198 "My Soul Gives Glory to My God" (Luke)
H-3 Chr-139, 145; Desc-77
S-1 #241-42. Orff arr. and desc.
2036 "Give Thanks" (Luke)
SP170
240 "Hark! the Herald Angels Sing" (Mic, Luke)
246 "Joy to the World" (Mic, Luke) (C)
H-3 Hbl-8, 29, 73; Chr-119; Desc-15; Org-6
S-1 #19-20. Trumpet descs.

**Additional Hymn Suggestions**

179 "O Sing a Song of Bethlehem" (Mic)
196 "Come, Thou Long-Expected Jesus" (Mic)
250 "Once in Royal David's City" (Mic)
518 "O Thou, in Whose Presence" (Mic)
2050 "Mothering God, You Gave Me Birth" (Mic)
209 "Blessed Be the God of Israel" (Mic, Heb, Luke)
214 "Savior of the Nations, Come" (Mic, Luke)
241 "That Boy-Child of Mary" (Mic, Luke)
441 "What Does the Lord Require" (Heb, Luke)
187 "Rise, Shine, You People (Heb)
475 "Come Down, O Love Divine" (Heb)
2147 "There Are Some Things I May Not Know" (Heb)
2196 "We Walk by Faith" (Heb)
197 "Ye Who Claim the Faith of Jesus" (Luke)
200 "Tell Out, My Soul" (Luke)
215 "To a Maid Engaged to Joseph" (Luke)
216 "Lo, How a Rose E'er Blooming" (Luke)
272 "Sing of Mary, Pure and Lowly" (Luke)
276 "The First One Ever" (Luke)
434 "*Cuando el Pobre*" ("When the Poor Ones") (Luke)
518 "O Thou, in Whose Presence" (Luke)
2092 "Like a Child" (Luke)
2093 "The Snow Lay on the Ground" (Luke)
2095 "Star-Child" (Luke)
2099 "Joseph Dearest, Joseph Mine" (Luke)
2122 "She Comes Sailing on the Wind" (Luke)
2151 "I'm So Glad Jesus Lifted Me" (Luke)
2155 "Blest Are They" (Luke)
3059 "Love Has Come" (Luke, Advent, Christmas)
3157 "Come, Let Us Dream" (Luke)

**Additional Contemporary Suggestions**

M1 "Ancient of Days" (Mic)
M24 "Jesus, We Crown You with Praise" (Mic)
M164 "Good to Me" (Mic, Luke)
WS3042 "Shout to the North" (Mic, Luke)
M99
WS3040 "You Are My All in All" (Mic, Heb, Luke)
SP220
S2091 "The King of Glory Comes" (Mic, Luke)
S2077 "You Alone Are Holy" (Heb)
S2005 "Arise, Shine" (Luke, Advent)
S2029 "Praise to the Lord" (Luke)
S2033 "Glory to God" ("*Gloria a Dios*") (Luke)
S2098 "The Virgin Mary Had a Baby Boy" (Luke)
S2272 "Holy Ground" (Luke)
SP86
S2056 "God Is So Good" (Luke)
WS3044 "Make Way" (Luke)
WS3106 "Your Grace Is Enough" (Luke)
M191
M142 "Let the River Flow" (Luke)
M165 "Friend of God" (Luke)
M227 "I Will Boast" (Luke)
SP77 "O Magnify the Lord" (Luke)

**Vocal Solos**

"He Shall Feed His Flock" (Mic)
V-2
V-8 p. 334
"Alleluia, Sing to Jesus" (Mic)
V-3 (3) p. 50
"The Virgin's Slumber Song" (Luke)
V-4 p. 28
"To Touch His Tiny Hand" (Luke)
V-10 p. 22

**Anthems**

"Joy to the World" (Mic, Luke)
Arr. Douglas J. Benton; Hope C-5827
SATB with organ, opt. brass, percussion, and handbells

"A Boy Was Born" (Mic, Luke)
Robert G. Farrell; Paraclete Press PPM01350
SATB *a cappella*

**Other Suggestions**

Visuals:
**O** Bethlehem, Christ feeding sheep, globe
**P** Mary, arm, toppled throne, feed, full/empty bowls
**E** Scroll, open Bible, cross/manger
**G** Pregnant women, greeting, Luke 1:42b
Greeting: BOW245 or BOW246 (Luke)
Canticle: UM199. "Canticle of Mary" ("Magnificat") (Luke)
Prayer of Confession: BOW478 (Luke)
Prayer: WSL6 (Luke)
Prayer: BOW256. The Annunciation to Mary (Luke)
Prayer: BOW257. The Visitation of Mary to Elizabeth (Luke)
Prayer: BOW511. For God's Reign (Mic, Luke)
Prayer of Intercession: BOW546. For Those Who Suffer (Luke)
Response: UM300. "O the Lamb" (Heb)
Offertory Prayer: WSL148 (Luke)
See BOW263 for An Advent Service of Lessons and Carols for additional ideas.

**Isaiah 9:2-7**

2 The people walking in darkness have seen a great light.
On those living in a pitch-dark land, light has dawned.
3 You have made the nation great;
you have increased its joy.
They rejoiced before you as with joy at the harvest,
as those who divide plunder rejoice.
4 As on the day of Midian, you've shattered the yoke that
burdened them,
the staff on their shoulders,
and the rod of their oppressor.
5 Because every boot of the thundering warriors,
and every garment rolled in blood
will be burned, fuel for the fire.
6 A child is born to us, a son is given to us,
and authority will be on his shoulders.
He will be named
Wonderful Counselor, Mighty God,
Eternal Father, Prince of Peace.
7 There will be vast authority and endless peace
for David's throne and for his kingdom,
establishing and sustaining it
with justice and righteousness
now and forever.
The zeal of the LORD of heavenly forces will do this.

**Psalm 96 (UM815)**

Sing to the LORD a new song!
Sing to the LORD, all the earth!
2 Sing to the LORD! Bless his name!
Share the news of his saving work every single day!
3 Declare God's glory among the nations;
declare his wondrous works among all people
4 because the LORD is great and so worthy of praise.
He is awesome beyond all other gods
5 because all the gods of the nations are just idols,
but it is the LORD who created heaven!
6 Greatness and grandeur are in front of him;
strength and beauty are in his sanctuary.
7 Give to the LORD, all families of the nations—
give to the LORD glory and power!
8 Give to the LORD the glory due his name!
Bring gifts!
Enter his courtyards!
9 Bow down to the LORD in his holy splendor!
Tremble before him, all the earth!
10 Tell the nations, "The LORD rules!
Yes, he set the world firmly in place;
it won't be shaken.
He will judge all people fairly."
11 Let heaven celebrate! Let the earth rejoice!
Let the sea and everything in it roar!
12 Let the countryside and everything in it celebrate!
Then all the trees of the forest too
will shout out joyfully
13 before the LORD because he is coming!
He is coming to establish justice on the earth!
He will establish justice in the world rightly.
He will establish justice among all people fairly.

**Titus 2:11-14**

11 The grace of God has appeared, bringing salvation to all
people. 12 It educates us so that we can live sensible, ethi-
cal, and godly lives right now by rejecting ungodly lives and
the desires of this world. 13 At the same time we wait for the
blessed hope and the glorious appearance of our great God
and savior Jesus Christ. 14 He gave himself for us in order to
rescue us from every kind of lawless behavior, and cleanse a
special people for himself who are eager to do good actions.

**Luke 2:1-20**

In those days Caesar Augustus declared that everyone
throughout the empire should be enrolled in the tax lists.
2 This first enrollment occurred when Quirinius governed
Syria. 3 Everyone went to their own cities to be enrolled.
4 Since Joseph belonged to David's house and family line,
he went up from the city of Nazareth in Galilee to David's
city, called Bethlehem, in Judea. 5 He went to be enrolled
together with Mary, who was promised to him in marriage
and who was pregnant. 6 While they were there, the time
came for Mary to have her baby. 7 She gave birth to her
firstborn child, a son, wrapped him snugly, and laid him
in a manger, because there was no place for them in the
guestroom.

8 Nearby shepherds were living in the fields, guarding their
sheep at night. 9 The Lord's angel stood before them, the
Lord's glory shone around them, and they were terrified.

10 The angel said, "Don't be afraid! Look! I bring good news
to you—wonderful, joyous news for all people. 11 Your savior
is born today in David's city. He is Christ the Lord. 12 This is
a sign for you: you will find a newborn baby wrapped snugly
and lying in a manger." 13 Suddenly a great assembly of the
heavenly forces was with the angel praising God. They said,
14 "Glory to God in heaven, and on earth peace among those
whom he favors."

15 When the angels returned to heaven, the shepherds said
to each other, "Let's go right now to Bethlehem and see
what's happened. Let's confirm what the Lord has revealed
to us." 16 They went quickly and found Mary and Joseph, and
the baby lying in the manger. 17 When they saw this, they
reported what they had been told about this child.
18 Everyone who heard it was amazed at what the shepherds
told them. 19 Mary committed these things to memory and
considered them carefully. 20 The shepherds returned home,
glorifying and praising God for all they had heard and seen.
Everything happened just as they had been told.

**Primary Hymns and Songs for the Day**

238 "Angels We Have Heard on High" (Luke) (O)
H-3 Hbl-47; Chr-31; Desc-43; Org-45
217 "Away in a Manger" (Luke)
H-3 Org-12
S-1 #30-32. Various treatments
S-2 #20. Desc.
218 "It Came Upon the Midnight Clear" (Luke)
H-3 Hbl-72; Chr-113; Desc-22; Org-19
S-2 #39. Desc.
237 "Sing We Now of Christmas" (Luke) (C)
H-3 Chr-140
S-1 #136. Orff instr. arr.
239 "Silent Night" (Luke) (C)
H-3 Hbl-92; Chr-171; Desc-99; Org-159
S-1 #322. Desc.
#323. Guitar/autoharp chords
S-2 #167. Handbell arr.

**Additional Hymn Suggestions**

3064 "On Christmas Night" (Isa, Luke)
2001 "We Sing to You, O God" (Pss)
2011 "We Sing of Your Glory" (*"Tuya Es la Gloria"*) (Pss)
2255 "In the Singing" (Titus, Comm.)
224 "Good Christian Friends, Rejoice" (Luke)
227 "The Friendly Beasts" (Luke)
229 "Infant Holy, Infant Lowly" (Luke)
230 "O Little Town of Bethlehem" (Luke)
234 "O Come, All Ye Faithful" (Luke)
235 "Rock-a-Bye, My Dear Little Boy" (Luke)
236 "While Shepherds Watched Their Flocks" (Luke)
241 "That Boy-Child of Mary" (Luke)
244 "'Twas in the Moon of Wintertime" (Luke)
245 "The First Noel" (Luke)
249 "There's a Song in the Air" (Luke)
2092 "Like a Child" (Luke)
2093 "The Snow Lay on the Ground" (Luke)
2097 "One Holy Night in Bethlehem" (Luke)
2099 "Joseph Dearest, Joseph Mine" (Luke)
2276 "Glory to God in the Highest" (Luke)
3057 "Glory in the Highest (*"Gloria in las Alturas"*) (Luke)
617 "I Come with Joy" (Comm.)

**Additional Contemporary Suggestions**

S2075 "King of Kings" (Isa)
SP94
S2204 "Light of the World" (Isa)
S2023 "How Majestic Is Your Name" (Isa)
SP14
S2071 "Jesus, Name Above All Names" (Isa)
SP76
UM174 "His Name Is Wonderful" (Isa)
SP90
M19 "Shine on Us" (Isa)
M129 "You Are Holy" ("Prince of Peace") (Isa)
M249 "Marvelous Light" (Isa)
WS3177 "Here I Am to Worship" (Isa, Luke)
M116
WS3060 "Jesus, Jesus, Oh, What a Wonderful Child" (Isa, Luke)
WS3003 "How Great Is Our God" (Pss)
M117
WS3042 "Shout to the North" (Pss)
M99
S2034 "Blessed Be the Name of the Lord" (Pss)
M12, UM63
S2037 "I Sing Praises to Your Name" (Pss)
SP27
S2074 "Shout to the Lord" (Pss)
M16; V-3 (2) p. 32 Vocal Solo
UM176 "Majesty" (Pss)
SP73
M251 "Grace Like Rain" (Titus)
S2258 "Sing Alleluia to the Lord" (Titus, Comm.)
SP93
S2088 "Lord, I Lift Your Name on High" (Luke)
M2
M132 "Wonderful Maker" (Luke)
M133 "O Praise Him" ("All This for a King") (Luke)
M231 "Glory in the Highest" (Luke)
M130 "Offering" (Christmas)

**Vocal Solos**

"Go, Tell It on the Mountain" (Luke)
V-3 (1) p. 10
"O Holy Night" (Luke)
V-8 p. 93
"In the First Light"
V-5(1) p. 28
"Sing Noel!" (Luke)
V-11 p. 13
"Sleep, Little Baby" (Luke)
V-10 p. 27

**Anthems**

"O Holy Night" (Luke)
Arr. Jay Althouse; Hope C-5853
SATB with keyboard

"Silent Night" (Luke)
Arr. Matthew Culloton; MorningStar MSM-50-0085
SATB with piano, opt. flute or violin

**Other Suggestions**

Visuals:
**O** Light, yoke, rod, infant Jesus, Isa 9:6b, crown
**P** All nature, gifts and offerings, gold
**E** Gold cross, glory, sacrifice
**G** Infant Jesus, manger, nativity scene, shepherds, angels

Introit: BOW213. "Christ Is Born" (Luke)
Greeting: BOW271 (Luke) or BOW273 (Titus)
Opening Prayer: BOW276 or WSL8 (Luke)
Blessing of the Nativity Scene: BOW280
Candle Response: S2090. "Light the Advent Candle" (Luke)
Canticle: UM83. "Canticle of God's Glory" (Luke)
Prayer: UM231. Christmas (Titus)
Offertory Prayer: WSL126 or WSL127 (Luke, Christmas)
Call to Communion: WS3055. "Come, Little Children" (Luke)
Christmas Eve Resources: BOW, pp. 56–57, BOW281, BOW284
Response: S2033. "Glory to God" (*"Gloria a Dios"*) (Luke)
Blessing: WSL7 (John 1, Christmas)
Alternate Scriptures for Christmas Day: Isa 52:7-10, Ps 98, Heb 1:1-4 (5-12), John 1:1-14

**1 Samuel 2:18-20, 26**

18 Now Samuel was serving the LORD. He was a young boy,
clothed in a linen priestly vest. 19 His mother would make a
small robe for him and take it to him every year when she
went up with her husband to offer the annual sacrifice. 20 Eli
would bless Elkanah and his wife: “May the LORD replace the
child of this woman that you gave back to the LORD.” Then
they would return home. . . .
26 Meanwhile, the boy Samuel kept growing up and was
more and more liked by both the LORD and the people.

---

**Psalm 148 (UM861)**

Praise the LORD!
Praise the LORD from heaven!
    Praise God on the heights!
2 Praise God, all of you who are his messengers!
    Praise God, all of you who comprise his heavenly forces!
3 Sun and moon, praise God!
    All of you bright stars, praise God!
4 You highest heaven, praise God!
    Do the same, you waters that are above the sky!
5 Let all of these praise the LORD’s name
    because God gave the command and they were created!
6 God set them in place always and forever.
    God made a law that will not be broken.
7 Praise the LORD from the earth,
    you sea monsters and all you ocean depths!
8 Do the same, fire and hail, snow and smoke,
    stormy wind that does what God says!
9 Do the same, you mountains, every single hill,
    fruit trees, and every single cedar!
10 Do the same, you animals—wild or tame—
    you creatures that creep along and you birds that fly!
11 Do the same, you kings of the earth and every single
        person,
    you princes and every single ruler on earth!
12 Do the same, you young men—young women too!—
    you who are old together with you who are young!
13 Let all of these praise the LORD’s name
    because only God’s name is high over all.
    Only God’s majesty is over earth and heaven.
14 God raised the strength of his people,
    the praise of all his faithful ones—
        that’s the Israelites,
        the people who are close to him.
Praise the LORD!

---

**Colossians 3:12-17**

12 Therefore, as God’s choice, holy and loved, put on compassion, kindness, humility, gentleness, and patience.
13 Be tolerant with each other and, if someone has a complaint
against anyone, forgive each other. As the Lord forgave you, so
also forgive each other. 14 And over all these things put on love,
which is the perfect bond of unity. 15 The peace of Christ must
control your hearts—a peace into which you were called in
one body. And be thankful people. 16 The word of Christ must
live in you richly. Teach and warn each other with all wisdom
by singing psalms, hymns, and spiritual songs. Sing to God
with gratitude in your hearts. 17 Whatever you do, whether in
speech or action, do it all in the name of the Lord Jesus and
give thanks to God the Father through him.

**Luke 2:41-52**

41 Each year his parents went to Jerusalem for the Passover
Festival. 42 When he was 12 years old, they went up to Jerusalem according to their custom. 43 After the festival was over,
they were returning home, but the boy Jesus stayed behind
in Jerusalem. His parents didn’t know it. 44 Supposing that
he was among their band of travelers, they journeyed on
for a full day while looking for him among their family and
friends. 45 When they didn’t find Jesus, they returned to
Jerusalem to look for him. 46 After three days they found him
in the temple. He was sitting among the teachers, listening to
them and putting questions to them. 47 Everyone who heard
him was amazed by his understanding and his answers.
48 When his parents saw him, they were shocked.
His mother said, “Child, why have you treated us like this?
Listen! Your father and I have been worried. We’ve been
looking for you!”
49 Jesus replied, “Why were you looking for me? Didn’t
you know that it was necessary for me to be in my Father’s
house?” 50 But they didn’t understand what he said to them.
51 Jesus went down to Nazareth with them and was obedient to them. His mother cherished every word in her heart.
52 Jesus matured in wisdom and years, and in favor with God
and with people.

**Primary Hymns and Songs for the Day**

250 "Once in Royal David's City" (Luke, Christmas) (O)
H-3 Hbl-83; Chr-68, 156; Desc-57; Org-63
S-1 #182-84. Various treatments

179 "O Sing a Song of Bethlehem" (Luke)
H-3 Hbl-15, 20, 34, 84; Chr-150; Org-67
S-2 #100-103. Various treatments

229 "Infant Holy, Infant Lowly" (Luke, Christmas)
H-3 Chr-113; Desc-102; Org-171
S-1 #345. Handbell/keyboard arr.

241 "That Boy-Child of Mary" (Luke, Christmas)
H-3 Chr-179
S-1 #45. Guitar/autoharp chords
S-2 #28. Flute desc.

251 "Go, Tell It on the Mountain" (Christmas) (C)
H-3 Hbl-17, 28, 61; Chr-73; Desc-45; Org-46

**Additional Hymn Suggestions**

679 "O Splendor of God's Glory Bright" (1 Sam)
2155 "Blest Are They" (1 Sam)
2008 "Let All Things Now Living" (Pss)
3018 "Creation Sings" (Pss)
62 "All Creatures of Our God and King" (Pss)
77 "How Great Thou Art" (Pss)
96 "Praise the Lord Who Reigns Above" (Pss)
561 "Jesus, United by Thy Grace" (Col)
643 "When Love Is Found" (Col)
645 "O Perfect Love" (Col)
2044 "My Gratitude Now Accept, O God" (*"Gracias, Señor"*) (Col)
2114 "At the Font We Start Our Journey" (Col, New Year)
2175 "Together We Serve" (Col)
2185 "For One Great Peace" (Col)
2213 "Healer of Our Every Ill" (Col)
2216 "When We Are Called to Sing Your Praise" (Col)
2220 "We Are God's People" (Col)
3057 "Glory in the Highest (*"Gloria in las alturas"*) (Luke)
222 *"Niño Lindo"* ("Child So Lovely") (Luke)
235 "Rock-a-Bye, My Dear Little Boy" (Luke, Christmas)
242 "Love Came Down at Christmas" (Luke, Christmas)
256 "We Would See Jesus" (Luke)
257 "We Meet You, O Christ" (Luke)
447 "Our Parent, by Whose Name" (Luke)
2092 "Like a Child" (Luke)
2197 "Lord of All Hopefulness" (Luke)
3065 "Some Children See Him" (Luke, Christmas)

**Additional Contemporary Suggestions**

S2029 "Praise to the Lord" (1 Sam)
S2035 "Praise, Praise, Praise the Lord" (Pss)
WS3034 "God of Wonders" (Pss)
M80
M59 "Let Everything That Has Breath" (Pss)
M127 "Indescribable" (Pss)
M238 "Cannons" (Pss)
M231 "Glory in the Highest" (Pss, Christmas)
M154 "Dwell" (Col)
S2036 "Give Thanks" (Col)
SP170
S2141 "There's a Song" (Col)
S2156 "Give Peace" (*"Da Pacem Cordium"*) (Col)
S2171 "Make Me a Channel of Your Peace" (Col)
S2186 "Song of Hope" (Col)
S2224 "Make Us One" (Col)
SP137
S2226 "Bind Us Together" (Col)
SP140
M245 "No Sweeter Name" (Col)

**Vocal Solos**

"Bright and Beautiful" (1 Sam, Pss)
V-3 (3) p. 10
"All Creatures of Our God and King" (Pss)
V-6 p. 55
"Because You Are God's Chosen Ones" (Col)
V-8 p. 286
"Gentle Jesus, Meek and Mild" (Luke, Christmas)
V-1 p. 11
"Jesus, What a Wonderful Child" (Luke, Christmas)
V-5(1) p. 48
"Sing for Christ Is Born" (Luke, Christmas)
V-10 p. 16
"Welcome to Our World" (Luke, Christmas)
WS3067
V-5(1) p. 34

**Anthems**

"Bring a Torch, Jeanette, Isabella" (Christmas)
Arr. Neil Harmon; Hinshaw HMC2311
SATB with piano or harp, oboe and clarinet

"On This Day Earth Shall Ring" (Christmas)
Arr. Neil Harmon; MorningStar MSM-50-1714
SATB with piano or harp, flute, handbells

**Other Suggestions**

Visuals:
**O** Twelve-year-old boy, growing children, graduated sizes (clothes)
**P** Stars, planets, moon; nature imagery, single horn
**E** Clothes, compassion, forgiveness, singing, Col 3:16, 17b
**G** Growing boy, parents, child with teachers, glue or cord

Introit: BOW212. "Christ Is Born" (Christmas)
Introit: S2128. "Come and Find the Quiet Center" (Col)
Greeting: BOW274 (Pss) or BOW275 (Christmas)
Opening Prayer: BOW278 (Luke)
Prayer of Praise: WSL69 (Pss)
Canticle: UM646. "Canticle of Love" (Col)
Prayer: BOW313 (Luke)
Prayer of Thanksgiving and Intercession: BOW279 (Luke)
Dismissal with Blessing: BOW, pp. 287-88

**Ecclesiastes 3:1-13**

There's a season for everything
and a time for every matter under the heavens:
2 a time for giving birth and a time for dying,
a time for planting and a time for uprooting what was planted,
3 a time for killing and a time for healing,
a time for tearing down and a time for building up,
4 a time for crying and a time for laughing,
a time for mourning and a time for dancing,
5 a time for throwing stones and a time for gathering stones,
a time for embracing and a time for avoiding embraces,
6 a time for searching and a time for losing,
a time for keeping and a time for throwing away,
7 a time for tearing and a time for repairing,
a time for keeping silent and a time for speaking,
8 a time for loving and a time for hating,
a time for war and a time for peace.

9 What do workers gain from all their hard work? 10 I have
observed the task that God has given human beings. 11 God
has made everything fitting in its time, but has also placed
eternity in their hearts, without enabling them to discover
what God has done from beginning to end.
12 I know that there's nothing better for them but to enjoy
themselves and do what's good while they live. 13 Moreover,
this is the gift of God: that all people should eat, drink, and
enjoy the results of their hard work.

---

**Psalm 8 (UM743)**

LORD, our LORD, how majestic
is your name throughout the earth!
You made your glory higher than heaven!
2 From the mouths of nursing babies
you have laid a strong foundation
because of your foes,
in order to stop vengeful enemies.
3 When I look up at your skies,
at what your fingers made—
the moon and the stars
that you set firmly in place—
4 what are human beings
that you think about them;
what are human beings
that you pay attention to them?
5 You've made them only slightly less than divine,
crowning them with glory and grandeur.
6 You've let them rule over your handiwork,
putting everything under their feet—
7 all sheep and all cattle,
the wild animals too,
8 the birds in the sky,
the fish of the ocean,
everything that travels the pathways of the sea.
9 LORD, our LORD, how majestic is your name throughout the earth!

**Revelation 21:1-6a**

Then I saw a new heaven and a new earth, for the former
heaven and the former earth had passed away, and the sea
was no more. 2 I saw the holy city, New Jerusalem, coming
down out of heaven from God, made ready as a bride beautifully dressed for her husband.
3 "Look! God's dwelling is here with humankind. He will
dwell with them, and they will be his peoples. God himself
will be with them as their God. 4 He will wipe away every tear
from their eyes. Death will be no more. There will be no
mourning, crying, or pain anymore, for the former things
have passed away."5 Then the one seated on the throne said,
"Look! I'm making all things new." He also said, "Write this
down, for these words are trustworthy and true." 6a Then he
said to me, "All is done. I am the Alpha and the Omega, the
beginning and the end."

---

**Matthew 25:31-46**

31 "Now when the Human One comes in his majesty and all
his angels are with him, he will sit on his majestic throne.
32 All the nations will be gathered in front of him. He will
separate them from each other, just as a shepherd separates
the sheep from the goats. 33 He will put the sheep on his right
side. But the goats he will put on his left.
34 "Then the king will say to those on his right, 'Come, you
who will receive good things from my Father. Inherit the
kingdom that was prepared for you before the world began.
35 I was hungry and you gave me food to eat. I was thirsty and
you gave me a drink. I was a stranger and you welcomed me.
36 I was naked and you gave me clothes to wear. I was sick and
you took care of me. I was in prison and you visited me.'
37 "Then those who are righteous will reply to him, 'Lord,
when did we see you hungry and feed you, or thirsty and
give you a drink? 38 When did we see you as a stranger and
welcome you, or naked and give you clothes to wear? 39 When
did we see you sick or in prison and visit you?'
40 "Then the king will reply to them, 'I assure you that when
you have done it for one of the least of these brothers and
sisters of mine, you have done it for me.'
41 "Then he will say to those on his left, 'Get away from me,
you who will receive terrible things. Go into the unending
fire that has been prepared for the devil and his angels. 42 I
was hungry and you didn't give me food to eat. I was thirsty
and you didn't give me anything to drink. 43 I was a stranger
and you didn't welcome me. I was naked and you didn't give
me clothes to wear. I was sick and in prison, and you didn't
visit me.'
44 "Then they will reply, 'Lord, when did we see you hungry or thirsty or a stranger or naked or sick or in prison and
didn't do anything to help you?' 45 Then he will answer, 'I
assure you that when you haven't done it for one of the least
of these, you haven't done it for me.' 46 And they will go away
into eternal punishment. But the righteous ones will go into
eternal life."

### Primary Hymns and Songs for the Day

117 "O God, Our Help in Ages Past" (Pss, Rev) (O)
H-3 Hbl-33, 80; Chr-143; Desc-93; Org-132
S-1 #293-96. Various treatments
707 "Hymn of Promise" (Eccl)
H-3 Chr-112; Org-117
S-1 #270. Desc.
77 "How Great Thou Art" (Pss)
H-3 Chr-103; Org-105
S-1 #163. Harm.
383 "This Is a Day of New Beginnings" (Rev)
H-3 Chr-196
2254 "In Remembrance of Me" (Matt, Comm.)
2284 "Joy in the Morning" (Rev) (C)

### Additional Hymn Suggestions

384 "Love Divine, All Loves Excelling" (Rev)
388 "O Come and Dwell in Me" (Rev)
510 "Come, Ye Disconsolate" (Rev)
524 "Beams of Heaven as I Go" (Rev)
533 "We Shall Overcome" (Rev)
569 "We've a Story to Tell to the Nations" (Rev)
722 "I Want to Be Ready" (Rev)
727 "O What Their Joy and Their Glory Must Be" (Rev)
2210 "Joy Comes with the Dawn" (Rev)
3094 "Come to Me" (Rev, Matt)
192 "There's a Spirit in the Air" (Rev, Matt)
428 "For the Healing of the Nations" (Rev, Matt)
434 "*Cuando el Pobre*" ("When the Poor Ones") (Matt)
591 "Rescue the Perishing" (Matt)
616 "Come, Sinners, to the Gospel Feast" (Matt, Comm.)
2048 "God Weeps" (Matt)
2094 "Carol of the Epiphany" (Matt)
2095 "Star-Child" (Matt)
2126 "All Who Hunger" (Matt)
2138 "Sunday's Palms Are Wednesday's Ashes" (Matt)
2175 "Together We Serve" (Matt)
2178 "Here Am I" (Matt)
2268 "As We Gather at Your Table" (Matt, Comm.)
3128 "Whatever You Do" (Matt)
3169 "You Feed Us, Gentle Savior" (Matt, Comm.)
3115 "Covenant Prayer" (New Year, Covenant Service)

### Additional Contemporary Suggestions

S2203 "In His Time" (Eccl)
M63 "I Could Sing of Your Love Forever" (Eccl)
M140 "We Will Dance" (Eccl)
M152 "Be Glorified" (Eccl)
M167 "The Happy Song" (Eccl)
WS3032 "Across the Lands" (Pss)
WS3034 "God of Wonders" (Pss)
M80
S2023 "How Majestic Is Your Name" (Pss)
SP14
M252 "God with Us" (Pss, Christmas)
M266 "You Have Saved Us" (Pss)
UM171 "There's Something About That Name" (Rev)
SP89
UM347 "Spirit Song" (Rev)
SP134
UM706 "Soon and Very Soon" (Rev)
S-2 #187. Piano Arr.
S2087 "We Will Glorify" (Rev)
SP68
S2132 "You Who Are Thirsty" (Rev)
S2194 "O Freedom" (Rev)
WS3189 "There Is a Higher Throne" (Rev)
M21 "Blessing, Honour and Glory" (Rev)
WS3003 "How Great Is Our God" (Rev)
M117
M129 "You Are Holy" ("Prince of Peace") (Rev)
M159 "All Who Are Thirsty" (Rev)
M221 "Happy Day" (Rev)
M240 "You Are" (Rev, Christmas)
SP60 "To Him Who Sits on the Throne" (Rev, Matt)
M24 "Jesus, We Crown You with Praise" (Rev, Matt)
M32 "Holy and Anointed One" (Rev, Matt)
M55 "Jehovah Reigns" (Rev, Matt)
M141 "Sing to the King" (Matt)
M263 "From the Inside Out" (Matt, New Year)
S2244 "People Need the Lord" (Matt)

### Vocal Solos

"I Will Sing of Thy Great Mercies" (Eccl)
V-4 p. 43
"My Lord, What a Mornin'" (Rev)
V-7 p. 68
"Reach Out to Your Neighbor" (Matt)
V-8 p. 372
"A Covenant Prayer" (New Year)
V-11 p. 6

### Anthems

"To Everything a Season" (Eccl)
Taylor Davis; Choristers Guild CGA-1347
SATB with piano, opt. oboe

"I Won't Let Go" (Eccl, Matt)
Mark Miller; Choristers Guild CGA-1348
SATB with piano

### Other Suggestions

Visuals:
**O** Seasons, birth/death, workers, time piece, joy, gift
**P** Pss 8:1, infants, moon, stars, people, crown, sheep, birds, sea
**E** Heaven/earth, bride, handkerchief, newness, Alpha/Omega
**G** Christ, angels, nations, sheep/goats, ministry, fire,

Covenant Services are often celebrated this night. Resources include BOW288, 291-94 and UMH607
Introit: WS3103. "Purify My Heart" (Matt, New Year)
Greeting: BOW294 (New Year) or BOW453 (Rev)
Opening Prayer: WSL64 (Pss)
Prayer of Confession: WSL87 (Matt)
Prayer for Illumination: WSL75 (Rev)
Prayer: BOW295 (New Year)
Prayer: UM531. For Overcoming Adversity (Rev)
Canticle: UM734. "Canticle of Hope" (Rev)
Affirmation of Faith: WSL80 (Matt)
Offertory Prayer: WSL98 (Matt)
Great Thanksgiving for New Year: BOW, pp. 58–59
For additional suggestions, consult *The Abingdon Worship Annual 2016*.

**Isaiah 60:1-6**

Arise! Shine! Your light has come;
the LORD's glory has shone upon you.
2 Though darkness covers the earth
and gloom the nations,
the LORD will shine upon you;
God's glory will appear over you.
3 Nations will come to your light
and kings to your dawning radiance.
4 Lift up your eyes and look all around:
they are all gathered; they have come to you.
Your sons will come from far away,
and your daughters on caregivers' hips.
5 Then you will see and be radiant;
your heart will tremble and open wide,
because the sea's abundance will be turned over to you;
the nations' wealth will come to you.
6 Countless camels will cover your land,
young camels from Midian and Ephah.
They will all come from Sheba,
carrying gold and incense,
proclaiming the LORD's praises.

---

**Psalm 72:1-7, 10-14 (UM795)**

God, give your judgments to the king.
Give your righteousness to the king's son.
2 Let him judge your people with righteousness
and your poor ones with justice.
3 Let the mountains bring peace to the people;
let the hills bring righteousness.
4 Let the king bring justice to people who are poor;
let him save the children of those who are needy,
but let him crush oppressors!
5 Let the king live as long as the sun,
as long as the moon,
generation to generation.
6 Let him fall like rain upon fresh-cut grass,
like showers that water the earth.
7 Let the righteous flourish throughout their lives,
and let peace prosper until the moon is no more.
. . . . . . . . . . . . . . . . . . . . . . . . .
10 Let the kings of Tarshish and the islands bring tribute;
let the kings of Sheba and Seba present gifts.
11 Let all the kings bow down before him;
let all the nations serve him.
12 Let it be so, because he delivers the needy who cry out,
the poor, and those who have no helper.
13 He has compassion on the weak and the needy;
he saves the lives of those who are in need.
14 He redeems their lives from oppression and violence;
their blood is precious in his eyes.

---

**Ephesians 3:1-12**

This is why I, Paul, am a prisoner of Christ for you Gentiles.
2 You've heard, of course, about the responsibility to dis-
tribute God's grace, which God gave to me for you, right?
3 God showed me his secret plan in a revelation, as I mentioned briefly before (4 when you read this, you'll understand my insight into the secret plan about Christ). 5 Earlier
generations didn't know this hidden plan that God has now
revealed to his holy apostles and prophets through the Spirit.
6 This plan is that the Gentiles would be coheirs and parts of
the same body, and that they would share with the Jews in
the promises of God in Christ Jesus through the gospel. 7 I
became a servant of the gospel because of the grace that God
showed me through the exercise of his power.
8 God gave his grace to me, the least of all God's people,
to preach the good news about the immeasurable riches of
Christ to the Gentiles. 9 God sent me to reveal the secret plan
that had been hidden since the beginning of time by God,
who created everything. 10 God's purpose is now to show the
rulers and powers in the heavens the many different varieties
of his wisdom through the church. 11 This was consistent with
the plan he had from the beginning of time that he accomplished through Christ Jesus our Lord. 12 In Christ we have
bold and confident access to God through faith in him.

---

**Matthew 2:1-12**

After Jesus was born in Bethlehem in the territory of Judea
during the rule of King Herod, magi came from the east
to Jerusalem. 2 They asked, "Where is the newborn king of
the Jews? We've seen his star in the east, and we've come to
honor him."
3 When King Herod heard this, he was troubled, and everyone in Jerusalem was troubled with him. 4 He gathered all the
chief priests and the legal experts and asked them where the
Christ was to be born. 5 They said, "In Bethlehem of Judea,
for this is what the prophet wrote:
6 *You, Bethlehem, land of Judah,*
*by no means are you least among the rulers of Judah,*
*because from you will come one who governs,*
*who will shepherd my people Israel."*
7 Then Herod secretly called for the magi and found out
from them the time when the star had first appeared. 8 He
sent them to Bethlehem, saying, "Go and search carefully for
the child. When you've found him, report to me so that I too
may go and honor him." 9 When they heard the king, they
went; and look, the star they had seen in the east went ahead
of them until it stood over the place where the child was.
10 When they saw the star, they were filled with joy. 11 They
entered the house and saw the child with Mary his mother.
Falling to their knees, they honored him. Then they opened
their treasure chests and presented him with gifts of gold,
frankincense, and myrrh. 12 Because they were warned in a
dream not to return to Herod, they went back to their own
country by another route.

**Primary Hymns and Songs for the Day**

220 "Angels from the Realms of Glory" (Matt) (O)
H-3 Chr-30, 48, 62; Desc-89; Org-121
S-1 #280. Desc. and harm.
219 "What Child Is This" (Matt)
H-3 Hbl-102; Chr-210; Desc-46; Org-47
S-1 #150. Guitar chords
254 "We Three Kings" (Matt)
H-3 Chr-208; Org-65
S-2 #97-98. Various treatments
623 "Here, O My Lord, I See Thee" (Matt, Comm.)
245 "The First Noel" (Matt) (C)
H-3 Hbl-95; Chr-182; Desc-100; Org-161
S-1 #328-30. Various treatments

**Additional Hymn Suggestions**

2172 "We Are Called" (Isa, Epiphany)
2236 "Gather Us In" (Isa, Epiphany)
187 "Rise, Shine, You People" (Isa)
679 "O Splendor of God's Glory Bright" (Isa)
725 "Arise, Shine Out, Your Light Has Come" (Isa)
157 "Jesus Shall Reign" (Pss)
203 "Hail to the Lord's Anointed" (Pss)
2177 "Wounded World that Cries for Healing" (Pss)
2178 "Here Am I" (Pss)
2182 "When God Restored our Common Life" (Pss, Comm.)
421 "Make Me a Captive Lord" (Eph)
568 "Christ for the World We Sing" (Eph)
573 "O Zion, Haste" (Eph)
206 "I Want to Walk as a Child of the Light" (Matt)
216 "Lo, How a Rose E'er Blooming" (Matt)
217 "Away in a Manger" (Matt)
221 "In the Bleak Midwinter" (Matt)
223 "Break Forth, O Beauteous Heavenly Light" (Matt)
237 "Sing We Now of Christmas" (Matt)
242 "Love Came Down at Christmas" (Matt)
243 "*De Tierra Lejana Venimos*" ("From a Distant Home") (Matt)
244 "'Twas in the Moon of Wintertime" (Matt)
247 "O Morning Star, How Fair and Bright" (Matt)
248 "On This Day Earth Shall Ring" (Matt)
249 "There's a Song in the Air" (Matt)
256 "We Would See Jesus" (Matt)
619 "Now the Silence" (Matt, Comm.)
2094 "Carol of the Epiphany" (Matt)
2095 "Star-Child" (Matt)
2096 "Rise Up, Shepherd, and Follow" (Matt)
3062 "Spirit-Child Jesus" (Matt, Epiphany)
3063 "If I Could Visit Bethlehem" (Matt, Epiphany)

**Additional Contemporary Suggestions**

S2173 "Shine, Jesus, Shine" (Epiphany)
SP142
M243 "Beautiful Savior" (Epiphany)
M19 "Shine on Us" (Isa, Epiphany)
M4 "Let it Rise" (Isa)
WS3177 "Here I Am to Worship" (Isa, Epiphany)
M116
M232 "Rising" (Isa, Epiphany)
WS3038 "Mighty to Save" (Isa)
M246
SP176 "Arise, Shine" (Isa)
M126 "Famous One" (Isa, Matt, Epiphany)
M235 "Sing, Sing, Sing" (Pss, Matt)
S2162 "Grace Alone" (Eph)
M100
S2018 "Honor and Praise" (Matt)
S2098 "The Virgin Mary Had a Baby Boy" (Matt)
SP103 "We Worship and Adore You" (Matt)
M133 "O Praise Him" ("All This for a King") (Matt)
UM186 "Alleluia" (Matt, Comm.)
SP108, S-2 #3-4. Desc. and Harm.

**Vocal Solos**

"The People That Walked in Darkness" (Isa)
V-2
"Behold that Star!" (Matt, Epiphany)
V-3 (1) p. 34
"A Scottish Christmas Song" (Matt, Epiphany)
V-4 p. 4
"The Kings" (Matt, Epiphany)
V-9 p. 13
"Fit for a King" (Matt)
V-10 p. 32

**Anthems**

"Star Carol" (Matt)
Robert A. Hobby; MorningStar MSM-50-2150
SATB with organ

"What Star Is This" (Matt)
Jay Althouse; MorningStar MSM-50-2110
SATB with keyboard

**Other Suggestions**

Visuals:
**O** Light/dark, nations, kings, dawn, babes in arms, gold/incense
**P** Scales, mountains/hills, poor, sun/moon, rain, grass, king
**E** Writing, Christ, all nations
**G** Wise men, star, Bethlehem, infant, Mary, gifts, escape

Introit: S2005, BOW216. "Arise, Shine" (Isa)
Greeting: BOW296 (Epiphany) or BOW304 (Isa)
Prayer of Confession: BOW492 (Eph)
Call to Prayer: S2118. "Holy Spirit, Come to Us" ("*Veni Sancte Spiritus*") (Pss)
Prayer: BOW297 or UM255 (Epiphany)
Great Thanksgiving for Epiphany: BOW, pp. 58-59
Canticle/Blessing: UM225. "Canticle of Simeon" (Matt) See S-1, p. 386.
Closing Prayer: WSL11 (Isa, Matt, Epiphany)
Alternate scriptures if today is celebrated at the 2nd Sunday after Christmas: Jer 31:7-14; Ps 147:12-20; Eph 1:3-14; John 1:(1-9)10-18.
For additional ideas, consult *The Abingdon Worship Annual 2016.*

# JANUARY 10, 2016

**Isaiah 43:1-7**

But now, says the LORD—
the one who created you, Jacob,
  the one who formed you, Israel:
Don't fear, for I have redeemed you;
  I have called you by name; you are mine.
2 When you pass through the waters, I will be with you;
  when through the rivers, they won't sweep over you.
When you walk through the fire, you won't be scorched
  and flame won't burn you.
3 I am the LORD your God,
  the holy one of Israel, your savior.
I have given Egypt as your ransom,
  Cush and Seba in your place.
4 Because you are precious in my eyes,
  you are honored, and I love you.
  I give people in your place,
    and nations in exchange for your life.
5 Don't fear,
  I am with you.
From the east I'll bring your children;
  from the west I'll gather you.
6 I'll say to the north, "Give them back!"
  and to the south, "Don't detain them."
Bring my sons from far away,
  and my daughters from the end of the earth,
7 everyone who is called by my name
  and whom I created for my glory,
  whom I have formed and made.

**Psalm 29 (UM761)**

You, divine beings! Give to the LORD—
  give to the LORD glory and power!
2 Give to the LORD the glory due his name!
  Bow down to the LORD in holy splendor!
3 The LORD's voice is over the waters;
  the glorious God thunders;
    the LORD is over the mighty waters.
4 The LORD's voice is strong;
  the LORD's voice is majestic.
5 The LORD's voice breaks cedar trees—
  yes, the LORD shatters the cedars of Lebanon.
6 He makes Lebanon jump around like a young bull,
  makes Sirion jump around like a young wild ox.
7 The LORD's voice unleashes fiery flames;
8 the LORD's voice shakes the wilderness—
    yes, the LORD shakes the wilderness of Kadesh.
9 The LORD's voice convulses the oaks,
  strips the forests bare,
    but in his temple everyone shouts, "Glory!"
10 The LORD sits enthroned over the floodwaters;
  the LORD sits enthroned—king forever!
11 Let the LORD give strength to his people!
  Let the LORD bless his people with peace!

**Acts 8:14-17**

14 When word reached the apostles in Jerusalem that
Samaria had accepted God's word, they commissioned
Peter and John to go to Samaria. 15 Peter and John went
down to Samaria where they prayed that the new believers
would receive the Holy Spirit. (16 This was because the Holy
Spirit had not yet fallen on any of them; they had only been
baptized in the name of the Lord Jesus.) 17 So Peter and John
laid their hands on them, and they received the Holy Spirit.

**Luke 3:15-17, 21-22**

15 The people were filled with expectation, and everyone
wondered whether John might be the Christ. 16 John replied
to them all, "I baptize you with water, but the one who is
more powerful than me is coming. I'm not worthy to loosen
the strap of his sandals. He will baptize you with the Holy
Spirit and fire. 17 The shovel he uses to sift the wheat from
the husks is in his hands. He will clean out his threshing area
and bring the wheat into his barn. But he will burn the husks
with a fire that can't be put out." . . .

21 When everyone was being baptized, Jesus also was baptized. While he was praying, heaven was opened 22 and the
Holy Spirit came down on him in bodily form like a dove.
And there was a voice from heaven: "You are my Son, whom I
dearly love; in you I find happiness."

**Primary Hymns and Songs for the Day**

139 "Praise to the Lord, the Almighty" (Pss) (O)
H-3 Hbl-89; Chr-163; Desc-69; Org-79
S-1 #218-22. Various treatments
252 "When Jesus Came to Jordan" (Luke)
347 "Spirit Song" (Luke)
SP134
512 "Stand By Me" (Isa)
H-3 Chr-177
3165 "Take Me to the Water" (Acts, Luke)
529 "How Firm a Foundation" (Isa) (C)
H-3 Hbl-27, 69; Chr-102; Desc-41; Org-41
S-1 #133. Harm.
#134. Performance note

**Additional Hymn Suggestions**

2051 "I Was There to Hear Your Borning Cry" (Isa, Luke)
2062 "The Lily of the Valley" (Isa, Luke)
2218 "You Are Mine" (Isa)
73 "O Worship the King" (Pss)
122 "God of the Sparrow, God of the Whale" (Pss)
193 "Jesus! The Name High over All" (Acts, Luke)
257 "We Meet You, O Christ" (Acts, Luke)
420 "Breathe on Me, Breath of God" (Acts, Luke, Baptism)
539 "O Spirit of the Living God" (Acts)
2247 "Wonder of Wonders" (Acts, Luke, Baptism)
2248 "Baptized in Water" (Acts, Luke, Baptism)
2251 "We Were Baptized in Christ Jesus" (Acts, Luke, Baptism)
168 "At the Name of Jesus" (Luke)
332 "Spirit of Faith, Come Down" (Luke)
500 "Spirit of God, Descend upon My Heart" (Luke)
604 "Praise and Thanksgiving Be to God" (Luke, Baptism)
605 "Wash, O God, Our Sons and Daughters" (Luke, Baptism)
606 "Come, Let Us Use the Grace Divine" (Luke, Baptism)
608 "This Is the Spirit's Entry Now" (Luke, Baptism)
609 "You Have Put On Christ" (Luke, Baptism)
610 "We Know That Christ Is Raised" (Luke, Baptism)
611 "Child of Blessing, Child of Promise" (Luke, Baptism)
2060 "God the Sculptor of the Mountains" (Luke)
2089 "Wild and Lone the Prophet's Voice" (Luke)
2117 "Spirit of God" (Luke)
2122 "She Comes Sailing on the Wind" (Luke)
2123 "Loving Spirit" (Luke)

**Additional Contemporary Suggestions**

WS3042 "Shout to the North" (Isa)
M99
S2006 "Lord God Almighty" (Isa)
S2107 "Wade in the Water" (Acts, Luke, Baptism)
S2250 "I've Just Come from the Fountain" (Acts, Luke)
S2253 "Water, River, Spirit, Grace" (Luke, Baptism)
S2071 "Jesus, Name Above All Names" (Luke)
SP76
S2139 "I Know the Lord's Laid His Hands on Me" (Luke)
WS3091 "Come, Holy Spirit" (Luke)
WS3164 "Down to the River to Pray" (Luke, Baptism)
M34 "I Will Never Be" ("The Same Again") (Luke)
M126 "Famous One" (Luke)
SP4 "Great and Mighty Is He" (Luke)
M11

**Vocal Solos**

"Spirit of Faith Come Down" (Luke)
V-1 p. 43
"Brighter than the Sun" (Acts, Luke, Baptism)
V-5(1) p. 57
"Waterlife" (Acts, Luke, Baptism)
V-5(3) p. 17
"This Is De Healin' Water" (Acts, Luke)
V-7 p. 52
"Stan' Still Jordan" (Luke)
V-7 p. 62

**Anthems**

"The Lily of the Valley" (Isa, Luke)
Arr. David Rasbach; Choristers Guild CGA-1370
SATB with piano

"Carol of the Baptism" (Luke)
George Brandon; MorningStar MSM-50-2002
Two-part mixed voices or SAB with organ

**Other Suggestions**

Visuals:
**O** Clay, water (baptism), fire
**P** Nature images as described
**E** Water, symbols of the Holy Spirit
**G** Water, Holy Spirit, praying hands, dove, flames

Today is an excellent day to schedule baptisms in a joyous celebration. You may also schedule a congregational reaffirmation of the baptismal covenant using Baptismal Covenant IV, p. 50 in UM. See BOW, 81-114 for the full range of baptismal covenant possibilities. See BOW, 173-75 and UM608-11 for musical responses.
Introit: S2118. "Holy Spirit, Come to Us" (Luke)
Greeting: BOW300 (Baptism, Pss)
Opening Prayer: WSL12 (Luke)
Prayer of Confession: BOW487 (Baptism, Isa)
Prayer: BOW301 or UM253 or WSL12 (Baptism, Luke)
Baptism Response: S2249, BOW175. "God Claims You"
Baptism Response: S2252, BOW173. "Come, Be Baptized"
Great Thanksgiving for Baptism of the Lord: BOW, pp. 58-59
Blessing: BOW565 (Isa)
See BOW, p. 299 for more Baptism of the Lord suggestions.
For additional suggestions, consult *The Abingdon Worship Annual 2016.*

**Isaiah 62:1-5**

For Zion's sake I won't keep silent,
and for Jerusalem's sake I won't sit still
until her righteousness shines out like a light,
and her salvation blazes like a torch.
2 Nations will see your righteousness,
all kings your glory.
You will be called by a new name,
which the LORD's own mouth will determine.
3 You will be a splendid garland in the LORD's hand,
a royal turban in the palm of God's hand.
4 You will no longer be called Abandoned,
and your land will no longer be called Deserted.
Instead, you will be called My Delight Is in Her,
and your land, Married.
Because the LORD delights in you,
your land will be cared for once again.
5 As a young man marries a young woman,
so your sons will marry you.
With the joy of a bridegroom because of his bride,
so your God will rejoice because of you.

**Psalm 36:5-10 (UM771)**

5 But your loyal love, LORD, extends to the skies;
your faithfulness reaches the clouds.
6 Your righteousness is like the strongest mountains;
your justice is like the deepest sea.
LORD, you save both humans and animals.
7 Your faithful love is priceless, God!
Humanity finds refuge in the shadow of your wings.
8 They feast on the bounty of your house;
you let them drink from your river of pure joy.
9 Within you is the spring of life.
In your light, we see light.
10 Extend your faithful love to those who know you;
extend your righteousness to those whose heart is right.

**1 Corinthians 12:1-11**

Brothers and sisters, I don't want you to be ignorant about
spiritual gifts. 2 You know that when you were Gentiles you
were often misled by false gods that can't even speak. 3 So
I want to make it clear to you that no one says, "Jesus is
cursed!" when speaking by God's Spirit, and no one can
say, "Jesus is Lord," except by the Holy Spirit. 4 There are
different spiritual gifts but the same Spirit; 5 and there are
different ministries and the same Lord; 6 and there are different activities but the same God who produces all of them
in everyone. 7 A demonstration of the Spirit is given to each
person for the common good. 8 A word of wisdom is given
by the Spirit to one person, a word of knowledge to another
according to the same Spirit, 9 faith to still another by the
same Spirit, gifts of healing to another in the one Spirit,
10 performance of miracles to another, prophecy to another,
the ability to tell spirits apart to another, different kinds of
tongues to another, and the interpretation of the tongues
to another. 11 All these things are produced by the one and
same Spirit who gives what he wants to each person.

**John 2:1-11**

On the third day there was a wedding in Cana of Galilee.
Jesus' mother was there, and 2 Jesus and his disciples were
also invited to the celebration. 3 When the wine ran out,
Jesus' mother said to him, "They don't have any wine."
4 Jesus replied, "Woman, what does that have to do with me?
My time hasn't come yet."
5 His mother told the servants, "Do whatever he tells you."
6 Nearby were six stone water jars used for the Jewish cleansing ritual, each able to hold about twenty or thirty gallons.
7 Jesus said to the servants, "Fill the jars with water," and
they filled them to the brim. 8 Then he told them, "Now draw
some from them and take it to the headwaiter," and they did.
9 The headwaiter tasted the water that had become wine. He
didn't know where it came from, though the servants who
had drawn the water knew.
The headwaiter called the groom 10 and said, "Everyone
serves the good wine first. They bring out the second-rate
wine only when the guests are drinking freely. You kept the
good wine until now." 11 This was the first miraculous sign
that Jesus did in Cana of Galilee. He revealed his glory, and
his disciples believed in him.

**Primary Hymns and Songs for the Day**

140 "Great Is Thy Faithfulness" (Isa, Pss) (O)
114 "Many Gifts, One Spirit" (1 Cor)
333 "I'm Gonna Sing When the Spirit Says Sing" (1 Cor)
2227 "We Are the Body of Christ" (1 Cor)
555 "Forward Through the Ages" (1 Cor) (C)
H-3 Hbl-59; Chr-156; Org-140

**Additional Hymn Suggestions**

79 "Holy God, We Praise Thy Name" (Isa)
*See esp. stanzas 5 and 7*
89 "Joyful, Joyful, We Adore Thee" (Isa)
155 "All Hail the Power of Jesus' Name" (Isa)
519 "Lift Every Voice and Sing" (Isa, Human Relations)
530 "Are Ye Able" (Isa, Human Relations)
569 "We've a Story to Tell to the Nations" (Isa, Human Relations)
714 "I Know Whom I Have Believed" (Isa)
717 "The Battle Hymn of the Republic" (Isa)
719 "My Lord, What a Morning" (Isa, MLK Day)
105 "God of Many Names" (Isa, Pss)
2062 "The Lily of the Valley" (Isa, Pss)
111 "How Can We Name a Love" (Pss)
115 "How Like a Gentle Spirit" (Pss)
119 "O God in Heaven" (Pss)
267 "O Love, How Deep" (Pss)
384 "Love Divine, All Loves Excelling" (Pss)
400 "Come, Thou Fount of Every Blessing" (Pss)
414 "Thou Hidden Love of God" (Pss)
502 "Thy Holy Wings, O Savior" (Pss)
2001 "We Sing to You, O God" (Pss)
2117 "Spirit of God" (Pss)
103 "Immortal, Invisible, God Only Wise" (1 Cor)
332 "Spirit of Faith, Come Down" (1 Cor)
550 "Christ, from Whom All Blessings Flow" (1 Cor)
551 "Awake, O Sleeper" (1 Cor)
554 "All Praise to Our Redeeming Lord" (1 Cor)
558 "We Are the Church" (1 Cor, Human Relations)
560 "Help Us Accept Each Other" (1 Cor, MLK Day)
566 "Blest Be the Dear Uniting Love" (1 Cor, MLK Day)
637 "*Una Espiga*" ("Sheaves of Summer") (1 Cor, Comm.)
2237 "As a Fire Is Meant for Burning" (1 Cor)
2243 "We All Are One in Mission" (1 Cor, MLK Day)
2245 "Within the Day-to-Day" ("A Hymn for Deacons") (1 Cor)
642 "As Man and Woman We Were Made" (Isa, John)
256 "We Would See Jesus" (John)
257 "We Meet You, O Christ" (John, MLK Day)
532 "Jesus, Priceless Treasure" (John)
596 "Blessed Jesus, at Thy Word" (John)
644 "Jesus, Joy of Our Desiring" (John)
647 "Your Love, O God, Has Called Us Here" (John)
2230 "Lord, We Come to Ask Your Blessing" (John)
3127 "I Have a Dream" (MLK Day)

**Additional Contemporary Suggestions**

WS3038 "Mighty to Save" (Isa, Epiphany)
M246
UM143 "On Eagle's Wings" (Pss)
S-2 #143. Stanzas for soloist
S2173 "Shine, Jesus, Shine" (Pss)
SP142
SP185 "The Steadfast Love of the Lord" (Pss)
M63 "I Could Sing of Your Love Forever" (Pss)
M74 "There Is Joy in the Lord" (Pss)
M103 "How Great Are You, Lord" (Pss)
M158 "Eagle's Wings" (Pss)
M189 "Your Love, Oh Lord" (Pss)
M243 "Beautiful Savior" (Pss, Epiphany)
UM620 "One Bread, One Body" (1 Cor, Comm.)
S2118 "Holy Spirit, Come to Us" (1 Cor)
S2223 "They'll Know We Are Christians" (1 Cor)
S2224 "Make Us One" (1 Cor)
SP137
S2226 "Bind Us Together" (1 Cor)
SP140
S2229 "We Are One in Christ Jesus" (1 Cor)
S2188 "The Family Prayer Song" (John)
M54

**Vocal Solos**

"Shine, Jesus, Shine" (Isa, John)
V-3 (2) p. 48
"On Eagle's Wings" (Pss)
V-3 (2) p. 2
V-3 (3) p. 4
"Spirit of Faith Come Down" (1 Cor)
V-1 p. 43
"I Feel the Spirit Moving" (1 Cor)
V-3 (1) p. 22
"He Turned the Water into Wine" (John)
V-8 p. 76

**Anthems**

"And the Father Will Dance" (Isa)
Mark Hayes; Hinshaw HMC637
SATB with piano

"Come, My Way, My Truth, My Life" (John)
Z. Randall Stroope; MorningStar MSM-50-6515
SATB with organ

**Other Suggestions**

Visuals:
**O** Crown, bride and groom, invitation, torch, sunrise
**P** Sky, clouds, mountains, wings, banquet, fountain
**E** "Many gifts, one spirit," ministries, unity
**G** Large clay water jars, water/wine/bread, wedding
You may wish to include some reference to Martin Luther King, Jr. Day, Jan. 18.
Introit: UM164. "Come, My Way, My Truth, My Life" (John)
Greeting: BOW303 (Isa) or BOW455 or WSL68 (1 Cor)
Opening Prayer: WSL70 (Pss)
Litany: UM106. God Is Able (MLK Day)
Litany: UM556. Litany for Christian Unity (1 Cor)
Litany: BOW423 (Human Relations)
Prayer: WSL192 (1 Cor)
Prayer: BOW311 (John) or BOW312 (Pss)
Prayer: BOW435 (MLK Day)
Poem: UM183. Jesu, Thy Boundless Love to Me (Pss)
Offertory Prayer: WSL116 (1 Cor)
Prayer of Thanksgiving: BOW555 (1 Cor)

**Nehemiah 8:1-3, 5-6, 8-10**
When the seventh month came and the people of Israel
were settled in their towns, all the people gathered together
in the area in front of the Water Gate. They asked Ezra the
scribe to bring out the Instruction scroll from Moses, according to which the LORD had instructed Israel.
2 So on the first day of the seventh month, Ezra the priest
brought the Instruction before the assembly. This assembly
was made up of both men and women and anyone who could
understand what they heard. 3 Facing the area in front of the
Water Gate, he read it aloud, from early morning until the
middle of the day. He read it in the presence of the men and
the women and those who could understand, and everyone
listened attentively to the Instruction scroll. . . .
5 Standing above all of the people, Ezra the scribe opened
the scroll in the sight of all of the people. And as he opened
it, all of the people stood up. 6 Then Ezra blessed the LORD,
the great God, and all of the people answered, "Amen!
Amen!" while raising their hands. Then they bowed down
and worshipped the LORD with their faces to the ground. . . .
8 They read aloud from the scroll, the Instruction from
God, explaining and interpreting it so the people could
understand what they heard.
9 Then Nehemiah the governor, Ezra the priest and scribe,
and the Levites who taught the people said to all of the
people, "This day is holy to the LORD your God. Don't mourn
or weep." They said this because all the people wept when
they heard the words of the Instruction.
10 "Go, eat rich food, and drink something sweet," he said
to them, "and send portions of this to any who have nothing
ready! This day is holy to our LORD. Don't be sad, because
the joy from the LORD is your strength!"

---

**Psalm 19 (UM750)**
Heaven is declaring God's glory;
  the sky is proclaiming his handiwork.
2 One day gushes the news to the next,
  and one night informs another
    what needs to be known. . . .

---

**1 Corinthians 12:12-31a**
12 Christ is just like the human body—a body is a unit and
has many parts; and all the parts of the body are one body,
even though there are many. 13 We were all baptized by one
Spirit into one body, whether Jew or Greek, or slave or free,
and we all were given one Spirit to drink. 14 Certainly the
body isn't one part but many. 15 If the foot says, "I'm not part
of the body because I'm not a hand," does that mean it's not
part of the body? 16 If the ear says, "I'm not part of the body
because I'm not an eye," does that mean it's not part of the
body? 17 If the whole body were an eye, what would happen to
the hearing? And if the whole body were an ear, what would
happen to the sense of smell? 18 But as it is, God has placed
each one of the parts in the body just like he wanted. 19 If all
were one and the same body part, what would happen to the
body? 20 But as it is, there are many parts but one body. 21 So
the eye can't say to the hand, "I don't need you," or in
turn, the head can't say to the feet, "I don't need you."
22 Instead, the parts of the body that people think are the
weakest are the most necessary. 23 The parts of the body that
we think are less honorable are the ones we honor the most.
The private parts of our body that aren't presentable are
the ones that are given the most dignity. 24 The parts of our
body that are presentable don't need this. But God has put
the body together, giving greater honor to the part with less
honor
25 so that there won't be division in the body and so the parts
might have mutual concern for each other. 26 If one part
suffers, all the parts suffer with it; if one part gets the glory,
all the parts celebrate with it. 27 You are the body of Christ
and parts of each other. 28 In the church, God has appointed
first apostles, second prophets, third teachers, then miracles,
then gifts of healing, the ability to help others, leadership
skills, different kinds of tongues. 29 All aren't apostles, are
they? All aren't prophets, are they? All aren't teachers, are
they? All don't perform miracles, do they? 30 All don't have
gifts of healing, do they? All don't speak in different tongues,
do they? All don't interpret, do they? 31a Use your ambition to
try to get the greater gifts.

---

**Luke 4:14-21**
14 Jesus returned in the power of the Spirit to Galilee, and
news about him spread throughout the whole countryside.
15 He taught in their synagogues and was praised by everyone.
16 Jesus went to Nazareth, where he had been raised. On
the Sabbath he went to the synagogue as he normally did
and stood up to read. 17 The synagogue assistant gave him the
scroll from the prophet Isaiah. He unrolled the scroll and
found the place where it was written:
18 *The Spirit of the Lord is upon me,*
  *because the Lord has anointed me.*
*He has sent me to preach good news to the poor,*
  *to proclaim release to the prisoners*
  *and recovery of sight to the blind,*
  *to liberate the oppressed,*
19  *and to proclaim the year of the Lord's favor.*
20 He rolled up the scroll, gave it back to the synagogue
assistant, and sat down. Every eye in the synagogue was fixed
on him. 21 He began to explain to them, "Today, this scripture
has been fulfilled just as you heard it."

**Primary Hymns and Songs for the Day**

662 "Stand Up and Bless the Lord" (Neh) (O)
H-3 Hbl-79; Chr-141; Desc-95; Org-143
S-1 #306-8. Various treatments
77 "How Great Thou Art" (Pss)
H-3 Chr-103; Org-105
S-1 #163. Harm.
620 "One Bread, One Body" (1 Cor, Comm.)
H-3 Chr-156
2223 "They'll Know We Are Christians" (1 Cor)
2236 "Gather Us In" (1 Cor, Luke)
57 "O For a Thousand Tongues to Sing" (Luke) (C)
H-3 Hbl-79; Chr-142; Desc-17; Org-12
S-1 #33-38. Various treatments

**Additional Hymn Suggestions**

600 "Wonderful Words of Life" (Neh)
603 "Come, Holy Ghost, Our Hearts Inspire" (Neh)
660 "God Is Here" (Neh)
2126 "All Who Hunger" (Neh)
2246 "Deep in the Shadows of the Past" (Neh)
2279 "The Trees of the Field" (Neh)
149 "*Cantemos al Señor*" ("Let's Sing to the Lord") (Pss)
150 "God Who Stretched the Spangled Heavens" (Pss)
685 "Now, on Land and Sea Descending" (Pss)
2012 "Let Us with a Joyful Mind" (Pss)
114 "Many Gifts, One Spirit" (1 Cor)
548 "In Christ There Is No East or West" (1 Cor)
549 "Where Charity and Love Prevail" (1 Cor)
550 "Christ, from Whom All Blessings Flow" (1 Cor)
554 "All Praise to Our Redeeming Lord" (1 Cor)
555 "Forward Through the Ages" (1 Cor)
557 "Blest Be the Tie That Binds" (1 Cor)
578 "God of Love and God of Power" (1 Cor, Luke)
2175 "Together We Serve" (1 Cor)
2181 "We Need a Faith" (1 Cor)
2220 "We Are God's People" (1 Cor)
2221 "In Unity We Lift Our Song" (1 Cor)
2225 "Who Is My Mother, Who Is My Brother" (1 Cor)
2237 "As a Fire Is Meant for Burning" (1 Cor)
2240 "One God and Father of Us All" (1 Cor)
2243 "We All Are One in Mission" (1 Cor)
2245 "Within the Day-to-Day" ("A Hymn for Deacons") (1 Cor)
2261 "Life-Giving Bread" (1 Cor, Comm.)
157 "Jesus Shall Reign" (Luke)
263 "When Jesus the Healer Passed Through Galilee" (Luke)
333 "I'm Gonna Sing When the Spirit Says Sing" (Luke)
340 "Come, Ye Sinners, Poor and Needy" (Luke)
568 "Christ for the World We Sing" (Luke)
581 "Lord, Whose Love Through Humble Service" (Luke)
2117 "Spirit of God" (Luke)
2139 "I Know the Lord's Laid His Hands on Me" (Luke)
2172 "We Are Called" (Luke)
2241 "The Spirit Sends Us Forth to Serve" (Luke) (C)
3001 "O For a Thousand Tongues to Sing" (Luke)

**Additional Contemporary Suggestions**

S2132 "You Who Are Thirsty" (Neh)
UM63 "Blessed Be the Name" (Neh)
M12, S2034, SF2034
M105 "Let My Words Be Few" (Neh)
S2002 "I Will Call Upon the Lord" (Pss)
SP224
S2066 "Praise the Name of Jesus" (Pss)
SP87
WS3034 "God of Wonders" (Pss)
M80
M58 "All Heaven Declares" (Pss)
M93 "Rock of Ages" (Pss)
M111 "The Heavens Shall Declare" (Pss)
M126 "Famous One" (Pss)
M127 "Indescribable" (Pss)
M134 "It Is You" (Pss)
M235 "Sing, Sing, Sing" (Pss)
M243 "Beautiful Savior" (Pss, Luke)
S2224 "Make Us One" (1 Cor)
SP137
S2229 "We Are One in Christ Jesus" (1 Cor)
S2227 "We Are the Body of Christ" (1 Cor)
S2232 "Come Now, O Prince of Peace" (1 Cor)
S2240 "One God and Father of Us All" (1 Cor)
S2260 "Let Us Be Bread" (1 Cor, Comm.)
S2019 "Holy" ("*Santo*") (Luke)
S2109 "Hosanna! Hosanna!" (Luke)
S2118 "Holy Spirit, Come to Us" (Luke)
S2119 "Where the Spirit of the Lord Is" (Luke)
WS3186 "Days of Elijah" (Luke)
M139
M142 "Let the River Flow" (Luke)
M267 "Hear Us from Heaven" (Luke)

**Vocal Solos**

"The Heavens Declare His Glory" (Pss)
V-8 p. 248
"One Bread, One Body" (1 Cor, Comm.)
V-3 (2) p. 40
"O For a Thousand Tongues to Sing" (Luke)
V-1 p. 32
V-6 p. 28

**Anthems**

"Gather Us In" (1 Cor, Luke)
Arr. Mark Hayes; Alfred 52503
SATB with piano

"The Spirit of the Lord Is Upon Me" (Luke)
Edward Elgar; Novello 29-0219
SATB with organ

**Other Suggestions**

Visuals:
**O** Open Bible, scroll, morning, assembly, weeping/joy
**P** Gold, honeycomb, runner, groom
**E** Teamwork, body, health, harmony, gifts
**G** Images of poor/captives/blind/freedom, Jubilee
Introit: WS3094. "Come to Me" (Luke)
Greeting: BOW303 (Neh)
Call to Worship: WSL68 (1 Cor)
Responsive Invocation: WSL36 (1 Cor)
Responsive Prayer of Confession: BOW488 (1 Cor, Luke)
Prayer: UM594 or UM602 (Neh, Pss)
Prayer: BOW315 (1 Cor)
Prayer for Illumination: WSL71 (Pss)
Offering Response: UM587. "Bless Thou the Gifts" (1 Cor)
Sung Benediction: S2072. "Amen, Amen" (Luke)

**Jeremiah 1:4-10**

4 The LORD's word came to me:
5 "Before I created you in the womb I knew you;
before you were born I set you apart;
I made you a prophet to the nations."
6 "Ah, LORD God," I said, "I don't know how to speak
because I'm only a child."
7 The LORD responded,
"Don't say, 'I'm only a child.'
Where I send you, you must go;
what I tell you, you must say.
8 Don't be afraid of them,
because I'm with you to rescue you,"
declares the LORD.
9 Then the LORD stretched out his hand,
touched my mouth, and said to me,
"I'm putting my words in your mouth.
10 This very day I appoint you over nations and empires,
to dig up and pull down,
to destroy and demolish,
to build and plant."

**Psalm 71:1-6 (UM794)**

I've taken refuge in you, LORD.
Don't let me ever be put to shame!
2 Deliver me and rescue me by your righteousness!
Bend your ear toward me and save me!
3 Be my rock of refuge
where I can always escape.
You commanded that my life be saved
because you are my rock and my fortress.
4 My God, rescue me from the power of the wicked;
rescue me from the grip of the wrongdoer and the
oppressor
5 because you are my hope, LORD.
You, LORD, are the one I've trusted since childhood.
6 I've depended on you from birth—
you cut the cord when I came from my mother's womb.
My praise is always about you.

**1 Corinthians 13:1-13**

If I speak in tongues of human beings and of angels but I
don't have love, I'm a clanging gong or a clashing cymbal.
2 If I have the gift of prophecy and I know all the mysteries
and everything else, and if I have such complete faith that I
can move mountains but I don't have love, I'm nothing. 3 If I
give away everything that I have and hand over my own body
to feel good about what I've done but I don't have love, I
receive no benefit whatsoever.
4 Love is patient, love is kind, it isn't jealous, it doesn't brag,
it isn't arrogant, 5 it isn't rude, it doesn't seek its own advan-
tage, it isn't irritable, it doesn't keep a record of complaints,
6 it isn't happy with injustice, but it is happy with the truth.
7 Love puts up with all things, trusts in all things, hopes for all
things, endures all things.
8 Love never fails. As for prophecies, they will be brought
to an end. As for tongues, they will stop. As for knowledge, it
will be brought to an end. 9 We know in part and we prophesy
in part; 10 but when the perfect comes, what is partial will be
brought to an end. 11 When I was a child, I used to speak like
a child, reason like a child, think like a child. But now that I
have become a man, I've put an end to childish things.
12 Now we see a reflection in a mirror; then we will see face-
to-face. Now I know partially, but then I will know completely
in the same way that I have been completely known. 13 Now
faith, hope, and love remain—these three things—and the
greatest of these is love.

**Luke 4:21-30**

21 He began to explain to them, "Today, this scripture has
been fulfilled just as you heard it."
22 Everyone was raving about Jesus, so impressed were they
by the gracious words flowing from his lips. They said, "This
is Joseph's son, isn't it?"
23 Then Jesus said to them, "Undoubtedly, you will quote
this saying to me: 'Doctor, heal yourself. Do here in your
hometown what we've heard you did in Capernaum.'" 24 He
said, "I assure you that no prophet is welcome in the prophet's hometown. 25 And I can assure you that there were many
widows in Israel during Elijah's time, when it didn't rain for
three and a half years and there was a great food shortage
in the land. 26 Yet Elijah was sent to none of them but only
to a widow in the city of Zarephath in the region of Sidon.
27 There were also many persons with skin diseases in Israel
during the time of the prophet Elisha, but none of them
were cleansed. Instead, Naaman the Syrian was cleansed."
28 When they heard this, everyone in the synagogue was
filled with anger. 29 They rose up and ran him out of town.
They led him to the crest of the hill on which their town had
been built so that they could throw him off the cliff. 30 But he
passed through the crowd and went on his way.

### Primary Hymns and Songs for the Day
578 "God of Love and God of Power" (Jer, Luke) (O)
399 "Take My Life and Let it Be" (Jer)
2032 "My Life Is in You, Lord" (Pss)
SP204
408 "The Gift of Love" (1 Cor)
H-3 Chr-200; Org-45
444 "O Young and Fearless Prophet" (Luke)
S-2 #27. Desc.
593 "Here I Am, Lord" (Jer, Luke) (C)
H-3 Chr-97; Org-54

### Additional Hymn Suggestions
529 "How Firm a Foundation" (Jer)
2046 "Womb of Life" (Jer)
3118 "Take This Moment, Sign, and Space" (Jer)
2050 "Mothering God, You Gave Me Birth" (Jer, 1 Cor)
2051 "I Was There to Hear Your Borning Cry" (Jer, Baptism)
194 "Morning Glory, Starlit Sky" (Jer, 1 Cor)
336 "Of All the Spirit's Gifts to Me" (Jer, 1 Cor)
463 "Lord, Speak to Me" (Jer, Luke)
585 "This Little Light of Mine" (Jer, Luke)
520 "Nobody Knows the Trouble I See" (Pss)
523 "*Saranam, Saranam*" ("Refuge") (Pss)
525 "We'll Understand It Better By and By" (Pss, 1 Cor)
110 "A Mighty Fortress Is Our God" (Pss, 1 Cor)
373 "Nothing Between" (1 Cor)
480 "O Love That Wilt Not Let Me Go" (1 Cor)
549 "Where Charity and Love Prevail" (1 Cor)
632 "Draw Us in the Spirit's Tether" (1 Cor, Comm.)
643 "When Love Is Found" (1 Cor, Comm.)
645 "O Perfect Love" (1 Cor, Comm.)
647 "Your Love, O God, Has Called Us Here" (1 Cor)
2213 "Healer of Our Every Ill" (1 Cor)
2228 "Sacred the Body" (1 Cor)
2260 "Let Us Be Bread" (1 Cor, Comm.)
3087 "O Christ, When You Ascended" (1 Cor)
3089 "O Living God" (1 Cor)
261 "Lord of the Dance" (Luke)
468 "Dear Jesus, in Whose Life I See" (Luke)
2027 "Now Praise the Hidden Love of God" (Luke)
2139 "Oh, I Know the Lord's Laid His Hands on Me" (Luke)
2120 "Spirit, Spirit of Gentleness" (Luke)
2172 "We Are Called" (Luke)
2236 "Gather Us In" (Luke)
582 "Whom Shall I Send" (Jer, Luke) (C)

### Additional Contemporary Suggestions
S2139 "I Know the Lord's Laid His Hands on Me" (Jer)
WS3184 "Word of God, Speak" (Jer)
M148
SP2 "Ah, Lord God" (Jer)
M91 "Take My Life" (Jer)
S2002 "I Will Call Upon the Lord" (Pss)
SP224
S2066 "Praise the Name of Jesus" (Pss)
SP87
M93 "Rock of Ages" (Pss)
S2179 "Live in Charity" ("*Ubi Caritas*") (1 Cor)
S2141 "There's a Song" (1 Cor)
S2085 "He Came Down" (1 Cor)
S2223 "They'll Know We Are Christians" (1 Cor)
S2224 "Make Us One" (1 Cor)
SP137
M53 "Let It Be Said of Us" (1 Cor)
M40 "More Love, More Power" (1 Cor)
M260 "I Will Rise" (1 Cor)
WS3186 "Days of Elijah" (Luke)
M139
WS3100 "Jesus Paid It All" (Luke)
M244 (lead sheet and bridge)
M249 "Marvelous Light" (Luke, Epiphany)

### Vocal Solos
"Take My Life, and Let It Be Consecrated" (Jer)
V-3 (3) p. 17
V-8 p. 262
"Borning Cry" (Jer, Baptism)
V-5(1) p. 10
"Steal Away to Heaven" (Pss)
V-3 (1) p. 17
"Prayer" (Pss)
V-9 p. 32
"Of Love I Sing" (1 Cor)
V-8 p. 106
"Lord of the Dance" (Luke)
V-3 (3) p. 34

### Anthems
"Awake, My Soul, and Sing" (Pss)
Allen Pote; MorningStar MSM-50-5340
SATB with keyboard

"Love Never Ends" (1 Cor)
Gradley Ellingboe; Kjos 9064
SATB, solo, and piano

### Other Suggestions
Visuals:
**O** Pregnancy, boy, Jer 1:7b or 9b, hand/mouth, nations
**P** Ear, Ps 71:3 or 5a, rock, fortress, rescue, youth
**E** Speak, cymbals, remove mts., love, child/adult, mirror
**G** Bible, Jesus speaking/walking, widows, famine, leper
Greeting: BOW314 (Jer, 1 Cor, Luke)
Opening Prayer: BOW462 (Pss, 1 Cor)
Litany: WSL22 (Luke)
Canticle: UM646. "Canticle of Love" (1 Cor)
Prayer of Confession: WSL90 (Jer, Luke)
Prayer: BOW437 (1 Cor)
Prayer of Thanksgiving: BOW552 (Jer, 1 Cor)
Great Thanksgiving for Epiphany: BOW, pp. 58-59
Communion Response: S2256. "Holy, Holy, Holy Lord"
Blessing: WSL176 (1 Cor)
For additional ideas, see *The Abingdon Worship Annual 2016.*

**Exodus 34:29-35**

29 Moses came down from Mount Sinai. As he came down
from the mountain with the two covenant tablets in his hand,
Moses didn't realize that the skin of his face shone brightly
because he had been talking with God. 30 When Aaron and
all the Israelites saw the skin of Moses' face shining brightly,
they were afraid to come near him. 31 But Moses called them
closer. So Aaron and all the leaders of the community came
back to him, and Moses spoke with them. 32 After that, all the
Israelites came near as well, and Moses commanded them
everything that the LORD had spoken with him on Mount
Sinai. 33 When Moses finished speaking with them, he put a
veil over his face. 34 Whenever Moses went into the LORD's
presence to speak with him, Moses would take the veil off
until he came out again. When Moses came out and told
the Israelites what he had been commanded, 35 the Israelites
would see that the skin of Moses' face was shining brightly.
So Moses would put the veil on his face again until the next
time he went in to speak with the LORD.

---

**Psalm 99 (UM819)**

The LORD rules—
    the nations shake!
    He sits enthroned on the winged heavenly creatures—
    the earth quakes!
2 The LORD is great in Zion;
    he is exalted over all the nations.
3 Let them thank your great and awesome name.
    He is holy!
4 Strong king who loves justice,
    you are the one who established what is fair.
    You worked justice and righteousness in Jacob.
5 Magnify the LORD, our God!
    Bow low at his footstool!
    He is holy!
6 Moses and Aaron were among his priests,
    Samuel too among those who called on his name.
They cried out to the LORD, and he himself answered them—
7 he spoke to them from a pillar of cloud.
They kept the laws and the rules God gave to them.
8 LORD our God, you answered them.
    To them you were a God who forgives
    but also the one who avenged their wrong deeds.
9 Magnify the LORD our God!
    Bow low at his holy mountain
    because the LORD our God is holy!

---

**2 Corinthians 3:12–4:2**

12 So, since we have such a hope, we act with great confidence. 13 We aren't like Moses, who used to put a veil over
his face so that the Israelites couldn't watch the end of what
was fading away. 14 But their minds were closed. Right up to
the present day the same veil remains when the old covenant
is read. The veil is not removed because it is taken away by
Christ. 15 Even today, whenever Moses is read, a veil lies over
their hearts. 16 But whenever someone turns back to the Lord,
the veil is removed. 17 The Lord is the Spirit, and where the
Lord's Spirit is, there is freedom. 18 All of us are looking with
unveiled faces at the glory of the Lord as if we were looking
in a mirror. We are being transformed into that same image
from one degree of glory to the next degree of glory. This
comes from the Lord, who is the Spirit.

4 This is why we don't get discouraged, given that we
received this ministry in the same way that we received God's
mercy. 2 Instead, we reject secrecy and shameful actions. We
don't use deception, and we don't tamper with God's word.
Instead, we commend ourselves to everyone's conscience in
the sight of God by the public announcement of the truth.

---

**Luke 9:28-36 (37-43a)**

28 About eight days after Jesus said these things, he took
Peter, John, and James, and went up on a mountain to pray.
29 As he was praying, the appearance of his face changed and
his clothes flashed white like lightning. 30 Two men, Moses
and Elijah, were talking with him. 31 They were clothed with
heavenly splendor and spoke about Jesus' departure, which
he would achieve in Jerusalem. 32 Peter and those with him
were almost overcome by sleep, but they managed to stay
awake and saw his glory as well as the two men with him.

33 As the two men were about to leave Jesus, Peter said to
him, "Master, it's good that we're here. We should construct
three shrines: one for you, one for Moses, and one for Elijah"—but he didn't know what he was saying. 34 Peter was still
speaking when a cloud overshadowed them. As they entered
the cloud, they were overcome with awe.

35 Then a voice from the cloud said, "This is my Son, my
chosen one. Listen to him!" 36 Even as the voice spoke, Jesus
was found alone. They were speechless and at the time told
no one what they had seen.

37 The next day, when Jesus, Peter, John, and James had
come down from the mountain, a large crowd met Jesus.
38 A man from the crowd shouted, "Teacher, I beg you to take
a look at my son, my only child. 39 Look, a spirit seizes him
and, without any warning, he screams. It shakes him and
causes him to foam at the mouth. It tortures him and rarely
leaves him alone. 40 I begged your disciples to throw it out,
but they couldn't."

41 Jesus answered, "You faithless and crooked generation,
how long will I be with you and put up with you? Bring your
son here." 42 While he was coming, the demon threw him
down and shook him violently. Jesus spoke harshly to the
unclean spirit, healed the child, and gave him back to his
father. 43a Everyone was overwhelmed by God's greatness.

### Primary Hymns and Songs for the Day

185 "When Morning Gilds the Skies" (Exod, Luke) (O)
H-3 Hbl-103; Chr-126, 216; Desc-68; Org-76
S-1 #208. Intro. and Interlude
S-2 #107. Trumpet desc.
#108-9. Harm. with desc.
2272 "Holy Ground" (Exod, Luke)
SP86
2173 "Shine, Jesus, Shine" (2 Cor, Transfiguration)
SP142
173 "Christ, Whose Glory Fills the Skies" (Luke)
H-3 Hbl-51; Chr-206; Desc-89; Org-120
S-1 #278-279. Harm.
258 "O Wondrous Sight! O Vision Fair" (Luke)
H-3 Hbl-93; Chr-84; Desc-102; Org-175
S-2 #191. Harm.
S-2 #191. Harm.
395 "Take Time to Be Holy" (2 Cor, Luke)
H-3 Chr-178
S-1 #159. Harm.
451 "Be Thou My Vision" (Luke) (C)
H-3 Hbl-15, 48; Chr-36; Org-153
S-1 #319. Arr. for organ and voices in canon

### Additional Hymn Suggestions

2103 "We Have Come at Christ's Own Bidding" (Luke) (O)
103 "Immortal, Invisible, God Only Wise" (Exod)
151 "God Created Heaven and Earth" (Exod)
648 "God the Spirit, Guide and Guardian" (Exod)
2077 "You Alone Are Holy" ("*Solo Tu*") (Exod, Luke)
2177 "Wounded World that Cries for Healing" (Pss)
2183 "Unsettled World" (Pss)
107 "*La Palabra Del Señor Es Recta*" ("Righteous and Just Is the Word of Our Lord") (Pss)
332 "Spirit of Faith, Come Down" (2 Cor)
355 "Depth of Mercy" (2 Cor)
3097 "Depth of Mercy" (2 Cor)
384 "Love Divine, All Loves Excelling" (2 Cor)
393 "Spirit of the Living God" (2 Cor)
SP131; S-1#212 Vocal Desc. idea
603 "Come, Holy Ghost, Our Souls Inspire" (2 Cor)
388 "O Come and Dwell in Me" (2 Cor)
396 "O Jesus, I Have Promised" (2 Cor, Luke)
679 "O Splendor of God's Glory Bright" (2 Cor)
188 "Christ Is the World's Light" (Luke)
260 "Christ, Upon the Mountain Peak" (Luke)
265 "O Christ, the Healer" (Luke)
617 "I Come with Joy" (Luke, Comm.)
623 "Here, O My Lord, I See Thee" (Luke, Comm.)
2102 "Swiftly Pass the Clouds of Glory" (Luke)
2103 "We Have Come at Christ's Own Bidding" (Luke)
2202 "Come Away with Me" (Luke, Comm.)

### Additional Contemporary Suggestions

S2005 "Arise, Shine" (Exod, Luke, Transfiguration)
M266 "You Have Saved Us" (Exod, Luke)
S2274 "Come, All You People" ("*Uyai Mose*") (Pss)
M126 "Famous One" (Pss)
M234 "Awesome Is the Lord Most High" (Pss)
M263 "From the Inside Out" (Pss)
S2119 "Where the Spirit of the Lord Is" (2 Cor)
M19 "Shine on Us" (2 Cor, Transfiguration)
M4 "Let it Rise" (2 Cor)
WS3105 "In Christ Alone" ("My Hope Is Found") (2 Cor, Transfiguration)
M138
UM349 "Turn Your Eyes upon Jesus" (Luke)
SP218
M36 "Awesome in This Place" (Luke)
M43 "We Declare Your Majesty" (Luke)
S2070 "He Is Exalted" (Luke)
SP66
S2018 "Honor and Praise" (Luke)
S2069 "All Hail King Jesus" (Transfiguration)
SP63
WS3003 "How Great Is Our God" (Luke, Transfiguration)
M117
M243 "Beautiful Savior" (Transfiguration)
SP4 "Great and Mighty Is He" (Transfiguration)
M11

### Vocal Solos

"Be Thou My Vision" (Exod, Luke)
Inclusive Text UM451
V-6 p. 13
"Shine, Jesus, Shine" (Luke, Transfiguration)
V-3 (2) p. 48
"I Saw the Lord, and All Beside Was Darkness" (Transfiguration)
V-8 p. 268

### Anthems

"Come, All You People" ("*Uyai Mose*") (Pss)
Arr. Kevin Holland; Choristers Guild CGA-1373
SATB with percussion

"Prayer of the Incarnation" (Luke)
John Butler; Paraclete Press PPM01333
SATB *a cappella*

### Other Suggestions

Visuals:
**O** Mountain, tablets, veil
**P** Throne, earthquake, footstool, cloud, mountain
**E** Veil, glory, mirror, transformer, Bible, 2 Cor 3:17b
**G** Mountain, prayer, dazzling light, 3 booths, cloud

Introit: S2273, BOW187. "Jesus, We Are Here" ("*Yesu Tawa Pano*") (Luke, Black History)
Greeting: BOW318 (Exod, Pss, Luke)
Prayer: UM259. Transfiguration (Luke) or UM477. For Illumination (2 Cor)
Prayers: WSL13 and BOW319 (Luke, Transfiguration)
Response to Prayer: UM168, stanza 4. "At the Name of Jesus" (Luke)
Litany: BOW496. The Ten Commandments (Exod)
Scripture Response: UM596, stanza 3. "Blessed Jesus, at Thy Word" (2 Cor)
Sung Benediction: BOW205. "Shine on Me" (Exod, Luke, Black History)

**Joel 2:1-2, 12-17**

Blow the horn in Zion;
give a shout on my holy mountain!
Let all the people of the land tremble,
for the day of the LORD is coming.
It is near—
[2]a day of darkness and no light,
a day of clouds and thick darkness!
Like blackness spread out upon the mountains,
a great and powerful army comes,
unlike any that has ever come before them,
or will come after them in centuries ahead.

. . . . . . . . . . . . . . . . . . . . . . . . .

[12]Yet even now, says the LORD,
return to me with all your hearts,
with fasting, with weeping, and with sorrow;
[13]tear your hearts
and not your clothing.
Return to the LORD your God,
for he is merciful and compassionate,
very patient, full of faithful love,
and ready to forgive.
[14]Who knows whether he will have a change of heart
and leave a blessing behind him,
a grain offering and a drink offering
for the LORD your God?
[15]Blow the horn in Zion;
demand a fast;
request a special assembly.
[16]Gather the people;
prepare a holy meeting;
assemble the elders;
gather the children,
even nursing infants.
Let the groom leave his room
and the bride her chamber.
[17]Between the porch and the altar
let the priests, the LORD's ministers, weep.
Let them say, "Have mercy, LORD, on your people,
and don't make your inheritance a disgrace,
an example of failure among the nations.
Why should they say among the peoples,
'Where is their God?' "

**Psalm 51:1-17 (UM 785)**

Have mercy on me, God, according to your faithful love!
Wipe away my wrongdoings according to your great
compassion!
[2] Wash me completely clean of my guilt;
purify me from my sin!

. . . . . . . . . . . . . . . . . . . . . . . . . . . . . . . . . . . . . . . . . . . . . .

[10] Create a clean heart for me, God;
put a new, faithful spirit deep inside me!
[11] Please don't throw me out of your presence;
please don't take your holy spirit away from me.
[12] Return the joy of your salvation to me
and sustain me with a willing spirit.
[13] Then I will teach wrongdoers your ways,
and sinners will come back to you.
[14]Deliver me from violence, God, God of my salvation,
so that my tongue can sing of your righteousness.
[15] Lord, open my lips,
and my mouth will proclaim your praise.
[16] You don't want sacrifices.
If I gave an entirely burned offering,
you wouldn't be pleased.
[17] A broken spirit is my sacrifice, God.
You won't despise a heart, God, that is broken and crushed.

**2 Corinthians 5:20b–6:10**

[20b] We beg you as Christ's representatives, "Be reconciled
to God!" [21] God caused the one who didn't know sin to be
sin for our sake so that through him we could become the
righteousness of God.
6 Since we work together with him, we are also begging you
not to receive the grace of God in vain. [2] He says, *I listened to
you at the right time, and I helped you on the day of salvation.* Look,
now is the right time! Look, now is the day of salvation!
[3] We don't give anyone any reason to be offended about
anything so that our ministry won't be criticized. [4] Instead,
we commend ourselves as ministers of God in every way.
We did this with our great endurance through problems,
disasters, and stressful situations. [5] We went through beatings,
imprisonments, and riots. We experienced hard work, sleep-
less nights, and hunger. [6] We displayed purity, knowledge,
patience, and generosity. We served with the Holy Spirit,
genuine love, [7] telling the truth, and God's power. We carried
the weapons of righteousness in our right hand and our left
hand. [8] We were treated with honor and dishonor and with
verbal abuse and good evaluation. We were seen as both fake
and real, [9] as unknown and well known, as dying—and look,
we are alive! We were seen as punished but not killed, [10] as
going through pain but always happy, as poor but making
many rich, and as having nothing but owning everything.

**Matthew 6:1-6, 16-21**

"Be careful that you don't practice your religion in front
of people to draw their attention. If you do, you will have no
reward from your Father who is in heaven.
[2] "Whenever you give to the poor, don't blow your trumpet
as the hypocrites do in the synagogues and in the streets so
that they may get praise from people. I assure you, that's the
only reward they'll get. [3] But when you give to the poor, don't
let your left hand know what your right hand is doing [4] so
that you may give to the poor in secret. Your Father who sees
what you do in secret will reward you.
[5] "When you pray, don't be like hypocrites. They love to pray
standing in the synagogues and on the street corners so that
people will see them. I assure you, that's the only reward they'll
get. [6] But when you pray, go to your room, shut the door, and
pray to your Father who is present in that secret place. Your
Father who sees what you do in secret will reward you." . . .
[16] "And when you fast, don't put on a sad face like the hypocrites. They distort their faces so people will know they are
fasting. I assure you that they have their reward. [17] When you
fast, brush your hair and wash your face. [18] Then you won't
look like you are fasting to people, but only to your Father
who is present in that secret place. Your Father who sees in
secret will reward you.
[19] "Stop collecting treasures for your own benefit on earth,
where moth and rust eat them and where thieves break in
and steal them. [20] Instead, collect treasures for yourselves
in heaven, where moth and rust don't eat them and where
thieves don't break in and steal them. [21] Where your treasure
is, there your heart will be also."

**Primary Hymns and Songs for the Day**
269 "Lord, Who Throughout These Forty Days" (Lent) (O)
H-3 Chr-106; Desc-65; Org-72
S-2 #105. Flute/violin desc.
#106. Harm.
453 "More Love to Thee, O Christ" (Matt)
H-3 Org-94
2128 "Come and Find the Quiet Center" (Matt)
2138 "Sunday's Palms Are Wednesday's Ashes" (Pss)
H-3 Hbl-14, 64; Chr-132, 203
S-2 #22. Desc.
402 "Lord, I Want to Be a Christian" (Joel, Matt) (C)
H-3 Chr-130

**Additional Hymn Suggestions**
379 "Blow Ye the Trumpet, Blow" (Joel)
121 "There's a Wideness in God's Mercy" (Joel)
2206 "Without Seeing You" (Joel, Ash Wednesday)
3098 "Dust and Ashes" (Joel, Pss, Ash Wednesday)
3097 "Depth of Mercy" (Pss)
355 "Depth of Mercy" (Pss)
382 "Have Thine Own Way, Lord" (Pss)
417 "O For a Heart to Praise My God" (Pss)
502 "Thy Holy Wings, O Savior" (Pss)
294 "Alas! and Did My Savior Bleed" (2 Cor)
359 "Alas! and Did My Savior Bleed" (2 Cor)
407 "Close to Thee" (2 Cor)
463 "Lord, Speak to Me" (2 Cor)
292 "What Wondrous Love Is This" (2 Cor) (C)
2196 "We Walk by Faith" (2 Cor, Matt)
627 "O the Depth of Love Divine" (2 Cor, Comm.)
2234 "Lead On, O Cloud of Presence" (2 Cor, Lent)
2278 "The Lord's Prayer" (Matt)
UM271, WS3068-WS3071
352 "It's Me, It's Me, O Lord" (Matt, Black History)
357 "Just as I Am, Without One Plea" (Matt)
378 "Amazing Grace" (Matt)
395 "Take Time to Be Holy" (Matt)
472 "Near to the Heart of God" (Matt)
492 "Prayer Is the Soul's Sincere Desire" (Matt)
496 "Sweet Hour of Prayer" (Matt)
2202 "Come Away with Me" (Matt)
2205 "The Fragrance of Christ" (Matt)
2262 "Let Us Offer to the Father" (Matt)

**Additional Contemporary Suggestions**
WS3042 "Shout to the North" (Joel, Pss)
M99
M224 "Because of Your Love" (Joel, Pss, Lent)
WS3103 "Purify My Heart" (Pss)
M90
M50 "Refiner's Fire" (Pss)
M91 "Take My Life" (Pss)
M151 "Lord You Have My Heart" (Pss)
M153 "Give Us Clean Hands" (Pss, Ash Wednesday, Comm.)
M251 "Grace Like Rain" (Pss, Lent)
M266 "You Have Saved Us" (Pss)
WS3188 "Hosanna" (Pss, Lent)
M268
M277 "How Great Is the Love" (Pss, Lent)
S2133 "Give Me a Clean Heart" (Pss)
S2154 "Please Enter My Heart, Hosanna" (Pss)
S2157 "Come and Fill Our Hearts" (Pss)
S2152 "Change My Heart, O God" (Pss)
SP195
S2055 "You Are My Hiding Place" (Pss, Matt)
S2086 "Open Our Eyes, Lord" (Pss, Matt)
SP199
M26 "The Power of Your Love" (Pss, Matt)
WS3008 "Open the Eyes of My Heart" (Pss, Matt)
M57
M67 "We Want to See Jesus Lifted High" (2 Cor)
M226 "Counting on God" (2 Cor.)
M227 "I Will Boast" (2 Cor.)
S2273 "Jesus, We Are Here" (Matt, Black History)
M38 "In the Secret" ("I Want to Know You") (Matt)
M115 "When It's All Been Said and Done" (Matt)
M156 "Be the Centre" (Matt)
M241 "As It Is in Heaven" (Matt)
WS3040 "You Are My All in All" (Matt, Lent)
SP220

**Vocal Solos**
"If with All Your Hearts" (Joel)
V-8 p. 277
"A Contrite Heart" (Pss)
V-4 p. 10
"Turn My Heart to You" (Pss)
V-5(2) p. 14
"The Heart of Worship" (Pss, Matt)
M71
"The Gospel of Grace" (Matt)
V-3 (1) p.44

**Anthems**
"Have Mercy on Me, O God" (Pss)
Carl Schalk; Augsburg 11-10937
SATB *a cappella*

"Just as I Am, I Come" (Matt)
Arr. Mary McDonald; Hope C-5843
SATB with piano

**Other Suggestions**
Visuals:
**O** Trumpet, alarm, dark, cloud, weeping, heart
**P** Blot, wash, heart, hyssop, snow, Pss 51:10, joy, sing
**E** Christ, cross, clock, suffer, serve, weep/joy
**G** Hands, prayer, closed door, oil/basin, moth/rust, treasure/heart, treasure box
Suggested Service of Worship: BOW321
Introit: S2138. "Sunday's Palms Are Wednesday's Ashes," stanza 1 (Pss)
Greeting: BOW328 (Joel)
Call to Prayer: S2207. "Lord, Listen to Your Children" (Matt)
Opening Prayer: UM353. Ash Wednesday (Joel, Pss)
Prayer of Confession: BOW475 (Pss)
Prayer of Confession: WSL14 (Joel, Ash Wednesday, Lent)
Sung Prayer: S2134. "Forgive Us, Lord" (Pss)
Prayer: WSL15 (Pss, Matt)
Offertory Prayer: WSL123 (Matt)
Prayer of Thanksgiving: BOW550 (Pss, Matt)
Closing Prayer: BOW567 (Matt)

**Deuteronomy 26:1-11**

Once you have entered the land the LORD your God is
giving you as an inheritance, and you take possession of it
and are settled there, 2 take some of the early produce of the
fertile ground that you have harvested from the land the
LORD your God is giving you, and put it in a basket. Then go
to the location the LORD your God selects for his name to
reside. 3 Go to the priest who is in office at that time and say
to him: "I am declaring right now before the LORD my God
that I have indeed arrived in the land the LORD swore to our
ancestors to give us."

4 The priest will then take the basket from you and place it
before the LORD your God's altar. 5 Then you should sol-
emnly state before the LORD your God:

"My father was a starving Aramean. He went down to Egypt,
living as an immigrant there with few family members, but
that is where he became a great nation, mighty and numerous. 6 The Egyptians treated us terribly, oppressing us and
forcing hard labor on us. 7 So we cried out for help to the
LORD, our ancestors' God. The LORD heard our call. God saw
our misery, our trouble, and our oppression. 8 The LORD
brought us out of Egypt with a strong hand and an outstretched arm, with awesome power, and with signs and wonders. 9 He brought us to this place and gave us this land—a
land full of milk and honey. 10 So now I am bringing the early
produce of the fertile ground that you, LORD, have given
me."

Set the produce before the LORD your God, bowing down
before the LORD your God. 11 Then celebrate all the good
things the LORD your God has done for you and your family—each one of you along with the Levites and the immigrants who are among you.

---

**Psalm 91:1-2, 9-16 (UM810)**

Living in the Most High's shelter,
camping in the Almighty's shade,
2 I say to the LORD, "You are my refuge, my stronghold!
You are my God—the one I trust!"

. . . . . . . . . . . . . . . . . . . . . . . . . .

9 Because you've made the LORD my refuge,
the Most High, your place of residence—
10 no evil will happen to you;
no disease will come close to your tent.
11 Because he will order his messengers to help you,
to protect you wherever you go.
12 They will carry you with their own hands
so you don't bruise your foot on a stone.
13 You'll march on top of lions and vipers;
you'll trample young lions and serpents underfoot.
14 God says, "Because you are devoted to me,
I'll rescue you.
I'll protect you because you know my name.
15 Whenever you cry out to me, I'll answer.
I'll be with you in troubling times.
I'll save you and glorify you.
16 I'll fill you full with old age.
I'll show you my salvation."

---

**Romans 10:8b-13**

8b *The word is near you, in your mouth and in your heart* (that is,
the message of faith that we preach). 9 Because if you confess
with your mouth "Jesus is Lord" and in your heart you have
faith that God raised him from the dead, you will be saved.
10 Trusting with the heart leads to righteousness, and confess-
ing with the mouth leads to salvation. 11 The scripture says,
*All who have faith in him won't be put to shame.* 12 There is no
distinction between Jew and Greek, because the same Lord is
Lord of all, who gives richly to all who call on him. 13 *All who
call on the Lord's name will be saved.*

---

**Luke 4:1-13**

Jesus returned from the Jordan River full of the Holy Spirit,
and was led by the Spirit into the wilderness. 2 There he was
tempted for forty days by the devil. He ate nothing during
those days and afterward Jesus was starving. 3 The devil said
to him, "Since you are God's Son, command this stone to
become a loaf of bread."

4 Jesus replied, "It's written, *People won't live only by bread.*"

5 Next the devil led him to a high place and showed him
in a single instant all the kingdoms of the world. 6 The devil
said, "I will give you this whole domain and the glory of all
these kingdoms. It's been entrusted to me and I can give it to
anyone I want. 7 Therefore, if you will worship me, it will all
be yours."

8 Jesus answered, "It's written, *You will worship the Lord your
God and serve only him.*"

9 The devil brought him into Jerusalem and stood him at
the highest point of the temple. He said to him, "Since you
are God's Son, throw yourself down from here; 10 for it's written: *He will command his angels concerning you, to protect you*
11 and *they will take you up in their hands so that you won't hit your
foot on a stone.*"

12 Jesus answered, "It's been said, *Don't test the Lord your
God.*" 13 After finishing every temptation, the devil departed
from him until the next opportunity.

**Primary Hymns and Songs for the Day**

110 "A Mighty Fortress Is Our God" (Pss) (O)
H-3 Chr-19; Desc-35; Org-34
S-1 #111-13. Various treatments

116 "The God of Abraham Praise" (Deut) (O)
H-3 Hbl-62, 95; Chr-59; Org-77
S-1 #211. Harm.

143 "On Eagle's Wings" (Pss)
S-2 #143. Stanzas for soloist

156 "I Love to Tell the Story" (Rom)
H-3 Chr-107

177 "He Is Lord" (Rom)
SP122

2105 "Jesus, Tempted in the Desert" (Luke)
H-3 Chr-53; Org-33
S-1 #109-10. Desc. and harm.

2112 "Jesus Walked This Lonesome Valley" (Luke) (C)

269 "Lord, Who Throughout These Forty Days" (Luke) (C)
H-3 Chr-106; Desc-65; Org-72
S-2 #105. Flute/violin desc.
#106. Harm.

**Additional Hymn Suggestions**

66 "Praise, My Soul, the King of Heaven" (Deut) (O)
2234 "Lead On, O Cloud of Presence" (Deut)
2238 "In the Midst of New Dimensions" (Deut)
97 "For the Fruits of This Creation" (Deut)
139 "Praise to the Lord, the Almighty" (Deut)
117 "O God, Our Help in Ages Past" (Pss)
130 "God Will Take Care of You" (Pss)
141 "Children of the Heavenly Father" (Pss)
377 "It Is Well with My Soul" (Pss)
502 "Thy Holy Wings, O Savior" (Pss)
523 "*Saranam, Saranam*" ("Refuge") (Pss)
2121 "O Holy Spirit, Root of Life" (Pss, Lent)
114 "Many Gifts, One Spirit" (Rom)
385 "Let Us Plead for Faith Alone" (Rom)
548 "In Christ There Is No East or West" (Rom)
555 "Forward Through the Ages" (Rom)
714 "I Know Whom I Have Believed" (Rom)
2140 "Since Jesus Came into My Heart" (Rom)
2160 "Into My Heart" (Rom)
2269 "Come, Share the Lord" ("We Gather Here") (Rom, Comm.)
3110 "By Grace We Have Been Saved" (Rom)
2196 "We Walk by Faith" (Rom, Luke)
2211 "Faith Is Patience in the Night" (Rom, Luke)
178 "Hope of the World" (Luke)
252 "When Jesus Came to Jordan" (Luke)
257 "We Meet You, O Christ" (Luke)
267 "O Love, How Deep" (Luke, Comm.)
395 "Take Time to Be Holy" (Luke)
410 "I Want a Principle Within" (Luke)
2123 "Loving Spirit" (Luke)
3073 "We Walk His Way" (Luke, Lent)

**Additional Contemporary Suggestions**

S2054 "Nothing Can Trouble" ("*Nada Te Turbe*") (Pss)
S2118 "Holy Spirit, Come to Us" (Pss)
WS3021 "Everlasting God" (Pss)
M182
WS3134 "Still" (Pss, Lent)
M216
M26 "The Power of Your Love" (Pss, Lent)
M28 "Who Can Satisfy My Soul Like You?" (Pss)
M60 "Better Is One Day" (Pss)
M79 "I Stand Amazed" (Pss, Lent)
M158 "Eagle's Wings" (Pss)
M257 "Came to My Rescue" (Pss)
M123 "Made Me Glad" (Pss, Luke)
S2053 "If It Had Not Been for the Lord" (Pss, Luke)
S2002 "I Will Call Upon the Lord" (Rom)
SP224
S2154 "Please Enter My Heart, Hosanna" (Rom)
S2056 "God Is So Good" (Rom)
WS3176 "Come, Now Is the Time to Worship" (Rom)
M56
M225 "At the Cross" (Rom, Lent)
M94 "That's Why We Praise Him" (Luke, Lent)
M277 "How Great Is the Love" (Lent)

**Vocal Solo**

"On Eagle's Wings" (Pss)
V-3 (2) p. 2
V-3 (3) p. 4
"It Is Well with My Soul" (Pss)
V-5(2) p. 35
"Prayer" (Pss)
V-9 p. 32
"Grace Greater than Our Sin" (Rom)
V-8 p. 180

**Anthems**

"Come, Share the Lord" (Rom)
Arr. Lloyd Larson; Hope C-5842
SATB with piano

"I Wonder As I Wander" (Luke)
Arr. J. Aaron McDermid; MorningStar MSM-50-1620
SATB *divisi a cappella*

**Other Suggestions**

Visuals:
**O** Basket with food/produce, hand, arm, wrapped gift
**P** Angels, stone, lion, snake, "deliverance"
**E** Faces, professing, multiracial, all ages, Christ
**G** Loaf bread, stone (also arranged as a wall), angels

Boy Scout Sunday is officially the Sunday before February 8, however The UMC celebrates it on the second Sunday of February.
Introit: S2138. "Sunday's Palms Are Wednesday's Ashes," stanza 1 (Lent)
Greeting: BOW327 (Joel, Pss)
Call to Prayer or Response to Psalm: S2053. "If It Had Not Been for the Lord" (Pss)
Prayer of Confession: BOW478 (Pss, Rom)
Prayer of Confession: WSL14 (Luke, Lent)
Prayer: WSL16 (Luke, Lent)
Prayer: BOW333 (Luke)
Prayer: BOW430. Rural Life Sunday (Deut)
Prayer: UM268. Lent (Deut)
Offertory Prayer: WSL118 (Deut)
Prayer of Thanksgiving: BOW552 (Deut)
Blessing: BOW561 (Pss)

### Genesis 15:1-12, 17-18

After these events, the LORD's word came to Abram in a
vision, "Don't be afraid, Abram. I am your protector. Your
reward will be very great."
2 But Abram said, "LORD God, what can you possibly give
me, since I still have no children? The head of my household
is Eliezer, a man from Damascus." 3 He continued, "Since you
haven't given me any children, the head of my household
will be my heir."
4 The LORD's word came immediately to him, "This man
will not be your heir. Your heir will definitely be your very
own biological child." 5 Then he brought Abram outside and
said, "Look up at the sky and count the stars if you think you
can count them. He continued, "This is how many children
you will have." 6 Abram trusted the LORD, and the LORD recognized Abram's high moral character.
7 He said to Abram, "I am the LORD, who brought you
out of Ur of the Chaldeans to give you this land as your
possession."
8 But Abram said, "LORD God, how do I know that I will
actually possess it?"
9 He said, "Bring me a three-year-old female calf, a three-
year-old female goat, a three-year-old ram, a dove, and a
young pigeon." 10 He took all of these animals, split them in
half, and laid the halves facing each other, but he didn't split
the birds. 11 When vultures swooped down on the carcasses,
Abram waved them off. 12 After the sun set, Abram slept
deeply. A terrifying and deep darkness settled over him. . . .
17 After the sun had set and darkness had deepened, a
smoking vessel with a fiery flame passed between the split-
open animals. 18 That day the LORD cut a covenant with
Abram: "To your descendants I give this land, from Egypt's
river to the great Euphrates."

---

### Psalm 27 (UM758)

The LORD is my light and my salvation.
Should I fear anyone?
The LORD is a fortress protecting my life.
Should I be frightened of anything?
2 When evildoers come at me trying to eat me up—
it's they, my foes and my enemies,
who stumble and fall!
3 If an army camps against me,
my heart won't be afraid.
If war comes up against me,
I will continue to trust in this:
4 I have asked one thing from the LORD—
it's all I seek:
to live in the LORD's house all the days of my life,
seeing the LORD's beauty
and constantly adoring his temple.
5 Because he will shelter me in his own dwelling
during troubling times;
he will hide me in a secret place in his own tent;
he will set me up high, safe on a rock.
6 Now my head is higher than the enemies surrounding me,
and I will offer sacrifices in God's tent—
sacrifices with shouts of joy!
I will sing and praise the LORD.
7 LORD, listen to my voice when I cry out—
have mercy on me and answer me!
8 Come, my heart says, seek God's face.
LORD, I do seek your face!
9 Please don't hide it from me!
Don't push your servant aside angrily—
you have been my help!
God who saves me,
don't neglect me!
Don't leave me all alone!
10 Even if my father and mother left me all alone,
the LORD would take me in.
11 LORD, teach me your way;
because of my opponents, lead me on a good path.
12 Don't give me over to the desires of my enemies,
because false witnesses and violent accusers
have taken their stand against me.
13 But I have sure faith
that I will experience the LORD's goodness
in the land of the living!
14 Hope in the LORD!
Be strong! Let your heart take courage!
Hope in the LORD!

---

### Philippians 3:17–4:1

17 Brothers and sisters, become imitators of me and watch
those who live this way—you can use us as models. 18 As I have
told you many times and now say with deep sadness, many
people live as enemies of the cross. 19 Their lives end with
destruction. Their god is their stomach, and they take pride
in their disgrace because their thoughts focus on earthly
things. 20 Our citizenship is in heaven. We look forward to a
savior that comes from there—the Lord Jesus Christ. 21 He
will transform our humble bodies so that they are like his glorious body, by the power that also makes him able to subject
all things to himself.
4 Therefore, my brothers and sisters whom I love and miss,
who are my joy and crown, stand firm in the Lord.

---

### Luke 13:31-35

31 At that time, some Pharisees approached Jesus and said,
"Go! Get away from here, because Herod wants to kill you."
32 Jesus said to them, "Go, tell that fox, 'Look, I'm throwing out demons and healing people today and tomorrow,
and on the third day I will complete my work. 33 However, it's
necessary for me to travel today, tomorrow, and the next day
because it's impossible for a prophet to be killed outside of
Jerusalem.'
34 "Jerusalem, Jerusalem, you who kill the prophets and
stone those who were sent to you! How often I have wanted
to gather your people just as a hen gathers her chicks under
her wings. But you didn't want that. 35 Look, your house is
abandoned. I tell you, you won't see me until the time comes
when you say, *Blessings on the one who comes in the Lord's name."*

**Primary Hymns and Songs for the Day**

116 "The God of Abraham Praise" (Gen) (O)
H-3 Hbl-62, 95; Chr-59; Org-77
S-1 #211. Harm.
140 "Great Is Thy Faithfulness" (Gen) (O)
H-3 Chr-87; Desc-39; Org-39
S-2 #59. Piano arr.
2064 "O Lord, You're Beautiful" (Pss)
295 "In the Cross of Christ I Glory" (Phil) (C)
H-3 Hbl-72; Chr-113; Desc-89; Org-119
S-1 #276-77. Harm. with desc.
396 "O Jesus, I Have Promised" (Phil) (C)
S-2 #9. Desc.
2001 "We Sing to You, O God" (Luke) (C)
H-3 Hbl-8, 53, 90; Chr-37; Desc-27; Org-24
S-1 #78-80. Various treatments

**Additional Hymn Suggestions**

2202 "Come Away with Me" (Gen, Luke, Lent) (O)
100 "God, Whose Love Is Reigning o'er Us" (Gen) (O)
132 "All My Hope Is Firmly Grounded" (Gen)
142 "If Thou But Suffer God to Guide Thee" (Gen)
451 "Be Thou My Vision" (Gen)
508 "Faith, While Trees Are Still in Blossom" (Gen)
124 "Seek the Lord" (Pss)
153 "Thou Hidden Source of Calm Repose" (Pss)
479 "Jesus, Lover of My Soul" (Pss)
580 "Lead On, O King Eternal" (Pss, Phil)
2053 "If It Had Not Been for the Lord" (Pss)
2214 "Lead Me, Guide Me" (Pss)
2218 "You Are Mine" (Pss)
2267 "Taste and See" (Pss, Comm.)
189 "Fairest Lord Jesus" (Phil)
286 "O Sacred Head, Now Wounded" (Phil)
417 "O For a Heart to Praise My God" (Phil)
419 "I Am Thine, O Lord" (Phil)
524 "Beams of Heaven as I Go" (Phil)
517 "By Gracious Powers" (Phil, Luke)
3073 "We Walk His Way" (Phil, Luke)
105 "God of Many Names" (Luke)
115 "How Like a Gentle Spirit" (Luke)
118 "The Care the Eagle Gives Her Young" (Luke)
141 "Children of the Heavenly Father" (Luke)
267 "O Love, How Deep" (Luke, Comm.)
2112 "Jesus Walked This Lonesome Valley" (Luke, Lent)
2123 "Loving Spirit" (Luke)
2236 "Gather Us In" (Luke)

**Additional Contemporary Suggestions**

UM123 "*El Shaddai*" (Gen)
UM523 "*Saranam, Saranam*" ("Refuge") (Pss)
S2002 "I Will Call Upon the Lord" (Pss)
SP224
S2054 "Nothing Can Trouble" ("*Nada Te Turbe*") (Pss)
S2144 "Someone Asked the Question" (Pss)
S2207 "Lord, Listen to Your Children" (Pss)
S2235-b "We Are Marching" ("*Siyahamba*") (Pss)
SP209 "The Lord Is My Light" (Pss)
M92 "All Things Are Possible" (Pss)
M123 "Made Me Glad" (Pss)
M250 "Our God Saves" (Pss)
M257 "Came to My Rescue" (Pss)
M258 "You Never Let Go" (Pss)
M70 "No Higher Calling" (Pss, Phil)
M83 "Just Let Me Say" (Pss, Phil)
WS3004 "Step by Step" (Pss, Phil, Luke)
M51
WS3105 "In Christ Alone" (Pss, Phil, Luke)
M138
M258 "You Never Let Go" (Pss, Luke)
UM143 "On Eagle's Wings" (Luke)
S-2 #143. Stanzas for soloist
UM261 "Lord of the Dance" (Luke)
M26 "The Power of Your Love" (Luke)

**Vocal Solos**

"Be Thou My Vision" (Gen)
V-6 p. 13
"Patiently Have I Waited for the Lord" (Pss)
V-4 p. 24
"The Lord Is My Light" (Pss)
V-8 p. 57
"Courage, My Heart" (Pss, Lent)
V-9 p. 20
"On Eagle's Wings" (Luke)
V-3 (2) p. 2
V-3 (3) p. 4
"Lord of the Dance" (Luke)
V-3 (3) p. 34

**Anthems**

"A Prayer of St. Patrick" (Phil)
Michael McCarthy; MorningStar MSM-50-9350
SSATTBB *a cappella* with soloists

"*Kyrie*" (Luke)
Mozart/Liebergen; Hinshaw HMC2335
SAB with keyboard, opt. 2 flutes

**Other Suggestions**

Visuals:
**O** Shield, stars, heifer, goat, ram, pigeon, fire, torch
**P** Light, army/war, sanctuary, tent, rock, singing, path
**E** Cross, "citizens," Christ, love, crown, Phil 4:1c
**G** Jerusalem, hen/chicks, Luke 13:35c
Greeting: BOW326 (Pss)
Call to Confession: S2138. "Sunday's Palms Are Wednesday's Ashes," stanza 2 (Pss)
Prayer of Confession: BOW490 (Phil, Rom)
Call to Prayer: S2200. "O Lord, Hear My Prayer" (Pss)
Prayer: UM531. For Overcoming Adversity (Pss)
Prayer: UM691. For Protection at Night (Luke)
Prayer: BOW336 or BOW398 (Luke)
Intercessory Prayer: BOW334 (Pss)
Response: S2277. "Lord, Have Mercy" (Lent)
Prayer of Thanksgiving: BOW553 (Pss, Luke)
Blessing: WSL165 or BOW565 (Pss)
Sung Benediction: S2279. "The Trees of the Field" (Pss)

**Isaiah 55:1-9**
All of you who are thirsty, come to the water!
Whoever has no money, come, buy food and eat!
Without money, at no cost, buy wine and milk!
2 Why spend money for what isn't food,
and your earnings for what doesn't satisfy?
Listen carefully to me and eat what is good;
enjoy the richest of feasts.
3 Listen and come to me;
listen, and you will live.
I will make an everlasting covenant with you,
my faithful loyalty to David.
4 Look, I made him a witness to the peoples,
a prince and commander of peoples.
5 Look, you will call a nation you don't know,
a nation you don't know will run to you
because of the LORD your God,
the holy one of Israel, who has glorified you.
6 Seek the LORD when he can still be found;
call him while he is yet near.
7 Let the wicked abandon their ways
and the sinful their schemes.
Let them return to the LORD so that he may have mercy on
them,
to our God, because he is generous with forgiveness.
8 My plans aren't your plans,
nor are your ways my ways, says the LORD.
9 Just as the heavens are higher than the earth,
so are my ways higher than your ways,
and my plans than your plans.

---

**Psalm 63:1-8 (UM788)**
God! My God! It's you—
I search for you!
My whole being thirsts for you!
My body desires you
in a dry and tired land,
no water anywhere.
2 Yes, I've seen you in the sanctuary;
I've seen your power and glory.
3 My lips praise you
because your faithful love
is better than life itself!
4 So I will bless you as long as I'm alive;
I will lift up my hands in your name.
5 I'm fully satisfied—
as with a rich dinner.
My mouth speaks praise with joy on my lips—
6 whenever I ponder you on my bed,
whenever I meditate on you
in the middle of the night—
7 because you've been a help to me and I shout for joy in
the protection of your wings.
8 My whole being clings to you;
your strong hand upholds me.

---

**1 Corinthians 10:1-13**
Brothers and sisters, I want you to be sure of the fact that
our ancestors were all under the cloud and they all went
through the sea. 2 All were baptized into Moses in the cloud
and in the sea. 3 All ate the same spiritual food, 4 and all
drank the same spiritual drink. They drank from a spiritual
rock that followed them, and the rock was Christ. 5 However,
God was unhappy with most of them, and they were struck
down in the wilderness. 6 These things were examples for us,
so we won't crave evil things like they did. 7 Don't worship
false gods like some of them did, as it is written, *The people sat
down to eat and drink and they got up to play.* 8 Let's not practice
sexual immorality, like some of them did, and twenty-three
thousand died in one day. 9 Let's not test Christ, like some of
them did, and were killed by the snakes. 10 Let's not grumble,
like some of them did, and were killed by the destroyer.
11 These things happened to them as an example and were
written as a warning for us to whom the end of time has
come. 12 So those who think they are standing need to watch
out or else they may fall. 13 No temptation has seized you that
isn't common for people. But God is faithful. He won't allow
you to be tempted beyond your abilities. Instead, with the
temptation, God will also supply a way out so that you will be
able to endure it.

---

**Luke 13:1-9**
Some who were present on that occasion told Jesus about
the Galileans whom Pilate had killed while they were offering
sacrifices. 2 He replied, "Do you think the suffering of these
Galileans proves that they were more sinful than all the other
Galileans? 3 No, I tell you, but unless you change your hearts
and lives, you will die just as they did. 4 What about those
eighteen people who were killed when the tower of Siloam
fell on them? Do you think that they were more guilty of
wrongdoing than everyone else who lives in Jerusalem? 5 No,
I tell you, but unless you change your hearts and lives, you
will die just as they did."
6 Jesus told this parable: "A man owned a fig tree planted
in his vineyard. He came looking for fruit on it and found
none. 7 He said to his gardener, 'Look, I've come looking for
fruit on this fig tree for the past three years, and I've never
found any. Cut it down! Why should it continue depleting
the soil's nutrients?' 8 The gardener responded, 'Lord, give it
one more year, and I will dig around it and give it fertilizer.
9 Maybe it will produce fruit next year; if not, then you can
cut it down.'"

**Primary Hymns and Songs for the Day**

121 "There's a Wideness in God's Mercy" (Isa) (O)
H-3 Chr-195; Desc-102; Org-179
2132 "You Who Are Thirsty" (Isa)
2196 "We Walk by Faith" (Isa)
H-3 Chr-21
396 "O Jesus, I Have Promised" (1 Cor)
S-2 #9. Desc.
413 "A Charge to Keep I Have" (1 Cor, Luke)
H-3 Desc-19; Org-14
S-1 #46. Choral harm.
127 "Guide Me, O Thou Great Jehovah" (Isa, 1 Cor) (C)
H-3 Hbl-25, 51, 58; Chr-89; Desc-26; Org-23
S-1 #76-77. Desc. and harm.

**Additional Hymn Suggestions**

124 "Seek the Lord" (Isa)
339 "Come, Sinners, to the Gospel Feast" (Isa)
340 "Come, Ye Sinners, Poor and Needy" (Isa)
350 "Come, All of You" (Isa)
375 "There Is a Balm in Gilead" (Isa)
510 "Come, Ye Disconsolate" (Isa)
629 "You Satisfy the Hungry Heart" (Isa)
2282 "I'll Fly Away" (Isa)
381 "Savior, Like a Shepherd Lead Us" (Pss)
475 "Come Down, O Love Divine" (Pss)
498 "My Prayer Rises to Heaven" (Pss)
506 "Wellspring of Wisdom" (Pss, 1 Cor, Luke)
2117 "Spirit of God" (Pss)
2216 "When We Are Called to Sing Your Praise" (Pss, Lent)
2267 "Taste and See" (Pss)
2001 "We Sing to You, O God" (Pss, 1 Cor)
410 "I Want a Principle Within" (1 Cor)
649 "How Shall They Hear the Word of God" (1 Cor)
416 "Come Out the Wilderness" (1 Cor, Luke)
519 "Lift Every Voice and Sing" (1 Cor, Luke)
438 "Forth in Thy Name, O Lord" (Luke)
2060 "God the Sculptor of the Mountains" (Luke)

**Additional Contemporary Suggestions**

S2132 "You Who Are Thirsty" (Isa)
M159 "All Who Are Thirsty" (Isa)
M32 "Holy and Anointed One" (Isa, Lent)
WS3004 "Step by Step" (Isa, Lent)
M51
WS3099 "Falling on My Knees" ("Hungry") (Isa, Pss, Lent)
M155
WS3092 "Come, Holy Spirit" (Isa, Pss)
WS3094 "Come to Me" (Isa, Pss)
M189 "Your Love, Oh Lord" (Isa, Pss)
UM143 "On Eagle's Wings" (Pss)
S-2 #143. Stanzas for soloist
S2025 "As the Deer" (Pss)
SP200
S2144 "Someone Asked the Question" (Pss)
S2159 "Jesus, Draw Me Close" (Pss)
M48
M29 "Draw Me Close" (Pss)
M158 "Eagle's Wings" (Pss)
M262 "Desert Song" (Pss)
S2066 "Praise the Name of Jesus" (1 Cor)
SP87

**Vocal Solos**

"There Is a Balm in Gilead" (Isa)
V-3 (1) p. 29
"Maybe the Rain" (Isa, Lent)
V-5(2) p. 27
"Just a Closer Walk with Thee" (Isa, Lent)
V-5(2) p. 31
V-8 p. 323
"For Those Tears I Died" (Isa, Lent)
V-8 p. 242
"On Eagle's Wings" (Pss)
V-3 (2) p. 2
V-3 (3) p. 4
"Wondrous Love" (Lent)
V-6 p. 47

**Anthems**

"A Rose Touched by the Sun's Warm Rays" (Isa)
Jean Berger; Augsburg 11-953 (AC p. 26)
SATB *a cappella*

"O Jesus, Every Moment" (Luke)
Philip W. J. Stopford; MorningStar MSM-50-5825
SATB with keyboard

**Other Suggestions**

Visuals:
**O** Water, wine/milk/honey, money, listen, Isa 55:6a
**P** Desert, lifted hands, food, bed, Pss 63:7b, wings
**E** Water/food, larger rock, bread/wine, baptism
**G** Fig branch or tree, figs, axe, cross
Introit: S2132. "You Who Are Thirsty" (Isa)
Greeting: BOW332 (Isa, 1 Cor)
Opening Prayer: BOW459 (Isa, Pss)
Opening Prayer: WSL17 (Isa, Pss, 1Cor, Lent)
Canticle: UM125. "Canticle of Covenant Faithfulness" (Isa)
Call to Confession: S2138. "Sunday's Palms Are Wednesday's Ashes," stanza 3 (Lent)
Prayer of Confession: BOW528. A Prayer of Susanna Wesley (Lent)
Sung Prayer: S2134. "Forgive Us, Lord" ("*Perdón, Señor*") (Pss, Lent)
Prayer: WSL28 (Isa, Pss)
Prayer: UM268. Lent (1 Cor)
Prayer: BOW336 (1 Cor, Luke)
Prayer: BOW530. A Prayer of Saint Thomas Aquinas (Isa, Pss)
Prayer: UM423. Finding Rest in God. (Pss)
Litany: UM106. God Is Able (1 Cor)
Blessing: BOW564 (Pss)
Blessing: WSL18 (Lent)

**Joshua 5:9-12**

9 Then the LORD said to Joshua, "Today I have rolled away from you the disgrace of Egypt." So the place was called Gilgal, as it is today.

10 The Israelites camped in Gilgal. They celebrated Passover on the evening of the fourteenth day of the month on the plains of Jericho. 11 On the very next day after Passover, they ate food produced in the land: unleavened bread and roasted grain. 12 The manna stopped on that next day, when they ate food produced in the land. There was no longer any manna for the Israelites. So that year they ate the crops of the land of Canaan.

---

**Psalm 32 (UM766)**

The one whose wrongdoing is forgiven,<br>
  whose sin is covered over, is truly happy!<br>
2 The one the LORD doesn't consider guilty—<br>
  in whose spirit there is no dishonesty—<br>
  that one is truly happy!<br>
3 When I kept quiet, my bones wore out;<br>
  I was groaning all day long—<br>
  every day, every night!—<br>
4 because your hand was heavy upon me.<br>
  My energy was sapped as if in a summer drought. *[Selah]*<br>
5 So I admitted my sin to you;<br>
  I didn't conceal my guilt.<br>
  "I'll confess my sins to the LORD, " is what I said.<br>
  Then you removed the guilt of my sin. *[Selah]*<br>
6 That's why all the faithful should pray to you during<br>
    troubled times,<br>
  so that a great flood of water won't reach them.<br>
7 You are my secret hideout!<br>
  You protect me from trouble.<br>
  You surround me with songs of rescue! *[Selah]*<br>
8 I will instruct you and teach you<br>
  about the direction you should go.<br>
  I'll advise you and keep my eye on you.<br>
9 Don't be like some senseless horse or mule,<br>
  whose movement must be controlled<br>
  with a bit and a bridle.<br>
    Don't be anything like that!<br>
10 The pain of the wicked is severe,<br>
  but faithful love surrounds the one who trusts the LORD.<br>
11 You who are righteous, rejoice in the LORD and be glad!<br>
  All you whose hearts are right, sing out in joy!

---

**2 Corinthians 5:16-21**

16 So then, from this point on we won't recognize people by human standards. Even though we used to know Christ by human standards, that isn't how we know him now. 17 So then, if anyone is in Christ, that person is part of the new creation. The old things have gone away, and look, new things have arrived!

18 All of these new things are from God, who reconciled us to himself through Christ and who gave us the ministry of reconciliation. 19 In other words, God was reconciling the world to himself through Christ, by not counting people's sins against them. He has trusted us with this message of reconciliation.

20 So we are ambassadors who represent Christ. God is negotiating with you through us. We beg you as Christ's representatives, "Be reconciled to God!" 21 God caused the one who didn't know sin to be sin for our sake so that through him we could become the righteousness of God.

---

**Luke 15:1-3, 11b-32**

All the tax collectors and sinners were gathering around Jesus to listen to him. 2 The Pharisees and legal experts were grumbling, saying, "This man welcomes sinners and eats with them."

3 Jesus told them this parable: . . .

11b "A certain man had two sons. 12 The younger son said to his father, 'Father, give me my share of the inheritance.' Then the father divided his estate between them. 13 Soon afterward, the younger son gathered everything together and took a trip to a land far away. There, he wasted his wealth through extravagant living.

14 "When he had used up his resources, a severe food shortage arose in that country and he began to be in need. 15 He hired himself out to one of the citizens of that country, who sent him into his fields to feed pigs. 16 He longed to eat his fill from what the pigs ate, but no one gave him anything. 17 When he came to his senses, he said, 'How many of my father's hired hands have more than enough food, but I'm starving to death! 18 I will get up and go to my father, and say to him, "Father, I have sinned against heaven and against you. 19 I no longer deserve to be called your son. Take me on as one of your hired hands." ' 20 So he got up and went to his father.

"While he was still a long way off, his father saw him and was moved with compassion. His father ran to him, hugged him, and kissed him. 21 Then his son said, 'Father, I have sinned against heaven and against you. I no longer deserve to be called your son.' 22 But the father said to his servants, 'Quickly, bring out the best robe and put it on him! Put a ring on his finger and sandals on his feet! 23 Fetch the fattened calf and slaughter it. We must celebrate with feasting 24 because this son of mine was dead and has come back to life! He was lost and is found!' And they began to celebrate.

25 "Now his older son was in the field. Coming in from the field, he approached the house and heard music and dancing. 26 He called one of the servants and asked what was going on. 27 The servant replied, 'Your brother has arrived, and your father has slaughtered the fattened calf because he received his son back safe and sound.' 28 Then the older son was furious and didn't want to enter in, but his father came out and begged him. 29 He answered his father, 'Look, I've served you all these years, and I never disobeyed your instruction. Yet you've never given me as much as a young goat so I could celebrate with my friends. 30 But when this son of yours returned, after gobbling up your estate on prostitutes, you slaughtered the fattened calf for him.' 31 Then his father said, 'Son, you are always with me, and everything I have is yours. 32 But we had to celebrate and be glad because this brother of yours was dead and is alive. He was lost and is found.'"

**Primary Hymns and Songs for the Day**

132 "All My Hope Is Firmly Grounded" (Josh) (O)
H-3 Chr-23, 78

579 "Lord God, Your Love Has Called Us Here" (2 Cor, One Great Hour) (O)
S-1 #57-61. Various treatments

2055 "You Are My Hiding Place" (Pss, Luke)

2083 "My Song Is Love Unknown" (2 Cor)
H-3 Chr-139, 158; Desc-90; Org-126
S-1 #284-85. Desc. and harm.

140 "Great Is Thy Faithfulness" (Luke)
H-3 Chr-87; Desc-39; Org-39
S-2 #59. Piano arr.

383 "This Is a Day of New Beginnings" (2 Cor, Luke, Comm.) (C)
H-3 Chr-196

384 "Love Divine, All Loves Excelling" (2 Cor, Luke) (C)
H-3 Chr-134; Desc-18; Org-13
S-1 #41-42. Desc. and harm.

**Additional Hymn Suggestions**

97 "For the Fruits of This Creation" (Josh)
138 "The King of Love My Shepherd Is" (Josh)
631 "O Food to Pilgrims Given" (Josh, Comm., One Great Hour)
2126 "All Who Hunger" (Josh, Comm.)
343 "Come Back Quickly to the Lord" (Josh, Luke)
160 "Rejoice, Ye Pure in Heart" (Pss)
161 "Rejoice, Ye Pure in Heart" (Pss)
2134 "Forgive Us, Lord" ("*Perdon, Señor*") (Pss, Luke)
292 "What Wondrous Love Is This" (2 Cor)
294 "Alas! and Did My Savior Bleed" (2 Cor)
359 "Alas! and Did My Savior Bleed" (2 Cor)
388 "O Come and Dwell in Me" (2 Cor)
545 "The Church's One Foundation" (2 Cor)
562 "Jesus, Lord, We Look to Thee" (2 Cor)
2046 "Womb of Life" (2 Cor)
2212 "My Life Flows On" ("How Can I Keep from Singing") (2 Cor)
98 "To God Be the Glory" (2 Cor)
2050 "Mothering God, You Gave Me Birth" (2 Cor, Luke)
3100 "Jesus Paid It All" (2 Cor, Luke, Lent)
115 "How Like a Gentle Spirit" (Luke)
120 "Your Love, O God" (Luke)
339 "Come, Sinners, to the Gospel Feast" (Luke)
340 "Come, Ye Sinners, Poor and Needy" (Luke)
348 "Softly and Tenderly Jesus Is Calling" (Luke)
434 "*Cuando el Pobre*" ("When the Poor Ones") (Luke, One Great Hour)
2047 "Bring Many Names" (Luke)
2149 "Living for Jesus" (Luke)
2197 "Lord of All Hopefulness" (Luke)
2214 "Lead Me, Guide Me" (Luke)
3072 "Cast Out, O Christ" (Luke)
3101 "Love Lifted Me" (Luke)

**Additional Contemporary Suggestions**

S2272 "Holy Ground" (Josh)
SP86
M36 "Awesome in this Place" (Josh)
S2032 "My Life Is in You, Lord" (Pss)
SP204
S2074 "Shout to the Lord" (Pss)
M16; V-3 (2) p. 32 Vocal Solo
S2053 "If It Had Not Been for the Lord" (Pss, Luke)
UM507 "Through It All" (Pss, Luke)
WS3027 "Hallelujah" ("Your Love Is Amazing") (Pss, Luke)
M118
M73 "My Redeemer Lives" (Pss, Lent)
M266 "You Have Saved Us" (2 Cor.)
M49 "Refresh My Heart" (2 Cor)
M94 "That's Why We Praise Him" (2 Cor, Luke)
M109 "He Knows My Name" (Luke)
M106 "I Come to the Cross" (Luke, Lent)
M142 "Let the River Flow" (Luke)
S2151 "I'm So Glad Jesus Lifted Me" (Luke)
M224 "Because of Your Love" (Luke)
WS3038 "Mighty to Save" (Luke)
M246
M256 "Forever Reign" (Luke)
WS3099 "Falling on My Knees" ("Hungry") (Luke)
M155
WS3102 "You Are My King" ("Amazing Love") (Luke)
M82

**Vocal Solos**

"Brighter than the Sun" (2 Cor, Baptism)
V-5(1) p. 57
"Softly and Tenderly" (Luke)
V-5(3) p. 52
"Strength to My Soul" (Luke)
V-8 p. 352
"So Art Thou With Me" (Luke, Lent)
V-9 p. 34

**Anthems**

"The Handiwork of God" (2 Cor)
Mark Miller: Choristers Guild CGA-1379
SATB with piano

"And the Father Will Dance" (Luke)
Mark Hayes; Hinshaw HMC637
SATB with piano

**Other Suggestions**

Visuals:
**O** Fruit, vegetable, grain, unleavened bread
**P** Praying hands, embracing arms, bridle/bit
**E** Butterfly/chrysalis, flowering bulbs, Spring flowers
**G** Rembrandt "Return of the Prodigal," embrace, lost/found, robe, ring, sandals, goat, calf

**One Great Hour of Sharing:** UMCOR materials, disaster relief
Greeting: BOW331 (Josh, Pss)
Greeting: BOW 424 (Luke, One Great Hour)
Call to Prayer: S2200. "O Lord, Hear My Prayer" (Luke, Lent)
Opening Prayer: BOW454 (Luke)
Canticle: UM646. "Canticle of Love" (Luke)
Prayer of Confession: BOW477 (Pss, Luke) or BOW489 (2 Cor)
Prayer: BOW522. For Purity (Lent, Luke)
Prayer: UM268. Lent (Josh)
Prayer: BOW337, UM639 or UM446 (Luke, One Great Hour)
Offertory Prayer: WSL111 (2 Cor)
Prayer of Thanksgiving: BOW558 (Luke, One Great Hour)
Blessing: BOW564 (2 Cor, Luke)
Sung Benediction: S2279. "The Trees of the Field" (Pss)

**Isaiah 43:16-21**

16 The LORD says—who makes a way in the sea
and a path in the mighty waters,
17 who brings out chariot and horse,
army and battalion;
they will lie down together and will not rise;
they will be extinguished, extinguished like a wick.
18 Don't remember the prior things;
don't ponder ancient history.
19 Look! I'm doing a new thing;
now it sprouts up; don't you recognize it?
I'm making a way in the desert,
paths in the wilderness.
20 The beasts of the field,
the jackals and ostriches, will honor me,
because I have put water in the desert
and streams in the wilderness
to give water to my people,
my chosen ones,
21 this people whom I formed for myself,
who will recount my praise.

---

**Psalm 126 (UM847)**

When the LORD changed Zion's circumstances for the better,
it was like we had been dreaming.
2 Our mouths were suddenly filled with laughter;
our tongues were filled with joyful shouts.
It was even said, at that time, among the nations,
"The LORD has done great things for them!"
3 Yes, the LORD has done great things for us,
and we are overjoyed.
4 LORD, change our circumstances for the better,
like dry streams in the desert waste!
5 Let those who plant with tears
reap the harvest with joyful shouts.
6 Let those who go out,
crying and carrying their seed,
come home with joyful shouts,
carrying bales of grain!

---

**Philippians 3:4b-14**

4b If anyone else has reason to put their confidence in physical advantages, I have even more:
5 I was circumcised on the eighth day.
I am from the people of Israel and the tribe of Benjamin.
I am a Hebrew of the Hebrews.
With respect to observing the Law, I'm a Pharisee.
6 With respect to devotion to the faith, I harassed the
church.
With respect to righteousness under the Law, I'm
blameless.
7 These things were my assets, but I wrote them off as a
loss for the sake of Christ. 8 But even beyond that, I consider
everything a loss in comparison with the superior value of
knowing Christ Jesus my Lord. I have lost everything for him,
but what I lost I think of as sewer trash, so that I might gain
Christ 9 and be found in him. In Christ I have a righteousness
that is not my own and that does not come from the Law but
rather from the faithfulness of Christ. It is the righteousness
of God that is based on faith. 10 The righteousness that I have
comes from knowing Christ, the power of his resurrection,
and the participation in his sufferings. It includes being
conformed to his death 11 so that I may perhaps reach the
goal of the resurrection of the dead.
12 It's not that I have already reached this goal or have
already been perfected, but I pursue it, so that I may grab
hold of it because Christ grabbed hold of me for just this
purpose. 13 Brothers and sisters, I myself don't think I've
reached it, but I do this one thing: I forget about the things
behind me and reach out for the things ahead of me. 14 The
goal I pursue is the prize of God's upward call in Christ Jesus.

---

**John 12:1-8**

Six days before Passover, Jesus came to Bethany, home of
Lazarus, whom Jesus had raised from the dead. 2 Lazarus
and his sisters hosted a dinner for him. Martha served and
Lazarus was among those who joined him at the table. 3 Then
Mary took an extraordinary amount, almost three-quarters of
a pound, of very expensive perfume made of pure nard. She
anointed Jesus' feet with it, then wiped his feet dry with her
hair. The house was filled with the aroma of the perfume.
4 Judas Iscariot, one of his disciples (the one who was about
to betray him), complained, 5 "This perfume was worth a
year's wages! Why wasn't it sold and the money given to the
poor?" (6 He said this not because he cared about the poor
but because he was a thief. He carried the money bag and
would take what was in it.)
7 Then Jesus said, "Leave her alone. This perfume was to
be used in preparation for my burial, and this is how she has
used it. 8 You will always have the poor among you, but you
won't always have me."

### Primary Hymns and Songs for the Day

126 "Sing Praise to God Who Reigns Above" (Isa) (O)
H-3 Hbl-92; Chr-173; Desc-76; Org-91
S-1 #237. Desc.
2182 "When God Restored Our Common Life" (Pss)
H-3 Chr-139; Desc-90; Org-123
298 "When I Survey the Wondrous Cross" (Phil)
H-3 Hbl-6, 102; Chr-213; Desc-49; Org-49
S-1 #155. Desc.
299 "When I Survey the Wondrous Cross" (Phil)
H-3 Hbl-47; Chr-214; Desc-90; Org-127
S-1 #288. Transposition to E-flat major
2161 "To Know You More" (Phil)
453 "More Love to Thee, O Christ" (John) (C)
H-3 Org-94

### Additional Hymn Suggestions

134 "O Mary, Don't You Weep" (Isa, Lent)
149 "*Cantemos al Señor*" ("Let's Sing unto the Lord") (Isa, Pss)
383 "This Is a Day of New Beginnings" (Isa, Phil)
388 "O Come and Dwell in Me" (Isa, Phil)
448 "Go Down, Moses" (Isa, Phil)
506 "Wellspring of Wisdom" (Isa)
509 "Jesus, Savior, Pilot Me" (Isa)
529 "How Firm a Foundation" (Isa) (O)
129 "Give to the Winds Thy Fears" (Pss)
203 "Hail to the Lord's Anointed" (Pss)
510 "Come, Ye Disconsolate" (Pss)
2210 "Joy Comes with the Dawn" (Pss)
2279 "The Trees of the Field" (Pss)
57 "O For a Thousand Tongues to Sing" (Pss, John)
59 "*Mil Voces Para Celebrar*" (Pss, John)
297 "Beneath the Cross of Jesus" (Phil)
363 "And Can It Be that I Should Gain" (Phil)
399 "Take My Life and Let It Be" (Phil)
410 "I Want a Principle Within" (Phil)
414 "Thou Hidden Love of God" (Phil)
505 "When Our Confidence Is Shaken" (Phil)
701 "When We All Get to Heaven" (Phil)
709 "Come, Let Us Join Our Friends Above" (Phil)
2208 "Guide My Feet" (Phil)
2213 "Healer of Our Every Ill" (Phil)
98 "To God Be the Glory" (Phil)
170 "O How I Love Jesus" (John)
172 "My Jesus, I Love Thee" (John)
175 "Jesus, the Very Thought of Thee" (John)
194 "Morning Glory, Starlit Sky" (John, Lent)
274 "Woman in the Night" (John)
276 "The First One Ever" (John)
444 "O Young and Fearless Prophet" (John)
532 "Jesus, Priceless Treasure" (John)
2205 "The Fragrance of Christ" (John)
2216 "When We Are Called to Sing Your Praise" (John)

### Additional Contemporary Suggestions

M49 "Refresh My Heart" (Isa)
M266 "You Have Saved Us" (Isa)
WS3001 "O For a Thousand Tongues to Sing" (Pss)
WS3108 "Trading My Sorrows" (Pss)
M75
M263 "From the Inside Out" (Pss)
UM394 "Something Beautiful" (Phil)
S2167 "More Like You" (Phil)
S2164 "Sanctuary" (Phil)
M52
S2163 "He Who Began a Good Work in You" (Phil)
SP180
WS3085 "The Power of the Cross" (Phil)
M222
M76 "The Wonderful Cross" (Phil)
M38 "In the Secret" ("I Want to Know You") (Phil)
M30 "Knowing You" ("All I Once Held Dear") (Phil)
M32 "Holy and Anointed One" (John)
S2165 "Cry of My Heart" (John)
M39
WS3083 "We Adore You, Jesus Christ" ("*Adoremus te Christe*") (John)

### Vocal Solos

"God Will Make a Way" (with "He Leadeth Me") (Isa)
V-3 (2) p. 9
"Here I Am" (Isa, Phil)
V-11 p. 19
"O For a Thousand Tongues to Sing" (Pss, John)
V-6 p. 28
V-1 p. 32
"Jesus Revealed in Me" (Phil)
V-8 p. 347
"And Can It Be that I Should Gain" (Phil)
V-1 p. 29

### Anthems

"Deep River" (Phil)
Arr. Matthew Culloton; MorningStar MSM-50-5912
SATB *divisi, a cappella*

"The Very Thought of Thee" (Mark)
Arr. Brian L. Hanson; Choristers Guild CGA-1375
SATB with piano

### Other Suggestions

Visuals:
**O** Sand, water, horse/chariot, wick, river, animals
**P** Laughter, joy, sheaves of wheat, water, baptism
**E** Trash can with "things," baptism, cross /black drape
**G** Perfume bottle, leather bag, anointing, baptism
Greeting: BOW453 (Pss)
Opening Prayer: BOW464 (Isa, Pss)
Canticle: UM135. "Canticle of Moses and Miriam" (Isa, Pss)
Prayer of Confession: BOW480 (Phil, Luke)
Response: S2113. "Lamb of God" (Lent)
Response: S2277. "Lord, Have Mercy" (Lent)
Prayer: WSL19 (Isa)
Intercessory Prayer: BOW519. For Others (Luke)
Blessing: BOW564 (Isa, John)
For additional suggestions, consult *The Abingdon Worship Annual 2016.*

**Luke 19:28-40 (Palms)**

[28] After Jesus said this, he continued on ahead, going up to
Jerusalem.
[29] As Jesus came to Bethphage and Bethany on the Mount
of Olives, he gave two disciples a task. [30] He said, "Go into the
village over there. When you enter it, you will find tied up
there a colt that no one has ever ridden. Untie it and bring it
here. [31] If someone asks, 'Why are you untying it?' just say, 'Its
master needs it.'" [32] Those who had been sent found it exactly
as he had said.
[33] As they were untying the colt, its owners said to them,
"Why are you untying the colt?"
[34] They replied, "Its master needs it." [35] They brought it to
Jesus, threw their clothes on the colt, and lifted Jesus onto it.
[36] As Jesus rode along, they spread their clothes on the road.
[37] As Jesus approached the road leading down from the
Mount of Olives, the whole throng of his disciples began
rejoicing. They praised God with a loud voice because of all
the mighty things they had seen. [38] They said,
"Blessings on the king who comes in the name of the Lord.
Peace in heaven and glory in the highest heavens."
[39] Some of the Pharisees from the crowd said to Jesus,
"Teacher, scold your disciples! Tell them to stop!"
[40] He answered, "I tell you, if they were silent, the stones
would shout."

---

**Psalm 118:1-2, 19-29 (Palms) (UM839)**

Give thanks to the LORD because he is good,
because his faithful love lasts forever.
[2] Let Israel say it:
"God's faithful love lasts forever!"
. . . . . . . . . . . . . . . . . . . . . . . . .
[19] Open the gates of righteousness for me
so I can come in and give thanks to the LORD!
[20] This is the LORD's gate;
those who are righteous enter through it.
[21] I thank you because you answered me,
because you were my saving help.
[22] The stone rejected by the builders
is now the main foundation stone!
[23] This has happened because of the LORD;
it is astounding in our sight!
[24] This is the day the LORD acted;
we will rejoice and celebrate in it!
[25] LORD, please save us!
LORD, please let us succeed!
[26] The one who enters in the LORD's name is blessed;
we bless all of you from the LORD's house.
[27] The LORD is God!
He has shined a light on us!
So lead the festival offering with ropes
all the way to the horns of the altar.
[28] You are my God—I will give thanks to you!
You are my God—I will lift you up high!
[29] Give thanks to the LORD because he is good,
because his faithful love lasts forever.

---

**Isaiah 50:4-9a (Passion)**

[4] The LORD God gave me an educated tongue
to know how to respond to the weary
with a word that will awaken them in the morning.
God awakens my ear in the morning to listen,
as educated people do.
[5] The LORD God opened my ear;
I didn't rebel; I didn't turn my back.
[6] Instead, I gave my body to attackers,
and my cheeks to beard pluckers.
I didn't hide my face
from insults and spitting.
[7] The LORD God will help me;
therefore, I haven't been insulted.
Therefore, I set my face like flint,
and knew I wouldn't be ashamed.
[8] The one who will declare me innocent is near.
Who will argue with me?
Let's stand up together.
Who will bring judgment against me?
Let him approach me.
[9a] Look! The LORD God will help me.

---

**Psalm 31:9-16 (Passion) (UM764)**

[9] Have mercy on me, LORD, because I'm depressed.
My vision fails because of my grief,
as do my spirit and my body.
[10] My life is consumed with sadness;
my years are consumed with groaning.
Strength fails me because of my suffering;
my bones dry up.
[11] I'm a joke to all my enemies,
still worse to my neighbors.
I scare my friends,
and whoever sees me in the street runs away!
[12] I am forgotten, like I'm dead,
completely out of mind;
I am like a piece of pottery, destroyed.
[13] Yes, I've heard all the gossiping,
terror all around;
so many gang up together against me,
they plan to take my life!
[14] But me? I trust you, LORD!
I affirm, "You are my God."
[15] My future is in your hands.
Don't hand me over to my enemies,
to all who are out to get me!
[16] Shine your face on your servant;
save me by your faithful love!

---

**Philippians 2:5-11 (Passion)**

[5] Adopt the attitude that was in Christ Jesus:
[6] Though he was in the form of God,
he did not consider being equal with God something
to exploit.
[7] But he emptied himself
by taking the form of a slave
and by becoming like human beings.
When he found himself in the form of a human,
[8] he humbled himself by becoming obedient to the
point of death,
even death on a cross.
[9] Therefore, God highly honored him
and gave him a name above all names,
[10] so that at the name of Jesus everyone
in heaven, on earth, and under the earth might bow

11and every tongue confess that
Jesus Christ is Lord, to the glory of God the Father.

**Luke 22:14–23:56 or Luke 23:1-49 (Passion)**

14When the time came, Jesus took his place at the table, and the apostles joined him. 15He said to them, "I have earnestly desired to eat this Passover with you before I suffer. 16I tell you, I won't eat it until it is fulfilled in God's kingdom." 17After taking a cup and giving thanks, he said, "Take this and share it among yourselves. 18I tell you that from now on I won't drink from the fruit of the vine until God's kingdom has come." 19After taking the bread and giving thanks, he broke it and gave it to them, saying, "This is my body, which is given for you. Do this in remembrance of me." 20In the same way, he took the cup after the meal and said, "This cup is the new covenant by my blood, which is poured out for you.

21"But look! My betrayer is with me; his hand is on this table. 22The Human One goes just as it has been determined. But how terrible it is for that person who betrays him." 23They began to argue among themselves about which of them it could possibly be who would do this.

24An argument broke out among the disciples over which one of them should be regarded as the greatest.

25But Jesus said to them, "The kings of the Gentiles rule over their subjects, and those in authority over them are called 'friends of the people.' 26But that's not the way it will be with you. Instead, the greatest among you must become like a person of lower status and the leader like a servant. 27So which one is greater, the one who is seated at the table or the one who serves at the table? Isn't it the one who is seated at the table? But I am among you as one who serves.

28"You are the ones who have continued with me in my trials. 29And I confer royal power on you just as my Father granted royal power to me. 30Thus you will eat and drink at my table in my kingdom, and you will sit on thrones overseeing the twelve tribes of Israel.

31"Simon, Simon, look! Satan has asserted the right to sift you all like wheat. 32However, I have prayed for you that your faith won't fail. When you have returned, strengthen your brothers and sisters."

33Peter responded, "Lord, I'm ready to go with you, both to prison and to death!"

34Jesus replied, "I tell you, Peter, the rooster won't crow today before you have denied three times that you know me."

35Jesus said to them, "When I sent you out without a wallet, bag, or sandals, you didn't lack anything, did you?"

They said, "Nothing."

36Then he said to them, "But now, whoever has a wallet must take it, and likewise a bag. And those who don't own a sword must sell their clothes and buy one. 37I tell you that this scripture must be fulfilled in relation to me: *And he was counted among criminals.* Indeed, what's written about me is nearing completion."

38They said to him, "Lord, look, here are two swords."

He replied, "Enough of that!"

39Jesus left and made his way to the Mount of Olives, as was his custom, and the disciples followed him. 40When he arrived, he said to them, "Pray that you won't give in to temptation." 41He withdrew from them about a stone's throw, knelt down, and prayed. 42He said, "Father, if it's your will, take this cup of suffering away from me. However, not my will but your will must be done." 43Then a heavenly angel appeared to him and strengthened him. 44He was in anguish and prayed even more earnestly. His sweat became like drops of blood falling on the ground. 45When he got up from praying, he went to the disciples. He found them asleep, overcome by grief. 46He said to them, "Why are you sleeping? Get up and pray so that you won't give in to temptation."

47While Jesus was still speaking, a crowd appeared, and the one called Judas, one of the Twelve, was leading them. He approached Jesus to kiss him.

48Jesus said to him, "Judas, would you betray the Human One with a kiss?"

49When those around him recognized what was about to happen, they said, "Lord, should we fight with our swords?" 50One of them struck the high priest's servant, cutting off his right ear.

51Jesus responded, "Stop! No more of this!" He touched the slave's ear and healed him.

52Then Jesus said to the chief priests, the officers of the temple guard, and the elders who had come to get him, "Have you come with swords and clubs to arrest me, as though I were a thief? 53Day after day I was with you in the temple, but you didn't arrest me. But this is your time, when darkness rules."

54After they arrested Jesus, they led him away and brought him to the high priest's house. Peter followed from a distance. 55When they lit a fire in the middle of the courtyard and sat down together, Peter sat among them.

56Then a servant woman saw him sitting in the firelight. She stared at him and said, "This man was with him too."

57But Peter denied it, saying, "Woman, I don't know him!"

58A little while later, someone else saw him and said, "You are one of them too."

But Peter said, "Man, I'm not!"

59An hour or so later, someone else insisted, "This man must have been with him, because he is a Galilean too."

60Peter responded, "Man, I don't know what you are talking about!" At that very moment, while he was still speaking, a rooster crowed. 61The Lord turned and looked straight at Peter, and Peter remembered the Lord's words: "Before a rooster crows today, you will deny me three times." 62And Peter went out and cried uncontrollably.

63The men who were holding Jesus in custody taunted him while they beat him. 64They blindfolded him and asked him repeatedly, "Prophesy! Who hit you?" 65Insulting him, they said many other horrible things against him.

66As morning came, the elders of the people, both chief priests and legal experts, came together, and Jesus was brought before their council.

67They said, "If you are the Christ, tell us!"

He answered, "If I tell you, you won't believe. 68And if I ask you a question, you won't answer. 69But from now on, *the Human One will be seated on the right side of the power of God.*"

70They all said, "Are you God's Son, then?"

He replied, "You say that I am."

71Then they said, "Why do we need further testimony? We've heard it from his own lips."

23 The whole assembly got up and led Jesus to Pilate and 2began to accuse him. They said, "We have found this man misleading our people, opposing the payment of taxes to Caesar, and claiming that he is the Christ, a king."

3 Pilate asked him, "Are you the king of the Jews?"
Jesus replied, "That's what you say."
4 Then Pilate said to the chief priests and the crowds, "I find
no legal basis for action against this man."
5 But they objected strenuously, saying, "He agitates the
people with his teaching throughout Judea—starting from
Galilee all the way here."
6 Hearing this, Pilate asked if the man was a Galilean.
7 When he learned that Jesus was from Herod's district, Pilate
sent him to Herod, who was also in Jerusalem at that time.
8 Herod was very glad to see Jesus, for he had heard about
Jesus and had wanted to see him for quite some time. He was
hoping to see Jesus perform some sign. 9 Herod questioned
Jesus at length, but Jesus didn't respond to him. 10 The chief
priests and the legal experts were there, fiercely accusing
Jesus. 11 Herod and his soldiers treated Jesus with contempt.
Herod mocked him by dressing Jesus in elegant clothes and
sent him back to Pilate. 12 Pilate and Herod became friends
with each other that day. Before this, they had been enemies.
13 Then Pilate called together the chief priests, the rulers,
and the people. 14 He said to them, "You brought this man
before me as one who was misleading the people. I have
questioned him in your presence and found nothing in this
man's conduct that provides a legal basis for the charges you
have brought against him. 15 Neither did Herod, because
Herod returned him to us. He's done nothing that deserves
death. 16 Therefore, I'll have him whipped, then let him go."
18 But with one voice they shouted, "Away with this man!
Release Barabbas to us." (19 Barabbas had been thrown into
prison because of a riot that had occurred in the city, and for
murder.)
20 Pilate addressed them again because he wanted to release
Jesus.
21 They kept shouting out, "Crucify him! Crucify him!"
22 For the third time, Pilate said to them, "Why? What
wrong has he done? I've found no legal basis for the death
penalty in his case. Therefore, I will have him whipped, then
let him go."
23 But they were adamant, shouting their demand that Jesus
be crucified. Their voices won out. 24 Pilate issued his deci-
sion to grant their request. 25 He released the one they asked
for, who had been thrown into prison because of a riot and
murder. But he handed Jesus over to their will.
26 As they led Jesus away, they grabbed Simon, a man from
Cyrene, who was coming in from the countryside. They put
the cross on his back and made him carry it behind Jesus. 27 A
huge crowd of people followed Jesus, including women, who
were mourning and wailing for him. 28 Jesus turned to the
women and said, "Daughters of Jerusalem, don't cry for me.
Rather, cry for yourselves and your children. 29 The time will
come when they will say, 'Happy are those who are unable to
become pregnant, the wombs that never gave birth, and the
breasts that never nursed a child.' 30 Then *they will say to the
mountains, 'Fall on us,' and to the hills, 'Cover us.'* 31 If they do
these things when the tree is green, what will happen when it
is dry?"
32 They also led two other criminals to be executed with
Jesus. 33 When they arrived at the place called The Skull, they
crucified him, along with the criminals, one on his right and
the other on his left. 34 Jesus said, "Father, forgive them, for
they don't know what they're doing." They drew lots as a way
of dividing up his clothing.
35 The people were standing around watching, but the leaders sneered at him, saying, "He saved others. Let him save
himself if he really is the Christ sent from God, the chosen
one."
36 The soldiers also mocked him. They came up to him,
offering him sour wine 37 and saying, "If you really are the
king of the Jews, save yourself." 38 Above his head was a notice
of the formal charge against him. It read "This is the king of
the Jews."
39 One of the criminals hanging next to Jesus insulted him:
"Aren't you the Christ? Save yourself and us!"
40 Responding, the other criminal spoke harshly to him,
"Don't you fear God, seeing that you've also been sentenced
to die? 41 We are rightly condemned, for we are receiving the
appropriate sentence for what we did. But this man has done
nothing wrong." 42 Then he said, "Jesus, remember me when
you come into your kingdom."
43 Jesus replied, "I assure you that today you will be with me
in paradise."
44 It was now about noon, and darkness covered the whole
earth until about three o'clock, 45 while the sun stopped shining. Then the curtain in the sanctuary tore down the middle.
46 Crying out in a loud voice, Jesus said, "Father, *into your
hands I entrust my life.*" After he said this, he breathed for the
last time.
47 When the centurion saw what happened, he praised God,
saying, "It's really true: this man was righteous." 48 All the
crowds who had come together to see this event returned to
their homes beating their chests after seeing what had happened. 49 And everyone who knew him, including the women
who had followed him from Galilee, stood at a distance
observing these things.
50 Now there was a man named Joseph who was a member
of the council. He was a good and righteous man. 51 He
hadn't agreed with the plan and actions of the council. He
was from the Jewish city of Arimathea and eagerly anticipated
God's kingdom. 52 This man went to Pilate and asked for
Jesus' body. 53 Taking it down, he wrapped it in a linen cloth
and laid it in a tomb carved out of the rock, in which no one
had ever been buried. 54 It was the Preparation Day for the
Sabbath, and the Sabbath was quickly approaching. 55 The
women who had come with Jesus from Galilee followed
Joseph. They saw the tomb and how Jesus' body was laid in
it, 56 then they went away and prepared fragrant spices and
perfumed oils. They rested on the Sabbath, in keeping with
the commandment.

## Primary Hymns and Songs for the Day

278 "Hosanna, Loud Hosanna" (Palms Gospel) (O)
H-3 Hbl-16, 22, 68; Chr-101; Desc-37
S-1 #115. Harm.
2109 "Hosanna! Hosanna!" (Palms Gospel)
291 "He Never Said a Mumbalin' Word" (Isa)
286 "O Sacred Head, Now Wounded" (Passion Gospel, Comm.)
H-3 Hbl-82; Chr-148; Desc-86; Org-111
2083 "My Song Is Love Unknown" (Palms/Passion Gospels) (C)
H-3 Chr-139, 158; Desc-90; Org-126
S-1 #284-85. Desc. and harm.
280 "All Glory, Laud, and Honor" (Palms Gospel) (C)
H-3 Hbl-45; Chr-22; Desc-96; Org-144
S-1 #309-10. Harm. with desc.

## Additional Hymn Suggestions

277 "Tell Me the Stories of Jesus" (Palms Gospel)
279 "*Mantos y Palmas*" ("Filled with Excitement") (Palms Gospel)
658 "This Is the Day the Lord Hath Made" (Pss 118)
2111 "We Sang Our Glad Hosannas" (Palms/Passion Gospels)
3082 "Who Is He" (Palms/Passion Gospels)
160 "Rejoice Ye Pure in Heart" (Phil) (O)
166 "All Praise to Thee, for Thou, O King Divine" (Phil)
168 "At the Name of Jesus" (Phil)
176 "Majesty" (Phil)
SP73
193 "Jesus! the Name High over All" (Phil)
536 "Precious Name" (Phil)
2100 "Thou Didst Leave Thy Throne" (Phil, Passion Gospel)
285 "To Mock Your Reign, O Dearest Lord" (Passion Gospel)
287 "O Love Divine, What Hast Thou Done" (Passion Gospel)
292 "What Wondrous Love Is This" (Passion Gospel)
294 "Alas! and Did My Savior Bleed" (Passion Gospel)
371 "I Stand Amazed in the Presence" (Passion Gospel)
527 "Do, Lord, Remember Me" (Passion Gospel)
581 "Lord, Whose Love Through Humble Service" (Passion Gospel)
614 "For the Bread Which You Have Broken" (Passion Gospel)
633 "The Bread of Life for All Is Broken" (Passion Gospel)
2106 "When Jesus Wept" (Passion Gospel)
2110 "Why Has God Forsaken Me?" (Passion Gospel)
2138 "Sunday's Palms Are Wednesday's Ashes" (Palms/Passion Gospels)
2209 "How Long, O Lord" (Passion Gospel)
2254 "In Remembrance of Me" (Passion Gospel, Comm.)
2263 "Broken for Me" (Passion Gospel, Comm.)
2261 "Life-Giving Bread" (Passion Gospel, Comm.)
3075 "Glory in the Cross" (Passion Gospel)

## Additional Contemporary Suggestions

WS3023 "Forever" (Ps 118)
M68
WS3078 "Hosanna" (Ps 118, Palms Gospel)
WS3079 "Hosanna" (Palms, Passion Gospels)
S2270 "I Will Enter His Gates" (Ps 118)
SP168
S2069 "All Hail King Jesus" (Palms Gospel)
SP63
S2075 "King of Kings" (Palms Gospel)
SP94
S2091 "The King of Glory Comes" (Palms Gospel)
S2109 "Hosanna! Hosanna!" (Palms Gospel)
S2154 "Please Enter My Heart, Hosanna" (Palms Gospel)
WS3008 "Open the Eyes of My Heart" (Isa)
M57
M243 "Beautiful Savior" (Ps 31, Passion Gospel)
S2023 "How Majestic Is Your Name" (Phil)
SP14
S2070 "He Is Exalted" (Phil)
SP66
S2071 "Jesus, Name Above All Names" (Phil)
SP76
WS3176 "Come, Now Is the Time to Worship" (Phil)
M56
M111 "The Heavens Shall Declare" (Phil, Palms Gospel)
M253 "Jesus Messiah" (Phil, Passion Gospel, Comm.)
M225 "At the Cross" (Phil, Passion Gospel)
S2113 "Lamb of God" (Passion Gospel)
UM628 "Eat This Bread" (Passion Gospel, Comm.)
UM640 "Take Our Bread" (Passion Gospel, Comm.)
M77 "Above All" (Passion Gospel)
V-3 (2) p. 17 Vocal Solo
WS3085 "The Power of the Cross" (Passion Gospel, Holy Week)
M222

## Vocal Solos

"Ride On, Ride On in Majesty!" (Palms Gospel)
V-5(2) p. 57
"Ride On, Jesus" (Palms Gospel)
V-7 p. 8
"The Shepherd Became a Lamb" (Palms/Passion Gospels)
V-10 p. 48

## Anthems

"Look Who's Coming" (Palms Gospel)
Michael Bedford; Choristers Guild CGA-1358
Unison with piano and opt. trumpet

"Hosanna! Blessed Is He! (Palms Gospel)
Arr. Hal H. Hopson; Choristers Guild CGA-1360
SATB and Unison choir with keyboard

## Other Suggestions

Visuals:

| | |
|---|---|
| **Palms G** | Palms, cloaks, colt, crowd, Jesus, stones |
| **Ps 118** | Gates, cornerstone, joy, light |
| **O** | Teacher, morning, cheek/beard, spitting, |
| **Ps 31** | Grief, starvation, broken jar, whispering |
| **E** | Jesus, manacles, Crucifixion, knees bent |
| **Passion G** | Rooster, 2 swords, pray, kiss, robe, whip |

Introit: WS3077. "Blessed Is He Who Comes in God's Name" (Palms Gospel)
Greeting: BOW330 (Luke)
Call to Worship: WSL21 (Palms Gospel)
Canticle: UM167. "Canticle of Christ's Obedience" (Phil)
Prayer of Confession: BOW484 (Luke)
Response: S2277. "Lord, Have Mercy" (Lent)
Affirmation of Faith: WSL76 (Phil, Passion Gospel)
Prayer: UM283 or UM403 (Passion Gospel)
Prayer: BOW335, BOW348-349, or BOW550 (Phil, Luke)
Intercessory Prayer: WSL26 (Luke 23)
Response: UM488. "Jesus, Remember Me" (Passion Gospel)
Offertory Prayer: WSL153 (Palms Gospel, Pss 118)
Blessing: BOW560 (Pss 31)
Blessing: WSL27 (Luke, Holy Week)

**Exodus 12:1-4 (5-10) 11-14**

The Lord said to Moses and Aaron in the land of Egypt, 2 "This month will be the first month; it will be the first month of the year for you. 3 Tell the whole Israelite community: On the tenth day of this month they must take a lamb for each household, a lamb per house. 4 If a household is too small for a lamb, it should share one with a neighbor nearby. You should divide the lamb in proportion to the number of people who will be eating it. 5 Your lamb should be a flawless year-old male. You may take it from the sheep or from the goats. 6 You should keep close watch over it until the fourteenth day of this month. At twilight on that day, the whole assembled Israelite community should slaughter their lambs. 7 They should take some of the blood and smear it on the two doorposts and on the beam over the door of the houses in which they are eating. 8 That same night they should eat the meat roasted over the fire. They should eat it along with unleavened bread and bitter herbs. 9 Don't eat any of it raw or boiled in water, but roasted over fire with its head, legs, and internal organs. 10 Don't let any of it remain until morning, and burn any of it left over in the morning. 11 This is how you should eat it. You should be dressed, with your sandals on your feet and your walking stick in your hand. You should eat the meal in a hurry. It is the Passover of the Lord. 12 I'll pass through the land of Egypt that night, and I'll strike down every oldest child in the land of Egypt, both humans and animals. I'll impose judgments on all the gods of Egypt. I am the Lord. 13 The blood will be your sign on the houses where you live. Whenever I see the blood, I'll pass over you. No plague will destroy you when I strike the land of Egypt.

14 "This day will be a day of remembering for you. You will observe it as a festival to the Lord. You will observe it in every generation as a regulation for all time.

**Psalm 116:1-4, 12-19 (UM116)**

I love the Lord because he hears
  my requests for mercy.
2 I'll call out to him as long as I live,
  because he listens closely to me.
3 Death's ropes bound me;
  the distress of the grave found me—
  I came face-to-face with trouble and grief.
4 So I called on the Lord's name:
  "Lord, please save me!"

. . . . . . . . . . . . . . . . . . . . . . . . . .

12 What can I give back to the Lord
  for all the good things he has done for me?
13 I'll lift up the cup of salvation.
  I'll call on the Lord's name.
14 I'll keep the promises I made to the Lord
  in the presence of all God's people.
15 The death of the Lord's faithful
  is a costly loss in his eyes.
16 Oh yes, Lord, I am definitely your servant!
  I am your servant and the son of your female servant—
  you've freed me from my chains.
17 So I'll offer a sacrifice of thanksgiving to you,
  and I'll call on the Lord's name.
18 I'll keep the promises I made to the Lord
  in the presence of all God's people,
19 in the courtyards of the Lord's house,
  which is in the center of Jerusalem.
Praise the Lord!

**1 Corinthians 11:23-26**

23 I received a tradition from the Lord, which I also handed on to you: on the night on which he was betrayed, the Lord Jesus took bread. 24 After giving thanks, he broke it and said, "This is my body, which is for you; do this to remember me." 25 He did the same thing with the cup, after they had eaten, saying, "This cup is the new covenant in my blood. Every time you drink it, do this to remember me." 26 Every time you eat this bread and drink this cup, you broadcast the death of the Lord until he comes.

**John 13:1-17, 31b-35**

Before the Festival of Passover, Jesus knew that his time had come to leave this world and go to the Father. Having loved his own who were in the world, he loved them fully.

2 Jesus and his disciples were sharing the evening meal. The devil had already provoked Judas, Simon Iscariot's son, to betray Jesus. 3 Jesus knew the Father had given everything into his hands and that he had come from God and was returning to God. 4 So he got up from the table and took off his robes. Picking up a linen towel, he tied it around his waist. 5 Then he poured water into a washbasin and began to wash the disciples' feet, drying them with the towel he was wearing. 6 When Jesus came to Simon Peter, Peter said to him, "Lord, are you going to wash my feet?"

7 Jesus replied, "You don't understand what I'm doing now, but you will understand later."

8 "No!" Peter said. "You will never wash my feet!"

Jesus replied, "Unless I wash you, you won't have a place with me."

9 Simon Peter said, "Lord, not only my feet but also my hands and my head!"

10 Jesus responded, "Those who have bathed need only to have their feet washed, because they are completely clean. You disciples are clean, but not every one of you." 11 He knew who would betray him. That's why he said, "Not every one of you is clean."

12 After he washed the disciples' feet, he put on his robes and returned to his place at the table. He said to them, "Do you know what I've done for you? 13 You call me 'Teacher' and 'Lord,' and you speak correctly, because I am. 14 If I, your Lord and teacher, have washed your feet, you too must wash each other's feet. 15 I have given you an example: Just as I have done, you also must do. 16 I assure you, servants aren't greater than their master, nor are those who are sent greater than the one who sent them. 17 Since you know these things, you will be happy if you do them." . . .

31b "Now the Human One has been glorified, and God has been glorified in him. 32 If God has been glorified in him, God will also glorify the Human One in himself and will glorify him immediately. 33 Little children, I'm with you for a little while longer. You will look for me—but, just as I told the Jewish leaders, I also tell you now—'Where I'm going, you can't come.'

34 "I give you a new commandment: Love each other. Just as I have loved you, so you also must love each other. 35 This is how everyone will know that you are my disciples, when you love each other."

**Primary Hymns and Songs for the Day**

579 "Lord God, Your Love Has Called Us Here" (John) (O)
S-1 #57-61. Various treatments
623 "Here, O My Lord, I See Thee" (Exod, Comm.)
S-1 #265. Desc.
432 "*Jesu, Jesu*" (John, footwashing)
H-3 Chr-114; Org-19
S-1 #63. Vocal part
2254 "In Remembrance of Me" (1 Cor, Comm.)
289 "Ah, Holy Jesus" (John) (C)
H-3 Chr-20; Desc-51
S-2 #81-85. Harms.
#86. Instrumental desc.
292 "What Wondrous Love Is This" (John) (C)
H-3 Hbl-102; Chr-212; Org-185
S-1 #347. Harm.

**Additional Hymn Suggestions**

2246 "Deep in the Shadows of the Past" (Exod)
2060 "God the Sculptor of the Mountains" (Exod)
506 "Wellspring of Wisdom" (Exod)
425 "O Crucified Redeemer" (Exod, 1 Cor, Comm.)
614 "For the Bread Which You Have Broken" (1 Cor, Comm.)
615 "For the Bread Which You Have Broken" (1 Cor, Comm.)
618 "Let Us Break Bread Together" (1 Cor, Comm.)
632 "Draw Us in the Spirit's Tether" (1 Cor, Comm.)
633 "The Bread of Life for All Is Broken" (1 Cor, Comm.)
635 "Because Thou Hast Said" (1 Cor, Comm.)
2050 "Mothering God, You Gave Me Birth" (1 Cor, Comm.)
2213 "Healer of Our Every Ill" (John)
2255 "In the Singing" (1 Cor, Comm.)
2263 "Broken for Me" (1 Cor, Comm.)
2269 "Come, Share the Lord" (1 Cor, Comm.)
190 "Who Is He in Yonder Stall" (John)
273 "Jesus' Hands Were Kind Hands" (John)
288 "Were You There" (John)
517 "By Gracious Powers" (John)
2111 "We Sang Our Glad Hosannas" (John, Holy Thursday)
2177 "Wounded World that Cries for Healing" (John)
2187 "Now It Is Evening" (John, Comm.)
2260 "Let Us Be Bread" (John, Comm.)
2268 "As We Gather at Your Table" (John, Comm.)
3074 "Jesus Is a Rock in a Weary Land" (John, Lent)

**Additional Contemporary Suggestions**

S2031 "We Bring the Sacrifice of Praise" (Pss)
SP1
S2002 "I Will Call Upon the Lord" (Pss)
SP224
S2068 "I Love You, Lord" (Pss)
SP72
M224 "Because of Your Love" (Pss)
M243 "Beautiful Savior" (Pss, Holy Week)
M252 "God with Us" (Pss)
M79 "I Stand Amazed" (Pss)
UM628 "Eat This Bread" (1 Cor, Comm.)
UM640 "Take Our Bread" (1 Cor, Comm.)
M253 "Jesus Messiah" (1 Cor, Comm.)
S2266 "Here Is Bread, Here Is Wine" (1 Cor, Comm.)
S2176 "Make Me a Servant" (John)
SP193
S2224 "Make Us One" (John)
SP137
S2223 "They'll Know We Are Christians" (John)
S2179 "Live in Charity" ("*Ubi Caritas*") (John)
S2226 "Bind Us Together" (John)
SP140

**Vocal Solos**

"King of Glory, King of Peace" (Pss, Lent)
V-9 p. 24
"In Remembrance" (John, Comm.)
V-5(2) p. 7
"He Breaks the Bread, He Pours the Wine" (John, Comm.)
V-10 p. 43

**Anthems**

"The Savior Prays Alone" (John)
Ken Medema; Alfred 42524
SATB with keyboard

"Ah, Holy Jesus" (John)
Arr. John Ferguson; Augsburg 11-10572
SATB with organ

**Other Suggestions**

Visuals:
**O** Lamb/blood/doorpost, sandals, staff, Exod 12:14
**P** Ear, snare, cup, open shackles, Pss 116:4b, 12, 13, or 15
**E** Broken loaf, cup, 1 Cor 11:24b or 25b
**G** Robe, towel/basin, footwashing, disciples, love
Suggested Service of Worship: BOW351 or BOW354
Greeting: BOW343 (John)
Call to Prayer: S2198. "Stay with Me" (Holy Thursday)
Prayer: BOW352. Confession and Pardon (Holy Thursday)
Prayer: UM283 or BOW349 (Holy Thursday, 2 Cor)
Response: S2275. "*Kyrie*" (Lent, Communion)
Offertory Prayer: WSL154 (John)
Call to Communion: S2265. "Time Now to Gather" (1 Cor)
Great Thanksgiving for Holy Thursday: BOW, pp. 64-65
Closing Prayer: WSL27 (John)
Dismissal with Blessing: BOW354 (Phil)
For additional suggestions, consult previous planners and *The Abingdon Worship Annual 2016*.

**Isaiah 52:13–53:12**

13 Look, my servant will succeed.
He will be exalted and lifted very high.
14 Just as many were appalled by you,
he too appeared disfigured, inhuman,
his appearance unlike that of mortals.
15 But he will astonish many nations.
Kings will be silenced because of him,
because they will see what they haven't seen before;
what they haven't heard before, they will ponder.
**53** Who can believe what we have heard,
and for whose sake has the LORD's arm been revealed?
2 He grew up like a young plant before us,
like a root from dry ground.
He possessed no splendid form for us to see,
no desirable appearance.
3 He was despised and avoided by others;
a man who suffered, who knew sickness well.
Like someone from whom people hid their faces,
he was despised, and we didn't think about him.
4 It was certainly our sickness that he carried,
and our sufferings that he bore,
but we thought him afflicted,
struck down by God and tormented.
5 He was pierced because of our rebellions
and crushed because of our crimes.
He bore the punishment that made us whole;
by his wounds we are healed.
6 Like sheep we had all wandered away,
each going its own way,
but the LORD let fall on him all our crimes.
7 He was oppressed and tormented,
but didn't open his mouth.
Like a lamb being brought to slaughter,
like a ewe silent before her shearers,
he didn't open his mouth.
8 Due to an unjust ruling he was taken away,
and his fate—who will think about it?
He was eliminated from the land of the living,
struck dead because of my people's rebellion.
9 His grave was among the wicked,
his tomb with evildoers,
though he had done no violence,
and had spoken nothing false.
10 But the LORD wanted to crush him
and to make him suffer.
If his life is offered as restitution,
he will see his offspring; he will enjoy long life.
The LORD's plans will come to fruition through him.
11 After his deep anguish he will see light, and he will be satisfied.
Through his knowledge, the righteous one, my servant,
will make many righteous,
and will bear their guilt.
12 Therefore, I will give him a share with the great,
and he will divide the spoil with the strong,
in return for exposing his life to death
and being numbered with rebels,
though he carried the sin of many
and pleaded on behalf of those who rebelled.

**Psalm 22 (UM752)**

My God! My God,
why have you left me all alone?
Why are you so far from saving me—
so far from my anguished groans?
2 My God, I cry out during the day,
but you don't answer;
even at nighttime I don't stop.
3 You are the holy one, enthroned.
You are Israel's praise.
4 Our ancestors trusted you—
they trusted you and you rescued them;
5 they cried out to you and they were saved;
they trusted you and they weren't ashamed.
6 But I'm just a worm, less than human;
insulted by one person, despised by another.
7 All who see me make fun of me—
they gape, shaking their heads:
8 "He committed himself to the LORD,
so let God rescue him;
let God deliver him
because God likes him so much."
9 But you are the one who pulled me from the womb,
placing me safely at my mother's breasts.
10 I was thrown on you from birth;
you've been my God
since I was in my mother's womb.
11 Please don't be far from me,
because trouble is near
and there's no one to help.
12 Many bulls surround me;
mighty bulls from Bashan encircle me.
13 They open their mouths at me
like a lion ripping and roaring!
14 I'm poured out like water.
All my bones have fallen apart.
My heart is like wax;
it melts inside me.
15 My strength is dried up
like a piece of broken pottery.
My tongue sticks to the roof of my mouth;
you've set me down in the dirt of death.
16 Dogs surround me;
a pack of evil people circle me like a lion—
oh, my poor hands and feet!
17 I can count all my bones!
Meanwhile, they just stare at me, watching me.
18 They divvy up my garments among themselves;
they cast lots for my clothes.
19 But you, LORD! Don't be far away!
You are my strength!
Come quick and help me!
20 Deliver me from the sword.
Deliver my life from the power of the dog.
21 Save me from the mouth of the lion.
From the horns of the wild oxen
you have answered me!
22 I will declare your name to my brothers and sisters;
I will praise you in the very center of the congregation!
23 All of you who revere the LORD—praise him!
All of you who are Jacob's descendants—honor him!
All of you who are all Israel's offspring—
stand in awe of him!
24 Because he didn't despise or detest
the suffering of the one who suffered—

he didn't hide his face from me.
No, he listened when I cried out to him for help.
25 I offer praise in the great congregation
because of you;
I will fulfill my promises
in the presence of those who honor God.
26 Let all those who are suffering eat and be full!
Let all who seek the LORD praise him!
I pray your hearts live forever!
27 Every part of the earth
will remember and come back to the LORD;
every family among all the nations will worship you.
28 Because the right to rule belongs to the LORD,
he rules all nations.
29 Indeed, all the earth's powerful
will worship him;
all who are descending to the dust
will kneel before him;
my being also lives for him.
30 Future descendants will serve him;
generations to come will be told about my LORD.
31 They will proclaim God's righteousness
to those not yet born,
telling them what God has done.

---

**Hebrews 10:16-25**

16 *This is the covenant that I will make with them.*
*After these days, says the Lord,*
*I will place my laws in their hearts*
*and write them on their minds.*
17 *And I won't remember their sins*
*and their lawless behavior anymore.*
18 When there is forgiveness for these things, there is no
longer an offering for sin.
19 Brothers and sisters, we have confidence that we can
enter the holy of holies by means of Jesus' blood, 20 through
a new and living way that he opened up for us through the
curtain, which is his body, 21 and we have a great high priest
over God's house.
22 Therefore, let's draw near with a genuine heart with
the certainty that our faith gives us, since our hearts are
sprinkled clean from an evil conscience and our bodies are
washed with pure water.
23 Let's hold on to the confession of our hope without
wavering, because the one who made the promises is reliable.
24 And let us consider each other carefully for the purpose
of sparking love and good deeds. 25 Don't stop meeting
together with other believers, which some people have got-
ten into the habit of doing. Instead, encourage each other,
especially as you see the day drawing near.

---

**John 18:1–19:42**

After he said these things, Jesus went out with his disciples
and crossed over to the other side of the Kidron Valley. He
and his disciples entered a garden there. 2 Judas, his betrayer,
also knew the place because Jesus often gathered there with
his disciples. 3 Judas brought a company of soldiers and some
guards from the chief priests and Pharisees. They came there
carrying lanterns, torches, and weapons. 4 Jesus knew everything that was to happen to him, so he went out and asked,
"Who are you looking for?"
5 They answered, "Jesus the Nazarene."
He said to them, "I Am." (Judas, his betrayer, was standing
with them.) 6 When he said, "I Am," they shrank back and fell to
the ground. 7 He asked them again, "Who are you looking for?"
They said, "Jesus the Nazarene."
8 Jesus answered, "I told you, 'I Am.' If you are looking for
me, then let these people go." 9 This was so that the word he
had spoken might be fulfilled: "I didn't lose anyone of those
whom you gave me."
10 Then Simon Peter, who had a sword, drew it and struck
the high priest's servant, cutting off his right ear. (The servant's name was Malchus.) 11 Jesus told Peter, "Put your sword
away! Am I not to drink the cup the Father has given me?"
12 Then the company of soldiers, the commander, and the
guards from the Jewish leaders took Jesus into custody. They
bound him 13 and led him first to Annas. He was the father-in-
law of Caiaphas, the high priest that year. (14 Caiaphas was the
one who had advised the Jewish leaders that it was better for
one person to die for the people.)
15 Simon Peter and another disciple followed Jesus. Because
this other disciple was known to the high priest, he went
with Jesus into the high priest's courtyard. 16 However, Peter
stood outside near the gate. Then the other disciple (the one
known to the high priest) came out and spoke to the woman
stationed at the gate, and she brought Peter in. 17 The servant
woman stationed at the gate asked Peter, "Aren't you one of
this man's disciples?"
"I'm not," he replied. 18 The servants and the guards had
made a fire because it was cold. They were standing around
it, warming themselves. Peter joined them there, standing by
the fire and warming himself.
19 Meanwhile, the chief priest questioned Jesus about his
disciples and his teaching. 20 Jesus answered, "I've spoken
openly to the world. I've always taught in synagogues and in
the temple, where all the Jews gather. I've said nothing in private. 21 Why ask me? Ask those who heard what I told them.
They know what I said."
22 After Jesus spoke, one of the guards standing there
slapped Jesus in the face. "Is that how you would answer the
high priest?" he asked.
23 Jesus replied, "If I speak wrongly, testify about what was
wrong. But if I speak correctly, why do you strike me?"
24 Then Annas sent him, bound, to Caiaphas the high priest.
25 Meanwhile, Simon Peter was still standing with the
guards, warming himself. They asked, "Aren't you one of his
disciples?"
Peter denied it, saying, "I'm not."
26 A servant of the high priest, a relative of the one whose
ear Peter had cut off, said to him, "Didn't I see you in the
garden with him?" 27 Peter denied it again, and immediately a
rooster crowed.
28 The Jewish leaders led Jesus from Caiaphas to the Roman
governor's palace. It was early in the morning. So that they
could eat the Passover, the Jewish leaders wouldn't enter the
palace; entering the palace would have made them ritually
impure.
29 So Pilate went out to them and asked, "What charge do
you bring against this man?"
30 They answered, "If he had done nothing wrong, we
wouldn't have handed him over to you."
31 Pilate responded, "Take him yourselves and judge him
according to your Law."
The Jewish leaders replied, "The Law doesn't allow us to

kill anyone." (32 This was so that Jesus' word might be fulfilled when he indicated how he was going to die.)

33 Pilate went back into the palace. He summoned Jesus and asked, "Are you the king of the Jews?"

34 Jesus answered, "Do you say this on your own or have others spoken to you about me?"

35 Pilate responded, "I'm not a Jew, am I? Your nation and its chief priests handed you over to me. What have you done?"

36 Jesus replied, "My kingdom doesn't originate from this world. If it did, my guards would fight so that I wouldn't have been arrested by the Jewish leaders. My kingdom isn't from here."

37 "So you are a king?" Pilate said.

Jesus answered, "You say that I am a king. I was born and came into the world for this reason: to testify to the truth. Whoever accepts the truth listens to my voice."

38 "What is truth?" Pilate asked.

After Pilate said this, he returned to the Jewish leaders and said, "I find no grounds for any charge against him. 39 You have a custom that I release one prisoner for you at Passover. Do you want me to release for you the king of the Jews?"

40 They shouted, "Not this man! Give us Barabbas!" (Barabbas was an outlaw.)

19 Then Pilate had Jesus taken and whipped. 2 The soldiers twisted together a crown of thorns and put it on his head, and dressed him in a purple robe. 3 Over and over they went up to him and said, "Greetings, king of the Jews!" And they slapped him in the face.

4 Pilate came out of the palace again and said to the Jewish leaders, "Look! I'm bringing him out to you to let you know that I find no grounds for a charge against him." 5 When Jesus came out, wearing the crown of thorns and the purple robe, Pilate said to them, "Here's the man."

6 When the chief priests and their deputies saw him, they shouted out, "Crucify, crucify!"

Pilate told them, "You take him and crucify him. I don't find any grounds for a charge against him."

7 The Jewish leaders replied, "We have a Law, and according to this Law he ought to die because he made himself out to be God's Son."

8 When Pilate heard this word, he was even more afraid. 9 He went back into the residence and spoke to Jesus, "Where are you from?" Jesus didn't answer. 10 So Pilate said, "You won't speak to me? Don't you know that I have authority to release you and also to crucify you?"

11 Jesus replied, "You would have no authority over me if it had not been given to you from above. That's why the one who handed me over to you has the greater sin." 12 From that moment on, Pilate wanted to release Jesus.

However, the Jewish leaders cried out, saying, "If you release this man, you aren't a friend of the emperor! Anyone who makes himself out to be a king opposes the emperor!"

13 When Pilate heard these words, he led Jesus out and seated him on the judge's bench at the place called Stone Pavement (in Aramaic, *Gabbatha*). 14 It was about noon on the Preparation Day for the Passover. Pilate said to the Jewish leaders, "Here's your king."

15 The Jewish leaders cried out, "Take him away! Take him away! Crucify him!"

Pilate responded, "What? Do you want me to crucify your king?"

"We have no king except the emperor," the chief priests answered. 16 Then Pilate handed Jesus over to be crucified.

The soldiers took Jesus prisoner. 17 Carrying his cross by himself, he went out to a place called Skull Place (in Aramaic, *Golgotha*). 18 That's where they crucified him—and two others with him, one on each side and Jesus in the middle. 19 Pilate had a public notice written and posted on the cross. It read "Jesus the Nazarene, the king of the Jews." 20 Many of the Jews read this sign, for the place where Jesus was crucified was near the city and it was written in Aramaic, Latin, and Greek. 21 Therefore, the Jewish chief priests complained to Pilate, "Don't write, 'The king of the Jews' but 'This man said, "I am the king of the Jews."'"

22 Pilate answered, "What I've written, I've written."

23 When the soldiers crucified Jesus, they took his clothes and his sandals, and divided them into four shares, one for each soldier. His shirt was seamless, woven as one piece from the top to the bottom. 24 They said to each other, "Let's not tear it. Let's cast lots to see who will get it." This was to fulfill the scripture,

*They divided my clothes among themselves,*
*and they cast lots for my clothing.*

That's what the soldiers did.

25 Jesus' mother and his mother's sister, Mary the wife of Clopas, and Mary Magdalene stood near the cross. 26 When Jesus saw his mother and the disciple whom he loved standing nearby, he said to his mother, "Woman, here is your son." 27 Then he said to the disciple, "Here is your mother." And from that time on, this disciple took her into his home.

28 After this, knowing that everything was already completed, in order to fulfill the scripture, Jesus said, "I am thirsty." 29 A jar full of sour wine was nearby, so the soldiers soaked a sponge in it, placed it on a hyssop branch, and held it up to his lips. 30 When he had received the sour wine, Jesus said, "It is completed." Bowing his head, he gave up his life.

31 It was the Preparation Day and the Jewish leaders didn't want the bodies to remain on the cross on the Sabbath, especially since that Sabbath was an important day. So they asked Pilate to have the legs of those crucified broken and the bodies taken down. 32 Therefore, the soldiers came and broke the legs of the two men who were crucified with Jesus. 33 When they came to Jesus, they saw that he was already dead so they didn't break his legs. 34 However, one of the soldiers pierced his side with a spear, and immediately blood and water came out. 35 The one who saw this has testified, and his testimony is true. He knows that he speaks the truth, and he has testified so that you also can believe. 36 These things happened to fulfill the scripture, *They won't break any of his bones.* 37 And another scripture says, *They will look at him whom they have pierced.*

38 After this Joseph of Arimathea asked Pilate if he could take away the body of Jesus. Joseph was a disciple of Jesus, but a secret one because he feared the Jewish authorities. Pilate gave him permission, so he came and took the body away. 39 Nicodemus, the one who at first had come to Jesus at night, was there too. He brought a mixture of myrrh and aloe, nearly seventy-five pounds in all. 40 Following Jewish burial customs, they took Jesus' body and wrapped it, with the spices, in linen cloths. 41 There was a garden in the place where Jesus was crucified, and in the garden was a new tomb in which no one had ever been laid. 42 Because it was the Jewish Preparation Day and the tomb was nearby, they laid Jesus in it.

**Primary Hymns and Songs for the Day**

289 "Ah, Holy Jesus" (John) (O)
H-3 Chr-20; Desc-51
S-2 #81-85. Harms.
#86. Instrumental desc.

290 "Go to Dark Gethsemane" (John) (O)
H-3 Hbl-18; Chr-74; Desc-89; Org-121
S-2 #150. Harm.

294 "Alas! and Did My Savior Bleed" (Isa, John)
H-3 Chr-21

359 "Alas! and Did My Savior Bleed" (Isa, John)

2180 "Why Stand So Far Away, My God?" (Pss)
H-3 Chr-139, 145; Desc-77
S-1 #241-42. Orff arr. and desc.

288 "Were You There" (John)

287 "O Love Divine, What Hast Thou Done" (John) (C)

**Additional Hymn Suggestions**

165 "Hallelujah! What a Savior" (Isa)
291 "He Never Said a Mumbalin' Word" (Isa)
520 "Nobody Knows the Trouble I See" (Pss)
2209 "How Long, O Lord" (Pss, Good Friday)
2267 "Taste and See" (Pss, Comm.)
419 "I Am Thine, O Lord" (Heb)
472 "Near to the Heart of God" (Heb)
2140 "Since Jesus Came into My Heart" (Heb)
2259 "Victim Divine" (Heb, John)
190 "Who Is He in Yonder Stall" (John)
267 "O Love, How Deep" (John)
274 "Woman in the Night" (John)
282 "'Tis Finished! The Messiah Dies" (John)
285 "To Mock Your Reign, O Dearest Lord" (John)
286 "O Sacred Head, Now Wounded" (John)
295 "In the Cross of Christ I Glory" (John)
298 "When I Survey the Wondrous Cross" (John)
363 "And Can It Be that I Should Gain" (John)
470 "My God, I Love Thee" (John)
633 "The Bread of Life for All Is Broken" (John, Comm.)
2083 "My Song Is Love Unknown" (Good Friday)
2100 "Thou Didst Leave Thy Throne" (John)
2102 "Swiftly Pass the Clouds of Glory" (John)
2106 "When Jesus Wept" (John)
2110 "Why Has God Forsaken Me?" (Good Friday)
2111 "We Sang Our Glad Hosannas" (John, Good Friday)
2149 "Living for Jesus" (John)
2263 "Broken for Me" (Good Friday, Comm.)
3080 "Lord, Is It I?" (John, Good Friday)
3084 "O Christ, You Hang upon a Cross" (John, Good Friday)

**Additional Contemporary Suggestions**

WS3081 "Now Behold the Lamb" (Isa, Good Friday)
WS3085 "The Power of the Cross" (Isa, John, Good Friday)
M222
M225 "At the Cross" (Isa, Good Friday)
M239 "Wholly Yours" (Isa)
M247 "The Stand" (Isa, John)
SP64 "Our God Reigns" (Isa)
M224 "Because of Your Love" (Heb)
M251 "Grace Like Rain" (Heb)
UM488 "Jesus, Remember Me" (John)
M24 "Jesus, We Crown You with Praise" (John, Good Friday)
M77 "Above All" (John, Good Friday)
V-3 (2) p. 17 Vocal Solo
M76 "The Wonderful Cross" (John, Good Friday)
S2198 "Stay with Me" ("*Nohu pu*") (Good Friday)
SP111 "There Is a Redeemer" (Good Friday)
M81 "Amazing Love" (Good Friday)
M274 "Revelation Song" (Good Friday)
M277 "How Great Is the Love" (Good Friday)
M278 "Jesus Died My Soul to Save" (John, Good Friday)

**Vocal Solos**

"He Was Cut Off Out of the Land of the Living" (recitative) (Isa)
"But Thou Didst Not Leave His Soul in Hell" (aria) (John)
V-2
"Steal Away to Heaven" (Pss, Good Friday)
V-3 (1) p. 17
"Lamb of God" (John, Good Friday)
V-5(2) p. 5
"Were You There?" (John, Good Friday)
V-7 p. 60
"I Wonder Why" (John, Good Friday)
V-8 p. 236
"O Love Divine, What Hast Thou Done!" (John)
V-1 p. 17
"Ah, Holy Jesus" (John)
V-6 p. 24

**Anthems**

"O Sorrow Deep" (John)
Robert W. Lehman; Paraclete Press PPM01310
SSATBB *a cappella*

"The Power of the Cross" (John)
Arr. Patti Drennan; Alfred 42522
SATB with piano and opt. oboe

**Other Suggestions**

Visuals:
**Gd. Fri.** Cross draped in black, altar stripped
**O** Crucifixion, root, Isa 53:3, lamb, shears, grave, light
**P** Worm, mocking, nursing child, spilled water, melted wax, dice
**E** Open Bible, heart, Crucifixion, water, Heb 10:23a
**G** Torch, sword, fire, cock crowing, robe, INRI, wine, branch, spear, linen cloth, tomb

Worship Service Ideas: BOW362, BOW365, or BOW366
Greeting: BOW329 (Heb)
Call to Worship: WSL22 (Isa, John)
Opening Prayer: WSL25 (John, Good Friday)
Prayer of Confession: WSL24 (John, Good Friday)
Sung Prayer: S2275. "*Kyrie*" (Lent, Communion)
Response: S2113. "Lamb of God" (Good Friday)
Response: S2277. "Lord, Have Mercy" (Good Friday)
Offertory Prayer: WSL155 (John)
Blessing: WSL27 (Good Friday)

**Acts 10:34-43**

34 Peter said, "I really am learning that God doesn't show
partiality to one group of people over another. 35 Rather, in
every nation, whoever worships him and does what is right
is acceptable to him. 36 This is the message of peace he sent
to the Israelites by proclaiming the good news through
Jesus Christ: He is Lord of all! 37 You know what happened
throughout Judea, beginning in Galilee after the baptism John
preached. 38 You know about Jesus of Nazareth, whom God
anointed with the Holy Spirit and endowed with power. Jesus
traveled around doing good and healing everyone oppressed
by the devil because God was with him. 39 We are witnesses of
everything he did, both in Judea and in Jerusalem. They killed
him by hanging him on a tree, 40 but God raised him up on the
third day and allowed him to be seen, 41 not by everyone but
by us. We are witnesses whom God chose beforehand, who ate
and drank with him after God raised him from the dead. 42 He
commanded us to preach to the people and to testify that he
is the one whom God appointed as judge of the living and the
dead. 43 All the prophets testify about him that everyone who
believes in him receives forgiveness of sins through his name."

**Psalm 118:1-2, 14-24 (UM839)**

Give thanks to the LORD because he is good,<br>
    because his faithful love lasts forever.<br>
2 Let Israel say it:<br>
    "God's faithful love lasts forever!"

. . . . . . . . . . . . . . . . . . . . . . . . .

14 The LORD was my strength and protection;<br>
    he was my saving help!<br>
15 The sounds of joyful songs and deliverance<br>
    are heard in the tents of the righteous:<br>
    "The LORD's strong hand is victorious!<br>
16 The LORD's strong hand is ready to strike!<br>
    The LORD's strong hand is victorious!"<br>
17 I won't die—no, I will live<br>
    and declare what the LORD has done.<br>
18 Yes, the LORD definitely disciplined me,<br>
    but he didn't hand me over to death.<br>
19 Open the gates of righteousness for me<br>
    so I can come in and give thanks to the LORD!<br>
20 This is the LORD's gate;<br>
    those who are righteous enter through it.<br>
21 I thank you because you answered me,<br>
    because you were my saving help.<br>
22 The stone rejected by the builders<br>
    is now the main foundation stone!<br>
23 This has happened because of the LORD;<br>
    it is astounding in our sight!<br>
24 This is the day the LORD acted;<br>
    we will rejoice and celebrate in it!

**1 Corinthians 15:19-26**

19 If we have a hope in Christ only in this life, then we
deserve to be pitied more than anyone else.

20 But in fact Christ has been raised from the dead. He's
the first crop of the harvest of those who have died. 21 Since
death came through a human being, the resurrection of the
dead came through one too. 22 In the same way that everyone
dies in Adam, so also everyone will be given life in Christ.
23 Each event will happen in the right order: Christ, the first
crop of the harvest, then those who belong to Christ at his
coming, 24 and then the end, when Christ hands over the
kingdom to God the Father, when he brings every form of
rule, every authority and power to an end. 25 It is necessary
for him to rule until *he puts all enemies under his feet.* 26 Death is
the last enemy to be brought to an end,

**John 20:1-18 (or Luke 24:1-12)**

Early in the morning of the first day of the week, while it was
still dark, Mary Magdalene came to the tomb and saw that the
stone had been taken away from the tomb. 2 She ran to Simon
Peter and the other disciple, the one whom Jesus loved, and
said, "They have taken the Lord from the tomb, and we don't
know where they've put him." 3 Peter and the other disciple left
to go to the tomb. 4 They were running together, but the other
disciple ran faster than Peter and was the first to arrive at the
tomb. 5 Bending down to take a look, he saw the linen cloths
lying there, but he didn't go in. 6 Following him, Simon Peter
entered the tomb and saw the linen cloths lying there. 7 He also
saw the face cloth that had been on Jesus' head. It wasn't with
the other clothes but was folded up in its own place. 8 Then
the other disciple, the one who arrived at the tomb first, also
went inside. He saw and believed. 9 They didn't yet understand
the scripture that Jesus must rise from the dead. 10 Then the
disciples returned to the place where they were staying.

11 Mary stood outside near the tomb, crying. As she cried,
she bent down to look into the tomb. 12 She saw two angels
dressed in white, seated where the body of Jesus had been,
one at the head and one at the foot. 13 The angels asked her,
"Woman, why are you crying?"

She replied, "They have taken away my Lord, and I don't
know where they've put him." 14 As soon as she had said this,
she turned around and saw Jesus standing there, but she
didn't know it was Jesus.

15 Jesus said to her, "Woman, why are you crying? Who are
you looking for?"

Thinking he was the gardener, she replied, "Sir, if you have carried him away, tell me where you have put him and I will get him."

16 Jesus said to her, "Mary."

She turned and said to him in Aramaic, "Rabbouni" (which means *Teacher*).

17 Jesus said to her, "Don't hold on to me, for I haven't yet
gone up to my Father. Go to my brothers and sisters and tell
them, 'I'm going up to my Father and your Father, to my
God and your God.'"

18 Mary Magdalene left and announced to the disciples, "I've
seen the Lord." Then she told them what he said to her.

**Luke 24:1-12**

Very early in the morning on the first day of the week, the
women went to the tomb, bringing the fragrant spices they
had prepared. 2 They found the stone rolled away from the
tomb, 3 but when they went in, they didn't find the body of
the Lord Jesus. 4 They didn't know what to make of this. Suddenly, two men were standing beside them in gleaming bright
clothing. 5 The women were frightened and bowed their faces
toward the ground, but the men said to them, "Why do you
look for the living among the dead? 6 He isn't here, but has
been raised. Remember what he told you while he was still in
Galilee, 7 that the Human One must be handed over to sinners, be crucified, and on the third day rise again." 8 Then they
remembered his words. 9 When they returned from the tomb,
they reported all these things to the eleven and all the others.
10 It was Mary Magdalene, Joanna, Mary the mother of James,
and the other women with them who told these things to the
apostles. 11 Their words struck the apostles as nonsense, and
they didn't believe the women. 12 But Peter ran to the tomb.
When he bent over to look inside, he saw only the linen cloth.
Then he returned home, wondering what had happened.

**Primary Hymns and Songs for the Day**
302 "Christ the Lord Is Risen Today" (John, Luke) (O)
H-3 Hbl-8, 51; Chr-49; Desc-31; Org-32
S-1 #104-8. Various treatments
702 "Sing with All the Saints in Glory" (1 Cor)
H-3 Hbl-25, 74; Chr-120; Desc-54; Org-58
S-1 #173-176. Various treatments
312 "Hail the Day That Sees Him Rise" (1 Cor, John)
H-3 Hbl-72; Chr-50; Desc-69; Org-78
S-1 #213. Desc.
303 "The Day of Resurrection" (John, Luke) (C)
H-3 Hbl-74; Chr-123; Desc-64; Org-71
S-1 #195-97. Various treatments

**Additional Hymn Suggestions**
2114 "At the Font We Start Our Journey" (Acts, Baptism)
257 "We Meet You, O Christ" (Acts)
319 "Christ Jesus Lay in Death's Strong Bands" (Acts, John)
662 "Stand Up and Bless the Lord" (Pss)
2084 "Come, Let Us with Our Lord Arise" (Pss, Easter)
308 "Thine Be the Glory" (1 Cor, John)
636 "Christian People, Raise Your Song" (1 Cor, Comm.)
2115 "Christ Has Risen" (1 Cor, John, Luke, Easter)
134 "O Mary, Don't You Weep" (John)
311 "Now the Green Blade Riseth" (John, Luke)
314 "In the Garden" (John, Luke)
315 "Come, Ye Faithful, Raise the Strain" (John, Luke)
316 "He Rose" (John, Luke)
317 "O Sons and Daughters, Let Us Sing" (John)
322 "Up from the Grave He Arose" (John)
324 "Hail Thee, Festival Day" (John, Luke)
2077 "You Alone Are Holy" ("*Solo Tu Eres Santo*") (Easter)
2211 "Faith Is Patience in the Night" (Easter)
2242 "Walk with Me" (John)
3090 "The Easter Song" (John, Luke)
318 "Christ Is Alive" (John, Luke)

**Additional Contemporary Suggestions**
M32 "Holy and Anointed One" (Acts)
S2043 "Alleluia" (Pss, 1 Cor, Easter)
S2270 "I Will Enter His Gates" (Pss)
SP168
WS3023 "Forever" (Pss)
M68
WS3027 "Hallelujah" ("Your Love Is Amazing") (Pss)
M118
WS2040 "You Are My All in All" (Pss, Easter)
SP220
S2088 "Lord, I Lift Your Name on High" (1 Cor, Easter)
M2
S2116 "Christ the Lord Is Risen" (1 Cor, Easter)
S2219 "Goodness Is Stronger than Evil" (1 Cor, Easter)
M17 "This Kingdom" (1 Cor)
UM186 "Alleluia" (John, Luke)
SP108, S-2 #3-4. Desc. and harm.
M77 "Above All" (John)
V-3 (2) p. 17 Vocal solo
WS3105 "In Christ Alone" ("My Hope Is Found") (Easter)
M138
S2039 "Holy, Holy" (Easter)
SP141
S2258 "Sing Alleluia to the Lord" (Easter, Comm.)
SP93

**Vocal Solos**
"Jesus Christ Is Risen Today" (Easter)
V-1 p. 50
"The First Day of my Life" (Easter)
V-11 p. 22
"Crown Him, the Risen King" (Easter)
V-10 p. 55
"I Know That My Redeemer Liveth" (1 Cor)
V-2
V-5(2) p. 22

**Anthems**
"O Sons and Daughters" (John)
Donald Livingston; Paraclete Press PPM01320
SATB *divisi* with organ, brass, percussion

"Ring the Easter Bells" (Easter)
Joseph M. Martin; Alfred 42512
SATB with keyboard and opt. handbells

**Other Suggestions**
Visuals: Flowers, butterfly, peacock
**Acts** Risen Christ, cross draped in white, all nations
**P** Right hand, gates, cornerstone, Pss 118:1a, b, 17, or 24
**E** Resurrection, fruit, empty tomb
**G** Stone, running feet, shroud, rolled napkin, weep/joy
Greeting: BOW382 (1 Cor) or WSL29 (Luke, John, Easter)
Introit: UM657 or UM658. "This Is the Day" (Pss)
Introit: WS3090. "The Easter Song" (John, Luke, Easter)
Introit: S2111. "We Sang Our Glad Hosannas" (John, Easter)
Prayer: UM320. Easter Vigil or Day (Easter)
Prayer: UM360. Freedom in Christ (1 Cor)
Intercessory Prayer: BOW399. Week 1 (Easter)
Response: UM179, stanza 4. "O Sing a Song of Bethlehem" (Acts)
Offertory Prayer: WSL119 (Easter)
Prayer of Thanksgiving and Intercession: BOW395 (John, Luke)
Great Thanksgiving for Easter: BOW, pp. 66-67 (Communion)
Closing Prayer: BOW396 (John)
Sung Benediction: S2237. "As a Fire Is Meant for Burning," stanza 3 (Easter)
Order of Worship for Easter Vigil: BOW369.

**Acts 5:27-32**
27 The apostles were brought before the council where the
high priest confronted them: 28 "In no uncertain terms, we
demanded that you not teach in this name. And look at you!
You have filled Jerusalem with your teaching. And you are
determined to hold us responsible for this man's death."
29 Peter and the apostles replied, "We must obey God rather
than humans! 30 The God of our ancestors raised Jesus from
the dead—whom you killed by hanging him on a tree. 31 God
has exalted Jesus to his right side as leader and savior so that
he could enable Israel to change its heart and life and to
find forgiveness for sins. 32 We are witnesses of such things,
as is the Holy Spirit, whom God has given to those who obey
him."

---

**Psalm 150 (UM862)**
Praise the LORD!
Praise God in his sanctuary!
    Praise God in his fortress, the sky!
2 Praise God in his mighty acts!
    Praise God as suits his incredible greatness!
3 Praise God with the blast of the ram's horn!
    Praise God with lute and lyre!
4 Praise God with drum and dance!
    Praise God with strings and pipe!
5 Praise God with loud cymbals!
    Praise God with clashing cymbals!
6 Let every living thing praise the LORD!
Praise the LORD!

---

**Revelation 1:4-8**
4 John, to the seven churches that are in Asia:
Grace and peace to you from the one who is and was and
is coming, and from the seven spirits that are before God's
throne, 5 and from Jesus Christ—the faithful witness, the
firstborn from among the dead, and the ruler of the kings of
the earth.
To the one who loves us and freed us from our sins by his
blood, 6 who made us a kingdom, priests to his God and
Father—to him be glory and power forever and always.
Amen.
7 Look, he is coming with the clouds! Every eye will see him,
including those who pierced him, and all the tribes of the
earth will mourn because of him. This is so. Amen. 8 "I am
the Alpha and the Omega," says the Lord God, "the one who
is and was and is coming, the Almighty."

---

**John 20:19-31**
19 It was still the first day of the week. That evening, while
the disciples were behind closed doors because they were
afraid of the Jewish authorities, Jesus came and stood among
them. He said, "Peace be with you." 20 After he said this, he
showed them his hands and his side. When the disciples saw
the Lord, they were filled with joy. 21 Jesus said to them again,
"Peace be with you. As the Father sent me, so I am sending
you." 22 Then he breathed on them and said, "Receive the
Holy Spirit. 23 If you forgive anyone's sins, they are forgiven; if
you don't forgive them, they aren't forgiven."
24 Thomas, the one called Didymus, one of the Twelve,
wasn't with the disciples when Jesus came. 25 The other disciples told him, "We've seen the Lord!"
But he replied, "Unless I see the nail marks in his hands,
put my finger in the wounds left by the nails, and put my
hand into his side, I won't believe."
26 After eight days his disciples were again in a house and
Thomas was with them. Even though the doors were locked,
Jesus entered and stood among them. He said, "Peace be
with you." 27 Then he said to Thomas, "Put your finger here.
Look at my hands. Put your hand into my side. No more
disbelief. Believe!"
28 Thomas responded to Jesus, "My Lord and my God!"
29 Jesus replied, "Do you believe because you see me? Happy
are those who don't see and yet believe."
30 Then Jesus did many other miraculous signs in his disciples' presence, signs that aren't recorded in this scroll.
31 But these things are written so that you will believe that
Jesus is the Christ, God's Son, and that believing, you will
have life in his name.

**Primary Hymns and Songs for the Day**

181 "Ye Servants of God" (Rev) (O)
H-3 Hbl-90, 105; Chr-221; Desc-49; Org-51
S-2 #71-74. Intro. and harms.
315 "Come, Ye Faithful, Raise the Strain" (Acts, John)
H-3 Hbl-53; Chr-57; Desc-94; Org-141
S-2 #161. Desc.
326 "The Head That Once Was Crowned" (Acts)
H-3 Chr-187, 207; Desc-95; Org-142
S-1 #305. Desc.
2010 "Praise Ye the Lord" (Pss)
718 "Lo, He Comes with Clouds Descending" (Rev)
H-3 Hbl-93; Chr-129; Desc-50; Org-53
S-1 #157. Desc.
2196 "We Walk by Faith" (John)
H-3 Chr-21
2206 "Without Seeing You" (John)
139 "Praise to the Lord, the Almighty" (Pss) (C)
H-3 Hbl-89; Chr-163; Desc-69; Org-79
S-1 #218-22. Various treatments

**Additional Hymn Suggestions**

257 "We Meet You, O Christ" (Acts)
96 "Praise the Lord Who Reigns Above" (Pss)
139 "Praise to the Lord, the Almighty" (Pss)
2008 "Let All Things Now Living" (Pss)
2020 "Praise the Lord with the Sound of Trumpet" (Pss)
2205 "The Fragrance of Christ" (Pss)
88 "Maker, in Whom We Live" (Rev)
90 "Ye Watchers and Ye Holy Ones" (Rev)
184 "Of the Father's Love Begotten" (Rev)
384 "Love Divine, All Loves Excelling" (Rev)
715 "Rejoice, the Lord Is King" (Rev)
716 "Rejoice, the Lord Is King" (Rev)
177 "He Is Lord" (John)
SP122
308 "Thine Be the Glory" (John)
317 "O Sons and Daughters, Let Us Sing" (John, Easter)
331 "Holy Spirit, Come Confirm Us" (John)
336 "Of All the Spirit's Gifts to Me" (John)
376 "*Dona Nobis Pacem*" (John)
420 "Breathe on Me, Breath of God" (John)
465 "Holy Spirit, Truth Divine" (John)
475 "Come Down, O Love Divine" (John)
500 "Spirit of God, Descend upon My Heart" (John)
505 "When Our Confidence Is Shaken" (John)
543 "O Breath of Life" (John)
623 "Here, O My Lord, I See Thee" (John, Comm.)
2046 "Womb of Life" (John)
2117 "Spirit of God" (John)
2147 "There Are Some Things I May Not Know" (John)
2211 "Faith Is Patience in the Night" (John)
2255 "In the Singing" (John, Comm.)
2115 "Christ Has Risen" (John, Easter)
3089 "O Living God" (John, Easter)
3107 "Just a Little Talk with Jesus" (John)
3110 "By Grace We Have Been Saved" (John)

**Additional Contemporary Suggestions**

S2070 "He Is Exalted" (Acts)
SP66
S2159 "Jesus, Draw Me Close" (Acts)
M48
SP18 "I Exalt You" (Acts)
S2078 "Alleluia" (Pss)
M59 "Let Everything That Has Breath" (Pss)
M127 "Indescribable" (Pss)
UM349 "Turn Your Eyes upon Jesus" (Rev, John)
SP218
S2087 "We Will Glorify" (Rev)
SP68
UM706 "Soon and Very Soon" (Rev)
S-2 #187. Piano arr.
M20 "Jesus Is Alive" (Rev, Easter)
M55 "Jehovah Reigns" (Rev)
UM328 "Surely the Presence of the Lord" (Rev)
SP243; S-2 #200. Stanzas for soloist
S2119 "Where the Spirit of the Lord Is" (John)
M26 "The Power of Your Love" (John)
S2086 "Open Our Eyes, Lord" (John)
SP199
S2266 "Here Is Bread, Here Is Wine" (John, Comm.)
WS3108 "Trading My Sorrows" (John)
M75

**Vocal Solos**

"Sing a Song of Joy" (Pss)
V-4 p. 2
"Come, O Thou Traveler Unknown" (John)
V-1 p. 21
"I Know That My Redeemer Lives" (John, Easter)
V-5(2) p. 22

**Anthems**

"*Dona Nobis Pacem*" (John)
Arr. John Behnke; MorningStar MSM-50-5255
SATB with keyboard

"Jazz Alleluia" (John, Easter)
Craig Curry; Alfred 42506
SATB with piano

**Other Suggestions**

Visuals:
**Acts** Cross draped in white
**P** Musical instruments, dancing
**E** Alpha/Omega, clouds, Christ descending, 7 flames
**G** Risen Christ, Holy Spirit, nails, kneel, closed door
Greeting: BOW381 (John) or BOW420 (Rev)
Opening Prayer: BOW394 (Acts)
Sung Prayer of Confession: S2138. "Sunday's Palms Are Wednesday's Ashes," stanza 3 (John)
Words of Assurance: S2169. "God, How Can We Forgive," stanza 2 (John)
Prayer: WSL34 (Rev, John)
Prayer: UM335. An Invitation to the Holy Spirit (John)
Prayer: UM594. Come, Divine Interpreter (Rev)
Responsive Prayer for Illumination: WSL73 (John)
Response: UM503. "Let It Breathe on Me" (John)
Offertory Prayer: WSL141 (John, Easter)
Blessing: BOW561 (John)

**Acts 9:1-6 (7-20)**

Meanwhile, Saul was still spewing out murderous threats
against the Lord's disciples. He went to the high priest,
2 seeking letters to the synagogues in Damascus. If he found
persons who belonged to the Way, whether men or women,
these letters would authorize him to take them as prisoners
to Jerusalem. 3 During the journey, as he approached Damascus, suddenly a light from heaven encircled him. 4 He fell to
the ground and heard a voice asking him, "Saul, Saul, why
are you harassing me?"
5 Saul asked, "Who are you, Lord?"
"I am Jesus, whom you are harassing," came the reply.
6 "Now get up and enter the city. You will be told what you
must do."
7 Those traveling with him stood there speechless; they
heard the voice but saw no one. 8 After they picked Saul up
from the ground, he opened his eyes but he couldn't see. So
they led him by the hand into Damascus. 9 For three days he
was blind and neither ate nor drank anything.
10 In Damascus there was a certain disciple named Ananias.
The Lord spoke to him in a vision, "Ananias!"
He answered, "Yes, Lord."
11 The Lord instructed him, "Go to Judas' house on Straight
Street and ask for a man from Tarsus named Saul. He is praying. 12 In a vision he has seen a man named Ananias enter
and put his hands on him to restore his sight."
13 Ananias countered, "Lord, I have heard many reports
about this man. People say he has done horrible things to
your holy people in Jerusalem. 14 He's here with authority
from the chief priests to arrest everyone who calls on your
name."
15 The Lord replied, "Go! This man is the agent I have chosen to carry my name before Gentiles, kings, and Israelites.
16 I will show him how much he must suffer for the sake of my
name."
17 Ananias went to the house. He placed his hands on
Saul and said, "Brother Saul, the Lord sent me—Jesus, who
appeared to you on the way as you were coming here. He
sent me so that you could see again and be filled with the
Holy Spirit." 18 Instantly, flakes fell from Saul's eyes and he
could see again. He got up and was baptized. 19 After eating,
he regained his strength.
He stayed with the disciples in Damascus for several days.
20 Right away, he began to preach about Jesus in the synagogues. "He is God's Son," he declared.

---

**Psalm 30 (UM762)**

I exalt you, LORD,
because you pulled me up;
you didn't let my enemies
celebrate over me.
2 LORD, my God, I cried out to you for help,
and you healed me. . . .

---

**Revelation 5:11-14**

11 Then I looked, and I heard the sound of many angels
surrounding the throne, the living creatures, and the elders.
They numbered in the millions—thousands upon thousands.
12 They said in a loud voice,
"Worthy is the slaughtered Lamb
to receive power, wealth, wisdom, and might,
and honor, glory, and blessing."
13 And I heard every creature in heaven and on earth and
under the earth and in the sea—I heard everything everywhere say,
"Blessing, honor, glory, and power belong
to the one seated on the throne
and to the Lamb
forever and always."
14 Then the four living creatures said, "Amen," and the elders
fell down and worshipped.

---

**John 21:1-19**

Later, Jesus himself appeared again to his disciples at the
Sea of Tiberias. This is how it happened: 2 Simon Peter,
Thomas (called Didymus), Nathanael from Cana in Galilee,
Zebedee's sons, and two other disciples were together.
3 Simon Peter told them, "I'm going fishing."
They said, "We'll go with you." They set out in a boat, but
throughout the night they caught nothing. 4 Early in the
morning, Jesus stood on the shore, but the disciples didn't
realize it was Jesus.
5 Jesus called to them, "Children, have you caught anything
to eat?"
They answered him, "No."
6 He said, "Cast your net on the right side of the boat and
you will find some."
So they did, and there were so many fish that they couldn't
haul in the net. 7 Then the disciple whom Jesus loved said
to Peter, "It's the Lord!" When Simon Peter heard it was
the Lord, he wrapped his coat around himself (for he was
naked) and jumped into the water. 8 The other disciples
followed in the boat, dragging the net full of fish, for they
weren't far from shore, only about one hundred yards.
9 When they landed, they saw a fire there, with fish on it,
and some bread. 10 Jesus said to them, "Bring some of the fish
that you've just caught." 11 Simon Peter got up and pulled the
net to shore. It was full of large fish, one hundred fifty-three
of them. Yet the net hadn't torn, even with so many fish.
12 Jesus said to them, "Come and have breakfast." None of the
disciples could bring themselves to ask him, "Who are you?"
They knew it was the Lord. 13 Jesus came, took the bread, and
gave it to them. He did the same with the fish. 14 This was
now the third time Jesus appeared to his disciples after he
was raised from the dead.
15 When they finished eating, Jesus asked Simon Peter,
"Simon son of John, do you love me more than these?"
Simon replied, "Yes, Lord, you know I love you."
Jesus said to him, "Feed my lambs." 16 Jesus asked a second
time, "Simon son of John, do you love me?"
Simon replied, "Yes, Lord, you know I love you."
Jesus said to him, "Take care of my sheep." 17 He asked a
third time, "Simon son of John, do you love me?"
Peter was sad that Jesus asked him a third time, "Do you
love me?" He replied, "Lord, you know everything; you know
I love you."
Jesus said to him, "Feed my sheep. 18 I assure you that when
you were younger you tied your own belt and walked around
wherever you wanted. When you grow old, you will stretch
out your hands and another will tie your belt and lead you
where you don't want to go." 19 He said this to show the kind
of death by which Peter would glorify God. After saying this,
Jesus said to Peter, "Follow me."

### Primary Hymns and Songs for the Day

173 "Christ, Whose Glory Fills the Skies" (Acts, John) (O)
H-3 Hbl-51; Chr-206; Desc-89; Org-120
S-1 #278-79. Harms.
355 "Depth of Mercy" (Acts)
H-3 Chr-63, 100
S-1 #53. Desc.
3097 "Depth of Mercy (Acts)
2086 "Open Our Eyes, Lord" (Acts)
SP199
378 "Amazing Grace" (Acts, Pss, Native American)
H-3 Hbl-14, 46; Chr-27; Desc-14; Org-4
S-2 #5-7. Various treatments
3104 "Amazing Grace" ("My Chains Are Gone") (Acts, Pss)
M205
2210 "Joy Comes with the Dawn" (Pss, John)
674 "See the Morning Sun Ascending" (Rev)
H-3 Chr-108; Desc-79; Org-96
S-1 #338 and 341. Descs.
453 "More Love to Thee, O Christ" (John) (C)
H-3 Org-94

### Additional Hymn Suggestions

162 "Alleluia, Alleluia" (Acts)
363 "And Can It Be that I Should Gain" (Acts)
571 "Go, Make of All Disciples" (Acts)
582 "Whom Shall I Send?" (Acts)
377 "It Is Well with My Soul" (Acts, Pss)
510 "Come, Ye Disconsolate" (Acts, Pss)
524 "Beams of Heaven as I Go" (Acts, Pss)
591 "Rescue the Perishing" (Acts, John)
2211 "Faith Is Patience in the Night" (Pss)
2284 "Joy in the Morning" (Pss)
79 "Holy God, We Praise Thy Name" (Rev)
90 "Ye Watchers and Ye Holy Ones" (Rev)
154 "All Hail the Power of Jesus' Name" (Rev)
155 "All Hail the Power of Jesus' Name" (Rev)
478 "*Jaya Ho*" ("Victory Hymn") (Rev)
638 "This Is the Feast of Victory" (Rev, Comm.)
655 "Fix Me, Jesus" (Rev)
719 "My Lord, What a Morning" (Rev)
2045 "Sing a New Song to the Lord" (Rev)
307 "Christ Is Risen" (John, Comm.)
344 "*Tú Has Venido a la Orilla*" ("Lord, You Have Come to the Lakeshore") (John)
432 "*Jesu, Jesu*" (John)
S-1 #63. Vocal part
2115 "Christ Has Risen" (John)
2254 "In Remembrance of Me" (John, Comm.)
2265 "Time Now to Gather" (John, Comm.)

### Additional Contemporary Suggestions

S2250 "I've Just Come from the Fountain" (Acts, Baptism)
M8 "Nobody Fills My Heart Like Jesus" (Acts)
M252 "God with Us" (Acts)
M251 "Grace Like Rain" (Acts, Pss)
WS3148 "Word of God, Speak" (Acts, John)
M148
S2144 "Someone Asked the Question" (Pss, Rev)
S2195 "In the Lord I'll Be Ever Thankful" (Pss)
WS3108 "Trading My Sorrows" (Pss)
M75
S2022 "Great Is the Lord" (Rev)
SP30
S2040 "Awesome God" (Rev)
SP11
S2028 "Clap Your Hands" (Rev)
SP147 "I Will Celebrate" (Rev)
M46
M10 "Salvation Belongs to Our God" (Rev)
M15 "Agnus Dei" (Rev)
M21 "Blessing, Honour and Glory" (Rev)
M27 "We Will Worship the Lamb of Glory" (Rev)
M43 "We Declare Your Majesty" (Rev)
M44 "Most Holy Lord" (Rev)
M58 "All Heaven Declares" (Rev)
M74 "There Is Joy in the Lord" (Rev)
M125 "Praise Adonai" (Rev)
M136 "Worthy Is the Lamb" (Rev)
UM347 "Spirit Song" (John)
SP134
UM640 "Take Our Bread" (John, Comm.)
S2038 "Father, I Adore You" (John)
S2165 "Cry of My Heart" (John)
M39
S2218 "You Are Mine" (John)
WS3004 "Step by Step" (John)
M51

### Vocal Solos

"It Is Well with My Soul" (Acts, Pss)
V-5(2) p. 35
"My Lord, What a Morning" (Rev)
V-3 (1) p. 39
"Worthy Is the Lamb" (Rev)
V-8 p. 228
"Did You Feel the Mountains Tremble?" (Rev)
M69

### Anthems

"Worthy Is the Lamb" (Rev)
Arr. Lloyd Larson; Hope C-5831
SATB with piano

"The Shepherd" (John)
James Kevin Gray; Paraclete Press PPM01337
SATB *a cappella*

### Other Suggestions

Visuals:
**Acts** Light, blindfold, healing hand, Act 9:4c or 10c
**P** Joy, singing, dancing, sackcloth, Pss 30:5c or 11a
**E** Lamb, praise, angel choir, four creatures
**G** Fish, bread, lamb, sheep, fire, boat, net, fish, ICTHUS
Introit: UM625. "Come, Let Us Eat" (John)
Introit: S2127. "Come and See" ("*Kyrie*") (John)
Greeting: BOW385 (Rev) or BOW425 (Pss)
Greeting: BOW455 or BOW425-426 (John, Native American)
Opening Prayer: BOW392 (Acts, John)
Opening Prayer: BOW468 (Rev, Native American)
Prayers: WSL32 (John, Easter)
Intercessory Prayer: BOW396 (John)
Offertory Prayer: WSL117 (John)
Closing Prayer: BOW521 (Acts, Native American)

**Acts 9:36-43**
36 In Joppa there was a disciple named Tabitha (in Greek
her name is Dorcas). Her life overflowed with good works
and compassionate acts on behalf of those in need. 37 About
that time, though, she became so ill that she died. After they
washed her body, they laid her in an upstairs room. 38 Since
Lydda was near Joppa, when the disciples heard that Peter
was there, they sent two people to Peter. They urged, "Please
come right away!" 39 Peter went with them. Upon his arrival,
he was taken to the upstairs room. All the widows stood
beside him, crying as they showed the tunics and other clothing Dorcas made when she was alive.
40 Peter sent everyone out of the room, then knelt and
prayed. He turned to the body and said, "Tabitha, get up!"
She opened her eyes, saw Peter, and sat up. 41 He gave her his
hand and raised her up. Then he called God's holy people,
including the widows, and presented her alive to them.
42 The news spread throughout Joppa, and many put their
faith in the Lord. 43 Peter stayed for some time in Joppa with
a certain tanner named Simon.

---

**Psalm 23 (UM754)**
The LORD is my shepherd.
  I lack nothing.
2 He lets me rest in grassy meadows;
  he leads me to restful waters;
    3 he keeps me alive.
He guides me in proper paths
  for the sake of his good name.
4 Even when I walk through the darkest valley,
  I fear no danger because you are with me.
Your rod and your staff—
  they protect me.
5 You set a table for me
  right in front of my enemies.
You bathe my head in oil;
  my cup is so full it spills over!
6 Yes, goodness and faithful love
  will pursue me all the days of my life,
  and I will live in the LORD's house
  as long as I live.

---

**Revelation 7:9-17**
9 After this I looked, and there was a great crowd that no
one could number. They were from every nation, tribe,
people, and language. They were standing before the throne
and before the Lamb. They wore white robes and held palm
branches in their hands. 10 They cried out with a loud voice:
"Victory belongs to our God
  who sits on the throne,
    and to the Lamb."
11 All the angels stood in a circle around the throne, and
around the elders and the four living creatures. They fell
facedown before the throne and worshipped God, 12 saying,
"Amen! Blessing and glory
  and wisdom and thanksgiving
  and honor and power and might
    be to our God forever and always. Amen."
13 Then one of the elders said to me, "Who are these people
wearing white robes, and where did they come from?"
14 I said to him, "Sir, you know."
Then he said to me, "These people have come out of great
hardship. They have washed their robes and made them
white in the Lamb's blood. 15 This is the reason they are
before God's throne. They worship him day and night in his
temple, and the one seated on the throne will shelter them.
16 They won't hunger or thirst anymore. No sun or scorch-
ing heat will beat down on them, 17 because the Lamb who is
in the midst of the throne will shepherd them. He will lead
them to the springs of life-giving water, and God will wipe
away every tear from their eyes."

---

**John 10:22-30**
22 The time came for the Festival of Dedication in Jerusalem. It was winter, 23 and Jesus was in the temple, walking in
the covered porch named for Solomon. 24 The Jewish opposition circled around him and asked, "How long will you test
our patience? If you are the Christ, tell us plainly."
25 Jesus answered, "I have told you, but you don't believe.
The works I do in my Father's name testify about me, 26 but
you don't believe because you don't belong to my sheep.
27 My sheep listen to my voice. I know them and they follow
me. 28 I give them eternal life. They will never die, and no
one will snatch them from my hand. 29 My Father, who has
given them to me, is greater than all, and no one is able to
snatch them from my Father's hand. 30 I and the Father are
one."

### Primary Hymns and Songs for the Day

88 "Maker, in Whom We Live" (Rev) (O)
H-3 Hbl-55; Chr-60; Desc-30; Org-27
S-1 #86-88. Various treatments
732 "Come, We That Love the Lord" (Rev) (O)
H-3 Chr-106, 167; Desc-97; Org-147
S-1 #311. Desc. and harm.
474 "Precious Lord, Take My Hand" (Acts, Pss)
H-3 Chr-164; Org-116
136 "The Lord's My Shepherd, I'll Not Want" (Pss, John)
H-3 Hbl-96; Chr-188, 189; Desc-24; Org-21
2113 "Lamb of God" (Pss, Rev, John)
2040 "Awesome God" (Rev)
SP11
381 "Savior, Like a Shepherd Lead Us" (Pss, John) (C)
H-3 Chr-167; Org-15
S-2 #29. Harm.
733 "Marching to Zion" (Rev) (C)
H-3 Chr-298

### Additional Hymn Suggestions

497 "Send Me, Lord" (Acts., Pss)
2140 "Since Jesus Came into My Heart" (Acts, Pss)
304 "Easter People, Raise Your Voices" (Acts, Rev)
306 "The Strife Is O'er, the Battle Done" (Acts, Rev)
128 "He Leadeth Me: O Blessed Thought" (Pss)
138 "The King of Love My Shepherd Is" (Pss)
3031 "God Leads Us Along" (Pss)
407 "Close to Thee" (Pss, John)
518 "O Thou, in Whose Presence" (Pss, John)
650 "Give Me the Faith Which Can Remove" (Pss, John)
2112 "Jesus Walked This Lonesome Valley" (Pss)
2206 "Without Seeing You" (Pss)
2214 "Lead Me, Guide Me" (Pss)
90 "Ye Watchers and Ye Holy Ones" (Rev)
154 "All Hail the Power of Jesus' Name" (Rev)
155 "All Hail the Power of Jesus' Name" (Rev)
176 "Majesty, Worship His Majesty" (Rev)
SP73
181 "Ye Servants of God" (Rev)
325 "Hail, Thou Once Despised Jesus" (Rev)
631 "O Food to Pilgrims Given" (Rev, Comm.)
655 "Fix Me, Jesus" (Rev)
638 "This Is the Feast of Victory" (Rev, Comm.)
674 "See the Morning Sun Ascending" (Rev)
2126 "All Who Hunger" (Rev, Comm.)
2264 "Come to the Table" (Rev, Comm.)
3088 "Easter Alleluia" (Rev, John)
175 "Jesus, the Very Thought of Thee" (John)
2137 "Would I Have Answered When You Called" (John)

### Additional Contemporary Suggestions

S2054 "Nothing Can Trouble" ("*Nada Te Turbe*") (Pss)
WS3014 "You Are Good" (Pss)
M124
WS3026 "God Is Good All the Time" (Pss)
M45
M72 "Jesus, Lover of My Soul" ("It's All about You") (Pss, John)
M125 "Praise Adonai" (Pss)
WS3096 "Gentle Shepherd" (Pss, Rev, John)
S2058 "Shepherd Me, O God" (Pss, Rev, John)
M160 "Enough" (Pss, Rev)
S2132 "You Who Are Thirsty" (Rev)
S2272 "Holy Ground" (Rev)
SP86
WS3093 "Fill My Cup, Lord" (Rev, Comm.)
UM641 refrain; S-2 #62. Stanzas for soloist
M21 "Blessing, Honour and Glory" (Rev, Easter)
M23 "Hallelujah to the Lamb" (Rev, Easter)
M27 "We Will Worship the Lamb of Glory" (Rev)
M35 "White as Snow" (Rev)
M44 "Most Holy Lord" (Rev)
M58 "All Heaven Declares" (Rev, Easter)
M159 "All Who Are Thirsty" (Rev)
M161 "Healing Rain" (Rev)
M168 "He Reigns" (Rev)
M144 "Light the Fire Again" (Rev)
UM99 "My Tribute" ("To God Be the Glory") (Rev, John)
V-8 p. 5 Vocal Solo

### Vocal Solos

"God, Our Ever Faithful Shepherd" (Pss)
V-4 p. 15
"The Lord Is My Shepherd" (Pss)
V-5(3) p. 30
"The New 23rd" (Pss)
V-8 p. 340
"My Shepherd Will Supply My Need" (Pss)
V-10 p. 4
"Ye Servants of God" (Rev)
V-1 p. 41
"Marchin' On Up" (Rev)
V-3 (3) p. 57

### Anthems

"Shepherd Me, O God" (Pss, Rev, John)
Arr. Mark Hayes; Hope C-5832
SATB with piano and opt. violin and cello

"Many Will Come" (Luke)
Thomas Keesecker; Choristers Guild CGA-1374
SATB *a cappella*

### Other Suggestions

Visuals:
**Acts** Shroud, basin/water, sewing, praying hands, touching
**P** Shepherd's crook, pasture, water, path, shadow, table/oil
**E** White robe/palms, angels, Lamb, water, wiped tears
**G** Winter, Jesus, sheep, John 10:27
Greeting: BOW389 (Acts, Rev)
Psalm: UM137. Psalm 23 (KJV)
Prayer of Confession: S2277. "Lord, Have Mercy" (Rev)
Call to Prayer: S2132. "You Who Are Thirsty" (Rev, Comm.)
Prayer: UM321 (Easter)
Prayer: WSL17 or UM460 (Pss)
Offertory Prayer: WSL134 (Pss)

**Acts 11:1-18**

The apostles and the brothers and sisters throughout Judea
heard that even the Gentiles had welcomed God's word.
2 When Peter went up to Jerusalem, the circumcised believers
criticized him. 3 They accused him, "You went into the home
of the uncircumcised and ate with them!"
4 Step-by-step, Peter explained what had happened. 5 "I was
in the city of Joppa praying when I had a visionary experience. In my vision, I saw something like a large linen sheet
being lowered from heaven by its four corners. It came all
the way down to me. 6 As I stared at it, wondering what it was,
I saw four-legged animals—including wild beasts—as well as
reptiles and wild birds. 7 I heard a voice say, 'Get up, Peter!
Kill and eat!' 8 I responded, 'Absolutely not, Lord! Nothing
impure or unclean has ever entered my mouth.' 9 The
voice from heaven spoke a second time, 'Never consider
unclean what God has made pure.' 10 This happened three
times, then everything was pulled back into heaven. 11 At that
moment three men who had been sent to me from Caesarea
arrived at the house where we were staying. 12 The Spirit told
me to go with them even though they were Gentiles. These
six brothers also went with me, and we entered that man's
house. 13 He reported to us how he had seen an angel standing in his house and saying, 'Send to Joppa and summon
Simon, who is known as Peter. 14 He will tell you how you
and your entire household can be saved.' 15 When I began
to speak, the Holy Spirit fell on them, just as the Spirit fell
on us in the beginning. 16 I remembered the Lord's words:
'John will baptize with water, but you will be baptized with
the Holy Spirit.' 17 If God gave them the same gift he gave us
who believed in the Lord Jesus Christ, then who am I? Could
I stand in God's way?"
18 Once the apostles and other believers heard this, they
calmed down. They praised God and concluded, "So then
God has enabled Gentiles to change their hearts and lives so
that they might have new life."

---

**Psalm 148 (UM861)**

Praise the LORD!
Praise the LORD from heaven!
    Praise God on the heights!
2 Praise God, all of you who are his messengers!
    Praise God, all of you who comprise his heavenly forces!
3 Sun and moon, praise God!
    All of you bright stars, praise God!
4 You highest heaven, praise God!
    Do the same, you waters that are above the sky!
5 Let all of these praise the LORD's name
    because God gave the command and they were created!
6 God set them in place always and forever.
    God made a law that will not be broken.
7 Praise the LORD from the earth,
    you sea monsters and all you ocean depths!
8 Do the same, fire and hail, snow and smoke,
    stormy wind that does what God says!
9 Do the same, you mountains, every single hill,
    fruit trees, and every single cedar!
10 Do the same, you animals—wild or tame—
    you creatures that creep along and you birds that fly!
11 Do the same, you kings of the earth and every single
        person,
    you princes and every single ruler on earth!
12 Do the same, you young men—young women too!—
    you who are old together with you who are young!
13 Let all of these praise the LORD's name
    because only God's name is high over all.
    Only God's majesty is over earth and heaven.
14 God raised the strength of his people,
    the praise of all his faithful ones—
        that's the Israelites,
        the people who are close to him.
Praise the LORD!

---

**Revelation 21:1-6**

Then I saw a new heaven and a new earth, for the former
heaven and the former earth had passed away, and the
sea was no more. 2 I saw the holy city, New Jerusalem, coming down out of heaven from God, made ready as a bride
beautifully dressed for her husband. 3 I heard a loud voice
from the throne say, "Look! God's dwelling is here with
humankind. He will dwell with them, and they will be his
peoples. God himself will be with them as their God. 4 He will
wipe away every tear from their eyes. Death will be no more.
There will be no mourning, crying, or pain anymore, for the
former things have passed away." 5 Then the one seated on
the throne said, "Look! I'm making all things new." He also
said, "Write this down, for these words are trustworthy and
true." 6 Then he said to me, "All is done. I am the Alpha and
the Omega, the beginning and the end. To the thirsty I will
freely give water from the life-giving spring."

---

**John 13:31-35**

31 When Judas was gone, Jesus said, "Now the Human One
has been glorified, and God has been glorified in him. 32 If
God has been glorified in him, God will also glorify the
Human One in himself and will glorify him immediately.
33 Little children, I'm with you for a little while longer. You
will look for me—but, just as I told the Jewish leaders, I also
tell you now—'Where I'm going, you can't come.'
34 "I give you a new commandment: Love each other. Just as
I have loved you, so you also must love each other. 35 This is
how everyone will know that you are my disciples, when you
love each other."

**Primary Hymns and Songs for the Day**

62 "All Creatures of Our God and King" (Pss, Comm.) (O)
H-3 Hbl-44; Chr-21; Desc-66; Org-73
S-1 #198-204. Various treatments
2008 "Let All Things Now Living" (Pss) (O)
H-3 Chr-125; Org-9
S-1 #327. Desc.
548 "In Christ There Is No East or West" (Acts) (C)
H-3 Chr-111; Desc-74; Org-88
S-1 #231-33. Various treaments
560 "Help Us Accept Each Other" (Acts, John)
H-3 Chr-97
S-2 #1. Desc.
726 "O Holy City, Seen of John" (Rev)
H-3 Chr-139, 145; Desc-77
S-1 #241-42. Orff arr. and desc.
727 "O What Their Joy and Their Glory Must Be" (Rev)
H-3 Hbl-49; Chr-132; Desc-83; Org-103
S-1 #255. Harm. and desc.
2223 "They'll Know We Are Christians" (John)
384 "Love Divine, All Loves Excelling" (Acts, Rev, John) (C)
H-3 Chr-134; Desc-18; Org-13
S-1 #41-42. Desc. and harm.

**Additional Hymn Suggestions**

393 "Spirit of the Living God" (Acts)
547 "O Church of God, United" (Acts)
552 "Here, O Lord, Your Servants Gather" (Acts, Comm.)
561 "Jesus, United by Thy Grace" (Acts)
605 "Wash, O God, Our Sons and Daughters" (Acts, Baptism)
608 "This Is the Spirit's Entry Now" (Acts, Baptism)
2117 "Spirit of God" (Acts)
77 "How Great Thou Art" (Pss)
2045 "Sing a New Song to the Lord" (Pss)
3018 "Creation Sings" (Pss)
383 "This Is a Day of New Beginnings" (Rev, Comm.)
388 "O Come and Dwell in Me" (Rev)
428 "For the Healing of the Nations" (Rev)
480 "O Love That Wilt Not Let Me Go" (Rev)
524 "Beams of Heaven as I Go" (Rev)
533 "We Shall Overcome" (Rev)
580 "Lead On, O King Eternal" (Rev)
722 "I Want to Be Ready" (Rev)
731 "Glorious Things of Thee Are Spoken" (Rev)
2142 "Blessed Quietness" (Rev)
2210 "Joy Comes with the Dawn" (Rev)
2284 "Joy in the Morning" (Rev)
510 "Come, Ye Disconsolate" (Rev, John)
191 "Jesus Loves Me" (John)
408 "The Gift of Love" (John)
549 "Where Charity and Love Prevail" (John)
632 "Draw Us in the Spirit's Tether" (John, Comm.)
2213 "Healer of Our Every Ill" (John)
2260 "Let Us Be Bread" (John, Comm.)

**Additional Contemporary Suggestions**

WS3004 "Step by Step" (Acts)
M51
UM347 "Spirit Song" (Acts, Rev)
SP134
S2224 "Make Us One" (Acts, John)
SP137
S2035 "Praise, Praise, Praise the Lord" (Pss)
WS3034 "God of Wonders" (Pss)
M80
M59 "Let Everything That Has Breath" (Pss)
M125 "Praise Adonai" (Pss)
M127 "Indescribable" (Pss)
UM706 "Soon and Very Soon" (Rev)
S-2 #187. Piano Arr.
M23 "Hallelujah to the Lamb" (Rev, Easter)
M32 "Holy and Anointed One" (Rev, Easter, John)
WS3003 "How Great Is Our God" (Rev)
M117
M159 "All Who Are Thirsty" (Rev)
S2132 "You Who Are Thirsty" (Rev)
S2087 "We Will Glorify" (Rev, John)
SP68
UM347 "Spirit Song" (Rev)
SP134
UM432 "*Jesu, Jesu*" (John)
S-1 #63. Vocal part
S2226 "Bind Us Together" (John)
SP140
S2179 "Live in Charity" ("*Ubi Caritas*") (John)

**Vocal Solos**

"Sing a Song of Joy" (Pss)
V-4 p. 2
"All Creatures of Our God and King" (Pss)
V-6 p. 55
"This Is My Commandment" (John)
V-8 p. 284

**Anthems**

"All Creatures of Our God and King" (Pss)
Arr. Nick Page; Choristers Guild CGA-1344
SATB *a cappella* with solo

"Sometimes a Light Surprises" (Rev)
Williams/Gossler; MorningStar MSM-50-8841
SATB with keyboard, opt. children's choir or soloist

**Other Suggestions**

Visuals:
**Acts** Sheet, animals, baptism, Holy Spirit, rebirth
**P** Creation, sun/moon/stars, angels, nature, all ages, praise
**E** Newness, marriage, home, unity, water, Alpha & Omega, baptism
**G** Newness, love, John 13:34a, b
Introit: WS3094. "Come to Me" (Rev)
Greeting: BOW378 (Pss)
Opening Prayer: BOW393 (Acts, Rev)
Canticle: UM734. "Canticle of Hope" (Rev)
Prayer for Illumination: WSL75 (Rev)
Call to Prayer: S2132. "You Who Are Thirsty" (Rev)
Prayer: BOW399. Week 5 (Easter)
Prayer: BOW503. For the Church (Acts, John)
Intercessory Prayer: BOW397 (Rev)
Litany: WSL197 or UM556 (Acts, John)
Blessing: BOW564 (John)

### Acts 16:9-15

9 A vision of a man from Macedonia came to Paul during the night. He stood urging Paul, "Come over to Macedonia and help us!" 10 Immediately after he saw the vision, we prepared to leave for the province of Macedonia, concluding that God had called us to proclaim the good news to them.

11 We sailed from Troas straight for Samothrace and came to Neapolis the following day. 12 From there we went to Philippi, a city of Macedonia's first district and a Roman colony. We stayed in that city several days. 13 On the Sabbath we went outside the city gate to the riverbank, where we thought there might be a place for prayer. We sat down and began to talk with the women who had gathered. 14 One of those women was Lydia, a Gentile God-worshipper from the city of Thyatira, a dealer in purple cloth. As she listened, the Lord enabled her to embrace Paul's message. 15 Once she and her household were baptized, she urged, "Now that you have decided that I am a believer in the Lord, come and stay in my house." And she persuaded us.

---

### Psalm 67 (UM791)

Let God grant us grace and bless us;  
  let God make his face shine on us, *[Selah]*  
  2 so that your way becomes known on earth,  
  so that your salvation becomes known among all the  
      nations.  
3 Let the people thank you, God!  
  Let all the people thank you!  
  4 Let the people celebrate  
    and shout with joy  
    because you judge the nations fairly  
    and guide all nations on the earth. *[Selah]*  
  5 Let the people thank you, God!  
  Let all the people thank you!  
6 The earth has yielded its harvest.  
  God blesses us—our God blesses us!  
7 Let God continue to bless us;  
  let the far ends of the earth honor him.

---

### Revelation 21:1-10, 22–22:5

Then I saw a new heaven and a new earth, for the former heaven and the former earth had passed away, and the sea was no more. 2 I saw the holy city, New Jerusalem, coming down out of heaven from God, made ready as a bride beautifully dressed for her husband. 3 I heard a loud voice from the throne say, "Look! God's dwelling is here with humankind. He will dwell with them, and they will be his peoples. God himself will be with them as their God. 4 He will wipe away every tear from their eyes. Death will be no more. There will be no mourning, crying, or pain anymore, for the former things have passed away." 5 Then the one seated on the throne said, "Look! I'm making all things new." He also said, "Write this down, for these words are trustworthy and true." 6 Then he said to me, "All is done. I am the Alpha and the Omega, the beginning and the end. To the thirsty I will freely give water from the life-giving spring. 7 Those who emerge victorious will inherit these things. I will be their God, and they will be my sons and daughters. 8 But for the cowardly, the faithless, the vile, the murderers, those who commit sexual immorality, those who use drugs and cast spells, the idolaters and all liars—their share will be in the lake that burns with fire and sulfur. This is the second death."

9 Then one of the seven angels who had the seven bowls full of the seven last plagues spoke with me. "Come," he said, "I will show you the bride, the Lamb's wife." 10 He took me in a Spirit-inspired trance to a great, high mountain, and he showed me the holy city, Jerusalem, coming down out of heaven from God. . . .

22 I didn't see a temple in the city, because its temple is the Lord God Almighty and the Lamb. 23 The city doesn't need the sun or the moon to shine on it, because God's glory is its light, and its lamp is the Lamb. 24 The nations will walk by its light, and the kings of the earth will bring their glory into it. 25 Its gates will never be shut by day, and there will be no night there. 26 They will bring the glory and honor of the nations into it. 27 Nothing unclean will ever enter it, nor anyone who does what is vile and deceitful, but only those who are registered in the Lamb's scroll of life.

22 Then the angel showed me the river of life-giving water, shining like crystal, flowing from the throne of God and the Lamb 2 through the middle of the city's main street. On each side of the river is the tree of life, which produces twelve crops of fruit, bearing its fruit each month. The tree's leaves are for the healing of the nations. 3 There will no longer be any curse. The throne of God and the Lamb will be in it, and his servants will worship him. 4 They will see his face, and his name will be on their foreheads. 5 Night will be no more. They won't need the light of a lamp or the light of the sun, for the Lord God will shine on them, and they will rule forever and always.

---

### John 14:23-29

23 Jesus answered, "Whoever loves me will keep my word. My Father will love them, and we will come to them and make our home with them. 24 Whoever doesn't love me doesn't keep my words. The word that you hear isn't mine. It is the word of the Father who sent me.

25 "I have spoken these things to you while I am with you. 26 The Companion, the Holy Spirit, whom the Father will send in my name, will teach you everything and will remind you of everything I told you.

27 "Peace I leave with you. My peace I give you. I give to you not as the world gives. Don't be troubled or afraid. 28 You have heard me tell you, 'I'm going away and returning to you.' If you loved me, you would be happy that I am going to the Father, because the Father is greater than me. 29 I have told you before it happens so that when it happens you will believe."

### Primary Hymns and Songs for the Day

103 "Immortal, Invisible, God Only Wise" (Rev) (O)
H-3 Hbl-15, 71; Chr-65; Desc-93; Org-135
S-1 #300. Harm.
723 "Shall We Gather at the River" (Acts, Rev)
H-3 Chr-169
79 "Holy God, We Praise Thy Name" (Pss)
H-3 Chr-78, 98; Desc-48; Org-48
S-1 #151-53. Harm. and descs.
2218 "You Are Mine" (John)
428 "For the Healing of the Nations" (Rev) (C)
H-3 Hbl-25, 51, 58; Chr-89; Desc-26; Org-23
S-1 #76-77. Desc. and harm.

### Additional Hymn Suggestions

589 "The Church of Christ, in Every Age" (Acts, John)
555 "Forward Through the Ages" (Acts)
2243 "We All Are One in Mission" (Acts)
3158 "Go to the World" (Acts)
3147 "Built on a Rock" (Acts, John)
67 "We, Thy People, Praise Thee" (Pss)
93 "Let All the World in Every Corner Sing" (Pss)
127 "Guide Me, O Thou Great Jehovah" (Rev)
206 "I Want to Walk as a Child of the Light" (Rev)
524 "Beams of Heaven as I Go" (Rev)
540 "I Love Thy Kingdom, Lord" (Rev)
623 "Here, O My Lord, I See Thee" (Rev, Comm.)
722 "I Want to Be Ready" (Rev)
725 "Arise, Shine Out, Your Light Has Come" (Rev)
726 "O Holy City, Seen of John" (Rev)
400 "Come, Thou Fount of Every Blessing" (Rev)
2142 "Blessed Quietness" (Rev)
2158 "Just a Closer Walk with Thee" (Rev)
2210 "Joy Comes with the Dawn" (Rev)
2284 "Joy in the Morning" (Rev)
569 "We've a Story to Tell to the Nations" (Rev) (C)
2282 "I'll Fly Away" (Rev) (C)
3089 "O Living God" (Rev, Easter)
3094 "Come to Me" (Rev, John)
350 "Come, All of You" (Rev, John)
380 "There's Within My Heart a Melody" (John)
408 "The Gift of Love" (John)
422 "Jesus, Thine All-Victorious Love" (John)
433 "All Who Love and Serve Your City" (John)
475 "Come Down, O Love Divine" (John)
549 "Where Charity and Love Prevail" (John)
634 "Now Let Us from This Table Rise" (John, Comm.)
647 "Your Love, O God, Has Called Us Here" (John)
2156 "Give Peace" ("*Da Pacem Cordium*") (John)
2187 "Now It Is Evening" (John, Evening)
2213 "Healer of Our Every Ill" (John)

### Additional Contemporary Suggestions

S2173 "Shine, Jesus, Shine" (Rev)
SP142
UM349 "Turn Your Eyes upon Jesus" (Rev)
SP218
S2132 "You Who Are Thirsty" (Rev)
S2194 "O Freedom" (Rev)
UM171 "There's Something About That Name" (Rev)
SP89
UM706 "Soon and Very Soon" (Rev)
S-2 #187. Piano Arr.
UM347 "Spirit Song" (Rev, John)
SP134
WS3189 "There Is a Higher Throne" (Rev)
M21 "Blessing, Honour and Glory" (Rev, Easter)
M28 "Who Can Satisfy My Soul Like You?" (Rev)
M31 "I See the Lord" (Rev)
M63 "I Could Sing of Your Love Forever" (Rev)
M69 "Did You Feel the Mountains Tremble?" (Rev)
M130 "Offering" (Rev)
M154 "Dwell" (John)
S2266 "Here Is Bread, Here Is Wine" (John, Comm.)
SP48 "Behold, What Manner of Love" (John)
M88 "Holy Spirit, Rain Down" (John)

### Vocal Solos

"Praise to the Lord, the Almighty" (Pss)
V-6 p. 18
"Come, Thou Fount of Every Blessing" (Rev)
V-3 (3) p. 22
V-6 p. 4
"Just a Closer Walk with Thee" (Rev)
V-5(2) p. 31
V-8 p. 323
"Gentle Like Jesus" (John)
V-8 p. 42

### Anthems

"The Music of Living" (Rev)
Dan Forrest; Hinshaw HMC2321
SATB with keyboard, opt. violin, horn, percussion

"*Dona Nobis Pacem*" (John)
Arr. Emily Lund; Hope C-5821
Two-part mixed with piano

### Other Suggestions

Visuals:
**Acts** Purple cloth, women witnessing, ship/sails, open/closed door
**P** Thanksgiving, first garden fruit, rogation
**E** Light/lamp, nations, open gates, sing, Lamb, book, water
**G** Love, Word, Trinity, Spirit, John 14:27, briefcase, lamp, heart

Introit: S2157. "Come and Fill Our Hearts" (John)
Greeting: BOW390 (John)
Greeting: BOW391 or BOW453 (Rev)
Opening Prayer: BOW473 (Acts, Rev, John)
Canticle: UM734. "Canticle of Hope" (Rev)
Prayer for Illumination: WSL75 (Rev)
Prayer: WSL50 (Acts, Rev, Baptism)
Prayer: BOW511. For God's Reign (Rev)
Prayer: BOW526. For the World and Its Peoples (Pss, Rev)
Litany: BOW495. A Litany for the Church and for the World (Pss, John)
Blessing: BOW560 or Psalm 67:1 (Pss)
Sung Benediction: WS3182. "Benediction Hymn" (Pss, John)
Sung Benediction: UM667. "Shalom" (John)

**Acts 1:1-11**
Theophilus, the first scroll I wrote concerned everything
Jesus did and taught from the beginning, 2 right up to the day
when he was taken up into heaven. Before he was taken up,
working in the power of the Holy Spirit, Jesus instructed the
apostles he had chosen. 3 After his suffering, he showed them
that he was alive with many convincing proofs. He appeared
to them over a period of forty days, speaking to them about
God's kingdom. 4 While they were eating together, he
ordered them not to leave Jerusalem but to wait for what the
Father had promised. He said, "This is what you heard from
me: 5 John baptized with water, but in only a few days you will
be baptized with the Holy Spirit."
6 As a result, those who had gathered together asked Jesus,
"Lord, are you going to restore the kingdom to Israel now?"
7 Jesus replied, "It isn't for you to know the times or seasons
that the Father has set by his own authority. 8 Rather, you
will receive power when the Holy Spirit has come upon you,
and you will be my witnesses in Jerusalem, in all Judea and
Samaria, and to the end of the earth."
9 After Jesus said these things, as they were watching, he
was lifted up and a cloud took him out of their sight. 10 While
he was going away and as they were staring toward heaven,
suddenly two men in white robes stood next to them. 11 They
said, "Galileans, why are you standing here, looking toward
heaven? This Jesus, who was taken up from you into heaven,
will come in the same way that you saw him go into heaven."

---

**Psalm 47 (UM781)**
Clap your hands, all you people!
  Shout joyfully to God with a joyous shout!
2 Because the LORD Most High is awesome,
  he is the great king of the whole world.
3 He subdues the nations under us,
  subdues all people beneath our feet.
4 He chooses our inheritance for us:
  the heights of Jacob, which he loves. *[Selah]*
5 God has gone up with a joyous shout—
  the LORD with the blast of the ram's horn.
6 Sing praises to God! Sing praises!
  Sing praises to our king! Sing praises
  7 because God is king of the whole world!
  Sing praises with a song of instruction!
8 God is king over the nations.
  God sits on his holy throne.
9 The leaders of all people are gathered
  with the people of Abraham's God
  because the earth's guardians belong to God;
    God is exalted beyond all.

---

**Ephesians 1:15-23**
15 Since I heard about your faith in the Lord Jesus and your
love for all God's people, this is the reason that 16 I don't stop
giving thanks to God for you when I remember you in my
prayers. 17 I pray that the God of our Lord Jesus Christ, the
Father of glory, will give you a spirit of wisdom and revelation that makes God known to you. 18 I pray that the eyes of
your heart will have enough light to see what is the hope of
God's call, what is the richness of God's glorious inheritance
among believers, 19 and what is the overwhelming greatness
of God's power that is working among us believers. This
power is conferred by the energy of God's powerful strength.
20 God's power was at work in Christ when God raised him
from the dead and sat him at God's right side in the heavens,
21 far above every ruler and authority and power and angelic
power, any power that might be named not only now but
in the future. 22 God put everything under Christ's feet and
made him head of everything in the church, 23 which is his
body. His body, the church, is the fullness of Christ, who fills
everything in every way.

---

**Luke 24:44-53**
44 Jesus said to them, "These are my words that I spoke to
you while I was still with you—that everything written about
me in the Law from Moses, the Prophets, and the Psalms
must be fulfilled." 45 Then he opened their minds to understand the scriptures. 46 He said to them, "This is what is written: the Christ will suffer and rise from the dead on the third
day, 47 and a change of heart and life for the forgiveness of
sins must be preached in his name to all nations, beginning
from Jerusalem. 48 You are witnesses of these things. 49 Look,
I'm sending to you what my Father promised, but you are to
stay in the city until you have been furnished with heavenly
power."
50 He led them out as far as Bethany, where he lifted his
hands and blessed them. 51 As he blessed them, he left them
and was taken up to heaven. 52 They worshipped him and
returned to Jerusalem overwhelmed with joy. 53 And they
were continuously in the temple praising God.

**Primary Hymns and Songs for the Day**

154 "All Hail the Power of Jesus' Name" (Acts) (O)
H-3 Hbl-45; Chr-22; Desc-24; Org-20
S-1 #66-70. Various treatments

155 "All Hail the Power of Jesus' Name" (Acts) (O)
H-3 Desc-29; Org-27
S-2 #50-51. Desc. and interlude

312 "Hail the Day That Sees Him Rise" (Acts) (O)
H-3 Hbl-72; Chr-50; Desc-69; Org-78
S-1 #213. Desc.

2028 "Clap Your Hands" (Pss)

2074 "Shout to the Lord" (Pss)
M16; V-3 (2) p. 32 Vocal solo

559 "Christ Is Made the Sure Foundation" (Eph)
H-3 Chr-49; Desc-103; Org-180
S-1 #346. Desc.

2086 "Open Our Eyes, Lord" (Eph)
SP199

384 "Love Divine, All Loves Excelling" (Luke) (C)
H-3 Chr-134; Desc-18; Org-13
S-1 #41-42. Desc. and harm.

---

**Additional Hymn Suggestions**

324 "Hail Thee, Festival Day" (Acts, Luke) (O)
313 "*Cristo Vive*" ("Christ Is Risen") (Acts, Luke)
319 "Christ Jesus Lay in Death's Strong Bands" (Acts)
494 "Kum Ba Yah" ("Come By Here") (Acts)
541 "See How Great a Flame Aspires" (Acts)
2247 "Wonder of Wonders" (Acts, Baptism)
2248 "Baptized in Water" (Acts, Baptism)
3089 "O Living God" (Acts)
157 "Jesus Shall Reign" (Pss, Eph)
188 "Christ Is the World's Light" (Acts, Pss)
325 "Hail, Thou Once Despised Jesus" (Pss, Eph)
326 "The Head That Once Was Crowned" (Pss, Eph)
327 "Crown Him with Many Crowns" (Pss, Eph, Luke)
178 "Hope of the World" (Eph)
368 "My Hope Is Built" (Eph)
711 "For All the Saints" (Eph)
2147 "There Are Some Things I May Not Know" (Eph)
2205 "The Fragrance of Christ" (Eph)
2220 "We Are God's People" (Eph)
2261 "Life-Giving Bread" (Eph, Comm.)
2279 "The Trees of the Field" (Eph)
3035 "Bless Christ Through Whom All Things Are Made" (Eph)
302 "Christ the Lord Is Risen Today" (Luke)
307 "Christ Is Risen" (Luke, Comm.)
2077 "You Alone Are Holy" ("*Solo Tu Eres Santo*") (Luke)
2084 "Come, Let Us with Our Lord Arise" (Luke)
2115 "Christ Has Risen" (Luke)
2117 "Spirit of God" (Luke)
2184 "Sent Out in Jesus' Name" (Luke) (C)
2282 "I'll Fly Away" (Luke, Ascension)
3087 "O Christ, When You Ascended" (Luke, Ascension)

---

**Additional Contemporary Suggestions**

S2125 "Come, Holy Spirit" (Acts)
SP132

M88 "Holy Spirit, Rain Down" (Acts, Luke)
M234 "Awesome Is the Lord Most High" (Acts, Luke)
S2070 "He Is Exalted" (Pss, Ascension)
SP66

M120 "Lord Most High" (Pss)
WS3023 "Forever" (Eph)
M68

WS3104 "Amazing Grace" ("My Chains Are Gone") (Eph)
M205

WS3105 "In Christ Alone" ("My Hope Is Found") (Eph, Ascension)
M138

M77 "Above All" (Eph, Ascension)
V-3 (2) p. 17 Vocal Solo

S2006 "Lord God Almighty" (Luke)
S2078 "Alleluia" (Luke, Ascension)
S2116 "Christ the Lord Is Risen" (Luke, Ascension)
S2088 "Lord, I Lift Your Name on High" (Luke, Ascension)
M2

WS3188 "Hosanna" (Ascension)
M268

---

**Vocal Solos**

"Jesus Christ Is Risen Today" (Acts, Luke)
V-1 p. 50
"Rejoice Now, My Spirit" (Pss)
V-9 p. 30
"In the First Light" (Ascension)
V-5(1) p. 28
"Ride On, Jesus" (Ascension)
V-7 p. 8

---

**Anthems**

"All Hail the Power of Jesus' Name" (Acts)
Arr. Marty Parks; Hope C-5836
SATB with keyboard (opt. Irish fiddle)

"Love Divine, All Loves Excelling" (Luke)
Mack Wilberg; Oxford 0-19-386490-8
SATB with organ

---

**Other Suggestions**

*These ideas may be used on May 8 as Ascension Sunday.*

Visuals:
- **Acts** Baptism, Holy Spirit, Ascension, mantel
- **P** Clasped hands, Ascension, trumpet, singing, feet
- **E** Praying, heart, Bible, Christ/throne, names, church
- **G** Mantel, Bible, witness, Ascension, worship, joy

Introit: S2118. "Holy Spirit, Come to Us" ("*Veni Sancte Spiritus*")
Greeting: BOW387 or BOW402 (Acts, Pss, Luke)
Call to Worship: WSL35 (Luke, Easter)
Opening Prayer: BOW392 (Acts)
Call to Prayer: S2273, BOW187. "Jesus, We Are Here" (Acts, Luke)
Prayer: BOW399. Week 7 (Easter)
Prayer: UM323 or BOW403 (Ascension)
Response to Prayer: S2276. "Glory to God in the Highest" (Pss, Eph)
Affirmation of Faith: WSL76 (Eph, Ascension)
Offertory Prayer: WSL131 (Eph, Easter)
Call to Communion: S2269. "Come, Share the Lord" (Eph)
Great Thanksgiving for Easter Season: BOW, pp. 66-67 (Comm.)

**Acts 16:16-34**

16 One day, when we were on the way to the place for prayer,
we met a slave woman. She had a spirit that enabled her to
predict the future. She made a lot of money for her owners
through fortune-telling. 17 She began following Paul and us,
shouting, "These people are servants of the Most High God!
They are proclaiming a way of salvation to you!" 18 She did
this for many days.
This annoyed Paul so much that he finally turned and said
to the spirit, "In the name of Jesus Christ, I command you to
leave her!" It left her at that very moment.
19 Her owners realized that their hope for making money
was gone. They grabbed Paul and Silas and dragged them
before the officials in the city center. 20 When her owners
approached the legal authorities, they said, "These people
are causing an uproar in our city. They are Jews 21 who promote customs that we Romans can't accept or practice."
22 The crowd joined in the attacks against Paul and Silas, so
the authorities ordered that they be stripped of their clothes
and beaten with a rod. 23 When Paul and Silas had been
severely beaten, the authorities threw them into prison and
ordered the jailer to secure them with great care. 24 When he
received these instructions, he threw them into the inner-
most cell and secured their feet in stocks.
25 Around midnight Paul and Silas were praying and singing hymns to God, and the other prisoners were listening to
them. 26 All at once there was such a violent earthquake that
it shook the prison's foundations. The doors flew open and
everyone's chains came loose. 27 When the jailer awoke and
saw the open doors of the prison, he thought the prisoners
had escaped, so he drew his sword and was about to kill himself. 28 But Paul shouted loudly, "Don't harm yourself! We're
all here!"
29 The jailer called for some lights, rushed in, and fell trembling before Paul and Silas. 30 He led them outside and asked,
"Honorable masters, what must I do to be rescued?"
31 They replied, "Believe in the Lord Jesus, and you will be
saved—you and your entire household." 32 They spoke the
Lord's word to him and everyone else in his house. 33 Right
then, in the middle of the night, the jailer welcomed them
and washed their wounds. He and everyone in his household
were immediately baptized. 34 He brought them into his
home and gave them a meal. He was overjoyed because he
and everyone in his household had come to believe in God.

---

**Psalm 97 (UM816)**

The LORD rules! Let the earth rejoice!
  Let all the islands celebrate!
2 Clouds and thick darkness surround God.
  His throne is built on righteousness and justice.
3 Fire proceeds before him,
  burning up his enemies on every side.
4 His lightning lights up the world;
  the earth sees it and trembles!
5 The mountains melt like wax before the LORD,
  before the LORD of the whole world!
6 Heaven has proclaimed God's righteousness,
  and all nations have seen his glory.
7 All those who worship images,
  those who are proud of idols,
  are put to shame.
All gods bow down to the LORD!
8 Zion has heard and celebrates,
  the towns of Judah rejoice,
  because of your acts of justice, LORD,
  9 because you, LORD, are the Most High
    over all the earth,
  because you are so superior to all other gods.
10 Those of you who love the LORD, hate evil!
  God guards the lives of his faithful ones,
  delivering them from the power of the wicked.
11 Light is planted like seed for the righteous person;
  joy too for those whose heart is right.
12 Rejoice in the LORD, righteous ones!
  Give thanks to his holy name!

---

**Revelation 22:12-14, 16-17, 20-21**

12 "Look! I'm coming soon. My reward is with me, to repay
all people as their actions deserve. 13 I am the alpha and the
omega, the first and the last, the beginning and the end.
14 Favored are those who wash their robes so that they may
have the right of access to the tree of life and may enter the
city by the gates. . . .
16 "I, Jesus, have sent my angel to bear witness to all of you
about these things for the churches. I'm the root and descen-
dant of David, the bright morning star. 17 The Spirit and the
bride say, 'Come!' Let the one who hears say, 'Come!' And let
the one who is thirsty come! Let the one who wishes receive
life-giving water as a gift." . . .
20 The one who bears witness to these things says, "Yes, I'm
coming soon." Amen. Come, Lord Jesus!
21 The grace of the Lord Jesus be with all.

---

**John 17:20-26**

20 "I'm not praying only for them but also for those who
believe in me because of their word. 21 I pray they will be one,
Father, just as you are in me and I am in you. I pray that they
also will be in us, so that the world will believe that you sent
me. 22 I've given them the glory that you gave me so that they
can be one just as we are one. 23 I'm in them and you are in
me so that they will be made perfectly one. Then the world
will know that you sent me and that you have loved them just
as you loved me.
24 "Father, I want those you gave me to be with me where I
am. Then they can see my glory, which you gave me because
you loved me before the creation of the world.
25 "Righteous Father, even the world didn't know you, but
I've known you, and these believers know that you sent me.
26 I've made your name known to them and will continue to
make it known so that your love for me will be in them, and I
myself will be in them."

**Primary Hymns and Songs for the Day**

731 "Glorious Things of Thee Are Spoken" (Rev) (O)
H-3 Hbl-61; Chr-72; Desc-17; Org-11
S-1 #27. Desc.
#28. Harm. in F major
610 "We Know That Christ Is Raised (Acts, Easter) (O)
H-3 Hbl-100; Chr-214; Desc- ; Org-37
S-1 #118-27. Various treatments
247 "O Morning Star, How Fair and Bright" (Pss, Rev)
H-3 Chr-147; Desc-104; Org-183
363 "And Can It Be that I Should Gain" (Acts)
2069 "All Hail King Jesus" (Rev)
SP63
2224 "Make Us One" (John)
SP137
561 "Jesus, United by Thy Grace" (John) (C)
H-3 Hbl-52, 73; Chr-90; Desc-92; Org-131
S-1 #291-292. Desc. and harm.
2223 "They'll Know We Are Christians" (John) (C)

**Additional Hymn Suggestions**

130 "God Will Take Care of You" (Acts)
266 "Heal Us, Emmanuel, Hear Our Prayer" (Acts)
367 "He Touched Me" (Acts)
458 "Dear Lord, for All in Pain" (Acts)
512 "Stand By Me" (Acts)
605 "Wash, O God, Our Sons and Daughters" (Acts)
606 "Come, Let Us Use the Grace Divine" (Acts)
608 "This Is the Spirit's Entry Now" (Acts, Baptism)
2146 "His Eye Is on the Sparrow" (Acts)
2247 "Wonder of Wonders" (Acts, Baptism)
2248 "Baptized in Water" (Acts, Baptism)
2249 "God Claims You" (Acts)
2251 "We Were Baptized in Christ Jesus" (Acts, Baptism)
3110 "By Grace We Have Been Saved" (Acts)
2062 "The Lily of the Valley" (Acts, Rev)
3094 "Come to Me" (Rev)
184 "Of the Father's Love Begotten" (Rev)
348 "Softly and Tenderly Jesus Is Calling" (Rev) (C)
569 "We've a Story to Tell to the Nations" (Rev)
723 "Shall We Gather at the River" (Rev)
730 "O Day of God, Draw Nigh" (Rev)
2018 "Honor and Praise" (Rev)
2076 "O Blessed Spring" (Rev)
2284 "Joy in the Morning" (Rev)
388 "O Come and Dwell in Me" (John)
445 "Happy the Home When God Is There" (John, Christian Home)
447 "Our Parent, by Whose Name" (John, Christian Home)
547 "O Church of God, United" (John)
557 "Blest Be the Tie That Binds" (John)
562 "Jesus, Lord, We Look to Thee" (John)
604 "Praise and Thanksgiving Be to God" (John)
2220 "We Are God's People" (John)
2238 "In the Midst of New Dimensions" (John)
2232 "Come Now, O Prince of Peace" ("*O-So-So*") (John)

**Additional Contemporary Suggestions**

S2250 "I've Just Come from the Fountain" (Acts)
M8 "Nobody Fills My Heart Like Jesus" (Acts)
M252 "God with Us" (Acts)
WS3104 "Amazing Grace" ("My Chains Are Gone") (Acts, Rev)
M205
M251 "Grace Like Rain" (Acts, Rev)
M62 "Rise Up and Praise Him" (Pss)
WS3023 "Forever" (Pss)
M68
M77 "Above All" (Pss)
V-3 (2) p. 17 Vocal Solo
M120 "Lord Most High" (Pss)
M134 "It Is You" (Pss)
S2022 "Great Is the Lord" (Pss)
SP30
S2070 "He Is Exalted" (Pss)
SP66
SP18 "I Exalt You" (Pss)
S2087 "We Will Glorify" (Rev)
SP68
S2132 "You Who Are Thirsty" (Rev)
S2192 "Freedom Is Coming" (Rev)
WS3189 "There Is a Higher Throne" (Rev)
M20 "Jesus Is Alive" (Rev)
M24 "Jesus, We Crown You with Praise" (Rev)
M32 "Holy and Anointed One" (Rev)
M55 "Jehovah Reigns" (Rev)
M63 "I Could Sing of Your Love Forever"
M69 "Do You Feel the Mountains Tremble?" (Rev)
WS3003 "How Great Is Our God" (Rev)
M117
M159 "All Who Are Thirsty" (Rev)
S2226 "Bind Us Together" (John)
SP140

**Vocal Solos**

"O Glorious Love" (Acts)
V-8 p. 306
"Softly and Tenderly" (Rev)
V-5(3) p. 52
"My Lord, What a Mornin'" (Rev)
V-7 p. 68

**Anthems**

"E'en So, Lord Jesus Quickly Come" (Rev)
Paul Manz; Concordia 98-1054
SATB *a cappella*

"He's Got the Whole World" (John)
Arr. Joel Ramey; Hope C-5848
SAB with piano, optional unison choir

**Other Suggestions**

*You may celebrate Ascension today, using May 5 ideas.*
Visuals:
**Acts** Fortune teller/money, rods/open shackles, chains, baptism
**P** Coast, clouds, lightning, shield/rescue
**E** Alpha/Omega, white robe, root, flame, bride, water, Rev 22:20b
**G** Jesus praying, hearts
Greeting: WSL33 (Easter)
Introit: WS3050. "Until Jesus Comes" (Rev)
Canticle: UM734. "Canticle of Hope" (Rev)
Baptism Response: UM609. "You Have Put On Christ" (Acts)
Prayer: BOW437 or 439 (Festival of the Christian Home)

**Acts 2:1-21**

When Pentecost Day arrived, they were all together in one
place. 2 Suddenly a sound from heaven like the howling of a
fierce wind filled the entire house where they were sitting.
3 They saw what seemed to be individual flames of fire alight-
ing on each one of them. 4 They were all filled with the Holy
Spirit and began to speak in other languages as the Spirit
enabled them to speak.

5 There were pious Jews from every nation under heaven
living in Jerusalem. 6 When they heard this sound, a crowd
gathered. They were mystified because everyone heard them
speaking in their native languages. 7 They were surprised and
amazed, saying, "Look, aren't all the people who are speaking Galileans, every one of them? 8 How then can each of
us hear them speaking in our native language? 9 Parthians,
Medes, and Elamites; as well as residents of Mesopotamia,
Judea, and Cappadocia, Pontus and Asia, 10 Phrygia and
Pamphylia, Egypt and the regions of Libya bordering Cyrene;
and visitors from Rome (both Jews and converts to Judaism),
11 Cretans and Arabs—we hear them declaring the mighty
works of God in our own languages!" 12 They were all surprised and bewildered. Some asked each other, "What does
this mean?" 13 Others jeered at them, saying, "They're full of
new wine!"

14 Peter stood with the other eleven apostles. He raised his
voice and declared, "Judeans and everyone living in Jerusalem! Know this! Listen carefully to my words! 15 These people
aren't drunk, as you suspect; after all, it's only nine o'clock in
the morning! 16 Rather, this is what was spoken through the
prophet Joel:

17 *In the last days, God says,*
*I will pour out my Spirit on all people.*
*Your sons and daughters will prophesy.*
*Your young will see visions.*
*Your elders will dream dreams.*
18 *Even upon my servants, men and women,*
*I will pour out my Spirit in those days,*
*and they will prophesy.*
19 *I will cause wonders to occur in the heavens above*
*and signs on the earth below,*
*blood and fire and a cloud of smoke.*
20 *The sun will be changed into darkness,*
*and the moon will be changed into blood,*
*before the great and spectacular day of the Lord comes.*
21 *And everyone who calls on the name of the Lord will be saved.*

---

**Psalm 104:24-34, 35b (UM826)**

LORD, you have done so many things!
You made them all so wisely!
The earth is full of your creations!
25 And then there's the sea, wide and deep,
with its countless creatures—
living things both small and large.
26 There go the ships on it,
and Leviathan, which you made, plays in it!
27 All your creations wait for you
to give them their food on time.
28 When you give it to them, they gather it up;
when you open your hand, they are filled completely full!
29 But when you hide your face, they are terrified;
when you take away their breath,
they die and return to dust.
30 When you let loose your breath, they are created,
and you make the surface of the ground brand-new
again.
31 Let the LORD's glory last forever!
Let the LORD rejoice in all he has made!
32 He has only to look at the earth, and it shakes.
God just touches the mountains, and they erupt in
smoke.
33 I will sing to the LORD as long as I live;
I will sing praises to my God while I'm still alive.
34 Let my praise be pleasing to him;
I'm rejoicing in the LORD!

. . . . . . . . . . . . . . . . . . . . . . . . . . .

35b But let my whole being bless the LORD!

---

**Romans 8:14-17**

14 All who are led by God's Spirit are God's sons and
daughters. 15 You didn't receive a spirit of slavery to lead you
back again into fear, but you received a Spirit that shows you
are adopted as his children. With this Spirit, we cry, "Abba,
Father." 16 The same Spirit agrees with our spirit, that we are
God's children. 17 But if we are children, we are also heirs. We
are God's heirs and fellow heirs with Christ, if we really suffer
with him so that we can also be glorified with him.

---

**John 14:8-17 (25-27)**

8 Philip said, "Lord, show us the Father; that will be enough
for us."

9 Jesus replied, "Don't you know me, Philip, even after I
have been with you all this time? Whoever has seen me has
seen the Father. How can you say, 'Show us the Father'?
10 Don't you believe that I am in the Father and the Father is
in me? The words I have spoken to you I don't speak on my
own. The Father who dwells in me does his works. 11 Trust me
when I say that I am in the Father and the Father is in me, or
at least believe on account of the works themselves. 12 I
assure you that whoever believes in me will do the works that
I do. They will do even greater works than these because I
am going to the Father. 13 I will do whatever you ask for in my
name, so that the Father can be glorified in the Son.
14 When you ask me for anything in my name, I will do it.

15 "If you love me, you will keep my commandments. 16 I will
ask the Father, and he will send another Companion, who
will be with you forever. 17 This Companion is the Spirit of
Truth, whom the world can't receive because it neither sees
him nor recognizes him. You know him, because he lives with
you and will be with you. . . .

25 "I have spoken these things to you while I am with you.
26 The Companion, the Holy Spirit, whom the Father will
send in my name, will teach you everything and will remind
you of everything I told you.

27 "Peace I leave with you. My peace I give you. I give to you
not as the world gives. Don't be troubled or afraid."

**Primary Hymns and Songs for the Day**

539 "O Spirit of the Living God" (Acts) (O)
H-3 Hbl-44; Chr-21; Desc-40; Org-40
S-1 #131-32. Intro. and desc.
347 "Spirit Song" (Acts)
SP134
475 "Come Down, O Love Divine" (Acts)
2142 "Blessed Quietness" (John)
384 "Love Divine, All Loves Excelling" (John) (C)
H-3 Chr-134; Desc-18; Org-13
S-1 #41-42. Desc. and harm.

**Additional Hymn Suggestions**

324 "Hail Thee, Festival Day" (Acts)
331 "Holy Spirit, Come, Confirm Us" (Acts)
332 "Spirit of Faith, Come Down" (Acts, Rom) (O)
537 "Filled with the Spirit's Power" (Acts)
538 "Wind Who Makes All Winds That Blow" (Acts)
541 "See How Great a Flame Aspires" (Acts, John)
544 "Like the Murmur of the Dove's Song" (Acts, John)
547 "O Church of God, United" (Acts)
552 "Here, O Lord, Your Servants Gather" (Acts)
2027 "Now Praise the Hidden God of Love" (Acts)
2117 "Spirit of God" (Acts, John, Pentecost)
2120 "Spirit, Spirit of Gentleness" (Acts, Pentecost)
2122 "She Comes Sailing on the Wind" (Acts, Pentecost)
2236 "Gather Us In" (Acts)
2237 "As a Fire Is Meant for Burning" (Acts)
2246 "Deep in the Shadows of the Past" (Acts, Pentecost)
2269 "Come, Share the Lord" (Acts, Comm.)
3109 "Living Spirit, Holy Fire" (Acts)
73 "O Worship the King" (Pss)
148 "Many and Great, O God" (Pss)
372 "How Can We Sinners Know" (Rom)
404 "Every Time I Feel the Spirit" (Rom)
414 "Thou Hidden Love of God" (Rom)
2050 "Mothering God, You Gave Me Birth" (Rom)
113 "Source and Sovereign, Rock and Cloud" (John)
188 "Christ Is the World's Light" (John)
350 "Come, All of You" (John)
364 "Because He Lives" (John)
380 "There's Within My Heart a Melody" (John)
2218 "You Are Mine" (John, Confirmation)
2123 "Loving Spirit" (Pentecost)
2238 "In the Midst of New Dimensions" (Pentecost) (C)
2241 "The Spirit Sends Us Forth to Serve" (Pentecost) (C)

**Additional Contemporary Suggestions**

WS3092 "Come, Holy Spirit" (Acts, Pentecost)
S2049 "God Is Here Today" ("Dios Está Aquí) (Acts)
S2272 "Holy Ground" (Acts)
SP86
M36 "Awesome in This Place" (Acts)
M144 "Light the Fire Again" (Acts)
M168 "He Reigns" (Acts, Pentecost)
M88 "Holy Spirit, Rain Down" (Acts, John)
UM393 "Spirit of the Living God" (Rom)
SP131; S-1#212 Vocal Desc. idea
S2039 "Holy, Holy" (Rom, Pentecost)
SP141
UM328 "Surely the Presence of the Lord" (Acts, Pentecost)
SP243; S-2 #200. Stanzas for soloist
UM334 "Sweet, Sweet Spirit" (Acts)
S2119 "Where the Spirit of the Lord Is" (Acts, Pentecost)
S2124 "Come, O Holy Spirit, Come" (Acts, Pentecost)
M4 "Let It Rise" (Pss, Pentecost)
S2156 "Give Peace" ("*Da Pacem Cordium*") (John)
S2157 "Come and Fill Our Hearts" (John)
SP48 "Behold, What Manner of Love" (John)
M13 "Be Glorified" (John)
M154 "Dwell" (John, Pentecost)

**Vocal Solos**

"Spirit of Faith Come Down" (Acts)
V-1 p. 43
"Ev'ry Time I Feel De Spirit" (Acts)
V-7 p. 78
"New Wind Blowin'" (Acts)
V-8 p. 192
"I Feel the Spirit Moving" (Acts, Rom)
V-3 (1) p.22

**Anthems**

"Come Down, Holy Spirit" (Acts)
Lee Dengler; HW Gray/Alfred 42496
SATB with piano and opt. C instrument

"There's Within My Heart a Melody" (John)
Luther B. Bridgers; Hope C5478
SATB with piano and opt. handbells

**Other Suggestions**

Visuals:
**Acts** Wind, flames, nature, wine, clock (9:00 a.m.), nations, blood
**P** Nature, ship/whale, open hand, volcano, joy
**E** Children, open shackles, adoption certificate, will
**G** Jesus, ministry, prayer, flames, Bible, John 14:27

*Consider beginning the service with a reflective mood, using meditative opening songs, such as S2118, S2125, S2156, and WS3091. After the Pentecost reading, move to more celebrative hymns of the Holy Spirit.*

Introit: WS3146 or UM543. "O Breath of Life" (Acts)
Greeting: BOW406 (Pentecost)
Responsive Invocation: WSL39 (Acts, Pentecost)
Opening Prayer: BOW404 or WSL37 (Pentecost)
Response: S2118. "Holy Spirit, Come to Us" (Acts)
Prayer: WSL38, UM574, UM542, or BOW407 (Pentecost)
Litany: UM556. Litany for Christian Unity (Acts)
Offertory Prayer: WSL132 (Pentecost)

**Proverbs 8:1-4, 22-31**

Doesn't Wisdom cry out
and Understanding shout?
2 Atop the heights along the path,
at the crossroads she takes her stand.
3 By the gate before the city,
at the entrances she shouts:
4 "I cry out to you, people;
my voice goes out to all of humanity."
. . . . . . . . . . . . . . . . . . . . . . . . .
22 The LORD created me at the beginning of his way,
before his deeds long in the past.
23 I was formed in ancient times,
at the beginning, before the earth was.
24 When there were no watery depths, I was brought forth,
when there were no springs flowing with water.
25 Before the mountains were settled,
before the hills, I was brought forth;
26 before God made the earth and the fields
or the first of the dry land.
27 I was there when he established the heavens,
when he marked out the horizon on the deep sea,
28 when he thickened the clouds above,
when he secured the fountains of the deep,
29 when he set a limit for the sea,
so the water couldn't go beyond his command,
when he marked out the earth's foundations.
30 I was beside him as a master of crafts.
I was having fun,
smiling before him all the time,
31 frolicking with his inhabited earth
and delighting in the human race.

---

**Psalm 8 (UM743)**

LORD, our LORD, how majestic
is your name throughout the earth!
You made your glory higher than heaven!
2 From the mouths of nursing babies
you have laid a strong foundation
because of your foes,
in order to stop vengeful enemies.
3 When I look up at your skies,
at what your fingers made—
the moon and the stars
that you set firmly in place—
4 what are human beings
that you think about them;
what are human beings
that you pay attention to them?
5 You've made them only slightly less than divine,
crowning them with glory and grandeur.
6 You've let them rule over your handiwork,
putting everything under their feet—
7 all sheep and all cattle,
the wild animals too,
8 the birds in the sky,
the fish of the ocean,
everything that travels the pathways of the sea.
9 LORD, our LORD, how majestic is your name throughout
the earth!

**Romans 5:1-5**

Therefore, since we have been made righteous through
his faithfulness combined with our faith, we have peace with
God through our Lord Jesus Christ. 2 We have access by faith
into this grace in which we stand through him, and we boast
in the hope of God's glory. 3 But not only that! We even take
pride in our problems, because we know that trouble produces endurance, 4 endurance produces character, and character produces hope. 5 This hope doesn't put us to shame,
because the love of God has been poured out in our hearts
through the Holy Spirit, who has been given to us.

---

**John 16:12-15**

12 "I have much more to say to you, but you can't handle
it now. 13 However, when the Spirit of Truth comes, he will
guide you in all truth. He won't speak on his own, but will say
whatever he hears and will proclaim to you what is to come.
14 He will glorify me, because he will take what is mine and
proclaim it to you. 15 Everything that the Father has is mine.
That's why I said that the Spirit takes what is mine and will
proclaim it to you."

**Primary Hymns and Songs for the Day**
61 "Come, Thou Almighty King" (John, Trinity) (O)
H-3 Hbl-28, 49, 53; Chr-56; Desc-57; Org-63
S-1 #185-86. Desc. and harm.
103 "Immortal, Invisible, God Only Wise" (Prov)
H-3 Hbl-15, 71; Chr-65; Desc-93; Org-135
S-1 #300. Harm.
2023 "How Majestic Is Your Name" (Pss)
SP14
368 "My Hope Is Built" (Rom)
H-3 Chr-191
S-2 #171-72. Trumpet and vocal descs.
64 "Holy, Holy, Holy" (Trinity) (C)
H-3 Hbl-68; Chr-99; Desc-80; Org-97
S-1 #245-48. Various treatments

**Additional Hymn Suggestions**
113 "Source and Sovereign, Rock and Cloud" (Prov)
539 "O Spirit of the Living God" (Prov)
62 "All Creatures of Our God and King" (Prov, Pss, Trinity)
77 "How Great Thou Art" (Prov, Pss)
92 "For the Beauty of the Earth" (Prov, Pss)
100 "God, Whose Love Is Reigning o'er Us" (Prov, Pss)
151 "God Created Heaven and Earth" (Prov, Pss)
152 "I Sing the Almighty Power of God" (Prov, Pss)
144 "This Is My Father's World" (Prov, Pss)
147 "All Things Bright and Beautiful" (Prov, Pss)
149 "*Cantemos al Señor*" ("Let's Sing unto the Lord") (Prov, Pss)
450 "Creator of the Earth and Skies" (Pss, John)
2012 "Let Us with a Joyful Mind" (Prov, Pss)
2060 "God the Sculptor of the Mountains" (Prov, Pss)
2046 "Womb of Life" (Prov, Trinity)
2047 "Bring Many Names" (Prov, Trinity)
2050 "Mothering God, You Gave Me Birth" (Prov)
369 "Blessed Assurance" (Rom)
422 "Jesus, Thine All-Victorious Love" (Rom)
480 "O Love That Wilt Not Let Me Go" (Rom)
2187 "Now It Is Evening" (Rom)
2196 "We Walk by Faith" (Rom)
2211 "Faith Is Patience in the Night" (Rom)
2213 "Healer of Our Every Ill" (Rom)
2255 "In the Singing" (Rom, Comm.)
613 "O Thou Who This Mysterious Bread" (Rom, John, Comm.)
651 "Come, Holy Ghost, Our Souls Inspire" (Rom, John)
332 "Spirit of Faith, Come Down" (Rom, John)
119 "O God in Heaven" (John, Trinity)
188 "Christ Is the World's Light" (John)
189 "Fairest Lord Jesus" (John)
475 "Come Down, O Love Divine" (John)
85 "We Believe in One True God" (Trinity)
619 "Now the Silence" (Trinity, Comm.)
2262 "Let Us Offer to the Father" (Trinity, Comm.)
2276 "Glory to God in the Highest" (Trinity)
3017 "Come, Join the Dance of Trinity" (Trinity)
2185 "For One Great Peace" (Peace with Justice)

**Additional Contemporary Suggestions**
WS3034 "God of Wonders" (Pss)
M80
WS3003 "How Great Is Our God" (Pss, Trinity)
M117
M165 "Friend of God"
M63 "I Could Sing of Your Love Forever" (Rom)
WS3104 "Amazing Grace" ("My Chains Are Gone") (Rom)
M205
WS3105 "In Christ Alone" ("My Hope Is Found") (Rom)
M138
S2258 "Sing Alleluia to the Lord" (Rom, Comm.)
SP93
S2266 "Here Is Bread, Here Is Wine" (Rom, Comm.)
UM393 "Spirit of the Living God" (John)
SP131; S-1#212 Vocal desc. idea
UM494 "*Kum Ba Yah*" ("Come By Here") (John)
S2006 "Lord God Almighty" (Trinity)
S2039 "Holy, Holy" (Trinity)
SP141
M7 "I Believe in Jesus" (Trinity)
S2186 "Song of Hope" (Peace with Justice, Benediction)

**Vocal Solos**
"Be Thou My Vision" (Prov)
V-6 p. 13
"Bright and Beautiful" (Prov, Pss)
V-3 (3) p. 10
"Redeeming Grace" (Rom)
V-4 p. 47
"Alleluia" (Trinity)
V-8 p. 358

**Anthems**
"*Santo*" (Trinity)
Arr. Mark Burrows; Choristers Guild CGA-1349
SATB with piano and opt. percussions

"Concerto on 'Holy, Holy, Holy'" (Trinity)
Arr. Patrick M. Liebergen; Jubilate/Alfred 42489
SATB with keyboard, opt. brass

**Other Suggestions**
*Today may also be celebrated as Heritage Sunday, in honor of May 24, Aldersgate Day. This year's theme, "Roots, Shoots, and Branches," recollects our historic relationship with the African Methodist Episcopal Church and the 200th anniversary of Bishop Francis Asbury's death.*
Visuals:
**O** Crossroads, gate, nature, outer space, circle, joy
**P** Space, baby, moon/stars, Adam/Eve, animals, bird, fish
**E** Kairos/chronos, heart, pouring, flames
**G** Jesus, Spirit, Bible, kairos/chronos, preaching
Greeting: BOW391 or BOW411 (Trinity)
Opening Prayer: WSL64 (Pss)
Opening Prayer: BOW511 (Peace with Justice)
Canticle: UM80 (Trinity) or UM112 (Prov)
Litany: BOW495 (Peace with Justice)
Litany: WSL53 (Rom)
Affirmation of Faith: UM881 or WSL79 (Trinity)
Prayer: BOW412 (Trinity)
Prayer: UM456, BOW428, 513-20, 526-27 (Peace with Justice)
Doxology: WSL3009. "Praise God for this Holy Ground" (Trinity)
Closing Prayer: UM76. Trinity Sunday (Trinity)
Blessing: WSL172 (Trinity)

**1 Kings 18:20-21, (22-29), 30-39**

20 Ahab sent the message to all the Israelites. He gathered
the prophets at Mount Carmel. 21 Elijah approached all the
people and said, "How long will you hobble back and forth
between two opinions? If the LORD is God, follow God. If
Baal is God, follow Baal." The people gave no answer.
22 Elijah said to the people, "I am the last of the LORD's
prophets, but Baal's prophets number four hundred fifty.
23 Give us two bulls. Let Baal's prophets choose one. Let them
cut it apart and set it on the wood, but don't add fire. I'll prepare the other bull, put it on the wood, but won't add fire.
24 Then all of you will call on the name of your god, and I
will call on the name of the LORD. The god who answers with
fire—that's the real God!"
All the people answered, "That's an excellent idea."
25 So Elijah said to the prophets of Baal, "Choose one of
these bulls. Prepare it first since there are so many of you.
Call on the name of your god, but don't add fire."
26 So they took one of the bulls that had been brought to
them. They prepared it and called on Baal's name from
morning to midday. They said, "Great Baal, answer us!" But
there was no sound or answer. They performed a hopping
dance around the altar that had been set up.
27 Around noon, Elijah started making fun of them: "Shout
louder! Certainly he's a god! Perhaps he is lost in thought or
wandering or traveling somewhere. Or maybe he is asleep
and must wake up!"
28 So the prophets of Baal cried with a louder voice and cut
themselves with swords and knives as was their custom. Their
blood flowed all over them. 29 As noon passed they went crazy
with their ritual until it was time for the evening offering.
Still there was no sound or answer, no response whatsoever.
30 Then Elijah said to all the people, "Come here!" All the
people closed in, and he repaired the LORD's altar that had
been damaged. 31 Elijah took twelve stones, according to
the number of the tribes of the sons of Jacob—to whom the
LORD's word came: "Your name will be Israel." 32 He built the
stones into an altar in the LORD's name, and he dug a trench
around the altar big enough to hold two seahs of dry grain.
33 He put the wood in order, butchered the bull, and placed
the bull on the wood. "Fill four jars with water and pour it on
the sacrifice and on the wood," he commanded. 34 "Do
it a second time!" he said. So they did it a second time. "Do
it a third time!" And so they did it a third time. 35 The water
flowed around the altar, and even the trench filled with
water. 36 At the time of the evening offering, the prophet
Elijah drew near and prayed: "LORD, the God of Abraham,
Isaac, and Israel, let it be known today that you are God in
Israel and that I am your servant. I have done all these things
at your instructions. 37 Answer me, LORD! Answer me so that
this people will know that you, LORD, are the real God and
that you can change their hearts." 38 Then the LORD's fire fell;
it consumed the sacrifice, the wood, the stones, and the dust.
It even licked up the water in the trench!
39 All the people saw this and fell on their faces. "The LORD
is the real God! The LORD is the real God!" they exclaimed.

---

**Psalm 96 (UM815)**

Sing to the LORD a new song!
  Sing to the LORD, all the earth!
2 Sing to the LORD! Bless his name!
  Share the news of his saving work every single day! . . .

---

**Galatians 1:1-12**

From Paul, an apostle who is not sent from human authority or commissioned through human agency, but sent
through Jesus Christ and God the Father who raised him
from the dead; 2 and from all the brothers and sisters with
me.
To the churches in Galatia.
3 Grace and peace to you from God the Father and the
Lord Jesus Christ. 4 He gave himself for our sins, so he could
deliver us from this present evil age, according to the will
of our God and Father. 5 To God be the glory forever and
always! Amen.
6 I'm amazed that you are so quickly deserting the one who
called you by the grace of Christ to follow another gospel.
7 It's not really another gospel, but certain people are confus-
ing you and they want to change the gospel of Christ. 8 However, even if we ourselves or a heavenly angel should ever
preach anything different from what we preached to you,
they should be under a curse. 9 I'm repeating what we've said
before: if anyone preaches something different from what
you received, they should be under a curse!
10 Am I trying to win over human beings or God? Or am I
trying to please people? If I were still trying to please people,
I wouldn't be Christ's slave. 11 Brothers and sisters, I want you
to know that the gospel I preached isn't human in origin. 12 I
didn't receive it or learn it from a human. It came through a
revelation from Jesus Christ.

---

**Luke 7:1-10**

After Jesus finished presenting all his words among the
people, he entered Capernaum. 2 A centurion had a servant
who was very important to him, but the servant was ill and
about to die. 3 When the centurion heard about Jesus, he
sent some Jewish elders to Jesus to ask him to come and heal
his servant. 4 When they came to Jesus, they earnestly pleaded
with Jesus. "He deserves to have you do this for him," they
said. 5 "He loves our people and he built our synagogue for
us."
6 Jesus went with them. He had almost reached the house
when the centurion sent friends to say to Jesus, "Lord, don't
be bothered. I don't deserve to have you come under my
roof. 7 In fact, I didn't even consider myself worthy to come
to you. Just say the word and my servant will be healed. 8 I'm
also a man appointed under authority, with soldiers under
me. I say to one, 'Go,' and he goes, and to another, 'Come,'
and he comes. I say to my servant, 'Do this,' and the servant
does it."
9 When Jesus heard these words, he was impressed with the
centurion. He turned to the crowd following him and said, "I
tell you, even in Israel I haven't found faith like this." 10 When
the centurion's friends returned to his house, they found the
servant restored to health.

**Primary Hymns and Songs for the Day**

475 "Come Down, O Love Divine" (1 Kgs) (O)
H-3 Chr-52; Org-30
S-1 #98-99. Descs.
3186 "Days of Elijah" (1 Kgs)
M139
650 "Give Me the Faith Which Can Remove" (1 Kgs, Luke)
S-1 #57-61. Various treatments
186 "Alleluia" (Gal, Luke)
SP108, S-2 #3-4. Desc. and harm.
467 "Trust and Obey" (Gal) (C)
H-3 Chr-202
S-1 #336. Harm.
430 "O Master, Let Me Walk with Thee" (Gal, Luke) (C)
H-3 Hbl-81; Chr-147; Desc-74; Org-87
S-2 #118. Desc.

**Additional Hymn Suggestions**

442 "Weary of All Trumpeting" (1 Kgs)
443 "O God Who Shaped Creation" (1 Kgs)
480 "O Love That Wilt Not Let Me Go" (1 Kgs)
501 "O Thou Who Camest from Above" (1 Kgs)
538 "Wind Who Makes All Winds That Blow" (1 Kgs)
539 "O Spirit of the Living God" (1 Kgs)
541 "See How Great a Flame Aspires" (1 Kgs)
719 "My Lord, What a Morning" (1 Kgs)
3147 "Built on a Rock" (1 Kgs)
203 "Hail to the Lord's Anointed" (1 Kgs, Pss)
422 "Jesus, Thine All-Victorious Love" (1 Kgs, Gal)
474 "Precious Lord, Take My Hand" (1 Kgs, Gal)
500 "Spirit of God, Descend upon My Heart" (1 Kgs, Gal)
77 "How Great Thou Art" (Pss)
176 "Majesty, Worship His Majesty" (Pss)
SP73
2001 "We Sing to You, O God" (Pss)
2011 "We Sing of Your Glory" (*"Tuya Es la Gloria"*) (Pss)
2045 "Sing a New Song to the Lord" (Pss)
433 "All Who Love and Serve Your City" (Pss, Gal)
410 "I Want a Principle Within" (Gal)
411 "Dear Lord, Lead Me Day by Day" (Gal)
413 "A Charge to Keep I Have" (Gal)
2225 "Who Is My Mother, Who Is My Brother" (Gal)
2269 "Come, Share the Lord" (Gal, Comm.)
3170 "What Feast of Love" (Gal, Comm.)
262 "Heal Me, Hands of Jesus" (Luke)
263 "When Jesus the Healer Passed Through Galilee" (Luke)
265 "O Christ, the Healer" (Luke)
266 "Heal Us, Emmanuel, Hear Our Prayer" (Luke)
273 "Jesus' Hands Were Kind Hands" (Luke)
385 "Let Us Plead for Faith Alone" (Luke)
508 "Faith, While Trees Are Still in Blossom" (Luke)
2196 "We Walk by Faith" (Luke)
2211 "Faith Is Patience in the Night" (Luke)
2213 "Healer of Our Every Ill" (Luke)

**Additional Contemporary Suggestions**

S2002 "I Will Call Upon the Lord" (1 Kgs)
SP224
S2040 "Awesome God" (1 Kgs)
SP11
WS3004 "Step by Step" (1 Kgs)
M51
WS3106 "Your Grace Is Enough" (1 Kgs)
M191
WS3003 "How Great Is Our God" (1 Kgs, Pss)
M117
UM393 "Spirit of the Living God" (1 Kgs, Luke)
SP131; S-1#212 Vocal Desc. idea
UM507 "Through It All" (1 Kgs, Luke)
M161 "Healing Rain" (1 Kgs, Luke)
S2022 "Great Is the Lord" (Pss)
SP30
S2037 "I Sing Praises to Your Name" (Pss)
SP27
S2070 "He Is Exalted" (Pss)
SP66
S2074 "Shout to the Lord" (Pss)
M16; V-3 (2) p. 32 Vocal Solo
WS3042 "Shout to the North" (Pss)
M99
M62 "Rise Up and Praise Him" (Pss)
M77 "Above All" (Pss)
V-3 (2) p. 17 Vocal Solo
M103 "How Great Are You, Lord" (Pss)
M234 "Awesome Is the Lord Most High" (Pss)
M252 "God with Us" (Pss)
M164 "Good to Me" (Luke)
M257 "Came to My Rescue" (Luke)
S2139 "Oh, I Know the Lord's Laid His Hands on Me" (Luke)
S2151 "I'm So Glad Jesus Lifted Me" (Luke)
WS3108 "Tradin' My Sorrows" (Luke)
M75
M177 "How Can I Keep from Singing" (Luke)

**Vocal Solos**

"My Lord, What a Morning" (1 Kgs)
V-3 (1) p. 39
"Great Is Thy Faithfulness" (1 Kgs)
V-8 p. 48
"My Prayer Rises to Heaven" (1 Kgs)
UM498

**Anthems**

"O Thou Who Camest from Above" (1 Kgs)
Philip W. J. Stopford; MorningStar MSM-50-5209
SATB with organ

"Great Is Thy Faithfulness" (1 Kgs)
Arr. Joseph M. Martin; Hope C-5657
SATB with keyboard

**Other Suggestions**

Visuals:
**O** 18:21b (limping), wood pile, 12 stones/altar, water jar, fire
**P** new song, singing, all nations, crown, nature
**E** crucifix/Resurrection, New Testament
**G** Jesus, centurian, healing
Introit: S2274. "Come, All You People" (*"Uyai Mose"*) (Pss)
Prayer: WSL12 (1 Kgs)
Canticle: UM91. "Canticle of Praise to God" (Pss)

**1 Kings 17:8-16 (17-24)**
8 The LORD's word came to Elijah: 9 Get up and go to
Zarephath near Sidon and stay there. I have ordered a widow
there to take care of you. 10 Elijah left and went to Zarephath.
As he came to the town gate, he saw a widow collecting sticks.
He called out to her, "Please get a little water for me in this
cup so I can drink." 11 She went to get some water. He then
said to her, "Please get me a piece of bread."
12 "As surely as the LORD your God lives," she replied, "I
don't have any food; only a handful of flour in a jar and a bit
of oil in a bottle. Look at me. I'm collecting two sticks so that
I can make some food for myself and my son. We'll eat the
last of the food and then die."
13 Elijah said to her, "Don't be afraid! Go and do what you
said. Only make a little loaf of bread for me first. Then bring
it to me. You can make something for yourself and your son
after that. 14 This is what Israel's God, the LORD, says: The jar
of flour won't decrease and the bottle of oil won't run out
until the day the LORD sends rain on the earth." 15 The widow
went and did what Elijah said. So the widow, Elijah, and
the widow's household ate for many days. 16 The jar of flour
didn't decrease nor did the bottle of oil run out, just as the
LORD spoke through Elijah.
17 After these things, the son of the widow, who was the
matriarch of the household, became ill. His sickness got
steadily worse until he wasn't breathing anymore. 18 She said
to Elijah, "What's gone wrong between us, man of God? Have
you come to me to call attention to my sin and kill my son?"
19 Elijah replied, "Give your son to me." He took her son
from her and carried him to the upper room where he was
staying. Elijah laid him on his bed. 20 Elijah cried out to the
LORD, "LORD my God, why is it that you have brought such
evil upon the widow that I am staying with by killing her
son?" 21 Then he stretched himself over the boy three times
and cried out to the LORD, "LORD my God, please give this
boy's life back to him." 22 The LORD listened to Elijah's voice
and gave the boy his life back. And he lived. 23 Elijah brought
the boy down from the upper room of the house and gave
him to his mother. Elijah said, "Look, your son is alive!"
24 "Now I know that you really are a man of God," the
woman said to Elijah, "and that the LORD's word is truly in
your mouth."

---

**Psalm 146 (UM858)**
Praise the LORD!
Let my whole being praise the LORD!
2 I will praise the LORD with all my life;
I will sing praises to my God as long as I live.
3 Don't trust leaders;
don't trust any human beings—
there's no saving help with them!
4 Their breath leaves them,
then they go back to the ground.
On that very same day, their plans die too.
5 The person whose help is the God of Jacob—
the person whose hope rests on the LORD their God—
is truly happy!
6 God: the maker of heaven and earth,
the sea, and all that is in them,
God: who is faithful forever,
7 who gives justice to people who are oppressed,
who gives bread to people who are starving!
The LORD: who frees prisoners.
8 The LORD: who makes the blind see.
The LORD: who straightens up those who are bent low.
The LORD: who loves the righteous.
9 The LORD: who protects immigrants,
who helps orphans and widows,
but who makes the way of the wicked twist and turn!
10 The LORD will rule forever!
Zion, your God will rule from one generation to the next!
Praise the LORD!

---

**Galatians 1:11-24**
11 Brothers and sisters, I want you to know that the gospel I
preached isn't human in origin. 12 I didn't receive it or learn
it from a human. It came through a revelation from Jesus
Christ.
13 You heard about my previous life in Judaism, how severely
I harassed God's church and tried to destroy it. 14 I advanced
in Judaism beyond many of my peers, because I was much
more militant about the traditions of my ancestors. 15 But
God had set me apart from birth and called me through his
grace. He was pleased 16 to reveal his Son to me, so that I
might preach about him to the Gentiles. I didn't immediately
consult with any human being. 17 I didn't go up to Jerusalem
to see the men who were apostles before me either, but I
went away into Arabia and I returned again to Damascus.
18 Then after three years I went up to Jerusalem to visit
Cephas and stayed with him fifteen days. 19 But I didn't see
any other of the apostles except James the brother of the
Lord. 20 Before God, I'm not lying about the things that I'm
writing to you! 21 Then I went into the regions of Syria and
Cilicia, 22 but I wasn't known personally by the Christian
churches in Judea. 23 They only heard a report about me:
"The man who used to harass us now preaches the faith
that he once tried to destroy." 24 So they were glorifying God
because of me.

---

**Luke 7:11-17**
11 A little later Jesus went to a city called Nain. His disciples
and a great crowd traveled with him. 12 As he approached
the city gate, a dead man was being carried out. He was his
mother's only son, and she was a widow. A large crowd from
the city was with her. 13 When he saw her, the Lord had compassion for her and said, "Don't cry." 14 He stepped forward
and touched the stretcher on which the dead man was being
carried. Those carrying him stood still. Jesus said, "Young
man, I say to you, get up." 15 The dead man sat up and began
to speak, and Jesus gave him to his mother.
16 Awestruck, everyone praised God. "A great prophet has
appeared among us," they said. "God has come to help his
people." 17 This news about Jesus spread throughout Judea
and the surrounding region.

**Primary Hymns and Songs for the Day**

60 "I'll Praise My Maker While I've Breath" (Pss) (O)
H-3 Chr-109; Org-105
S-2 #141. Harm.
141 "Children of the Heavenly Father" (1 Kgs, Luke)
H-3 Chr-46; Desc-102
S-2 #180-85. Various treatments
2213 "Healer of Our Every Ill" (1 Kgs, Luke)
129 "Give to the Winds Thy Fears" (1 Kgs, Pss, Luke) (C)
H-3 Chr-71; Desc-39; Org-39
S-1 #129. Desc.
383 "This Is a Day of New Beginnings" (1 Kgs, Gal, Luke, Comm.) (C)
H-3 Chr-196

**Additional Hymn Suggestions**

266 "Heal Us, Emmanuel, Hear Our Prayer" (1 Kgs)
350 "Come, All of You" (1 Kgs, Comm.)
352 "It's Me, It's Me, O Lord" (1 Kgs)
434 "*Cuando el Pobre*" ("When the Poor Ones") (1 Kgs, Pss)
2211 "Faith Is Patience in the Night" (1 Kgs)
3093 "Fill My Cup, Lord" (1 Kgs, Comm.)
UM641 refrain; S-2 #62. Stanzas for soloist
178 "Hope of the World" (1 Kgs, Pss)
57 "O For a Thousand Tongues to Sing" (Pss)
59 "*Mil Voces Para Celebrar*" (Pss)
66 "Praise, My Soul, the King of Heaven" (Pss)
140 "Great Is Thy Faithfulness" (Pss)
2177 "Wounded World that Cries for Healing" (Pss)
2182 "When God Restored Our Common Life" (Pss)
3001 "O For a Thousand Tongues to Sing" (Pss)
331 "Holy Spirit, Come, Confirm Us" (Gal, Luke)
382 "Have Thine Own Way, Lord" (Gal)
388 "O Come and Dwell in Me" (Gal)
463 "Lord, Speak to Me" (Gal)
582 "Whom Shall I Send?" (Gal)
2140 "Since Jesus Came into My Heart" (Gal)
2149 "Living for Jesus" (Gal)
2153 "I'm Gonna Live So God Can Use Me" (Gal)
162 "Alleluia, Alleluia" (Luke)
261 "Lord of the Dance" (Luke)
263 "When Jesus the Healer Passed Through Galilee" (Luke)
265 "O Christ, the Healer" (Luke)
304 "Easter People, Raise Your Voices" (Luke)
311 "Now the Green Blade Riseth" (Luke)
384 "Love Divine, All Loves Excelling" (Luke)
444 "O Young and Fearless Prophet" (Luke)
2115 "Christ Has Risen" (Luke)
3074 "Jesus Is a Rock in a Weary Land" (Luke)
3086 "Day of Arising" (Luke)

**Additional Contemporary Suggestions**

WS3094 "Come to Me" (1 Kgs)
WS3186 "Days of Elijah" (1 Kgs)
M139
S2029 "Praise to the Lord" (Pss)
S2032 "My Life Is in You, Lord" (Pss)
SP204
S2144 "Someone Asked the Question" (Pss)
SP32 "Bless the Lord, O My Soul" (Pss)
M64 "Hear Our Praises" (Pss)
WS3034 "God of Wonders" (Pss)
M80
S2036 "Give Thanks" (Pss)
SP170
S2186 "Song of Hope" (Pss)
S2139 "Oh, I Know the Lord's Laid His Hands on Me" (Gal)
WS3102 "You Are My King" ("Amazing Love") (Gal)
M82
WS3023 "Forever" (Gal)
M68
WS3108 "Trading My Sorrows" (Gal, Luke)
M75
S2116 "Christ the Lord Is Risen" (Luke)

**Vocal Solos**

"O For a Thousand Tongues to Sing" (Pss)
V-1 p. 32
V-6 p. 28
"Jesus, Thou Art Watching Ever" (Pss)
V-4 p. 6
"Lord of the Dance" (Luke)
V-3 (3) p. 34

**Anthems**

"Children of the Heavenly Father" (1 Kgs, Luke)
Arr. Jeremy S. Bakken; Choristers Guild CGA-1380
Unison/Two-part with piano

"How Blest Are They" (Pss)
Claude Bass; MorningStar 50-5201
SATB with piano

**Other Suggestions**

Visuals:
**O** Water vessel, sticks, meal/oil, child (sick/healed)
**P** praise/singing, creation, justice (scales), food, open shackles, woman/child
**E** Paul, shackles, Christ, Peter
**G** Jesus, woman, bier/bearers, man sitting up, hug
Greeting: BOW453 (Pss, 1 Kgs, Luke)
Opening Prayer: BOW459 (Gal) or BOW464 (1 Kgs, Luke)
Prayer of Confession: BOW478 or BOW479 (Gal)
Prayer: WSL28 (Luke)
Blessing: BOW561 (Pss)

**1 Kings 21:1-21a**

Now it happened sometime later that Naboth from Jezreel had a vineyard in Jezreel that was next to the palace of King Ahab of Samaria. 2 Ahab ordered Naboth, "Give me your vineyard so it can become my vegetable garden, because it is right next to my palace. In exchange for it, I'll give you an even better vineyard. Or if you prefer, I'll pay you the price in silver."

3 Naboth responded to Ahab, "LORD forbid that I give you my family inheritance!"

4 So Ahab went to his palace, irritated and upset at what Naboth had said to him—because Naboth had said, "I won't give you my family inheritance!" Ahab lay down on his bed and turned his face away. He wouldn't eat anything.

5 His wife Jezebel came to him. "Why are you upset and not eating any food?" she asked.

6 He answered her, "I was talking to Naboth. I said, 'Sell me your vineyard. Or if you prefer, I'll give you another vineyard for it.' But he said, 'I won't give you my vineyard!'"

7 Then his wife Jezebel said to him, "Aren't you the one who rules Israel? Get up! Eat some food and cheer up. I'll get Naboth's vineyard for you myself." 8 So she wrote letters in Ahab's name, putting his seal on them. She sent them to the elders and officials who lived in the same town as Naboth. 9 This is what she wrote in the letters: "Announce a fast and place Naboth at the head of the people. 10 Then bring in two liars in front of him and have them testify as follows: 'You cursed God and king!' Then take Naboth outside and stone him so he dies."

11 The elders and the officials who lived in Naboth's town did exactly as Jezebel specified in the letters that she had sent. 12 They announced a fast and placed Naboth at the head of the people. 13 Then the two liars came and sat in front of him. They testified against Naboth in front of the people, "Naboth cursed God and king!" So the people took Naboth outside the town and stoned him so that he died.

14 It was then reported to Jezebel, "Naboth was stoned. He's dead." 15 As soon as Jezebel heard that Naboth had been stoned to death, she said to Ahab, "Get up and take ownership of the vineyard of Naboth, which he had refused to sell to you. Naboth is no longer alive; he's dead." 16 When Ahab heard that Naboth had died, he got up and went down to Naboth's vineyard to take ownership of it.

17 The LORD's word came to Elijah from Tishbe: 18 Get up and go down to meet Israel's King Ahab in Samaria. He is in Naboth's vineyard. He has gone down to take ownership of it. 19 Say the following to him: This is what the LORD says: So, you've murdered and are now taking ownership, are you? Then tell him: This is what the LORD says: In the same place where the dogs licked up Naboth's blood, they will lick up your own blood.

20 Ahab said to Elijah, "So you've found me, my old enemy!"

"I found you," Elijah said, "because you've enslaved yourself by doing evil in the LORD's eyes. 21a So I am now bringing evil on you!"

**Psalm 5:1-8 (UM742)**

Hear my words, LORD!
  Consider my groans!
2 Pay attention to the sound of my cries, my king and my God,
  because I am praying to you! . . .

**Galatians 2:15-21**

15 We are born Jews—we're not Gentile sinners. 16 However, we know that a person isn't made righteous by the works of the Law but rather through the faithfulness of Jesus Christ. We ourselves believed in Christ Jesus so that we could be made righteous by the faithfulness of Christ and not by the works of the Law—because no one will be made righteous by the works of the Law. 17 But if it is discovered that we ourselves are sinners while we are trying to be made righteous in Christ, then is Christ a servant of sin? Absolutely not! 18 If I rebuild the very things that I tore down, I show that I myself am breaking the Law. 19 I died to the Law through the Law, so that I could live for God. 20 I have been crucified with Christ and I no longer live, but Christ lives in me. And the life that I now live in my body, I live by faith, indeed, by the faithfulness of God's Son, who loved me and gave himself for me. 21 I don't ignore the grace of God, because if we become righteous through the Law, then Christ died for no purpose.

**Luke 7:36–8:3**

36 One of the Pharisees invited Jesus to eat with him. After he entered the Pharisee's home, he took his place at the table. 37 Meanwhile, a woman from the city, a sinner, discovered that Jesus was dining in the Pharisee's house. She brought perfumed oil in a vase made of alabaster. 38 Standing behind him at his feet and crying, she began to wet his feet with her tears. She wiped them with her hair, kissed them, and poured the oil on them. 39 When the Pharisee who had invited Jesus saw what was happening, he said to himself, If this man were a prophet, he would know what kind of woman is touching him. He would know that she is a sinner.

40 Jesus replied, "Simon, I have something to say to you."

"Teacher, speak," he said.

41 "A certain lender had two debtors. One owed enough money to pay five hundred people for a day's work. The other owed enough money for fifty. 42 When they couldn't pay, the lender forgave the debts of them both. Which of them will love him more?"

43 Simon replied, "I suppose the one who had the largest debt canceled."

Jesus said, "You have judged correctly."

44 Jesus turned to the woman and said to Simon, "Do you see this woman? When I entered your home, you didn't give me water for my feet, but she wet my feet with tears and wiped them with her hair. 45 You didn't greet me with a kiss, but she hasn't stopped kissing my feet since I came in. 46 You didn't anoint my head with oil, but she has poured perfumed oil on my feet. 47 This is why I tell you that her many sins have been forgiven; so she has shown great love. The one who is forgiven little loves little."

48 Then Jesus said to her, "Your sins are forgiven."

49 The other table guests began to say among themselves, "Who is this person that even forgives sins?"

50 Jesus said to the woman, "Your faith has saved you. Go in peace."

8 Soon afterward, Jesus traveled through the cities and villages, preaching and proclaiming the good news of God's kingdom. The Twelve were with him, 2 along with some women who had been healed of evil spirits and sicknesses. Among them were Mary Magdalene (from whom seven demons had been thrown out), 3 Joanna (the wife of Herod's servant Chuza), Susanna, and many others who provided for them out of their resources.

**Primary Hymns and Songs for the Day**

162 "Alleluia, Alleluia" (Gal) (O)
441 "What Does the Lord Require" (1 Kgs, Gal, Luke)
H-3 Chr-211
473 "Lead Me, Lord" (Pss)
356 "*Pues Si Vivimos*" ("When We Are Living") (Gal)
S-1 #320. Orff instr. arr.
H-3 Chr-218; Org-155
340 "Come, Ye Sinners, Poor and Needy" (Luke)
S-1 #283. Choral harm.
2196 "We Walk by Faith" (Gal) (C)
H-3 Chr-21

**Additional Hymn Suggestions**

107 "*La Palabra Del Señor Es Recta*" ("Righteous and Just Is the Word of Our Lord") (1 Kgs, Pss)
435 "O God of Every Nation" (1 Kgs, Pss)
577 "God of Grace and God of Glory" (1 Kgs, Pss)
3098 "Dust and Ashes" (1 Kgs, Pss)
108 "God Hath Spoken by the Prophets" (1 Kgs, Luke)
139 "Praise to the Lord, the Almighty" (Pss)
411 "Dear Lord, Lead Me Day by Day" (Pss)
498 "My Prayer Rises to Heaven" (Pss)
2214 "Lead Me, Guide Me" (Pss)
2242 "Walk with Me" (Pss, Luke)
294 "Alas! and Did My Savior Bleed" (Gal)
341 "I Sought the Lord" (Gal)
351 "Pass Me Not, O Gentle Savior" (Gal)
385 "Let Us Plead for Faith Alone" (Gal)
414 "Thou Hidden Love of God" (Gal)
2211 "Faith Is Patience in the Night" (Gal)
378 "Amazing Grace" (Gal, Luke)
3110 "By Grace We Have Been Saved" (Gal)
266 "Heal Us, Emmanuel, Hear Our Prayer" (Luke)
274 "Woman in the Night" (Luke)
339 "Come, Sinners, to the Gospel Feast" (Luke)
365 "Grace Greater than Our Sin" (Luke)
367 "He Touched Me" (Luke)
390 "Forgive Our Sins as We Forgive" (Luke)
452 "My Faith Looks Up to Thee" (Luke)
616 "Come, Sinners, to the Gospel Feast" (Luke)
2101 "Two Fishermen" (Luke)
2130 "The Summons" (Luke)
2169 "God, How Can We Forgive" (Luke)
3101 "Love Lifted Me" (Luke)

**Additional Contemporary Suggestions**

WS3186 "Days of Elijah" (1 Kgs)
M139
S2162 "Grace Alone" (Gal)
M100
S2108 "O How He Loves You and Me!" (Gal)
SP113
WS3187 "We Fall Down" (Gal)
M66
M162 "Grace Flows Down" (Gal)
WS3027 "Hallelujah" ("Your Love Is Amazing") (Gal, Luke)
M118
WS3102 "You Are My King" ("Amazing Love") (Gal, Luke)
M82
WS3104 "Amazing Grace" ("My Chains Are Gone") (Gal, Luke)
M205
M251 "Grace Like Rain" (Gal, Luke)
M252 "God with Us" (Gal, Luke)
M3 "Jesus, Your Name" (Luke)
M7 "I Believe in Jesus" (Luke)
M150 "Everyday" (Luke)
UM394 "Something Beautiful" (Luke)
S2129 "I Have Decided to Follow Jesus" (Luke)
S2151 "I'm So Glad Jesus Lifted Me" (Luke)
WS3094 "Come to Me" (Luke)
WS3099 "Falling on My Knees" (Luke)
M155

**Vocal Solos**

"And Can It Be That I Should Gain" (Gal)
V-1 p. 29
"The Gospel of Grace" (Gal, Luke)
V-3 (1) p.44
"Redeeming Grace" (Gal, Luke)
V-4 p. 47
"Oh, What Love!" (Gal, Luke)
V-8 p. 144
"Grace Greater than Our Sin" (Gal)
V-8 p. 180
"Jesus, My All to Heaven Is Gone" (Luke)
V-9 p. 39

**Anthems**

"Wherever I May Wander" (Gal)
Arr. Daniel Nelson; Paraclete Press PPM01322
SATB with piano

"None Other Lamb" (Gal, Luke)
Larry B. Peterson; Curtis Music Press C9307
SATB *divisi* with organ

**Other Suggestions**

Visuals:
**O** Vineyard, garden, bed, sad, seal, stones, money
**P** Weeping, prayer, bowing, straight path, ruler
**E** Christ, build/destroy, cross, justify(margin)
**G** Table, broken jar, woman/hair/feet, Jesus
Greeting: BOW454 (Luke)
Act of Congregational Centering: BOW471 (Luke)
Opening Prayer: BOW462 (Luke)
Call to Prayer: S2048. "God Weeps" (1 Kgs)
Prayer of Confession: BOW481 or WSL93 (1 Kgs)
Sung Confession: S2134. "Forgive Us, Lord" ("*Perdón, Señor*") (Luke)
Prayer: UM403. For True Life (Pss)
Prayer: BOW515. For the Nation (1 Kgs)
Sung Prayer: S2201. "Prayers of the People"
Sung Benediction: UM665. "Go Now in Peace" (Luke)

**1 Kings 19:1-15a**
Ahab told Jezebel all that Elijah had done, how he had
killed all Baal's prophets with the sword. 2 Jezebel sent a messenger to Elijah with this message: "May the gods do whatever they want to me if by this time tomorrow I haven't made
your life like the life of one of them."
3 Elijah was terrified. He got up and ran for his life. He
arrived at Beer-sheba in Judah and left his assistant there.
4 He himself went farther on into the desert a day's journey.
He finally sat down under a solitary broom bush. He longed
for his own death: "It's more than enough, LORD! Take my
life because I'm no better than my ancestors." 5 He lay down
and slept under the solitary broom bush.
Then suddenly a messenger tapped him and said to him,
"Get up! Eat something!" 6 Elijah opened his eyes and saw
flatbread baked on glowing coals and a jar of water right by
his head. He ate and drank, and then went back to sleep.
7 The LORD's messenger returned a second time and tapped
him. "Get up!" the messenger said. "Eat something, because
you have a difficult road ahead of you." 8 Elijah got up, ate
and drank, and went refreshed by that food for forty days
and nights until he arrived at Horeb, God's mountain.
9 There he went into a cave and spent the night.
The LORD's word came to him and said, "Why are you here,
Elijah?"
10 Elijah replied, "I've been very passionate for the LORD
God of heavenly forces because the Israelites have abandoned your covenant. They have torn down your altars, and
they have murdered your prophets with the sword. I'm the
only one left, and now they want to take my life too!"
11 The LORD said, "Go out and stand at the mountain before
the LORD. The LORD is passing by." A very strong wind tore
through the mountains and broke apart the stones before
the LORD. But the LORD wasn't in the wind. After the wind,
there was an earthquake. But the LORD wasn't in the earthquake. 12 After the earthquake, there was a fire. But the LORD
wasn't in the fire. After the fire, there was a sound. Thin.
Quiet. 13 When Elijah heard it, he wrapped his face in his
coat. He went out and stood at the cave's entrance. A voice
came to him and said, "Why are you here, Elijah?"
14 He said, "I've been very passionate for the LORD God of
heavenly forces because the Israelites have abandoned your
covenant. They have torn down your altars, and they have
murdered your prophets with the sword. I'm the only one
left, and now they want to take my life too."
15a The LORD said to him, "Go back through the desert to
Damascus."

---

**Psalm 42 (UM777)**
Just like a deer that craves
streams of water,
my whole being craves you, God.
2 My whole being thirsts for God,
for the living God.
When will I come and see God's face? . . .

---

**Galatians 3:23-29**
23 Before faith came, we were guarded under the Law,
locked up until faith that was coming would be revealed,
24 so that the Law became our custodian until Christ so that
we might be made righteous by faith.
25 But now that faith has come, we are no longer under a
custodian.
26 You are all God's children through faith in Christ Jesus.
27 All of you who were baptized into Christ have clothed yourselves with Christ. 28 There is neither Jew nor Greek; there
is neither slave nor free; nor is there male and female, for
you are all one in Christ Jesus. 29 Now if you belong to Christ,
then indeed you are Abraham's descendants, heirs according
to the promise.

---

**Luke 8:26-39**
26 Jesus and his disciples sailed to the Gerasenes' land,
which is across the lake from Galilee. 27 As soon as Jesus got
out of the boat, a certain man met him. The man was from
the city and was possessed by demons. For a long time, he
had lived among the tombs, naked and homeless. 28 When
he saw Jesus, he shrieked and fell down before him. Then
he shouted, "What have you to do with me, Jesus, Son of the
Most High God? I beg you, don't torture me!" 29 He said this
because Jesus had already commanded the unclean spirit to
come out of the man. Many times it had taken possession of
him, so he would be bound with leg irons and chains and
placed under guard. But he would break his restraints, and
the demon would force him into the wilderness.
30 Jesus asked him, "What is your name?"
"Legion," he replied, because many demons had entered
him. 31 They pleaded with him not to order them to go back
into the abyss. 32 A large herd of pigs was feeding on the hillside. The demons begged Jesus to let them go into the pigs.
Jesus gave them permission, 33 and the demons left the man
and entered the pigs. The herd rushed down the cliff into
the lake and drowned.
34 When those who tended the pigs saw what happened,
they ran away and told the story in the city and in the
countryside. 35 People came to see what had happened. They
came to Jesus and found the man from whom the demons
had gone. He was sitting at Jesus' feet, fully dressed and
completely sane. They were filled with awe. 36 Those people
who had actually seen what had happened told them how the
demon-possessed man had been delivered. 37 Then everyone
gathered from the region of the Gerasenes asked Jesus to
leave their area because they were overcome with fear. So he
got into the boat and returned across the lake. 38 The man
from whom the demons had gone begged to come along
with Jesus as one of his disciples. Jesus sent him away, saying,
39 "Return home and tell the story of what God has done for
you." So he went throughout the city proclaiming what Jesus
had done for him.

**Primary Hymns and Songs for the Day**

548 "In Christ There Is No East or West" (Gal) (O)
H-3 Chr-111; Desc-74; Org-88
S-1 #231-233. Various treaments
2025 "As the Deer" (Pss)
SP200
2248 "Baptized in Water" (Gal)
H-3 Hbl-77; Chr-136; Desc-21; Org-16
S-1 #50-51. Flute and vocal descs.
2151 "I'm So Glad Jesus Lifted Me" (Luke)
3072 "Cast Out, O Christ" (Luke)
620 "One Bread, One Body" (Gal, Comm.) (C)
H-3 Chr-156

**Additional Hymn Suggestions**

127 "Guide Me, O Thou Great Jehovah" (1 Kgs)
358 "Dear Lord and Father of Mankind" (1 Kgs)
2117 "Spirit of God" (1 Kgs)
2120 "Spirit, Spirit of Gentleness" (1 Kgs)
129 "Give to the Winds Thy Fears" (1 Kgs, Pss)
130 "God Will Take Care of You" (1 Kgs, Pss)
142 "If Thou But Suffer God to Guide Thee" (1 Kgs, Pss)
361 "Rock of Ages" (1 Kgs, Pss)
2052 "The Lone Wild Bird" (1 Kgs, Pss)
2123 "Loving Spirit" (1 Kgs, Pss)
3093 "Fill My Cup, Lord" (1 Kgs, Pss)
115 "How Like A Gentle Spirit" (1 Kgs, Pss, Gal, Luke)
141 "Children of the Heavenly Father" (1 Kgs, Pss, Luke)
375 "There Is a Balm in Gilead" (1 Kgs, Pss, Luke)
507 "Through It All" (1 Kgs, Luke)
2213 "Healer of Our Every Ill" (1 Kgs, Luke)
589 "The Church of Christ, in Every Age" (Gal)
604 "Praise and Thanksgiving Be to God" (Gal)
2181 "We Need a Faith" (Gal)
2196 "We Walk by Faith" (Gal)
2211 "Faith Is Patience in the Night" (Gal)
2225 "Who Is My Mother, Who Is My Brother" (Gal)
2247 "Wonder of Wonders" (Gal, Baptism)
2269 "Come, Share the Lord" (Gal, Comm.)
3110 "By Grace We Have Been Saved" (Gal, Luke)
140 "Great Is Thy Faithfulness" (Luke)
193 "Jesus! the Name High over All" (Luke)
262 "Heal Me, Hands of Jesus" (Luke)
263 "When Jesus the Healer Passed Through Galilee" (Luke)
307 "Christ Is Risen" (Luke)
444 "O Young and Fearless Prophet" (Luke)
585 "This Little Light of Mine" (Luke)
2142 "Blessed Quietness" (Luke)
2191 "Eternal Father, Strong to Save" (Luke)
3101 "Love Lifted Me" (Luke)

**Additional Contemporary Suggestions**

WS3186 "Days of Elijah" (1 Kgs)
M139
S2066 "Praise the Name of Jesus" (Pss)
SP87
S2080 "All I Need Is You" (Pss)
S2159 "Jesus, Draw Me Close" (Pss)
M48
S2165 "Cry of My Heart" (Pss)
M39
S2167 "More Like You" (Pss)
M28 "Who Can Satisfy My Soul Like You?" (Pss)
M29 "Draw Me Close" (Pss)
M30 "Knowing You" ("All I Once Held Dear") (Pss)
M33 "Jesus, You Are My Life" (Pss)
M60 "Better Is One Day" (Pss)
WS3112 "Breathe" (Pss)
M61
M83 "Just Let Me Say" (Pss)
M107 "Show Me Your Ways" (Pss)
M110 "Love You So Much" (Pss)
M160 "Enough" (Pss)
WS3154 "Draw the Circle Wide" (Gal)
S2039 "Holy, Holy" (Gal)
SP141
S2249 "God Claims You" (Gal, Baptism)
WS3104 "Amazing Grace" ("My Chains Are Gone") (Luke)
M205
WS3108 "Trading My Sorrows" (Luke)
M75
M251 "Grace Like Rain" (Luke)
M252 "God with Us" (Luke)

**Vocal Solos**

"There Is a Balm in Gilead" (1 Kgs)
V-3 (1) p. 29
"So Art Thou with Me" (Pss)
V-9 p. 34
"One Bread, One Body" (Gal, Comm.)
V-3 (2) p. 40
"I Heard About a Man" (Luke)
V-8 p. 72

**Anthems**

"Balm in Gilead" (1 Kgs, Pss, Luke)
Arr. Mark Shepperd; Augsburg 11-10923
SATB with keyboard

"Eternal Father, Strong to Save" (Luke)
Arr. Dan Forrest; Hinshaw HMC2353
SATB *divisi* with keyboard

**Other Suggestions**

Visuals:
**O** Run, tree, cake/stone/jar, overturned altar
**P** Deer, stream, tears, procession, waterfall, waves
**E** Shackles, ruler, switch, child, baptism, unity
**G** Tombstone, man(naked/clothed), chains, pigs
Greeting: BOW327 (1 Kgs)
Opening Prayer: WSL38 (2 Kgs), BOW464 (Luke) or BOW469 (Pss)
Prayer of Confession: WSL92 (2 Kgs)
Call to Prayer: BOW194. "Teach Me to Hear in Silence" (1 Kgs)
Prayer: WSL19 (1 Kgs, Luke) or WSL17 (1 Kgs, Pss, Luke)
Prayers: BOW491 and UM392 (1 Kgs, Luke)
Prayer: UM423. Finding Rest in God (1 Kgs, Pss)
Prayer: BOW505 (Gal)
Prayers: WSL201 and BOW441 (Father's Day)
Blessing: BOW564 (Pss)

**2 Kings 2:1-2, 6-14**

Now the LORD was going to take Elijah up to heaven in a
windstorm, and Elijah and Elisha were leaving Gilgal. [2] Elijah
said to Elisha, "Stay here, because the LORD has sent me to
Bethel."

But Elisha said, "As the LORD lives and as you live, I won't
leave you." So they went down to Bethel. . . .

[6] Elijah said to Elisha, "Stay here, because the LORD has sent
me to the Jordan."

But Elisha said, "As the LORD lives and as you live, I won't
leave you." So both of them went on together. [7] Fifty members from the group of prophets also went along, but they
stood at a distance. Both Elijah and Elisha stood beside the
Jordan River. [8] Elijah then took his coat, rolled it up, and hit
the water. Then the water was divided in two! Both of them
crossed over on dry ground. [9] When they had crossed, Elijah
said to Elisha, "What do you want me to do for you before
I'm taken away from you?"

Elisha said, "Let me have twice your spirit."

[10] Elijah said, "You've made a difficult request. If you can
see me when I'm taken from you, then it will be yours. If you
don't see me, it won't happen."

[11] They were walking along, talking, when suddenly a fiery
chariot and fiery horses appeared and separated the two of
them. Then Elijah went to heaven in a windstorm.

[12] Elisha was watching, and he cried out, "Oh, my father,
my father! Israel's chariots and its riders!" When he could no
longer see him, Elisha took hold of his clothes and ripped
them in two.

[13] Then Elisha picked up the coat that had fallen from Elijah.
He went back and stood beside the banks of the Jordan River.
[14] He took the coat that had fallen from Elijah and hit the
water. He said, "Where is the LORD, Elijah's God?" And when
he hit the water, it divided in two! Then Elisha crossed over.

---

**Psalm 77:1-2, 11-20 (UM798)**

I cry out loud to God—
out loud to God so that he can hear me!
[2] During the day when I'm in trouble I look for my Lord.
At night my hands are still outstretched and don't grow numb;
my whole being refuses to be comforted.

. . . . . . . . . . . . . . . . . . . . . . . . .

[11] But I will remember the LORD's deeds;
yes, I will remember your wondrous acts from times long past.
[12] I will meditate on all your works;
I will ponder your deeds.
[13] God, your way is holiness!
Who is as great a god as you, God?
[14] You are the God who works wonders;
you have demonstrated your strength among all peoples.
[15] With your mighty arm you redeemed your people;
redeemed the children of Jacob and Joseph. *[Selah]*
[16] The waters saw you, God—
the waters saw you and reeled!
Even the deep depths shook!
[17] The clouds poured water,
the skies cracked thunder;
your arrows were flying all around!
[18] The crash of your thunder was in the swirling storm;
lightning lit up the whole world;
the earth shook and quaked.
[19] Your way went straight through the sea;
your pathways went right through the mighty waters.
But your footprints left no trace!
[20] You led your people like sheep
under the care of Moses and Aaron.

---

**Galatians 5:1, 13-25**

Christ has set us free for freedom. Therefore, stand firm
and don't submit to the bondage of slavery again. . . .

[13] You were called to freedom, brothers and sisters; only
don't let this freedom be an opportunity to indulge your
selfish impulses, but serve each other through love. [14] All the
Law has been fulfilled in a single statement: *Love your neighbor
as yourself.* [15] But if you bite and devour each other, be careful
that you don't get eaten up by each other!

[16] I say be guided by the Spirit and you won't carry out your
selfish desires. [17] A person's selfish desires are set against the
Spirit, and the Spirit is set against one's selfish desires. They
are opposed to each other, so you shouldn't do whatever you
want to do. [18] But if you are being led by the Spirit, you aren't
under the Law. [19] The actions that are produced by selfish
motives are obvious, since they include sexual immorality,
moral corruption, doing whatever feels good, [20] idolatry, drug
use and casting spells, hate, fighting, obsession, losing your
temper, competitive opposition, conflict, selfishness, group
rivalry, [21] jealousy, drunkenness, partying, and other things
like that. I warn you as I have already warned you, that those
who do these kinds of things won't inherit God's kingdom.

[22] But the fruit of the Spirit is love, joy, peace, patience, kind-
ness, goodness, faithfulness, [23] gentleness, and self-control.
There is no law against things like this. [24] Those who belong to
Christ Jesus have crucified self with its passions and its desires.

[25] If we live by the Spirit, let's follow the Spirit. [26] Let's not
become arrogant, make each other angry, or be jealous of
each other.

---

**Luke 9:51-62**

[51] As the time approached when Jesus was to be taken up into
heaven, he determined to go to Jerusalem. [52] He sent messengers on ahead of him. Along the way, they entered a Samaritan
village to prepare for his arrival, [53] but the Samaritan villagers
refused to welcome him because he was determined to go to
Jerusalem. [54] When the disciples James and John saw this, they
said, "Lord, do you want us to call fire down from heaven to
consume them?" [55] But Jesus turned and spoke sternly to them,
[56] and they went on to another village.

[57] As Jesus and his disciples traveled along the road, someone said to him, "I will follow you wherever you go."

[58] Jesus replied, "Foxes have dens and the birds in the sky
have nests, but the Human One has no place to lay his head."

[59] Then Jesus said to someone else, "Follow me."

He replied, "Lord, first let me go and bury my father."

[60] Jesus said to him, "Let the dead bury their own dead. But
you go and spread the news of God's kingdom."

[61] Someone else said to Jesus, "I will follow you, Lord, but
first let me say good-bye to those in my house."

[62] Jesus said to him, "No one who puts a hand on the plow
and looks back is fit for God's kingdom."

**Primary Hymns and Songs for the Day**

117 "O God, Our Help in Ages Past" (Pss) (O)
H-3 Hbl-33, 80; Chr-143; Desc-93; Org-132
S-1 #293-96. Various treatments

393 "Spirit of the Living God" (2 Kgs, Gal)
SP131; S-1#212 Vocal desc. idea

500 "Spirit of God, Descend upon My Heart" (2 Kgs, Gal)
H-3 Chr-175; Desc-77; Org-94
S-2 #125-28. Various treatments

703 "Swing Low, Sweet Chariot" (2 Kgs)
H-3 Chr-177

2107 "Wade in the Water" (2 Kgs, Gal)

336 "Of All the Spirit's Gifts to Me" (Gal)
S-2 #121. Desc.

465 "Holy Spirit, Truth Divine" (Gal)
H-3 Chr-63, 100
S-1 #53. Desc.

396 "O Jesus, I Have Promised" (Luke) (C)
S-2 #9. Desc.

**Additional Hymn Suggestions**

2052 "The Lone Wild Bird" (2 Kgs)
141 "Children of the Heavenly Father" (2 Kgs, Pss)
651 "Come, Holy Ghost, Our Souls Inspire" (2 Kgs, Gal)
2117 "Spirit of God" (2 Kgs, Gal)
593 "Here I Am, Lord" (2 Kgs, Luke)
77 "How Great Thou Art" (Pss)
117 "O God, Our Help in Ages Past" (Pss)
152 "I Sing the Almighty Power of God" (Pss)
700 "Abide with Me" (Pss)
2209 "How Long, O Lord" (Pss)
2216 "When We Are Called to Sing Your Praise" (Pss)
2217 "By the Babylonian Rivers" (Pss)
389 "Freely, Freely" (Gal, Comm.)
549 "Where Charity and Love Prevail" (Gal)
579 "Lord God, Your Love Has Called Us Here" (Gal)
2135 "When Cain Killed Abel" (Gal)
2213 "Healer of Our Every Ill" (Gal)
2254 "In Remembrance of Me" (Gal, Comm.)
206 "I Want to Walk as a Child of the Light" (Luke)
338 "Where He Leads Me" (Luke)
398 "Jesus Calls Us" (Luke)
402 "Lord, I Want to Be a Christian" (Luke)
407 "Close to Thee" (Luke)
415 "Take Up Thy Cross" (Luke) (C)
616 "Come, Sinners, to the Gospel Feast" (Luke, Comm.)
2100 "Thou Didst Leave Thy Throne" (Luke)
2101 "Two Fishermen" (Luke)
2127 "Come and See" ("*Kyrie*") (Luke)
2137 "Would I Have Answered When You Called" (Luke)
3161 "Gracious Creator of Sea and of Land" (Luke)

**Additional Contemporary Suggestions**

WS3186 "Days of Elijah" (1 Kgs)
M139
M69 "Did You Feel the Mountains Tremble?" (2 Kgs)
WS3034 "God of Wonders" (2 Kgs, Pss)
M80
WS3003 "How Great Is Our God" (Pss)
M117
WS3004 "Step by Step" (Pss, Luke)
M51
WS3117 "Rule of Life" (Gal)
WS3121 "If You Believe and I Believe" (Gal)
WS3148 "There's a Spirit of Love in This Place" (Gal)
S2118 "Holy Spirit, Come to Us" (Gal)
S2171 "Make Me a Channel of Your Peace" (Gal)
S2179 "Live in Charity" ("*Ubi Caritas*") (Gal)
S2145 "I've Got Peace Like a River" (Gal)
UM432 "*Jesu, Jesu*" (Gal)
S-1 #63. Vocal part
S2165 "Cry of My Heart" (Luke)
M39
S2218 "You Are Mine" (Luke)
WS3160 "We Will Follow" ("*Somlandela*") (Luke)
M41 "You're Worthy of My Praise" (Luke)
M108 "Lead Me, Lord" (Luke)

**Vocal Solos**

"Swing Low, Sweet Chariot!" (2 Kgs)
V-7 p. 36
"I Feel the Spirit Moving" (2 Kgs, Gal)
V-3 (1) p.22
"Because You Are God's Chosen Ones" (Gal)
V-8 p. 286

**Anthems**

"I've Got Peace Like a River" (Gal)
Arr. Joel Raney; Hope C-5833
SATB with piano (opt. four-hand piano)

"Will You Come and Follow Me" (Luke)
John Bell; GIA G4384
SATB with keyboard

**Other Suggestions**

Visuals:
**O** Tornado, mantel, parted water, torn clothes
**P** Prayer, arm, rain, clouds, storm, sea, Exodus
**E** Open shackles, love, brokenness, warning
**G** Jesus, fire, fox, nest, pillow, coffin, plow

Call to Worship: S2118. "Holy Spirit, Come to Us" ("*Veni Sancte Spiritus*") (Gal)
Greeting: BOW300 (Pss) or BOW456 (Pss, Luke)
Act of Congregational Centering: BOW470 (Gal)
Opening Prayer: BOW465 (Gal)
Call to Prayer: S2207. "Lord, Listen to Your Children" (2 Kgs)
Prayer of Confession: BOW477 (Gal)
Prayer: WSL182 or BOW337 (Gal)
Prayer: WSL198 (1 Kgs, Change of Pastoral Appointment)
Prayer of Thanksgiving: BOW550 (Pss, Luke)
Dismissal: BOW559 (Gal)
Blessing: WSL40 (2 Kgs)

**2 Kings 5:1-14**

Naaman, a general for the king of Aram, was a great man
and highly regarded by his master, because through him the
LORD had given victory to Aram. This man was a mighty warrior, but he had a skin disease. 2 Now Aramean raiding parties
had gone out and captured a young girl from the land of
Israel. She served Naaman's wife.
3 She said to her mistress, "I wish that my master could
come before the prophet who lives in Samaria. He would
cure him of his skin disease." 4 So Naaman went and told his
master what the young girl from the land of Israel had said.
5 Then Aram's king said, "Go ahead. I will send a letter to
Israel's king."
So Naaman left. He took along ten kikkars of silver, six
thousand shekels of gold, and ten changes of clothing. 6 He
brought the letter to Israel's king. It read, "Along with this
letter I'm sending you my servant Naaman so you can cure
him of his skin disease."
7 When the king of Israel read the letter, he ripped his
clothes. He said, "What? Am I God to hand out death and
life? But this king writes me, asking me to cure someone of
his skin disease! You must realize that he wants to start a fight
with me."
8 When Elisha the man of God heard that Israel's king had
ripped his clothes, he sent word to the king: "Why did you
rip your clothes? Let the man come to me. Then he'll know
that there's a prophet in Israel."
9 Naaman arrived with his horses and chariots. He stopped
at the door of Elisha's house. 10 Elisha sent out a messenger
who said, "Go and wash seven times in the Jordan River.
Then your skin will be restored and become clean."
11 But Naaman went away in anger. He said, "I thought for
sure that he'd come out, stand and call on the name of the
LORD his God, wave his hand over the bad spot, and cure the
skin disease. 12 Aren't the rivers in Damascus, the Abana and
the Pharpar, better than all Israel's waters? Couldn't I wash
in them and get clean?" So he turned away and proceeded to
leave in anger.
13 Naaman's servants came up to him and spoke to him:
"Our father, if the prophet had told you to do something
difficult, wouldn't you have done it? All he said to you was,
'Wash and become clean.'" 14 So Naaman went down and
bathed in the Jordan seven times, just as the man of God had
said. His skin was restored like that of a young boy, and he
became clean.

---

**Psalm 30 (UM7762)**

I exalt you, LORD,
because you pulled me up;
you didn't let my enemies
celebrate over me.
2 LORD, my God, I cried out to you for help,
and you healed me. . . .

---

**Galatians 6:(1-6), 7-16**

Brothers and sisters, if a person is caught doing something
wrong, you who are spiritual should restore someone like
this with a spirit of gentleness. Watch out for yourselves so
you won't be tempted too. 2 Carry each other's burdens and
so you will fulfill the law of Christ. 3 If anyone thinks they are
important when they aren't, they're fooling themselves.
4 Each person should test their own work and be happy with
doing a good job and not compare themselves with others.
5 Each person will have to carry their own load.
6 Those who are taught the word should share all good
things with their teacher. 7 Make no mistake, God is not
mocked. A person will harvest what they plant. 8 Those who
plant only for their own benefit will harvest devastation from
their selfishness, but those who plant for the benefit of the
Spirit will harvest eternal life from the Spirit. 9 Let's not get
tired of doing good, because in time we'll have a harvest if
we don't give up. 10 So then, let's work for the good of all
whenever we have an opportunity, and especially for those in
the household of faith.
11 Look at the large letters I'm making with my own hand-
writing! 12 Whoever wants to look good by human standards
will try to get you to be circumcised, but only so they won't
be harassed for the cross of Christ. 13 Those who are circumcised don't observe the Law themselves, but they want you to
be circumcised, so they can boast about your physical body.
14 But as for me, God forbid that I should boast about
anything except for the cross of our Lord Jesus Christ. The
world has been crucified to me through him, and I have
been crucified to the world. 15 Being circumcised or not
being circumcised doesn't mean anything. What matters is a
new creation. 16 May peace and mercy be on whoever follows
this rule and on God's Israel.

---

**Luke 10:1-11, 16-20**

After these things, the Lord commissioned seventy-two others and sent them on ahead in pairs to every city and place
he was about to go. 2 He said to them, "The harvest is bigger
than you can imagine, but there are few workers. Therefore,
plead with the Lord of the harvest to send out workers for
his harvest. 3 Go! Be warned, though, that I'm sending you
out as lambs among wolves. 4 Carry no wallet, no bag, and no
sandals. Don't even greet anyone along the way. 5 Whenever
you enter a house, first say, 'May peace be on this house.'
6 If anyone there shares God's peace, then your peace will
rest on that person. If not, your blessing will return to you.
7 Remain in this house, eating and drinking whatever they set
before you, for workers deserve their pay. Don't move from
house to house. 8 Whenever you enter a city and its people
welcome you, eat what they set before you. 9 Heal the sick
who are there, and say to them, 'God's kingdom has come
upon you.' 10 Whenever you enter a city and the people
don't welcome you, go out into the streets and say, 11 'As a
complaint against you, we brush off the dust of your city that
has collected on our feet. But know this: God's kingdom has
come to you.'

. . . . . . . . . . . . . . . . . . . . . . . . . . . . . . . . . . . . . . . . . . . .

16 Whoever listens to you listens to me. Whoever rejects you
rejects me. Whoever rejects me rejects the one who sent me."
17 The seventy-two returned joyously, saying, "Lord, even the
demons submit themselves to us in your name."
18 Jesus replied, "I saw Satan fall from heaven like lightning.
19 Look, I have given you authority to crush snakes and scorpi-
ons underfoot. I have given you authority over all the power
of the enemy. Nothing will harm you. 20 Nevertheless, don't
rejoice because the spirits submit to you. Rejoice instead that
your names are written in heaven."

**Primary Hymns and Songs for the Day**

66 "Praise, My Soul, the King of Heaven" (2 Kgs, Pss) (O)
H-3 Hbl-88; Chr-162; Desc-67; Org-75
S-1 #205. Harm.
#206. Desc.
2210 "Joy Comes with the Dawn" (Pss)
295 "In the Cross of Christ I Glory" (Pss, Gal)
H-3 Hbl-72; Chr-113; Desc-89; Org-119
S-1 #276-77. Harm. with desc.
298 "When I Survey the Wondrous Cross" (Gal)
H-3 Hbl-6, 102; Chr-213; Desc-49; Org-49
S-1 #155. Desc.
299 "When I Survey the Wondrous Cross" (Gal)
H-3 Hbl-47; Chr-214; Desc-90; Org-127
S-1 #288. Transposition to E-flat major
584 "Lord, You Give the Great Commission" (Luke) (C)
H-3 Hbl-61; Chr-132; Org-2
S-1 #4-5. Instrumental and vocal descs.
2184 "Sent Out in Jesus' Name" ("*Enviado Soy de Dios*") (C)

**Additional Hymn Suggestions**

2236 "Gather Us In" (2 Kgs, Luke) (O)
605 "Wash, O God, Our Sons and Daughters" (2 Kgs, Baptism)
732 "Come, We That Love the Lord" (Pss)
733 "Marching to Zion" (Pss)
2194 "O Freedom" (Pss)
2211 "Faith Is Patience in the Night" (Pss)
2284 "Joy in the Morning" (Pss)
163 "Ask Ye What Great Thing I Know" (Gal)
296 "Sing, My Tongue, the Glorious Battle" (Gal)
297 "Beneath the Cross of Jesus" (Gal)
301 "Jesus, Keep Me Near the Cross" (Gal)
308 "Thine Be the Glory" (Gal)
553 "And Are We Yet Alive" (Gal)
557 "Blest Be the Tie That Binds" (Gal)
561 "Jesus, United by Thy Grace" (Gal)
562 "Jesus, Lord, We Look to Thee" (Gal)
2213 "Healer of Our Every Ill" (Gal, Luke)
2225 "Who Is My Mother, Who Is My Brother" (Gal)
2269 "Come, Share the Lord" (Gal, Luke, Comm.)
497 "Send Me, Lord" (Luke)
569 "We've a Story to Tell to the Nations" (Luke)
573 "O Zion, Haste" (Luke)
593 "Here I Am, Lord" (Luke)
649 "How Shall They Hear the Word of God" (Luke)
2185 "For One Great Peace" (Luke)
2254 "In Remembrance of Me" (Luke, Comm.)
437 "This Is My Song" (Independence Day)
696 "America the Beautiful" (Independence Day)

**Additional Contemporary Suggestions**

UM393 "Spirit of the Living God" (2 Kgs)
SP131; S-1#212 Vocal Desc. idea
S2253 "Water, River, Spirit, Grace" (2 Kgs, Baptism)
S2144 "Someone Asked the Question" (Pss)
S2195 "In the Lord I'll Be Ever Thankful" (Pss)
UM706 "Soon and Very Soon" (Pss)
S-2 #187. Piano Arr.
WS3108 "Trading My Sorrows" (Pss)
M75
SP18 "I Exalt You" (Pss)
M5 "The River Is Here" (Pss)
M49 "Refresh My Heart" (Gal)
M53 "Let It Be Said of Us" (Gal)
M76 "The Wonderful Cross" (Gal)
M266 "You Have Saved Us" (Gal)
S2224 "Make Us One" (Gal, Comm.)
SP137
S2222 "The Servant Song" (Gal)
S2171 "Make Me a Channel of Your Peace" (Luke)
S2186 "Song of Hope" (Luke)
M86 "With All of My Heart" (Luke)
SP187
WS3186 "Days of Elijah" (Luke)
M139

**Vocal Solos**

"Standin' in De Need of Prayer" (2 Kgs, Pss)
V-7 p. 40
"Marchin' On Up" (Pss)
V-3 (3) p. 57
"Brighter than the Sun" (Gal, Baptism)
V-5(1) p. 57
"Make Me a Channel of Your Peace" (Gal, Luke)
V-3 (2) p. 25
V-3 (3) p. 28
"Reach Out to Your Neighbor" (Gal, Luke)
V-8 p. 372

**Anthems**

"I Saw the Cross of Jesus" (Gal)
Victor C. Johnson; Choristers Guild CGA-1346
SATB with piano

"America the Beautiful" (Independence Day)
Arr. Michael McCarthy; MorningStar MSM-50-7075
SSAATBB with organ or brass quintet

**Other Suggestions**

Visuals:
**O** Letter, torn clothes, healing, water/river
**P** Oil/cruet, joy/dance, mourn/sackcloth
**E** Pairs, harvest/workers, cross, butterfly/chrysalis
**G** Oil, no. 72/pairs, harvest, lamb/wolf, ministry, reject, joy

Introit: BOW199, S2271. "Come! Come! Everybody Worship" (Pss)
Greeting: BOW453 (Pss) or BOW458 (Luke)
Act of Congregational Centering: BOW473 (Pss, Gal)
Prayer of Confession: BOW490 (2 Kgs)
Prayer: BOW337 or BOW518 (Gal)
Prayer: UM429. For Our Country (Independence Day)
Prayers: BOW515-517 and BOW 442 (Independence Day)
Offertory Prayer: WSL121 (Gal)
Prayer of Thanksgiving: BOW550 (Gal)
Closing Prayer: BOW567 (Gal)

**Amos 7:7-17**

7 This is what the LORD showed me: The LORD was standing
by a wall, with a plumb line in his hand. 8 The LORD said to
me, "Amos, what do you see?"

"A plumb line," I said.

Then the LORD said,

"See, I am setting a plumb line
in the middle of my people Israel.
I will never again forgive them.
9 The shrines of Isaac will be made desolate,
and the holy places of Israel will be laid waste,
and I will rise against the house of Jeroboam with
the sword."

10 Then Amaziah, the priest of Bethel, reported to Israel's
King Jeroboam, "Amos has plotted against you within the
house of Israel. The land isn't able to cope with everything
that he is saying. 11 Amos has said, 'Jeroboam will die by the
sword, and Israel will be forced out of its land.'"

12 Amaziah said to Amos, "You who see things, go, run away
to the land of Judah, eat your bread there, and prophesy
there; 13 but never again prophesy at Bethel, for it is the
king's holy place and his royal house."

14 Amos answered Amaziah, "I am not a prophet, nor am I a
prophet's son; but I am a shepherd, and a trimmer of sycamore
trees. 15 But the LORD took me from shepherding the flock, and
the LORD said to me, 'Go, prophesy to my people Israel.'

16 "Now then hear the LORD's word.
You say, 'Don't prophesy against Israel, and don't preach
against the house of Isaac.'
17 "Therefore, the LORD proclaims:
'Your wife will become a prostitute in the city,
and your sons and your daughters will fall by
the sword,
and your land will be measured and divided up;
you yourself will die in an unclean land,
and Israel will surely be taken away from its land.'"

---

**Psalm 82 (UM804)**

God takes his stand in the divine council;
he gives judgment among the gods:
2 "How long will you judge unjustly
by granting favor to the wicked? *[Selah]*
3 Give justice to the lowly and the orphan;
maintain the right of the poor and the destitute!
4 Rescue the lowly and the needy.
Deliver them from the power of the wicked!
5 They don't know; they don't understand;
they wander around in the dark.
All the earth's foundations shake.
6 I hereby declare, "You are gods,
children of the Most High—all of you!
7 But you will die like mortals;
you will fall down like any prince."
8 Rise up, God! Judge the earth
because you hold all nations in your possession!

---

**Colossians 1:1-14**

From Paul, an apostle of Christ Jesus by God's will, and
Timothy our brother.

2 To the holy and faithful brothers and sisters in Christ in
Colossae.

Grace and peace to you from God our Father.

3 We always give thanks to God, the Father of our Lord
Jesus Christ, when we pray for you. 4 We've done this since we
heard of your faith in Christ Jesus and your love for all God's
people. 5 You have this faith and love because of the hope
reserved for you in heaven. You previously heard about this
hope through the true message, the good news, 6 which has
come to you. This message has been bearing fruit and growing among you since the day you heard and truly understood
God's grace, in the same way that it is bearing fruit and growing in the whole world. 7 You learned it from Epaphras, who
is the fellow slave we love and Christ's faithful minister for
your sake. 8 He informed us of your love in the Spirit.

9 Because of this, since the day we heard about you, we
haven't stopped praying for you and asking for you to be
filled with the knowledge of God's will, with all wisdom and
spiritual understanding. 10 We're praying this so that you
can live lives that are worthy of the Lord and pleasing to
him in every way: by producing fruit in every good work and
growing in the knowledge of God; 11 by being strengthened
through his glorious might so that you endure everything
and have patience; 12 and by giving thanks with joy to the
Father. He made it so you could take part in the inheritance,
in light granted to God's holy people. 13 He rescued us from
the control of darkness and transferred us into the kingdom
of the Son he loves. 14 He set us free through the Son and
forgave our sins.

---

**Luke 10:25-37**

25 A legal expert stood up to test Jesus. "Teacher," he said,
"what must I do to gain eternal life?"

26 Jesus replied, "What is written in the Law? How do you
interpret it?"

27 He responded, "*You must love the Lord your God with all your
heart, with all your being, with all your strength, and with all your
mind, and love your neighbor as yourself.*"

28 Jesus said to him, "You have answered correctly. Do this
and you will live."

29 But the legal expert wanted to prove that he was right, so
he said to Jesus, "And who is my neighbor?"

30 Jesus replied, "A man went down from Jerusalem to Jericho. He encountered thieves, who stripped him naked, beat
him up, and left him near death. 31 Now it just so happened
that a priest was also going down the same road. When he
saw the injured man, he crossed over to the other side of the
road and went on his way. 32 Likewise, a Levite came by that
spot, saw the injured man, and crossed over to the other side
of the road and went on his way. 33 A Samaritan, who was on
a journey, came to where the man was. But when he saw him,
he was moved with compassion. 34 The Samaritan went to him
and bandaged his wounds, tending them with oil and wine.
Then he placed the wounded man on his own donkey, took
him to an inn, and took care of him. 35 The next day, he took
two full days' worth of wages and gave them to the innkeeper.
He said, 'Take care of him, and when I return, I will pay you
back for any additional costs.' 36 What do you think? Which
one of these three was a neighbor to the man who encountered thieves?"

37 Then the legal expert said, "The one who demonstrated
mercy toward him."

Jesus told him, "Go and do likewise."

**Primary Hymns and Songs for the Day**

577 "God of Grace and God of Glory" (Pss) (O)
H-3 Hbl-25, 51, 58; Chr-89; Desc-26; Org-23
S-1 #76-77. Desc. and harm.
441 "What Does the Lord Require" (Amos)
H-3 Chr-211
257 "We Meet You, O Christ" (Luke)
S-2 #166. Desc.
2168 "Love the Lord Your God" (Luke)
2130 "The Summons" (Luke)
H-3 Chr-220
356 "*Pues Si Vivimos*" ("When We Are Living") (Col, Luke) (C)
S-1 #320. Orff instr. arr.
H-3 Chr-218; Org-155

**Additional Hymn Suggestions**

108 "God Hath Spoken by the Prophets" (Amos)
730 "O Day of God, Draw Nigh" (Amos)
2177 "Wounded World that Cries for Healing" (Amos)
2180 "Why Stand So Far Away, My God?" (Amos, Pss)
717 "The Battle Hymn of the Republic" (Amos, Pss)
708 "Rejoice in God's Saints" (Amos, Col)
126 "Sing Praise to God Who Reigns Above" (Pss)
142 "If Thou But Suffer God to Guide Thee" (Pss)
428 "For the Healing of the Nations" (Pss)
437 "This Is My Song" (Pss)
2047 "Bring Many Names" (Pss)
411 "Dear Lord, Lead Me Day by Day" (Col)
541 "See How Great a Flame Aspires" (Col)
2050 "Mothering God, You Gave Me Birth" (Col)
2181 "We Need a Faith" (Col)
2185 "For One Great Peace" (Col)
192 "There's a Spirit in the Air" (Col, Luke)
351 "Pass Me Not, O Gentle Savior" (Luke)
402 "Lord, I Want to Be a Christian" (Luke)
417 "O For a Heart to Praise My God" (Luke)
427 "Where Cross the Crowded Ways of Life" (Luke)
500 "Spirit of God, Descend upon My Heart" (Luke)
2138 "Sunday's Palms Are Wednesday's Ashes" (Luke)
2213 "Healer of Our Every Ill" (Luke)
2254 "In Remembrance of Me" (Luke, Comm.)
3128 "Whatever You Do" (Luke)

**Additional Contemporary Suggestions**

WS3106 "Your Grace Is Enough" (Amos, Col, Luke)
M191
S2036 "Give Thanks" (Pss, Col)
SP170
S2195 "In the Lord I'll Be Ever Thankful" (Col)
M87 "Let the Peace of God Reign" (Col)
S2161 "To Know You More" (Luke)
S2167 "More Like You" (Luke)
S2171 "Make Me a Channel of Your Peace" (Luke)
S2179 "Live in Charity" ("*Ubi Caritas*") (Luke)
S2188 "The Family Prayer Song" ("As for Me and My House") (Luke)
M54
UM123 "*El Shaddai*" (Luke)
UM432 "*Jesu, Jesu*" (Luke)
S-1 #63. Vocal part
WS3116 "Love the Lord" (Luke)
M270
M40 "More Love, More Power" (Luke)
M41 "You're Worthy of My Praise" (Luke)
M49 "Refresh My Heart" (Luke)
M53 "Let It Be Said of Us" (Luke)
M62 "Rise Up and Praise Him" (Luke)
M83 "Just Let Me Say" (Luke)
M86 "With All of My Heart" (Luke)
SP187
M98 "Take This Life" (Luke)

**Vocal Solos**

"God Weeps" (Amos, Pss)
S2048
"Make Me a Channel of Your Peace" (Col, Luke)
V-3 (2) p. 25
S2171
"A Song About Me" (Luke)
V-8 p. 364
"This Is My Commandment" (Luke)
V-8 p. 284
"Spirit of God" (Luke)
V-8 p. 170
"He Breaks the Bread, He Pours the Wine" (Luke, Comm.)
V-10 p. 43

**Anthems**

"Guide Us, Lord" (Col)
Mark Patterson: Choristers Guild CGA-1357
Unison/two-part with piano and opt. viola

"Children of the Heavenly Father" (Col, Luke)
Arr. Bradley Ellingboe; Kjos 8787
SATB *a cappella*

**Other Suggestions**

Visuals:
**O** Wall, plumb line, sword, scales of justice
**P** Scales, ministry with poor, children, earthquake
**E** Pray, Bible, fruit/globe, joy, light, rescue
**G** Briefcase, bloody clothes, bandages, oil, wine, coins
Introit: S2271, BOW199. "Come! Come! Everybody Worship" (Col)
Opening Prayer: BOW310 (Pss, Luke)
Prayer of Confession: WSL90 or BOW476 (Luke)
Prayer: BOW344 (Col)
Affirmation of Faith: WSL78 (Col)
Offertory Prayer: WSL123 (Luke)
Prayer of Thanksgiving: BOW555 (Luke)
Closing Prayer: BOW567 (Luke)
Responsive Benediction: WSL177 (Luke)
Sung Benediction: S2281. "May You Run and Not Be Weary" (Col)

**Amos 8:1-12**

This is what the LORD God showed me: a basket of summer
fruit. 2 He said, "Amos, what do you see?"
I said, "A basket of summer fruit."
Then the LORD said to me,
"The end has come upon my people Israel;
I will never again forgive them.
3 On that day, the people will wail the temple songs,"
says the LORD God;
"there will be many corpses,
thrown about everywhere.
Silence."
4 Hear this, you who trample on the needy and destroy
the poor of the land,
5 saying,
"When will the new moon
be over so that we may sell grain,
and the Sabbath
so that we may offer wheat for sale,
make the ephah smaller, enlarge the shekel,
and deceive with false balances,
6 in order to buy the needy for silver
and the helpless for sandals,
and sell garbage as grain?"
7 The LORD has sworn by the pride of Jacob:
Surely I will never forget what they have done.
8 Will not the land tremble on this account,
and all who live in it mourn,
as it rises and overflows like the Nile,
and then falls again, like the River of Egypt?
9 On that day, says the LORD God,
I will make the sun go down at noon,
and I will darken the earth in broad daylight.
10 I will turn your feasts into sad affairs
and all your singing into a funeral song;
I will make people wear mourning clothes
and shave their heads;
I will make it like the loss of an only child,
and the end of it like a bitter day.
11 The days are surely coming, says the LORD God,
when I will send hunger and thirst on the land;
neither a hunger for bread, nor a thirst for water,
but of hearing the LORD 's words.
12 They will wander from sea to sea,
and from north to east;
they will roam all around, seeking the LORD's word,
but they won't find it.

---

**Psalm 52**

Hey, powerful person!
Why do you brag about evil?
God's faithful love lasts all day long.
2 Your tongue devises destruction:
it's like a sharpened razor, causing deception.
3 You love evil more than good;
you love lying more than speaking what is right. *[Selah]*
4 You love all destructive words;
you love the deceiving tongue.
5 But God will take you down permanently;
he will snatch you up,
tear you out of your tent,
and uproot you from the land of the living! *[Selah]*
6 The righteous will see and be in awe;
they will laugh at those people:
7 "Look at them! They didn't make God their refuge.
Instead, they trusted in their own great wealth.
They sought refuge in it—to their own destruction!"
8 But I am like a green olive tree in God's house;
I trust in God's faithful love forever and always.
9 I will give thanks to you, God, forever,
because you have acted.
In the presence of your faithful people,
I will hope in your name because it's so good.

---

**Colossians 1:15-28**

15 The Son is the image of the invisible God,
the one who is first over all creation,
16 Because all things were created by him:
both in the heavens and on the earth,
the things that are visible and the things that are
invisible.
Whether they are thrones or powers,
or rulers or authorities,
all things were created through him and for him.
17 He existed before all things,
and all things are held together in him.
18 He is the head of the body, the church,
who is the beginning,
the one who is firstborn from among the dead
so that he might occupy the first place in everything.
19 Because all the fullness of God was pleased to live in him,
20 and he reconciled all things to himself through him—
whether things on earth or in the heavens.
He brought peace through the blood of his cross.
21 Once you were alienated from God and you were enemies
with him in your minds, which was shown by your evil actions.
22 But now he has reconciled you by his physical body through
death, to present you before God as a people who are holy,
faultless, and without blame. 23 But you need to remain well
established and rooted in faith and not shift away from the
hope given in the good news that you heard. This message has
been preached throughout all creation under heaven. And I,
Paul, became a servant of this good news.
24 Now I'm happy to be suffering for you. I'm completing
what is missing from Christ's sufferings with my own body.
I'm doing this for the sake of his body, which is the church.
25 I became a servant of the church by God's commission,
which was given to me for you, in order to complete God's
word. 26 I'm completing it with a secret plan that has been
hidden for ages and generations but which has now been
revealed to his holy people. 27 God wanted to make the glorious riches of this secret plan known among the Gentiles,
which is Christ living in you, the hope of glory. 28 This is what
we preach as we warn and teach every person with all wisdom
so that we might present each one mature in Christ.

---

**Luke 10:38-42**

38 While Jesus and his disciples were traveling, Jesus entered
a village where a woman named Martha welcomed him as a
guest. 39 She had a sister named Mary, who sat at the Lord's feet
and listened to his message. 40 By contrast, Martha was preoc-
cupied with getting everything ready for their meal. So Martha
came to him and said, "Lord, don't you care that my sister has
left me to prepare the table all by myself? Tell her to help me."
41 The Lord answered, "Martha, Martha, you are worried and
distracted by many things. 42 One thing is necessary. Mary has
chosen the better part. It won't be taken away from her."

**Primary Hymns and Songs for the Day**

103 "Immortal, Invisible, God Only Wise" (Col) (O)
H-3 Hbl-15, 71; Chr-65; Desc-93; Org-135
S-1 #300. Harm.

433 "All Who Love and Serve Your City" (Amos, Luke)
H-3 Chr-26, 65; Org-19
S-1 #62. Desc.

441 "What Does the Lord Require" (Amos)
H-3 Chr-211

562 "Jesus, Lord, We Look to Thee" (Amos, Col, Luke)
S-2 #165. Desc.

377 "It Is Well with My Soul" (Col) (C)
H-3 Chr-113

**Additional Hymn Suggestions**

592 "When the Church of Jesus" (Amos)
719 "My Lord, What a Morning" (Amos)
2048 "God Weeps" (Amos, Pss)
2180 "Why Stand So Far Away, My God?" (Amos, Pss)
3098 "Dust and Ashes" (Amos, Pss)
84 "Thank You, Lord" (Pss)
184 "Of the Father's Love Begotten" (Amos, Col)
187 "Rise, Shine, You People" (Col)
297 "Beneath the Cross of Jesus" (Col)
301 "Jesus, Keep Me Near the Cross" (Col)
305 "*Camina, Pueblo de Dios*" ("Walk On, O People of God") (Col)
359 "Alas! and Did My Savior Bleed" (Col)
362 "Nothing but the Blood" (Col)
370 "Victory in Jesus" (Col)
453 "More Love to Thee, O Christ" (Col)
511 "Am I a Soldier of the Cross" (Col)
2004 "Praise the Source of Faith and Learning" (Col)
2121 "O Holy Spirit, Root of Life" (Col)
2166 "Christ Beside Me" (Col)
2220 "We Are God's People" (Col)
2237 "As a Fire Is Meant for Burning" (Col)
2261 "Life-Giving Bread" (Col, Comm.)
2269 "Come, Share the Lord" (Col, Comm.)
3035 "Bless Christ Through Whom All Things Are Made" (Col)
3110 "By Grace We Have Been Saved" (Col)
274 "Woman in the Night" (Luke)
358 "Dear Lord and Father of Mankind" (Luke) *(Alternate Text–"Parent of Us All")*
396 "O Jesus, I Have Promised (Luke)
399 "Take My Life, and Let It Be" (Luke)
407 "Close to Thee" (Luke)
451 "Be Thou My Vision" (Luke)
532 "Jesus, Priceless Treasure" (Luke)
2128 "Come and Find the Quiet Center" (Luke)
2153 "I'm Gonna Live So God Can Use Me" (Luke)
2175 "Together We Serve" (Luke)
2202 "Come Away with Me" (Luke)
3109 "Living Spirit, Holy Fire" (Luke)
3118 "Take This Moment, Sign, and Space" (Luke)

**Additional Contemporary Suggestions**

WS3023 "Forever" (Pss)
M68
WS3027 "Hallelujah" ("Your Love Is Amazing") (Pss)
M118
M189 "Your Love, Oh Lord" (Pss)
S2065 "More Precious than Silver" (Pss, Luke)
SP99
S2164 "Sanctuary" (Col)
M52
S2173 "Shine, Jesus, Shine" (Col)
SP142
S2272 "Holy Ground" (Col)
SP86
WS3032 "Across the Lands" (Col)
M94 "That's Why We Praise Him" (Col)
M122 "Every Move I Make" (Luke)
S2159 "Jesus, Draw Me Close" (Luke)
M48
UM349 "Turn Your Eyes upon Jesus" (Luke)
SP218

**Vocal Solos**

"Did You Feel the Mountains Tremble?" (Amos, Pss)
M69
"It Is Well with My Soul" (Col)
V-5(2) p. 35
"Jesus Revealed in Me" (Col)
V-8 p. 347
"Be Thou My Vision" (Col, Luke)
V-6 p. 13
"Take My Life" (Luke)
V-3 (3) p. 17
V-8 p. 262

**Anthems**

"Rise, Shine!" (Col, Luke)
Dale Wood; Augsburg 11-10737
SATB with organ

"Jesus, Priceless Treasure" (Luke)
Brad Nix; Jubliate/Alfred 42507
SATB with keyboard

**Other Suggestions**

Visuals:
**O** Basket/fruit, new moon, silver, sandals, sackcloth
**P** Uprooted tree, wealth, olive tree, joy, laugh
**E** Risen Christ, glue, blood/cross, service
**G** Pots/pans, dust cloth, mop, dishes, Jesus/two women

Greeting: BOW307 or BOW457 (Col)
Act of Congregational Centering: BOW471 (Luke)
Opening Prayer: BOW468 (Amos, Col)
Sung Confession: UM450. "Creator of the Earth and Skies" (Amos)
Prayer of Confession: WSL90 (Amos) or BOW489 (Col)
Prayer of Confession: WSL96 or BOW478 (Luke)
Prayer: UM446. Serving the Poor (Amos)
Affirmation of Faith: WSL76 or UM888 (Col)
Prayer of Thanksgiving: BOW552 (Amos, Pss, Col)

**Hosea 1:2-10**
2 When the LORD first spoke through Hosea, the LORD said
to him,"Go, marry a prostitute and have children of prostitution, for the people of the land commit great prostitution
by deserting theLORD." 3 So Hosea went and took Gomer,
Diblaim's daughter, and she became pregnant and bore him
a son. 4 The LORD said to him, "Name him Jezreel; for in a
little while I will punish the house of Jehu for the blood of
Jezreel, and I will destroy the kingdom of the house of Israel.
5 On that day I will break the bow of Israel in the Jezreel
Valley." 6 Gomer became pregnant again and gave birth to a
daughter. Then the LORD said to Hosea, "Name her No Compassion, because I will no longer have compassion on the
house of Israel or forgive them. 7 But I will have compassion
on the house of Judah. I, the LORD their God, will save them;
I will not save them by bow, or by sword, or by war, or by
horses, or by horsemen." 8 When Gomer finished nursing No
Compassion, she became pregnant and gave birth to a son.
9 Then the LORD said, "Name him Not My People because
you are not my people, and I am not your God."

10 Yet the number of the people of Israel will be like the
sand of the sea, which can be neither measured nor numbered; and in the place where it was said to them, "You are
not my people," it will be said to them, "Children of the
living God."

---

**Psalm 85 (UM806)**
LORD, you've been kind to your land;
you've changed Jacob's circumstances for the better.
2 You've forgiven your people's wrongdoing;
you've covered all their sins. *[Selah]*
3 You've stopped being furious;
you've turned away from your burning anger.
4 You, the God who can save us, restore us!
Stop being angry with us!
5 Will you be mad at us forever?
Will you prolong your anger from one generation to
the next?
6 Won't you bring us back to life again
so that your people can rejoice in you?
7 Show us your faithful love, LORD!
Give us your salvation!
8 Let me hear what the LORD God says,
because he speaks peace to his people and to his
faithful ones.
Don't let them return to foolish ways.
9 God's salvation is very close to those who honor him
so that his glory can live in our land.
10 Faithful love and truth have met;
righteousness and peace have kissed.
11 Truth springs up from the ground;
righteousness gazes down from heaven.
12 Yes, the LORD gives what is good,
and our land yields its produce.
13 Righteousness walks before God,
making a road for his steps.

---

**Colossians 2:6-15 (16-19)**
6 So live in Christ Jesus the Lord in the same way as you
received him. 7 Be rooted and built up in him, be established
in faith, and overflow with thanksgiving just as you were
taught. 8 See to it that nobody enslaves you with philosophy
and foolish deception, which conform to human traditions
and the way the world thinks and acts rather than Christ.
9 All the fullness of deity lives in Christ's body. 10 And you
have been filled by him, who is the head of every ruler and
authority. 11 You were also circumcised by him. This wasn't
performed by human hands—the whole body was removed
through this circumcision by Christ. 12 You were buried with
him through baptism and raised with him through faith in
the power of God, who raised him from the dead. 13 When
you were dead because of the things you had done wrong
and because your body wasn't circumcised, God made you
alive with Christ and forgave all the things you had done
wrong. 14 He destroyed the record of the debt we owed, with
its requirements that worked against us. He canceled it by
nailing it to the cross. 15 When he disarmed the rulers and
authorities, he exposed them to public disgrace by leading
them in a triumphal parade.

16 So don't let anyone judge you about eating or drinking
or about a festival, a new moon observance, or sabbaths.
17 These religious practices are only a shadow of what was
coming—the body that cast the shadow is Christ. 18 Don't let
anyone who wants to practice harsh self-denial and worship
angels rob you of the prize. They go into detail about what
they have seen in visions and have become unjustifiably
arrogant by their selfish way of thinking. 19 They don't stay
connected to the head. The head nourishes and supports the
whole body through the joints and ligaments, so the body
grows with a growth that is from God.

---

**Luke 11:1-13**
Jesus was praying in a certain place. When he finished,
one of his disciples said, "Lord, teach us to pray, just as John
taught his disciples."
2 Jesus told them, "When you pray, say:
'Father, uphold the holiness of your name.
Bring in your kingdom.
3 Give us the bread we need for today.
4 Forgive us our sins,
for we also forgive everyone who has wronged us.
And don't lead us into temptation.'"
5 He also said to them, "Imagine that one of you has a
friend and you go to that friend in the middle of the night.
Imagine saying, 'Friend, loan me three loaves of bread
6 because a friend of mine on a journey has arrived and
I have nothing to set before him.' 7 Imagine further that
he answers from within the house, 'Don't bother me. The
door is already locked, and my children and I are in bed. I
can't get up to give you anything.' 8 I assure you, even if he
wouldn't get up and help because of his friendship, he will
get up and give his friend whatever he needs because of his
friend's brashness. 9 And I tell you: Ask and you will receive.
Seek and you will find. Knock and the door will be opened to
you. 10 Everyone who asks, receives. Whoever seeks, finds. To
everyone who knocks, the door is opened.

11 "Which father among you would give a snake to your
child if the child asked for a fish? 12 If a child asked for an
egg, what father would give the child a scorpion? 13 If you
who are evil know how to give good gifts to your children,
how much more will the heavenly Father give the Holy Spirit
to those who ask him?"

**Primary Hymns and Songs for the Day**

545 "The Church's One Foundation" (Col) (O)
546 "The Church's One Foundation" (Col) (O)
H-3 Hbl-94; Chr-180; Desc-16; Org-9
S-1 #25-26. Desc. and harm.
2169 "God, How Can We Forgive" (Hos, Pss, Luke)
H-3 Hbl-62, 95; Chr-59; Org-77
S-1 #211. Harm.
405 "Seek Ye First" (Luke)
SP182
S2278 "The Lord's Prayer" (Luke)
UM271, WS3068-WS3071
430 "O Master, Let Me Walk with Thee" (Col) (C)
H-3 Hbl-81; Chr-147; Desc-74; Org-87
S-2 #118. Desc.

**Additional Hymn Suggestions**

108 "God Hath Spoken by the Prophets" (Hos)
582 "Whom Shall I Send?" (Hos)
117 "O God, Our Help in Ages Past" (Pss)
119 "O God in Heaven" (Pss)
390 "Forgive Our Sins as We Forgive" (Pss, Col, Luke)
2180 "Why Stand So Far Away, My God?" (Hos, Pss)
2209 "How Long, O Lord" (Hos, Pss)
2217 "By the Babylonian Rivers" (Hos, Pss)
2234 "Lead On, O Cloud of Presence" (Hos, Pss)
162 "Alleluia, Alleluia" (Col)
306 "The Strife Is O'er, the Battle Done" (Col)
377 "It Is Well with My Soul" (Col)
407 "Close to Thee" (Col)
521 "I Want Jesus to Walk with Me" (Col)
559 "Christ Is Made the Sure Foundation" (Col)
610 "We Know That Christ Is Raised" (Col, Baptism)
2220 "We Are God's People" (Col)
2251 "We Were Baptized in Christ Jesus" (Col, Baptism)
2261 "Life-Giving Bread" (Col, Comm.)
2269 "Come, Share the Lord" (Col, Luke, Comm.)
192 "There's a Spirit in the Air" (Luke)
399 "Take My Life, and Let It Be" (Luke)
406 "Canticle of Prayer" (Luke)
437 "This Is My Song" (Luke)
440 "Let There Be Light" (Luke)
492 "Prayer Is the Soul's Sincere Desire" (Luke)
2138 "Sunday's Palms Are Wednesday's Ashes" (Luke)
2196 "We Walk by Faith" (Luke)
2202 "Come Away with Me" (Luke) (O)
2205 "The Fragrance of Christ" (Luke)
2262 "Let Us Offer to the Father" (Luke, Comm.)

**Additional Contemporary Suggestions**

SP146 "Revive Us, Oh Lord" (Pss)
M49 "Refresh My Heart" (Pss)
M144 "Light the Fire Again" (Pss)
M145 "Move Me Again" (Pss)
M242 "Salvation Is Here"
WS3040 "You Are My All in All" (Col, Luke)
SP220
S2171 "Make Me a Channel of Your Peace" (Luke)
S2207 "Lord, Listen to Your Children" (Luke)
M17 "This Kingdom" (Luke)
M115 "When It's All Been Said and Done" (Luke)
WS3004 "Step by Step" (Luke)
M51
WS3094 "Come to Me" (Luke)

**Vocal Solos**

"Patiently Have I Waited for the Lord" (Pss)
V-4 p. 24
"It Is Well with My Soul" (Col)
V-5(2) p. 35
"The Lord's Prayer" (Luke)
V-8 p. 39
"O Father in Heaven" (Luke)
V-8 p. 122
"Breathe" (Luke)
WS3112, M61

**Anthems**

"It Is Well with My Soul " (Col)
David Schwoebel; MorningStar MSM-50-5110
SATB with piano

"Seek Ye First" (Luke)
Arr. Douglas Wagner; Hope C5196
SATB with keyboard and opt. handbells

**Other Suggestions**

Visuals:
**O** Broken bow, newborn, sand
**P** Revival, kiss, growing plants, sky, harvest, path
**E** Roots, building, Christ, cross/crown, eraser
**G** Jesus, pray, three loaves, lock, open door, gifts, Trinity

Introit: S2273, BOW187. "Jesus, We Are Here" (Luke)
Call to Worship or Litany: WSL58 (Luke)
Opening Prayer: BOW314 (Col) or BOW467 (Luke)
Call to Prayer: S2200. "O Lord, Hear My Prayer" (Luke)
Prayer of Confession: BOW475 (Pss)
Sung Confession: S2013. "Bless the Lord" (Hos, Pss)
Canticle: UM270/UM271, WS3068–WS3071. "The Lord's Prayer" (Luke)
Prayer: BOW529. A Prayer of Saint Patrick (Col)
Prayer: WSL55 (Luke)
Prayer: UM894 or UM895. The Lord's Prayer (Luke)
Prayer: S2201. "Prayers of the People" (Luke)
Response: S2207. "Lord, Listen to Your Children" (Luke)
Litany: UM106. God Is Able (Luke)
Baptism Response: S2251, stanza 2. "We Were Baptized in Christ Jesus" (Col)
Offertory Prayer: WSL122 (Luke)
Blessing: BOW561 (Hos, Pss)

**Hosea 11:1-11**

When Israel was a child, I loved him,
and out of Egypt I called my son.
2 The more I called them,
the further they went from me;
they kept sacrificing to the Baals,
and they burned incense to idols.
3 Yet it was I who taught Ephraim to walk;
I took them up in my arms,
but they did not know that I healed them.
4 I led them
with bands of human kindness,
with cords of love.
I treated them like those
who lift infants to their cheeks;
I bent down to them and fed them.
5 They will return to the land of Egypt,
and Assyria will be their king,
because they have refused to return to me.
6 The sword will strike wildly in their cities;
it will consume the bars of their gates
and will take everything because of their schemes.
7 My people are bent on turning away from me;
and though they cry out to the Most High,
he will not raise them up.
8 How can I give you up, Ephraim?
How can I hand you over, Israel?
How can I make you like Admah?
How can I treat you like Zeboiim?
My heart winces within me;
my compassion grows warm and tender.
9 I won't act on the heat of my anger;
I won't return to destroy Ephraim;
for I am God and not a human being,
the holy one in your midst;
I won't come in harsh judgment.
10 They will walk after the LORD,
who roars like a lion.
When he roars,
his children will come trembling from the west.
11 They will come trembling like a bird,
and like a dove from the land of Assyria;
and I will return them to their homes, says the LORD.

**Psalm 107:1-9, 43 (UM830)**

"Give thanks to the LORD because he is good,
because his faithful love lasts forever!"
2 That's what those who are redeemed by the LORD say,
the ones God redeemed from the power of their enemies,
3 the ones God gathered from various countries,
from east and west, north and south.
4 Some of the redeemed had wandered into the desert,
into the wasteland.
They couldn't find their way to a city or town.
5 They were hungry and thirsty;
their lives were slipping away.
6 So they cried out to the LORD in their distress,
and God delivered them from their desperate
circumstances.
7 God led them straight to human habitation.
8 Let them thank the LORD for his faithful love
and his wondrous works for all people,
9 because God satisfied the one who was parched
with thirst,
and he filled up the hungry with good things!
. . . . . . . . . . . . . . . . . . . . . . . . .
43 Whoever is wise will pay attention to these things,
carefully considering the LORD's faithful love.

**Colossians 3:1-11**

Therefore, if you were raised with Christ, look for the
things that are above where Christ is sitting at God's right
side. 2 Think about the things above and not things on earth.
3 You died, and your life is hidden with Christ in God. 4 When
Christ, who is your life, is revealed, then you also will be
revealed with him in glory.
5 So put to death the parts of your life that belong to the
earth, such as sexual immorality, moral corruption, lust, evil
desire, and greed (which is idolatry). 6 The wrath of God is
coming upon disobedient people because of these things.
7 You used to live this way, when you were alive to these
things. 8 But now set aside these things, such as anger, rage,
malice, slander, and obscene language. 9 Don't lie to each
other. Take off the old human nature with its practices
10 and put on the new nature, which is renewed in knowledge
by conforming to the image of the one who created it. 11 In
this image there is neither Greek nor Jew, circumcised nor
uncircumcised, barbarian, Scythian, slave nor free, but Christ
is all things and in all people.

**Luke 12:13-21**

13 Someone from the crowd said to him, "Teacher, tell my
brother to divide the inheritance with me."
14 Jesus said to him, "Man, who appointed me as judge or
referee between you and your brother?"
15 Then Jesus said to them, "Watch out! Guard yourself
against all kinds of greed. After all, one's life isn't determined by one's possessions, even when someone is very
wealthy." 16 Then he told them a parable: "A certain rich
man's land produced a bountiful crop. 17 He said to himself,
What will I do? I have no place to store my harvest! 18 Then
he thought, Here's what I'll do. I'll tear down my barns
and build bigger ones. That's where I'll store all my grain
and goods. 19 I'll say to myself, You have stored up plenty of
goods, enough for several years. Take it easy! Eat, drink, and
enjoy yourself. 20 But God said to him, 'Fool, tonight you will
die. Now who will get the things you have prepared for yourself?' 21 This is the way it will be for those who hoard things
for themselves and aren't rich toward God."

### Primary Hymns and Songs for the Day

126 "Sing Praise to God Who Reigns Above" (Hos) (O)
H-3 Hbl-92; Chr-173; Desc-76; Org-91
S-1 #237. Desc.
2123 "Loving Spirit" (Hos, Pss)
H-3 Chr-67
S-2 #63-64. Desc. and harm.
433 "All Who Love and Serve Your City" (Luke)
H-3 Chr-26, 65; Org-19
S-1 #62. Desc.
102 "Now Thank We All Our God" (Hos, Pss, Col) (C)
H-3 Hbl-78; Chr-140; Desc-81; Org-98
S-1 #252-54. Various treatments

### Additional Hymn Suggestions

100 "God, Whose Love Is Reigning o'er Us" (Hos)
121 "There's a Wideness in God's Mercy" (Hos)
66 "Praise, My Soul, the King of Heaven" (Hos, Pss)
73 "O Worship the King" (Hos, Pss)
127 "Guide Me, O Thou Great Jehovah" (Hos, Pss)
140 "Great Is Thy Faithfulness" (Hos, Pss)
142 "If Thou But Suffer God to Guide Thee" (Hos, Pss)
2180 "Why Stand So Far Away, My God?" (Hos, Pss)
2209 "How Long, O Lord" (Hos, Pss)
2234 "Lead On, O Cloud of Presence" (Hos, Pss)
443 "O God Who Shaped Creation" (Hos, Luke)
350 "Come, All of You" (Pss, Comm.)
2264 "Come to the Table" (Pss, Comm.)
2012 "Let Us with a Joyful Mind" (Pss, Col)
720 "Wake, Awake, for Night Is Flying" (Pss, Luke)
114 "Many Gifts, One Spirit" (Col)
548 "In Christ There Is No East or West" (Col)
557 "Blest Be the Tie That Binds" (Col)
560 "Help Us Accept Each Other" (Col)
610 "We Know That Christ Is Raised" (Col)
617 "I Come with Joy" (Col, Comm.)
620 "One Bread, One Body" (Col, Comm.)
2082 "Woke Up This Morning" (Col)
2225 "Who Is My Mother, Who Is My Brother" (Col)
2247 "Wonder of Wonders" (Col, Baptism)
2269 "Come, Share the Lord" (Col, Comm.)
373 "Nothing Between" (Col, Luke)
399 "Take My Life, and Let It Be" (Col, Luke)
407 "Close to Thee" (Col, Luke)
413 "A Charge to Keep I Have" (Luke)
434 "*Cuando el Pobre*" ("When the Poor Ones") (Luke)
522 "Leave It There" (Luke)

### Additional Contemporary Suggestions

M125 "Praise Adonai" (Hos)
M262 "Desert Song" (Hos, Pss)
S2031 "We Bring the Sacrifice of Praise" (Pss)
SP1
S2036 "Give Thanks" (Pss)
SP170
S2132 "You Who Are Thirsty" (Pss)
WS3023 "Forever" (Pss)
M68
WS3027 "Hallelujah" ("Your Love Is Amazing") (Pss)
WS3042 "Shout to the North" (Pss)
M99
WS3014 "You Are Good" (Pss)
M124
M159 "All Who Are Thirsty" (Pss)
M160 "Enough"
M189 "Your Love, Oh Lord" (Pss)
M236 "Say So" (Pss)
M30 "Knowing You" ("All I Once Held Dear") (Col)
M33 "Jesus, You Are My Life" (Col)
M38 "In the Secret" ("I Want to Know You") (Col)
M53 "Let It Be Said of Us" (Col)
M91 "Take My Life" (Col)
M151 "Lord, You Have My Heart" (Col)
S2152 "Change My Heart, O God" (Col)
SP195
S2161 "To Know You More" (Col)
S2167 "More Like You" (Col)
S2080 "All I Need Is You" (Col, Luke)
S2159 "Jesus, Draw Me Close" (Col, Luke)
M48
WS3040 "You Are My All in All" (Col, Luke)
SP220
WS3099 "Falling on My Knees" ("Hungry") (Luke)
M155
UM405 "Seek Ye First" (Luke)
SP182
M115 "When It's All Been Said and Done" (Luke)
M156 "Be the Centre" (Luke)
M227 "I Will Boast" (Luke)

### Vocal Solos

"Maybe the Rain" (Hos, Pss)
V-5(2) p. 27
"Ho! Everyone Who Is Thirsty" (Pss)
V-8 p. 244
"One Bread, One Body" (Col, Comm.)
V-3 (2) p. 40
"Waterlife" (Col, Baptism)
V-5(3) p. 17

### Anthems

"Psalm 107" (Pss)
Robert C. Clatterbuck; Hope Publishing A-510
SATB with keyboard

"Treasures in Heaven" (Luke)
Allen Pote; Hinshaw HMC1059
SATB with keyboard

### Other Suggestions

Visuals:
**O** Child, incense, cords/bands, heart, lion, birds/dove
**P** N/S/E/W, desert, food/drink, straight path, Pss 107:2a
**E** Christ, crown, Bible, baptism, white robe, open shackles
**G** Will, possessions, barns, grain, party, death
Act of Congregational Centering: BOW472 (Hos)
Opening Prayer: BOW459 (Col) or BOW463 (Hos)
Prayer of Confession: BOW484 (Hos, Luke)
Sung Prayer: S2013. "Bless the Lord" (Hos, Pss)
Prayer: UM705 or UM529 or BOW514 (Col)
Prayer: BOW520. For Peace (Hos, Col)
Prayer of Thanksgiving: BOW551 (Hos)
Response: S2276 or WS3057. "Glory in the Highest" (Col)
Responsive Closing Prayer: WSL166 (Luke)
Blessing: BOW566. Sarum Blessing (Col)

**Isaiah 1:1, 10-20**

The vision about Judah and Jerusalem that Isaiah, Amoz's son, saw in the days of Judah's kings Uzziah, Jotham, Ahaz, and Hezekiah.

. . . . . . . . . . . . . . . . . . . . . . . . . . . . . . . . . . . . . . . . . .

10 Hear the LORD's word, you leaders of Sodom.
Listen to our God's teaching,
people of Gomorrah!
11 What should I think about all your sacrifices?
says the LORD.
I'm fed up with entirely burned offerings of rams
and the fat of well-fed beasts.
I don't want the blood of bulls, lambs, and goats.
12 When you come to appear before me,
who asked this from you,
this trampling of my temple's courts?
13 Stop bringing worthless offerings.
Your incense repulses me.
New moon, sabbath, and the calling of an assembly—
I can't stand wickedness with celebration!
14 I hate your new moons and your festivals.
They've become a burden that I'm tired of bearing.
15 When you extend your hands,
I'll hide my eyes from you.
Even when you pray for a long time,
I won't listen.
Your hands are stained with blood.
16 Wash! Be clean!
Remove your ugly deeds from my sight.
Put an end to such evil;
17 learn to do good.
Seek justice:
help the oppressed;
defend the orphan;
plead for the widow.
18 Come now, and let's settle this,
says the LORD.
Though your sins are like scarlet,
they will be white as snow.
If they are red as crimson,
they will become like wool.
19 If you agree and obey,
you will eat the best food of the land.
20 But if you refuse and rebel,
you will be devoured by the sword.
The LORD has said this.

**Psalm 50:1-8, 22-23 (UM 783)**

From the rising of the sun to where it sets,
God, the LORD God, speaks,
calling out to the earth.
2 From Zion, perfect in beauty,
God shines brightly.
3 Our God is coming;
he won't keep quiet.
A devouring fire is before him;
a storm rages all around him.
4 God calls out to the skies above
and to the earth in order to judge his people:
5 "Bring my faithful to me,
those who made a covenant with me by sacrifice."
6 The skies proclaim his righteousness
because God himself is the judge. Selah
7 "Listen, my people, I will now speak;
Israel, I will now testify against you.
I am God—your God!
8 I'm not punishing you for your sacrifices
or for your entirely burned offerings,
which are always before me. . . .
22 So consider this carefully, all you who forget God,
or I'll rip you to pieces with no one to deliver you:
23 The one who offers a sacrifice of thanksgiving is the one
who honors me.
And it is to the one who charts the correct path that I will
show divine salvation."

**Hebrews 11:1-3, 8-16**

Faith is the reality of what we hope for, the proof of what we don't see. 2 The elders in the past were approved because they showed faith.

3 By faith we understand that the universe has been created by a word from God so that the visible came into existence from the invisible. . . .

8 By faith Abraham obeyed when he was called to go out to a place that he was going to receive as an inheritance. He went out without knowing where he was going.

9 By faith he lived in the land he had been promised as a stranger. He lived in tents along with Isaac and Jacob, who were coheirs of the same promise. 10 He was looking forward to a city that has foundations, whose architect and builder is God.

11 By faith even Sarah received the ability to have a child, though she herself was barren and past the age for having children, because she believed that the one who promised was faithful. 12 So descendants were born from one man (and he was as good as dead). They were as many as the number of the stars in the sky and as countless as the grains of sand on the seashore. 13 All of these people died in faith without receiving the promises, but they saw the promises from a distance and welcomed them. They confessed that they were strangers and immigrants on earth. 14 People who say this kind of thing make it clear that they are looking for a homeland. 15 If they had been thinking about the country that they had left, they would have had the opportunity to return to it. 16 But at this point in time, they are longing for a better country, that is, a heavenly one. Therefore, God isn't ashamed to be called their God—he has prepared a city for them.

**Luke 12:32-40**

32 "Don't be afraid, little flock, because your Father delights in giving you the kingdom. 33 Sell your possessions and give to those in need. Make for yourselves wallets that don't wear out—a treasure in heaven that never runs out. No thief comes near there, and no moth destroys. 34 Where your treasure is, there your heart will be too.

35 "Be dressed for service and keep your lamps lit. 36 Be like people waiting for their master to come home from a wedding celebration, who can immediately open the door for him when he arrives and knocks on the door. 37 Happy are those servants whom the master finds waiting up when he arrives. I assure you that, when he arrives, he will dress himself to serve, seat them at the table as honored guests, and wait on them. 38 Happy are those whom he finds alert, even if he comes at midnight or just before dawn. 39 But know this, if the homeowner had known what time the thief was coming, he wouldn't have allowed his home to be broken into. 40 You also must be ready, because the Human One is coming at a time when you don't expect him."

**Primary Hymns and Songs for the Day**

529 "How Firm a Foundation" (Heb, Luke) (O)
H-3 Hbl-27, 69; Chr-102; Desc-41; Org-41
S-1 #133. Harm.
#134. Performance note
508 "Faith, While Trees Are Still in Blossom" (Heb)
H-3 Chr-67
S-2 #63-64. Desc. and harm.
710 "Faith of Our Fathers" (Heb)
H-3 Hbl-57; Chr-63; Desc-93; Org-133
577 "God of Grace and God of Glory" (Luke) (C)

**Additional Hymn Suggestions**

343 "Come Back Quickly to the Lord" (Isa, Comm.)
413 "A Charge to Keep I Have" (Isa)
436 "The Voice of God Is Calling" (Isa)
2174 "What Does the Lord Require of You" (Isa)
2177 "Wounded World that Cries for Healing" (Isa)
2178 "Here Am I" (Isa)
2182 "When God Restored our Common Life" (Isa)
440 "Let There Be Light" (Isa, Pss)
441 "What Does the Lord Require" (Isa, Pss)
450 "Creator of the Earth and Skies" (Isa, Pss)
103 "Immortal, Invisible, God Only Wise" (Pss)
122 "God of the Sparrow, God of the Whale" (Pss)
124 "Seek the Lord" (Pss)
2236 "Gather Us In" (Pss, Comm.)
132 "All My Hope Is Firmly Grounded" (Heb)
332 "Spirit of Faith, Come Down" (Heb)
385 "Let Us Plead for Faith Alone" (Heb)
507 "Through It All" (Heb)
711 "For All the Saints" (Heb)
2196 "We Walk by Faith" (Heb)
2206 "Without Seeing You" (Heb)
2211 "Faith Is Patience in the Night" (Heb)
2246 "Deep in the Shadows of the Past" (Heb)
2283 "For All the Saints" (Heb)
519 "Lift Every Voice and Sing" (Heb, Luke)
712 "I Sing a Song of the Saints of God" (Heb, Luke)
714 "I Know Whom I Have Believed" (Heb, Luke)
129 "Give to the Winds Thy Fears" (Luke)
395 "Take Time to Be Holy" (Luke)
634 "Now Let Us from This Table Rise" (Luke, Comm.)
719 "My Lord, What a Morning" (Luke)
720 "Wake, Awake, for Night Is Flying" (Luke)
722 "I Want to Be Ready" (Luke)
730 "O Day of God, Draw Nigh" (Luke) (C)
2140 "Since Jesus Came into My Heart" (Luke)
2218 "You Are Mine" (Luke)

**Additional Contemporary Suggestions**

S2186 "Song of Hope" (Isa)
M35 "White as Snow" (Isa)
M244 "Jesus Paid It All" (Isa)
M71 "The Heart of Worship" (Isa, Pss)
S2024 "From the Rising of the Sun" (Pss)
S2031 "We Bring the Sacrifice of Praise" (Pss)
SP1
S2029 "Praise to the Lord" (Pss)
S2049 "God Is Here Today" ("*Dios Está Aquí*") (Pss)
WS3023 "Forever" (Pss)
M68
M79 "I Stand Amazed" (Pss)
M134 "It Is You" (Pss)
M211 "I Will Not Forget You" (Pss)
UM405 "Seek Ye First" (Luke)
SP182
S2080 "All I Need Is You" (Luke)
WS3040 "You Are My All in All" (Luke)
SP220
WS3105 "In Christ Alone" ("My Hope Is Found") (Luke)
M138
M115 "When It's All Been Said and Done" (Luke)
M141 "Sing to the King" (Luke)
M156 "Be the Centre" (Luke)
M226 "Counting on God" (Luke)

**Vocal Solos**

"Spirit of Faith Come Down" (Heb)
V-1 p. 43
"My Lord, What a Morning" (Luke)
V-3 (1) p. 39
"Seek Ye First" (Luke)
V-8 p. 145

**Anthems**

"From the Rising of the Sun" (Pss)
Raymond Weidner; Paraclete Press PP01308
SATB *a cappella*

"Keep Your Lamps" (Luke)
Andre Thomas; Hinshaw HMC000
SATB with piano

**Other Suggestions**

Visuals:
**O** Bloody hands, wash hands, scarlet/snow/wool
**P** Sunrise/set, fire, storm, heaven/earth, praise
**E** Creation, crowd, tents, T-square, baby, star/sand
**G** Flock, purse, wedding banquet, lit lamp, clock
Greeting: BOW325 (Isa) or BOW331 (Pss)
Opening Prayer: BOW252 (Isa, Luke) or BOW254 (Luke)
Prayer of Confession: BOW479 (Isa)
Words of Assurance: BOW325 (Isa)
Response: S2277. "Lord, Have Mercy" (Isa)
Prayer: UM676. For a New Day (Pss, Luke)
Prayer: BOW528. A Prayer of Susanna Wesley (Luke)
Offertory Prayer: WSL123 (Luke)
Blessing: WSL164 or BOW561 (Heb)

**Isaiah 5:1-7**

Let me sing for my loved one
a love song for his vineyard.
My loved one had a vineyard on a fertile hillside.
2 He dug it,
cleared away its stones,
planted it with excellent vines,
built a tower inside it,
and dug out a wine vat in it.
He expected it to grow good grapes—
but it grew rotten grapes.
3 So now, you who live in Jerusalem, you people of Judah,
judge between me and my vineyard:
4 What more was there to do for my vineyard
that I haven't done for it?
When I expected it to grow good grapes,
why did it grow rotten grapes?
5 Now let me tell you what I'm doing to my vineyard.
I'm removing its hedge,
so it will be destroyed.
I'm breaking down its walls,
so it will be trampled.
6 I'll turn it into a ruin;
it won't be pruned or hoed,
and thorns and thistles will grow up.
I will command the clouds not to rain on it.
7 The vineyard of the LORD of heavenly forces is the house of Israel,
and the people of Judah are the plantings in which God delighted.
God expected justice, but there was bloodshed;
righteousness, but there was a cry of distress!

**Psalm 80:1-2, 8-19 (UM801)**

Shepherd of Israel, listen!
You, the one who leads Joseph as if he were a sheep.
You, who are enthroned upon the winged heavenly creatures.
Show yourself 2 before Ephraim, Benjamin, and Manasseh!
Wake up your power!
Come to save us!

. . . . . . . . . . . . . . . . . . . . . . . . . . .

8 You brought a vine out of Egypt.
You drove out the nations and planted it.
9 You cleared the ground for it;
then it planted its roots deep, filling the land.
10 The mountains were covered by its shade;
the mighty cedars were covered by its branches.
11 It sent its branches all the way to the sea;
its shoots went all the way to the Euphrates River.
12 So why have you now torn down its walls
so that all who come along can pluck its fruit,
13 so that any boar from the forest can tear it up,
so that the bugs can feed on it?
14 Please come back, God of heavenly forces!
Look down from heaven and perceive it!
Attend to this vine,
15 this root that you planted with your strong hand,
this son whom you secured as your very own.
16 It is burned with fire. It is chopped down.
They die at the rebuke coming from you.
17 Let your hand be with the one on your right side—
with the one whom you secured as your own—
18 then we will not turn away from you!
Revive us so that we can call on your name.
19 Restore us, LORD God of heavenly forces!
Make your face shine so that we can be saved!

**Hebrews 11:29–12:2**

29 By faith they crossed the Red Sea as if they were on dry
land, but when the Egyptians tried it, they were drowned.
30 By faith Jericho's walls fell after the people marched
around them for seven days.
31 By faith Rahab the prostitute wasn't killed with the disobedient because she welcomed the spies in peace.
32 What more can I say? I would run out of time if I told you
about Gideon, Barak, Samson, Jephthah, David, Samuel, and
the prophets. 33 Through faith they conquered kingdoms,
brought about justice, realized promises, shut the mouths
of lions, 34 put out raging fires, escaped from the edge of the
sword, found strength in weakness, were mighty in war, and
routed foreign armies. 35 Women received back their dead
by resurrection. Others were tortured and refused to be
released so they could gain a better resurrection.
36 But others experienced public shame by being taunted
and whipped; they were even put in chains and in prison.
37 They were stoned to death, they were cut in two, and they
died by being murdered with swords. They went around
wearing the skins of sheep and goats, needy, oppressed, and
mistreated. 38 The world didn't deserve them. They wandered around in deserts, mountains, caves, and holes in the
ground.
39 All these people didn't receive what was promised,
though they were given approval for their faith. 40 God
provided something better for us so they wouldn't be made
perfect without us.
**12** So then let's also run the race that is laid out in front of
us, since we have such a great cloud of witnesses surrounding
us. Let's throw off any extra baggage, get rid of the sin that
trips us up, 2 and fix our eyes on Jesus, faith's pioneer and
perfecter. He endured the cross, ignoring the shame, for the
sake of the joy that was laid out in front of him, and sat down
at the right side of God's throne.

**Luke 12:49-56**

49 "I came to cast fire upon the earth. How I wish that it was
already ablaze! 50 I have a baptism I must experience. How I
am distressed until it's completed! 51 Do you think that I have
come to bring peace to the earth? No, I tell you, I have come
instead to bring division. 52 From now on, a household of
five will be divided—three against two and two against three.
53 Father will square off against son and son against father;
mother against daughter and daughter against mother; and
mother-in-law against daughter-in-law and daughter-in-law
against mother-in-law."
54 Jesus also said to the crowds, "When you see a cloud form-
ing in the west, you immediately say, 'It's going to rain.' And
indeed it does. 55 And when a south wind blows, you say, 'A
heat wave is coming.' And it does. 56 Hypocrites! You know
how to interpret conditions on earth and in the sky. How is it
that you don't know how to interpret the present time?"

### Primary Hymns and Songs for the Day

529 "How Firm a Foundation" (Heb, Luke) (O)
H-3 Hbl-27, 69; Chr-102; Desc-41; Org-41
S-1 #133. Harm.
#134. Performance note
511 "Am I a Soldier of the Cross" (Heb, Luke)
H-3 Chr-27
S-1 #22-23. Desc. and harm.
2208 "Guide My Feet" (Heb)
730 "O Day of God, Draw Nigh" (Isa, Pss, Luke) (C)
H-3 Hbl-79; Chr-141; Desc-95; Org-143
S-1 #306-8. Various treatments

### Additional Hymn Suggestions

435 "O God of Every Nation" (Isa, Pss)
443 "O God Who Shaped Creation" (Isa, Pss)
450 "Creator of the Earth and Skies" (Isa, Pss)
506 "Wellspring of Wisdom" (Isa, Pss)
2136 "Out of the Depths" (Isa, Pss)
2169 "God, How Can We Forgive" (Isa, Pss)
2177 "Wounded World that Cries for Healing" (Isa, Pss)
2183 "Unsettled World" (Isa, Pss)
275 "The Kingdom of God" (Isa, Luke)
119 "O God in Heaven" (Pss, Heb)
79 "Holy God, We Praise Thy Name" (Heb)
206 "I Want to Walk as a Child of the Light" (Heb)
385 "Let Us Plead for Faith Alone" (Heb)
577 "God of Grace and God of Glory" (Heb)
636 "Christian People, Raise Your Song" (Heb)
708 "Rejoice in God's Saints" (Heb)
710 "Faith of Our Fathers" (Heb)
711 "For All the Saints" (Heb)
727 "O What Their Joy and Glory Must Be" (Heb)
2211 "Faith Is Patience in the Night" (Heb)
2238 "In the Midst of New Dimensions" (Heb)
2246 "Deep in the Shadows of the Past" (Heb)
2283 "For All the Saints" (Heb)
517 "By Gracious Powers" (Heb, Luke)
142 "If Thou But Suffer God to Guide Thee" (Luke)
433 "All Who Love and Serve Your City" (Luke)
541 "See How Great a Flame Aspires" (Luke)
578 "God of Love and God of Power" (Luke)
700 "Abide with Me" (Luke)
719 "My Lord, What a Morning" (Luke)
2102 "Swiftly Pass the Clouds of Glory" (Luke)
2212 "My Life Flows On" (Luke)

### Additional Contemporary Suggestions

M50 "Refiner's Fire" (Isa)
WS3103 "Purify My Heart" (Isa, Pss)
M90
M144 "Light the Fire Again" (Pss)
UM706 "Soon and Very Soon" (Heb)
S-2 #187. Piano Arr.
S2208 "Guide My Feet" (Heb)
M34 "I Will Never Be" (the Same Again) (Heb)
M38 "In the Secret" ("I Want to Know You") (Heb)
M53 "Let It Be Said of Us" (Heb)
M78 "Once Again" (Heb)
M76 "The Wonderful Cross" (Heb)
S2163 "He Who Began a Good Work in You" (Heb)
SP180
S2281 "May You Run and Not Be Weary" (Heb)
SP158 "The Battle Belongs to the Lord" (Luke)
M17 "This Kingdom" (Luke)
WS3042 "Shout to the North" (Luke)
M99
WS3186 "Days of Elijah" (Luke)
M139

### Vocal Solos

"Come, O Thou Traveler Unknown" (Heb, Luke)
V-1 p. 21
"Guide My Feet, Lord" (Heb, Luke)
V-7 p. 15
"My Lord, What a Morning" (Luke)
V-3 (1) p. 39

### Anthems

"Soon and Very Soon" (Heb)
Arr. Jack Schrader; Hope C-5825
Two-part mixed with piano

"Ain'-a That Good News" (Luke)
Arr. Mark Patterson; Choristers Guild CGA-1029
Unison/Two-part with piano

### Other Suggestions

Visuals:
**O** Vine/grapes, stones, tower, hedge, vat, wall
**P** Shepherd, vine/grapes, wall, fire, shears
**E** Walls, lions, fire, rising, weights, race, cross
**G** Fire, baptism, cross, wall, division, clock
Greeting: BOW243 (Luke)
Opening Prayer: BOW250 or BOW252 (Isa, Luke)
Prayer of Confession: BOW483 (Heb)
Sung Confession: S2134. "Forgive Us, Lord" (Isa, Pss)
Prayer: UM677. Listen, Lord (A Prayer) (Pss)
Prayer: UM574 or BOW345 (Heb)
Prayer: WSL45. Use last paragraph "Give us faith" (Heb)
Prayer of Thanksgiving: BOW554 (Heb, Luke)
Dismissal with Blessing: WSL162 or BOW265 (Heb)
Sung Benediction: M87. "Let the Peace of God Reign" (Heb)

**Jeremiah 1:4-10**

4 The LORD's word came to me:
5 "Before I created you in the womb I knew you;
before you were born I set you apart;
I made you a prophet to the nations."
6 "Ah, LORD God," I said, "I don't know how to speak
because I'm only a child."
7 The LORD responded,
"Don't say, 'I'm only a child.'
Where I send you, you must go;
what I tell you, you must say.
8 Don't be afraid of them,
because I'm with you to rescue you,"
declares the LORD.
9 Then the LORD stretched out his hand,
touched my mouth, and said to me,
"I'm putting my words in your mouth.
10 This very day I appoint you over nations and empires,
to dig up and pull down,
to destroy and demolish,
to build and plant."

**Psalm 71:1-6 (UM794)**

I've taken refuge in you, LORD.
Don't let me ever be put to shame!
2 Deliver me and rescue me by your righteousness!
Bend your ear toward me and save me!
3 Be my rock of refuge
where I can always escape.
You commanded that my life be saved
because you are my rock and my fortress.
4 My God, rescue me from the power of the wicked;
rescue me from the grip of the wrongdoer and the
oppressor
5 because you are my hope, LORD.
You, LORD, are the one I've trusted since childhood.
6 I've depended on you from birth—
you cut the cord when I came from my mother's womb.
My praise is always about you.

**Hebrews 12:18-29**

18 You haven't drawn near to something that can be
touched: a burning fire, darkness, shadow, a whirlwind, 19 a
blast of a trumpet, and a sound of words that made the ones
who heard it beg that there wouldn't be one more word.
20 They couldn't stand the command, *If even a wild animal
touches the mountain, it must be stoned.* 21 The sight was so fright-
ening that Moses said, "I'm terrified and shaking!"
22 But you have drawn near to Mount Zion, the city of the
living God, heavenly Jerusalem, to countless angels in a festival gathering, 23 to the assembly of God's firstborn children
who are registered in heaven, to God the judge of all, to the
spirits of the righteous who have been made perfect, 24 to
Jesus the mediator of the new covenant, and to the sprinkled
blood that speaks better than Abel's blood.
25 See to it that you don't resist the one who is speaking.
If the people didn't escape when they refused to listen to
the one who warned them on earth, how will we escape if
we reject the one who is warning from heaven? 26 His voice
shook the earth then, but now he has made a promise: *Still
once more I will shake not only the earth but heaven also.* 27 The
words "still once more" reveal the removal of what is
shaken—the things that are part of this creation—so that
what isn't shaken will remain. 28 Therefore, since we are
receiving a kingdom that can't be shaken, let's continue to
express our gratitude. With this gratitude, let's serve in a way
that is pleasing to God with respect and awe, 29 because our
God really is a consuming fire.

**Luke 13:10-17**

10 Jesus was teaching in one of the synagogues on the Sabbath. 11 A woman was there who had been disabled by a spirit
for eighteen years. She was bent over and couldn't stand
up straight. 12 When he saw her, Jesus called her to him and
said, "Woman, you are set free from your sickness." 13 He
placed his hands on her and she straightened up at once and
praised God.
14 The synagogue leader, incensed that Jesus had healed on
the Sabbath, responded, "There are six days during which
work is permitted. Come and be healed on those days, not
on the Sabbath day."
15 The Lord replied, "Hypocrites! Don't each of you on the
Sabbath untie your ox or donkey from its stall and lead it
out to get a drink? 16 Then isn't it necessary that this woman,
a daughter of Abraham, bound by Satan for eighteen long
years, be set free from her bondage on the Sabbath day?"
17 When he said these things, all his opponents were put to
shame, but all those in the crowd rejoiced at all the extraordinary things he was doing.

**Primary Hymns and Songs for the Day**

662 "Stand Up and Bless the Lord" (Heb) (O)
H-3 Hbl-79; Chr-141; Desc-95; Org-143
S-1 #306-8. Various treatments
731 "Glorious Things of Thee Are Spoken" (Heb)
H-3 Hbl-61; Chr-72; Desc-17; Org-11
S-1 #27. Desc.
#28. Harm. in F major
261 "Lord of the Dance" (Luke)
H-3 Chr-106; Org-81
273 "Jesus' Hands Were Kind Hands" (Luke)
S-2 #17-19. Various treatments
593 "Here I Am, Lord" (Jer) (C)
H-3 Chr-97; Org-54

**Additional Hymn Suggestions**

399 "Take My Life, and Let it Be" (Jer)
463 "Lord, Speak to Me" (Jer)
497 "Send Me, Lord" (Jer)
529 "How Firm a Foundation" (Jer)
582 "Whom Shall I Send" (Jer)
649 "How Shall They Hear the Word of God" (Jer)
2046 "Womb of Life" (Jer)
2052 "The Lone Wild Bird" (Jer)
2123 "Loving Spirit" (Jer)
2172 "We Are Called" (Jer)
3118 "Take This Moment, Sign, and Space" (Jer)
2050 "Mothering God, You Gave Me Birth" (Jer, Pss)
2051 "I Was There to Hear Your Borning Cry" (Jer, Pss)
430 "O Master, Let Me Walk with Thee" (Jer, Luke)
443 "O God Who Shaped Creation" (Jer., Luke)
578 "God of Love and God of Power" (Jer, Luke)
2178 "Here Am I" (Jer, Luke)
102 "Now Thank We All Our God" (Pss)
117 "O God, Our Help in Ages Past" (Pss)
139 "Praise to the Lord, the Almighty" (Pss) (O)
361 "Rock of Ages, Cleft for Me" (Pss)
523 "*Saranam, Saranam*" ("Refuge") (Pss)
103 "Immortal, Invisible, God Only Wise" (Heb)
704 "Steal Away to Jesus" (Heb)
733 "Marching to Zion" (Heb)
726 "O Holy City, Seen of John" (Heb)
2009 "O God Beyond All Praising" (Heb)
2011 "We Sing of Your Glory" ("*Tuya Es la Gloria*") (Heb)
2140 "Since Jesus Came into My Heart" (Heb)
2195 "In the Lord I'll Be Ever Thankful" (Heb)
2247 "Wonder of Wonders" (Heb, Baptism)
262 "Heal Me, Hands of Jesus" (Luke)
263 "When Jesus the Healer Passed Through Galilee" (Luke)
266 "Heal Us, Emmanuel, Hear Our Prayer" (Luke)
444 "O Young and Fearless Prophet" (Luke)
2213 "Healer of Our Every Ill" (Luke)

**Additional Contemporary Suggestions**

S2139 "I Know the Lord's Laid His Hands on Me" (Jer, Luke)
WS3184 "Word of God, Speak" (Jer)
M148
S2002 "I Will Call upon the Lord" (Pss)
SP224
S2032 "My Life Is in You, Lord" (Pss)
SP204
S2066 "Praise the Name of Jesus" (Pss)
SP87
M93 "Rock of Ages" (Pss)
M105 "Let My Words Be Few" (Heb)
S2040 "Awesome God" (Heb)
SP11
S2039 "Holy, Holy" (Heb)
SP141
UM171 "There's Something About That Name" (Heb)
SP89
S2064 "O Lord, You're Beautiful" (Luke)
S2151 "I'm So Glad Jesus Lifted Me" (Luke)
S2244 "People Need the Lord" (Luke)
WS3104 "Amazing Grace" ("My Chains Are Gone") (Luke)

**Vocal Solos**

"Be Thou My Vision" (Jer)
V-6 p. 13
"Prayer" (Pss)
V-9 p. 32
"Steal Away to Heaven" (Heb)
V-3 (1) p. 17
"Great Day!" (Heb)
V-7 p. 14
"Lord of the Dance" (Luke)
V-3 (3) p. 34

**Anthems**

"I Was There to Hear Your Borning Cry" (Jer, Pss)
Arr. John Helgen; Kjos 8826
SAATB with keyboard and C instrument

"Steal Away to Jesus" (Heb)
Arr. Edward Eicker; MorningStar MSM-50-6530
SATB *a cappella*

**Other Suggestions**

Visuals:
**O** Pregnant, young boy, hand to mouth, fear
**P** Rescue, rock, fortress, Pss 71:5, newborn
**E** Fire, darkness, storm, trumpet, stones, angels, throne, Christ, New Testament, praise
**G** Jesus, woman/cane/praise, donkey/water, open shackles
Introit: S2117. "Spirit of God" (Jer)
Prayer of Confession: WSL90 (Jer)
Prayer of Confession: BOW482 (Heb, Luke)
Prayer: BOW504. For the Church (Heb)
Prayer: BOW526. For the World (Jer, Pss, Luke)
Litany: BOW432 (Jer)
Blessing: BOW565 (Jer)

**Jeremiah 2:4-13**

4 Listen to the LORD's word,
people of Judah,
all you families of the Israelite household.
5 This is what the LORD says:
What wrong did your ancestors find in me
that made them wander so far?
They pursued what was worthless
and became worthless.
6 They didn't ask,
"Where's the LORD who brought us up from the land of Egypt,
who led us through the wilderness,
in a land of deserts and ravines,
in a land of drought and darkness,
in a land of no return,
where no one survives?"
7 I brought you into a land of plenty,
to enjoy its gifts and goodness,
but you ruined my land;
you disgraced my heritage.
8 The priests didn't ask,
"Where's the LORD?"
Those responsible for the Instruction didn't know me;
the leaders rebelled against me;
the prophets spoke in the name of Baal,
going after what has no value.
9 That is why I will take you to court
and charge even your descendants,
declares the LORD.
10 Look to the west as far as the shores of Cyprus
and to the east as far as the land of Kedar.
Ask anyone there:
Has anything this odd ever taken place?
11 Has a nation switched gods,
though they aren't really gods at all?
Yet my people have exchanged their glory
for what has no value.
12 Be stunned at such a thing, you heavens;
shudder and quake,
declares the LORD.
13 My people have committed two crimes:
They have forsaken me, the spring of living water.
And they have dug wells, broken wells that can't hold water.

**Psalm 81:1, 10-16 (UM803)**

Rejoice out loud to God, our strength!
Shout for joy to Jacob's God!
. . . . . . . . . . . . . . . . . . . . . . . . . .
10 I am the LORD your God,
who brought you up from Egypt's land.
Open your mouth wide—I will fill it up!
11 But my people wouldn't listen to my voice.
Israel simply wasn't agreeable toward me.
12 So I sent them off to follow their willful hearts;
they followed their own advice.
13 How I wish my people would listen to me!
How I wish Israel would walk in my ways!
14 Then I would subdue their enemies in a second;
I would turn my hand against their foes.
15 Those who hate the LORD would grovel before me,
and their doom would last forever!
16 But I would feed you with the finest wheat.
I would satisfy you with honey from the rock."

**Hebrews 13:1-8, 15-16**

Keep loving each other like family. 2 Don't neglect to open
up your homes to guests, because by doing this some have
been hosts to angels without knowing it. 3 Remember prisoners as if you were in prison with them, and people who are
mistreated as if you were in their place. 4 Marriage must be
honored in every respect, with no cheating on the relationship, because God will judge the sexually immoral person
and the person who commits adultery. 5 Your way of life
should be free from the love of money, and you should be
content with what you have. After all, he has said, *I will never*
*leave you or abandon you.* 6 This is why we can confidently say,

*The LORD is my helper,*
*and I won't be afraid.*
*What can people do to me?*

7 Remember your leaders who spoke God's word to you. Imi-
tate their faith as you consider the way their lives turned out. 8
Jesus Christ is the same yesterday, today, and forever! . . .
15 So let's continually offer up a sacrifice of praise through
him, which is the fruit from our lips that confess his name.
16 Don't forget to do good and to share what you have
because God is pleased with these kinds of sacrifices.

**Luke 14:1, 7-14**

One Sabbath, when Jesus went to share a meal in the home
of one of the leaders of the Pharisees, they were watching
him closely. . . .
7 When Jesus noticed how the guests sought out the best
seats at the table, he told them a parable. 8 "When someone
invites you to a wedding celebration, don't take your seat in
the place of honor. Someone more highly regarded than you
could have been invited by your host. 9 The host who invited
both of you will come and say to you, 'Give your seat to this
other person.' Embarrassed, you will take your seat in the
least important place. 10 Instead, when you receive an invitation, go and sit in the least important place. When your host
approaches you, he will say, 'Friend, move up here to a better
seat.' Then you will be honored in the presence of all your
fellow guests. 11 All who lift themselves up will be brought low,
and those who make themselves low will be lifted up."
12 Then Jesus said to the person who had invited him,
"When you host a lunch or dinner, don't invite your friends,
your brothers and sisters, your relatives, or rich neighbors.
If you do, they will invite you in return and that will be your
reward. 13 Instead, when you give a banquet, invite the poor,
crippled, lame, and blind. 14 And you will be blessed because
they can't repay you. Instead, you will be repaid when the just
are resurrected."

**Primary Hymns and Songs for the Day**

2236 "Gather Us In" (Luke, Comm.) (O)
2031 "We Bring the Sacrifice of Praise" (Heb) (O)
SP1
432 "*Jesu, Jesu*" (Heb, Luke)
H-3 Chr-114; Org-19
S-1 #63. Vocal part
616 "Come, Sinners, to the Gospel Feast" (Luke, Comm.)
S-1 #164-66. Various treatments
629 "You Satisfy the Hungry Heart" (Pss, Comm.)
S-1 #144. Four-part setting of refrain
557 "Blest Be the Tie That Binds" (Heb) (C)
H-3 Hbl-49; Chr-14; Desc-27; Org-25

**Additional Hymn Suggestions**

151 "God Created Heaven and Earth" (Jer)
439 "We Utter Our Cry" (Jer.)
649 "How Shall They Hear the Word of God" (Jer)
443 "O God Who Shaped Creation" (Jer, Pss)
450 "Creator of the Earth and Skies" (Jer, Pss)
2048 "God Weeps" (Jer, Pss)
2172 "We Are Called" (Jer, Pss)
2279 "The Trees of the Field" (Pss)
96 "Praise the Lord Who Reigns Above" (Pss)
57 "O For a Thousand Tongues to Sing" (Pss, Luke)
523 "*Saranam, Saranam*" (Heb)
529 "How Firm a Foundation" (Heb)
579 "Lord God, Your Love Has Called Us Here" (Heb, Luke)
2009 "O God Beyond All Praising" (Heb)
2094 "Carol of the Epiphany" (Heb)
2130 "The Summons" (Heb)
2178 "Here Am I" (Heb)
2181 "We Need a Faith" (Heb)
3033 "God of Great and God of Small" (Heb)
3147 "Built on a Rock" (Heb)
2175 "Together We Serve" (Heb, Luke)
2254 "In Remembrance of Me" (Heb, Luke, Comm.)
2268 "As We Gather at Your Table" (Heb, Luke, Comm.)
2269 "Come, Share the Lord" (Heb, Comm.)
166 "All Praise to Thee, for Thou, O King Divine" (Luke)
194 "Morning Glory, Starlit Sky" (Luke)
339 "Come, Sinners, to the Gospel Feast" (Luke)
340 "Come, Ye Sinners, Poor and Needy" (Luke)
568 "Christ for the World We Sing" (Luke)
581 "Lord, Whose Love Through Humble Service" (Luke)
2155 "Blest Are They" (Luke)
2197 "Lord of All Hopefulness" (Luke)
2263 "Broken for Me" (Luke, Comm.)
2265 "Time Now to Gather" (Luke, Comm.)
3149 "A Place at the Table" (Luke, Comm.)

**Additional Contemporary Suggestions**

S2132 "You Who Are Thirsty" (Jer, Pss)
S2006 "Lord God Almighty" (Pss)
S2074 "Shout to the Lord" (Pss)
M16; V-3 (2) p. 32 Vocal solo
S2144 "Someone Asked the Question" (Pss)
WS3108 "Trading My Sorrows" (Pss)
M75
M123 "Made Me Glad" (Pss)
S2179 "Live in Charity" ("*Ubi Caritas*") (Heb)
M24 "Jesus, We Crown You with Praise" (Heb)
M79 "I Stand Amazed" (Heb)
M211 "I Will Not Forget You" (Heb)
M229 "Forevermore" (Heb)
S2176 "Make Me a Servant" (Heb, Luke)
SP193
S2131 "Humble Thyself in the Sight of the Lord" (Heb, Luke)
SP223
WS3117 "Rule of Life" (Heb, Luke)
WS3151 "The Jesus in Me" (Heb, Luke)
S2222 "The Servant Song" (Luke)

**Vocal Solos**

"Praise the Lord, He Never Changes" (Heb)
V-8 p. 62
"The Heart of Worship" (Heb)
M71
"Author of Life Divine" (Luke, Comm.)
V-1 p. 39
"In Remembrance of Me" (Luke, Comm.)
S2254

**Anthems**

"Song of Gentleness" (Heb, Luke)
Douglas Wagner; Beckenhorst Press BP1192
Unison with keyboard or handbells

"Many Will Come" (Luke)
Thomas Keesecker; Choristers Guild CGA-1374
SATB *a cappella*

**Other Suggestions**

Visuals:
**O** Exodus, abundance, fountain, broken cistern
**P** Singing, Exodus, hard hearts, wheat, honey/rock
**E** Welcome, prison ministry, marriage certificate, money, Heb 13:6 or 8, Jesus
**G** Meal, marriage feast, table, poor, maimed, lame, blind
Greeting: BOW452 (Pss)
Litany: WSL49 (Pss, Luke)
Opening Prayer: BOW465 or WSL54 (Heb)
Canticle: UM646. "Canticle of Love" (Heb)
Prayers of Confession: UM893 (Jer, Pss, Heb)
Prayer of Confession: BOW489 (Heb, Luke)
Prayer: WSL205 (Luke)
Prayer: BOW511. For God's Reign (Luke)
Prayer: BOW512. For Guidance (Heb)
Reading: UM886. World Methodist Social Affirmation (Luke)
Offertory Prayer: WSL103 (Heb)
Invitation to Communion: S2264. "Come to the Table" (Luke)
Closing Prayer: WSL174 (Luke, Comm.)
Blessing: WSL169 (Luke, Comm.)

# INDEX OF SCRIPTURES REFERENCED

**Old Testament**

**New Testament**

# WORSHIP PLANNING SHEET 1

Date: ____________________ Color: ______________

Preacher: ____________________________________________

Liturgist: ____________________________________________

Selected Scripture: ____________________________________

| Selected Hymns | No. | Placement |
|---|---|---|
| | | |
| | | |
| | | |
| | | |

Psalter # ____________________

Keyboard Selections

| Title | Composer | Placement |
|---|---|---|
| | | |
| | | |
| | | |

Anthems

| Title | Choir | Composer | Placement |
|---|---|---|---|
| | | | |
| | | | |

Vocal Solos

| Title | Singer | Composer | Placement |
|---|---|---|---|
| | | | |
| | | | |

Other Ideas:

Acolytes: ____________________________________________

Head Usher: __________________________________________

Altar Guild Contact: ___________________________________

Other Participants: ____________________________________

# WORSHIP PLANNING SHEET 2

Date: ________________ Sunday: __________________ Color: ______________________________

Preacher: ______________________________________________________________

Liturgist: ______________________________________________________________

Opening Voluntary Composer

______________________________________________________________

______________________________________________________________

Hymn Tune Name No.

______________________________________________________________

Opening Prayer: ______________________________________________________

Prayer for Illumination: _______________________________________________

First Lesson: _________________________________________________________

Psalter: ______________________________________________________________

Second Lesson: _______________________________________________________

Gospel Lesson: _______________________________________________________

Hymn Tune Name No.

______________________________________________________________

Response to the Word: _________________________________________________

Prayers of the People: _________________________________________________

Offertory Composer

______________________________________________________________

Communion Setting: ___________________________________________________

Communion Hymns Tune Name No.

______________________________________________________________

______________________________________________________________

Closing Hymn Tune Name No.

______________________________________________________________

Benediction: _________________________________________________________

Closing Voluntary Composer

______________________________________________________________

# CONTEMPORARY WORSHIP PLANNING SHEET

Because of the diversity in orders of worship, you will want to adjust this planning sheet to meet the needs of your worship planning team. A common order used would consist of three to four opening praise choruses and lively hymns, a time of informal prayers of the congregation along with songs of prayer, reading of the primary scripture for the day, a drama or video to illustrate the day's theme, a message from the preacher, a testimony on the theme for the day (if a drama or video was not presented earlier), followed by closing songs appropriate to the mood of the service and the message. Any offering would usually be taken early in the service, and Holy Communion would normally take place following the message. Special music (solos, duets, instrumental music) can be used wherever it best expresses the theme of the service.

Date: ______________________ Sunday: ______________________

Thematic Emphasis or Topic: ______________________

Color: ______________________ Visual Focus: ______________________

Opening Songs:

______________________

______________________

Prayer Songs:

______________________

Scripture Selection(s):

______________________

Drama or Video:

______________________

Message Title:

______________________

Testimony: ______________________

Special Music:

______________________

Closing Songs:

______________________

Preacher: ______________________ Music Leader: ______________________

Worship Facilitator: ______________________ Prayer Leader: ______________________

# PLANNING NOTES

## PLANNING NOTES

# PLANNING NOTES